DUPLICITOUS

*How We the People can
Reclaim America!*

Michael Beaumont
Randy E. King

Duplicitous
How We the People can Reclaim America
©2014 Michael Beaumont, Randy E King

Published by
Road Scholar Publishing Group, LLC
Scottsdale, Arizona USA
Reboh@cox.net

ISBN-13: 978-0-692258-20-0

Other books by Randy E King:
• Left-Center-Right: What is Best for America?
• Is Anybody Listening? Real Teens - True Stories - Young People Hoping to Make a Difference

You can email the author: rking23@cox.net or call: 480.766.8533
Visit: restoreourpride.us / storiesofusa.com

Edited by: Susan Kohler
Cover & Interior Design: Fusion Creative Works, www.fusioncw.com
Printed and bound in the United States of America

DEDICATION

FROM MICHAEL BEAUMONT:

"When we try to pick out anything by itself, we find it hitched to everything else in the universe"

— John Muir

As my favorite quote from John Muir (Father of the National Parks) implies, we are influenced by others in our life. Many people have helped shape my personal and political philosophies, including: my mother, Joseph Westbrook and Randy King. Also, I truly admire those out there who are living the concepts within this book – which means that they have a strong viewpoint and are actively doing things that positively improve our Nation and our society. First, Shannon Smith operates a non-profit organization based in Southern California to improve our children's health and wellness. She was inspired by a young man named Zachary Cove – both were hospitalized and treated for cancer. Second, Bruce Crocker is a science teacher in Southern California. He uses his talents, knowledge and passion to not only educate his students, including myself, but to instill a desire to learn, appreciate life, and excel in whatever we do. Third, Jesus has been a large influence in my life. He gives me strength to stand firm, encouragement to serve, and discernment to know truth from fiction. Just as we are influenced by others, we in turn help shape the lives of others. There are three that I have committed myself to. To my godchildren Emili and Joseph: Challenges lie ahead, but I know you will overcome them. To my lovely daughter Natalie, you are the love of my life. You inspire me, and I wish nothing but the best for you.

FROM RANDY KING:

"He who knows nothing is closer to the truth than he whose mind is filled with falsehoods and errors."

— Thomas Jefferson

This book is dedicated to every American that goes the extra mile to ensure the legacy of the Constitution of our great Nation, so that its laws, ideals and values can continue to be passed on to future generations. To my parents, who are great Patriots in which their love for America are renowned. To my wife Linda, for her continued love and support during all of my writings. Susan Kohler, an experienced author in her own right was involved in editing this book. Shiloh Schroeder has now developed the visual artistry and organization of a number of my books. John Braden developed the Restore Our Pride logo, which truly captures our current State of the Union and our desire to protect what makes this country great. Thank you God for giving me the strength and wisdom to hear the calling to collaborate on this book.

ABOUT THE AUTHORS

MICHAEL BEAUMONT, MIT

"I believe America is unique and rare, not because of its government, but because of our shared values of Liberty, Hard Work, Compassion, Respect for Life, and Personal Responsibility. We must all play our part in protecting what makes America great."

— Michael Beaumont

Since he was very young, Michael Beaumont has been passionate about his work within the fields of science, technology, marketing and education. Determined to be a school teacher like his father, he became a professional math and science tutor before he even entered junior high school. He has always worked hard on his academics receiving the Presidential Academic Fitness Award twice (from Presidents Reagan and Bush) and voted Who's Who Among American High School Students. He also received scholarship awards for foreign language and community service for his efforts in learning three languages and volunteering much of his free time to several civic, governmental and faith-based community organizations.

It was partially by accident that he became an entrepreneur. A friend asked if he could build a website for him. He obliged and eventually helped manage the entire successful business. He felt the call to become an entrepreneur. He developed his skills in website design and marketing. As an entrepreneur, he has provided educational, marketing and technical support to many small and medium-sized businesses across the country. In order to do his job well, he must develop and execute not only an effective marketing plan that will improve the visibility of a business online, but also create systems that improve customer relations and business operations. He toils many long hours and has had many success stories along the way. He received an award from a local chamber of commerce for Entrepreneur of the Year. He has developed websites that get thousands of visitors daily without paid advertising and has numerous websites that rank #1 in search engines.

In May 2010, he teamed up with Randy E. King to develop a marketing platform for his youth focused **American Pride eBook**. The original concept was to educate people about what it means to be American and to provide a way for the general public to tell their stories - **StoriesofUSA.com** was born. Since then things have developed in ways that neither of them expected. **Dream2Achieve**, a youth leadership program was developed. **Left-Center-Right: What is BEST for America?**, the first collaborative book which was authored by Randy E King, encouraged Americans to develop a personal and political philosophy. **Is Anybody Listening? Real Teens, True Stories – Young People Hoping to Make a Difference**, the second book which was authored by Randy E King and Dr Vickie Christensen, focused on teen leadership. *Duplicitous – How We the People Can Reclaim America* - which is authored by Randy E King and Michael Beaumont represents the third book inspired by this partnership. This book takes a sober look at the divisive world we live in today, yet it shows people how to take a stand and get involved in order to make our Nation a better place to live and work. The mission of this partnership includes: educate people about what it means to be American, teach them how to be successful in America, and develop youth leadership programs.

On a more personal note, he has lived abroad for two years and has explored much of the United States. He loves to learn and is fascinated by cultures and languages. Also, he has seen the face of death and has lived to tell his personal story about it. In the winter of 2014, his appendix burst. By the time he entered the hospital emergency room, his blood pressure was 90 over 40 and most of his major organs were shutting down. Two weeks later he emerged from this near death experience with a drive and conviction to ensure that his daughter, and others who are willing, understand **the importance of taking a stand, getting involved, and making a positive difference in our communities.**

RANDY E KING

"Knowledge and awareness do not have a political party. In most of our schools, however, this is not the case. Our true enemy is ignorance and apathy. I don't know and I don't care attitude will break America. This book is about your personal awareness of the Past – Present – Future & the Inspiration to keep America Great"

— Randy E. King

Randy King for almost thirty years has been a leader within America's small business and membership driven communities. He was a senior leader with the US Chamber of Commerce (one of the most influential organizations in the United States) for fifteen years and part of the National Training Council with the US Chamber. He was appointed the National Sr. Director to develop the "Major Metro" project that is still in place today.

Randy is currently a Division Director for National Write Your Congressman (NWYC) - a non-partisan membership-based organization related to Congressional communications, legislative research & civic advocacy. He manages 18-25 legislative research consultants in 15% of all Congressional districts, and NWYC accounts for 37% of all constituent pressure that Congress receives. He has been on the advisory council to the CEOs of the US Green Chamber of Commerce and Welcome Home Troops (a non-profit organization that provides transition and integration support for American Military Service Members, Veterans and their Families). He is the co-producer of the world renowned, StoriesofUSA.com (an interactive 14 language site for young Americans to understand the history of our American Heritage).

Randy has consulted with the National Federation of Independent Business (NFIB) - the nation's most influential small business advocacy group in Washington DC. He has conducted fundraising seminars for the Arizona GOP. He has been the keynote speaker at numerous chamber of commerce and Fortune 500 company functions and has facilitated board retreats for chambers and associations, including the American Chamber of Commerce Executives (ACCE) & Western Association of Chamber Executives (WACE). His speeches specialize in operational management, dues and non-dues development, business leadership, performance and civic advocacy. He was President/CEO of the tourism driven Key Largo Chamber of Commerce.

Randy authored 9 books on business development, leadership, successful entrepreneurship, and civic advocacy. He has authored a children's book on what America means to our youth, co-authored a book on teen leadership, and has several audio education programs & "White Papers" on staff performance. He has been interviewed on hundreds of talk radio shows nationwide and internationally. He served as a faculty member at one of the top university-based leadership academies in the country - the US Chamber of Commerce Institute of Organizational Management (IOM). He has worked with the YMCA's "Youth and Government" Y-Leaders program and the Student Governmental Affairs Program (SGAP). He has been a founder of successful computer software and sales/marketing companies.

Randy's grass roots efforts through his training seminars, books, CDs, white papers, websites, operational management & leadership, public legislative policy, civic advocacy, and dues / non-dues development, have developed strong community and business ties that allow him to feel the pulse and concerns of American citizens. Randy lives in Arizona with his wife Linda.

CONTENTS

INTRODUCTION

"I have been impressed with the urgency of doing. Knowing is not enough; we must apply. Being willing is not enough, we must do."
—Leonardo da Vinci

The world changed on September 11, 2001. I still remember what I was doing that day. I woke up in the morning and headed towards the university that I was attending to finish my Masters Degree. The university is located near Los Angeles International Airport. Normally I listen to the news, but for some unknown reason, I was listening to music on the radio instead. As I was driving on the freeway, it felt like something was wrong. Something was missing. After I found out about what happened in New York, I realized that what was missing was a lack of airplanes in the sky. It is kind of like wearing a watch or a wedding ring. You eventually forget that you have it on until you need it.

Just like the attack on Pearl Harbor in 1941, the shooting of JFK in 1963 or Neil Armstrong landing on the Moon in 1969, everyone alive at that time had a story to tell related to what they were doing the day something momentous, for good or for bad, happened to America. In the case of fulfilling President John F. Kennedy's call to action - *"this nation should commit itself to achieving the goal, before this decade is out, of landing a man on the Moon and returning him safely to*

Earth," on July 20,1969, our world did change. **We proved that when we pull together as a nation, we can accomplish great things.** However, working together is not enough. **We must pull in the right direction.** What is that right direction?

In the aftermath of the September 11 terrorist attack, Americans rallied behind President George W. Bush. His approval rating soared to 90% (Gallup). The Nation wanted the President to act. . . and act he did. During his tenure, the US invaded both Iraq and Afghanistan, lowered taxes, and created the Department of Homeland Security, whose task was to coordinate national security issues. As time passed, people's moods soured, political tensions increased, and the national economy took a dive. Around the time GW Bush left office, his approval rating dropped to 25% (Gallup). Next, President Barack H. Obama took office with an approval rating of 69% (Gallup). During his tenure, the US significantly increased federal government spending, passed the Patient Protection and Affordable Health Care Act (nicknamed Obama Care), and raised taxes. His approval ratings sank to 38% in mid-October 2011 (Gallup).

After researching a number of issues related to writing this book, I had more questions than answers. How safe are we? Is the United States of America finished as a first world country? Is the quest for money, power and personal security stronger than the desire to help our neighbor? Can the Republicans and Democrats settle their differences and actually get something done that benefits the general population? Are the US Constitution and the Rule of Law still being followed in a way that benefits Americans? Most importantly, **can one person still make a positive change in our Nation or are we destined to mediocrity?**

Some would think that person a fool who thinks that one person can actually change the world. There are over 7 billion people on this planet and you are but one person. From the international banks and corporations that own everything to the central governments who are making backroom deals, the common person is controlled, manipulated and taken advantage of on a daily basis. There is no possible way for one man (or woman) to achieve any type of success or justice. There are too many obstacles in the way. It is all too easy to fall into this line of thinking. That someone is out to get you. That Big Business or Big Government is purposely and methodically keeping you down and preventing you from achieving your dreams.

Duplicitous has been defined as "**marked by deliberate deceptiveness especially by pretending one set of feelings and acting under the influence of another.**" Is there deliberate deceptiveness within our governmental and political systems? Regardless of a person's political philosophy, most Americans agree that this great Nation has a real problem. Part of that problem is the use of secrecy, unrestrained power, and backdoor deals that undermine the value and sovereignty of **We the People**.

George Orwell's *1984* is about a society ruled by a powerful elite that maintains control through government surveillance and mind control. *"Even the one plan that was practicable, suicide, they had no intention of carrying out. To hang on from day to day and from week to week, spinning out a present that had no future, seemed an unconquerable instinct, just as one's lungs will always draw the next breath so long as there is air available."* Some believe that this Big Brother concept has become a reality. That we are but pawns in a cruel game of life. That there is no hope for a bright future.

This reminds me of a quote from French author and philosopher, Albert Camus, *"In the depth of winter I finally learned that there was in me an invincible summer."* One concept I pull away from this is that **the cure for despair is passion.** If you are passionate about something, you will become focused to do what it takes to accomplish your goals and your mission. You will turn your dreams into reality.

It is true that there are obstacles in your way that prevent you from becoming successful – some real and some imagined. To learn how to overcome those personal obstacles that stand in your way, I highly recommend **Left-Center-Right: What is BEST for America?.**

Duplicitous takes a different path. Its primary goal is to educate you on the root causes of the social and political strife in our country, and on the flip side of this coin, to offer practical personal, professional and technical solutions and strategies that when implemented properly will empower you as an individual, a teenager, a corporation, a non-profit organization, or a politician to **Reclaim America!** It is much more than a how-to book. It is for learning about and preserving our Nation. The US Constitution, the fundamental law of this country and part of what makes this country great, starts with three important words ... "**We the People.**" It is our responsibility as a free and informed society to do what it takes to fight for liberty, justice and freedom. I have two simple questions to ask you the reader. **What type of society do you want your children and grandchildren to inherit? How close are we to fulfilling that vision?**

As a result of significant research, we have determined that there are three types of Americans: Apathetic (those who don't care), Concerned (those who care but do nothing), and Responsible (those who care and do something). Which one are you?

If you are not interested in liberty, freedom and justice, this book IS NOT for you. If you are looking for a comic book version of our political system, this book IS NOT for you. If you truly want to understand how our system works and how you can be an active part of it, then this book IS for you.

This book is designed to educate and inform you on how Americans can reclaim this country for the betterment of themselves and their local communities. In its essence, this book discusses the importance of finding a balance between too little government (which leads to anarchy) and too much government (which leads to oligarchy). It places the many political-related events into proper context, in that government officials will always attempt to ignore laws in order to benefit themselves and their friends. **The US Constitution is specifically designed to allow We the People to develop rules and maintain comprehensive accountability so that no one person or group is above the law.**

This book is organized into three sections. The first section describes our public face as a Nation. The second section describes the darker, more sinister, and often unspoken dangerous side of an uncontrolled government, and the third section describes practical solutions on how to create real social and political change. At the end of the day, remember that **You Can Make a Difference!**

SPOTLIGHT ON STEVE JOBS

At the end of most chapters in this book, an individual is highlighted. Each person is chosen for specific reasons. First, they are real life examples of concepts described within that particular chapter. Second, each had a specific vision, but more importantly, they communicated their ideas in such ways that others paid attention. Third, they had what it takes to make a positive difference in our Nation. By learning what made these people passionately steadfast and influential, we can learn how and why to get involved and be influential ourselves so that we too can leave our own positive legacy.

Steve Jobs is the Thomas Edison of our modern era. Just as Edison improved the lives of individuals who lived in the Industrial Age with his many patented inventions, Jobs has forever transformed the lives of those who live in the Information Age. He is the inventor of the iPod, iTunes, iMac, iPhone, iPad, and Pixar.

Steven Paul Jobs (February 24, 1955 – October 5, 2011) was born in San Francisco and was adopted by Paul and Clara Jobs. His biological parents – Abdulfattah Jandali, a Syrian Muslim graduate student who later became a political science professor, and Joanne Simpson, an American graduate student who went on to become a speech therapist – later married, giving birth to and raising his biological sister, the novelist Mona Simpson. He attended Cupertino Junior High School and Homestead High School, and frequented after-school lectures at Hewlett-Packard in Palo Alto, California. He was soon hired there and worked with Steve Wozniak as a summer employee.

In 1972, he graduated from high school and enrolled in Reed College in Portland, Oregon. His parents were working multiple jobs just to afford sending him to college. Not wanting his parents to sacrifice so much on his behalf, he dropped out after only one semester. Jobs found this a liberating experience. He was no longer shackled by the concerns of having to do well in college to obtain a piece of paper that tells the world that he is intelligent and capable. Still wanting to expand his base of knowledge, he continued to audit the courses he was interested in at Reed College, such as calligraphy. In the autumn of 1974, he returned to California and began attending meetings of the Homebrew Computer Club with Wozniak. He took a job as a technician at Atari in order to save money for a spiritual retreat to India. He was on his way to see Shri Neem Kairolie Baba (a devotee of the Hindu deity Hanuman), but Baba died before his arrival. He abruptly ended his pilgrimage and concluded: *"We weren't going to find a place where we could go for a month to be enlightened. It was one of the first times that **I started to realize that maybe Thomas Edison did a lot more to improve the world than Karl Marx and Neem Kairolie Baba put together.**"*

After his retreat to India, he was given the task of creating a circuit board for the game *Breakout*. Atari offered $100 for each chip that was eliminated in the machine. Steve Jobs had little interest or knowledge in circuit board design and made a deal with Wozniak to split the bonus evenly between them if Wozniak could minimize the number of chips. Wozniak reduced the number of chips by 50 for a total winnings of $5000. However, Jobs told Wozniak that Atari had only paid him $750 and that his share was $375.

In 1976, Steve Jobs, Steve Wosniak and Ronald Wayne started Apple Computer. In 1983, Jobs lured PepsiCo CEO John Sculley to work for him in his own unique way - *"Do you want to sell sugar water for the rest of your life or come with me and change the world?"*

After an industry-wide sales slump, an internal power struggle ensued. In May 1985, Steve Jobs was stripped of his duties. This did not stop Steve Jobs. In 1986, Jobs purchased The Graphics Group from George Lucas for $10 million. After struggling for many years, Jobs contracted this business, now named Pixar, with Disney to make computer-animated feature films. In 1995, Pixar released *Toy Story*, which eventually had a worldwide gross of almost $362 million. Over the next ten plus years, under Pixar's creative chief John Lasseter, the company would produce: *A Bug's Life, Toy Story 2, Monsters, Inc., Finding Nemo, The Incredibles, Cars, Ratatouille, WALL-E, Up, Toy Story 3, Cars 2, Brave* and *Monster's University*. Seven of them received, and two others were nominated for, the Academy Award for Best Animated Feature - an award introduced in 2001. On January 24, 2006, Steve Jobs announced that Disney had agreed to purchase Pixar in an all-stock transaction worth $7.4 billion. Once the deal closed, Steve Jobs became The Walt Disney Company's largest single shareholder with approximately 7% of the company's stock, and joined the company's board of directors.

In 1996, Steve Jobs returned to Apple and soon became CEO. Under this new leadership, Apple developed and released iMac, iTunes, iPod, iPhone and iPad. On August 9, 2011, Apple, if only for a brief time, was the most valuable company in the world. Steve Jobs did not set out to become rich, he wanted to change the world through technology.

Steve Jobs' contribution to the world is Apple, Pixar, his other enterprises, and his 338 patented inventions. He gave the world better computers, better telephones, and better music players. In a lot of cases, he created better jobs, too. Did he do it because he was a nice guy? Because he was greedy? Or because he was a maniacally single-minded competitor who got up every morning possessed by an unspeakable rage to destroy his rivals? Whatever drove Steve Jobs, it drove him to create superior products at better prices, and the world loves him for it.

Steve Jobs was a very private person. Unless he was promoting one of his new products, he avoided publicity. So it was a very rare occurrence that he delivered the commencement address for the 2005 class at Stanford University. This was his one and only time to do such a thing. The speech provides a very powerful and very personal narrative into the life and thoughts of Steven Paul Jobs. In it **he discusses his being adopted as a baby, not having enough money to go to college, getting fired from Apple and through it all following his passion, thinking differently, and above all else, not giving up on his dreams.**

Stanford University Commencement Address
June 12, 2005

"I'm honored to be with you today at your commencement from one of the finest universities in the world. Truth be told, I never graduated from college. And this is the closest I've ever gotten to a college graduation. Today I want to tell you three stories from my life. That's it. No big deal. Just three stories.

The first story is about connecting the dots.

I dropped out of Reed College after the first 6 months, but then stayed around as a drop-in for another 18 months or so before I really quit. So why did I drop out?

It started before I was born. My biological mother was a young, unwed college graduate student, and she decided to put me up for adoption. She felt very strongly that I should be adopted by college graduates, so everything was all set for me to be adopted at birth by a lawyer and his wife. Except that when I popped out they decided at the last minute that they really wanted a girl. So my parents, who were on a waiting list, got a call in the middle of the night asking: "We have an unexpected baby boy; do you want him?" They said: "Of course." My biological mother later found out that my mother had never graduated from college and that my father had never graduated from high school. She refused to sign the final adoption papers. She only relented a few months later when my parents promised that I would go to college. This was the start of my life.

And 17 years later I did go to college. But I naively chose a college that was almost as expensive as Stanford, and all of my working-class parents' savings were being spent on my college tuition. After six months, I couldn't see the value in it. I had no idea what I wanted to do with my life and no idea how college was going to help me figure it out. And here I was spending all of the money my parents had saved their entire life. So I decided to drop out and trust that it would all work out OK. It was pretty scary at the time, but looking back it was one of the best decisions I ever made. The minute I dropped out I could stop taking the required classes that didn't interest me, and begin dropping in on the ones that looked far more interesting.

It wasn't all romantic. I didn't have a dorm room, so I slept on the floor in friends' rooms, I returned coke bottles for the 5¢ deposits to buy food with, and I would walk the 7 miles across town every Sunday night to get one good meal a week at the Hare Krishna temple. I loved it. And much of what I stumbled into by following my curiosity and intuition turned out to be priceless later on. Let me give you one example:

Reed College at that time offered perhaps the best calligraphy instruction in the country. Throughout the campus every poster, every label on every drawer, was beautifully hand calligraphed. Because I had dropped out and didn't have to take the normal classes, I decided to take a calligraphy class to learn how to do this. I learned about serif and san serif typefaces, about varying the amount of space between different letter combinations, about what makes great typography great. It was beautiful, historical, artistically subtle in a way that science can't capture, and I found it fascinating.

None of this had even a hope of any practical application in my life. But ten years later, when we were designing the first Macintosh computer, it all came back to me. And we designed it all into the Mac. It was the first computer with beautiful typography. If I had never dropped in on that single course in college, the Mac would have never had multiple typefaces or proportionally spaced fonts. And since Windows just copied the Mac, it's likely that no personal computer would have them. If I had never dropped out, I would have never dropped in on that calligraphy class, and personal computers might not have the wonderful typography that they do. Of course it was impossible to connect the dots looking forward when I was in college. But it was very, very clear looking backwards ten years later.

Again, you can't connect the dots looking forward; you can only connect them looking backwards. So you have to trust that the dots will somehow connect in your future. You have to trust in something - your gut, destiny, life, karma, whatever. **Because believing that the dots will connect down the road will give you the confidence to follow your heart even when it leads you off the well-worn path, and that will make all the difference.**

My second story is about love and loss.

I was lucky - I found what I loved to do early in life. Woz and I started Apple in my parent's garage when I was 20. We worked hard, and in 10 years Apple had grown from just the two of us in a garage into a $2 billion company with over 4000 employees. We had just released our finest creation - the Macintosh - a year earlier, and I had just turned 30. And then I got fired. How can you get fired from a company you started? Well, as Apple grew we hired someone who I thought was very talented to run the company with me, and for the first year or so things went well. But then our visions of the future began to diverge and eventually we had a falling out. When we did, our Board of Directors sided with him. So at 30 I was out. And very publicly out. What had been the focus of my entire adult life was gone, and it was devastating.

I really didn't know what to do for a few months. I felt that I had let the previous generation of entrepreneurs down - that I had dropped the baton as it was being passed to me. I met with David Packard and Bob Noyce and tried to apologize for screwing up so badly. I was a very public failure, and I even thought about running away from the valley. But something slowly began to dawn on me - I still loved what I did. The turn of events at Apple had not changed that one bit. I had been rejected, but I was still in love. And so I decided to start over.

I didn't see it then, but it turned out that getting fired from Apple was the best thing that could have ever happened to me. The heaviness of being successful was replaced by the lightness of being a beginner again, less sure about everything. It freed me to enter one of the most creative periods of my life.

During the next five years, I started a company named NeXT, another company named Pixar, and fell in love with an amazing woman who would become my wife.

Pixar went on to create the world's first computer animated feature film, Toy Story, and is now the most successful animation studio in the world. In a remarkable turn of events, Apple bought NeXT, I returned to Apple, and the technology we developed at NeXT is at the heart of Apple's current renaissance. And Laurene and I have a wonderful family together.

I'm pretty sure none of this would have happened if I hadn't been fired from Apple. It was awful tasting medicine, but I guess the patient needed it. **Sometimes life hits you in the head with a brick. Don't lose faith.** I'm convinced that the only thing that kept me going was that I loved what I did. You've got to find what you love. And that is as true for your work as it is for your lovers. Your work is going to fill a large part of your life, and the only way to be truly satisfied is to do what you believe is great work. And the only way to do great work is to love what you do. If you haven't found it yet, keep looking. And don't settle. As with all matters of the heart, you'll know when you find it. And, like any great relationship, it just gets better and better as the years roll on. So keep looking. Don't settle.

My third story is about death.

When I was 17, I read a quote that went something like: "If you live each day as if it was your last, someday you'll most certainly be right." It made an impression on me, and since then, for the past 33 years, I have looked in the mirror every morning and asked myself: "If today were the last day of my life, would I want to do what I am about to do today?" And whenever the answer has been "No" for too many days in a row, I know I need to change something.

Remembering that I'll be dead soon is the most important tool I've ever encountered to help me make the big

choices in life. Because almost everything - all external expectations, all pride, all fear of embarrassment or failure - these things just fall away in the face of death, leaving only what is truly important. Remembering that you are going to die is the best way I know to avoid the trap of thinking you have something to lose. You are already naked. There is no reason not to follow your heart.

About a year ago I was diagnosed with cancer. I had a scan at 7:30 in the morning, and it clearly showed a tumor on my pancreas. I didn't even know what a pancreas was. The doctors told me this was almost certainly a type of cancer that is incurable, and that I should expect to live no longer than three to six months. My doctor advised me to go home and get my affairs in order, which is doctor's code for prepare to die. It means to try to tell your kids everything you thought you'd have the next 10 years to tell them in just a few months. It means to make sure everything is buttoned up so that it will be as easy as possible for your family. It means to say your goodbyes.

I lived with that diagnosis all day. Later that evening I had a biopsy, where they stuck an endoscope down my throat, through my stomach and into my intestines, put a needle into my pancreas and got a few cells from the tumor. I was sedated, but my wife, who was there, told me that when they viewed the cells under a microscope the doctors started crying because it turned out to be a very rare form of pancreatic cancer that is curable with surgery. I had the surgery and thankfully I'm fine now.

This was the closest I've been to facing death, and I hope it's the closest I get for a few more decades. Having lived through it, I can now say this to you with a bit more certainty than when death was a useful but purely intellectual concept:

No one wants to die. Even people who want to go to heaven don't want to die to get there. And yet death is the destination we all share. No one has ever escaped it. And that is as it should be, because Death is very likely the single best invention of Life. It is Life's change agent. It clears out the old to make way for the new. Right now the new is you, but someday not too long from now, you will gradually become the old and be cleared away. Sorry to be so dramatic, but it is quite true.

Your time is limited, so don't waste it living someone else's life. Don't be trapped by dogma - which is living with the results of other people's thinking. Don't let the noise of others' opinions drown out your own inner voice. And most important, have the courage to follow your heart and intuition. They somehow already know what you truly want to become. Everything else is secondary.

When I was young, there was an amazing publication called The Whole Earth Catalog, which was one of the bibles of my generation. It was created by a fellow named Stewart Brand not far from here in Menlo Park, and he brought it to life with his poetic touch. This was in the late 1960's, before personal computers and desktop publishing, so it was all made with typewriters, scissors, and polaroid cameras. It was sort of like Google in paperback form, 35 years before Google came along: it was idealistic, and overflowing with neat tools and great notions.

Stewart and his team put out several issues of The Whole Earth Catalog, and then when it had run its course, they put out a final issue. It was the mid-1970s, and I was your age. On the back cover of their final issue was a photograph of an early morning country road, the kind you might find yourself hitchhiking on if you were so adventurous. Beneath it were the words: "Stay Hungry. Stay Foolish." It was their farewell message as they signed off. Stay Hungry. Stay Foolish. And I have always wished that for myself. And now, as you graduate to begin anew, I wish that for you.

Stay Hungry. Stay Foolish.
Thank you all very much."

Chapter 1

PERCEPTION IS REALITY

"Everything you see or hear or experience in any way at all is specific to you. You create a universe by perceiving it, so everything in the universe you perceive is specific to you."

— **Douglas Adams**

Let me start by asking a question. If a person owns a home that is equipped with air conditioning, cable or satellite TV, DVD player, refrigerator, microwave oven, stereo and automatic dishwasher, and he/she owns a car, cell phone and has enough food to eat, would you consider this person to be living in poverty? According to the US Census Bureau, over the last 20 years, there has been an average of 11.3 to 15.1% of the population considered to be poor. Also, according to recent (~2005) government reports related to America's poor, 43% own homes, 80% have air conditioning (compared to 36% in 1970), ~75% own a car, 97% own a color television, 62% have cable or satellite TV, 89% own a microwave, ~33% have an automatic dishwasher and 89% report that they have enough to eat. It is true that there are some in America who truly are destitute and they truly need our help, but are the poor of today truly worse off than even the middle class of the 1940's?

Rich and poor are relative terms, just like warm and cool. I have several friends who live in Texas. The median house price throughout the state has been between $140,000 and $180,000 between 2000 and 2014. However, I have spent much of my life within a short drive of Disneyland, California. I could usually hear its nightly fireworks display when I was home.

At the height of the housing boom in 2006, the median house price in Orange County, CA, was $709,000. If a person in Texas and a person in Orange County obtained $0 fee, 0% interest 30-year loans from the bank, the Texan would have a mortgage payment of about $500 per month [180,000 ÷ 360], whereas the person from Orange County would have a mortgage payment around $1970 per month [709,000 ÷ 360].

Is the person in California wealthier because he owns a house that is worth $700,000 or is the person in Texas wealthier because he has an extra $1500 a month to purchase other things? The answer to this question depends on how you perceive it, and things are not always as they seem.

Taylor Armstrong was a cast member of the reality TV show *Housewives of Beverly Hills*. This show is about glitz, glamor and drama which offers a glimpse inside the world of luxurious wealth and pampered privilege. On September 2, 2010 (9.02.10), the city of Beverly Hills hosted a star-studded celebration honoring the date that matches its well-known zip code. Russell and Taylor Armstrong were at the center of the media's attention. Photographers and videographers were fighting each other to get images of this famous couple. They seemed to be a happily married wealthy couple.

On July 15, 2011, Taylor Armstrong filed for divorce. On August 15, 2011, Russell Armstrong was found dead. It was ruled a suicide. One day later, Russel Armstrong's business associate, Alan Schram, was also found dead. This too was ruled a suicide. Reports came in about their shady business dealings they did to fund their lavish lifestyle. Diane Diamond posted an in-depth report about the Armstrong's activities: Guilty plea to tax evasion in 1995, bankruptcy in 2005, and multiple lawsuits alleging fraud.

As the old saying goes, do not judge a book by its cover. You need to ask the right questions and find out what is really going on. Many reporters and bloggers will duplicate an article without verifying its veracity. There are many consumers of news who, due to complacency or the desire to promote an agenda, will believe the lies before they believe the truth. They live in their own reality, and they are comfortable there. No matter what evidence you show them to the contrary that their facts are incorrect, they will disregard them. I have a special name for this kind of person: Guardian. They are the protector of their own ego. **For some, being right is more important than being correct.**

Case in point, on September 11, 2001, airplanes flew into both towers of the World Trade Center in New York. There are many videos and eye witness testimonies describing the events of that day. On October 29, 2004, Osama bin Laden made a television appearance taking credit for the deaths of almost 3000 people. Despite all this evidence, there are people who believe that either 9/11 was an inside job committed by the President George W. Bush administration or that the events never even took place. There is a 2004 French TV documentary and similarly named paperback book called *Le 11 septembre n'a pas eu lieu* (September 11 did not occur). The premise of the movie is that 9/11 was a government conspiracy designed to gain political advantage. The Guardian style personality may truly believe that President George W. Bush and Vice President Richard Cheney wanted to start a war in the Middle East to steal their oil and to make themselves wealthy, and all they needed to do was to convince the American people. The Guardian will ignore any evidence to the contrary, especially if it proves that they have made incorrect assumptions.

Even with all the problematic issues related to perception, it does serve a purpose. I read a story several years ago that went something like this: A man driving an ice cream truck is passing through a residential part of town, takes a wrong turn, and before he realizes what is happening, he begins to drive through a tunnel. The top part of his vehicle begins to scrape the bottom of the bridge he is driving under. Soon, his truck becomes stuck in the tunnel. The driver stops for a moment, puts the car in reverse and tries to drive out of his predicament backwards, but he is unsuccessful. The vehicle does not move. So he turns off the engine, pulls out his cell phone and calls the police to help him out. When the police arrive on the scene, they close the road, redirect traffic and call for a tow truck. Soon the tow truck appears on the scene. The driver of the ice cream truck, the police and the tow truck driver try for over half an hour to extract the vehicle from the tunnel without success. It is at this time a 9 year old boy walks past the accident. Curious, he walks up to the drawn out yellow police tape that is designed to keep him and others away. After a few minutes of watching, a police officer walks over to the child. The police officer says, *"Where are your parents?"* The boy answers, *"I was on my way to the store when I saw this accident. I was curious."* The police officer tells him in a professional tone to move on out of the area. The boy then says, *"But I can help. I know how to get that truck out of the tunnel."* The police officer now curious, says *"What is your idea?"* The boy says in an excited tone, *"Flatten the tires!"* The police officer, realizing that the boy is right, walks over to the other men who are showing signs of exhaustion and tells them to let the air out of the tires. Within a couple minutes, the truck lowers a few inches and is able to be extracted from the tunnel.

Every person has their own way of looking at the world. As previously discussed (see Introduction), Steve Jobs wanted to change the world, and he did. Most people are appreciative of his efforts. However, there is another man who wanted to change the world. He became Chancellor of Germany in 1933. He strengthened its military and began to expand its Nation's boundaries starting in 1939. It took the combined efforts of the United States of America, Great Britain and Russia to finally stop this person's extremely aggressive behavior. I will not honor this person by mentioning his name. Those who know history of the 1940s understand exactly who I am talking about. I will simply call him H. He, like Steve Jobs, wanted to change the world. Where Jobs was admired, H was despised by hundreds of millions of people.

How is it that a man like Steve Jobs is loved by so many and H is hated by so many? The answer has to do with perception. Steve Jobs made people's lives easier, more entertaining and more convenient with all the products developed through Apple and Pixar. H made people's lives more difficult. He wanted to impose his form of government on a large group of people in Europe. He did this through military action that resulted in the deaths of millions of people.

WHAT IS PERCEPTION AND HOW DOES IT WORK?

Perception, as defined by Stephen P. Robbins (Ph.D., University of Arizona, Management and Organizational Behavior), *"is a process by which individuals organize and interpret their sensory impressions in order to give meaning to their environment."*

We, by nature, interpret what we see, hear, taste, smell and feel, in order to make sense out of and categorize the experience. A person's behavior is shaped by perceptions not by facts, and there are multiple factors that can influence one's perceptions:

1. Time
2. Mind-set
3. Personality
4. Environment
5. Personal History
6. Intentions / Motivations
7. Appearance, personality, attitude, and situation of the person, place, or object being perceived

When one person comes in contact with another, both people perceive the encounter, generalize and make quick judgments. Right, wrong, good, bad or indifferent, we make many decisions and judgment calls on a daily basis. If we had to thoroughly analyze every single event in our often repetitious lives, we would spend most of our time analyzing a situation rather than experiencing it. Our perceptions are like any other tool. They could help us or they could hurt us, depending on how they are used.

TRADITIONAL MORALITY, NEW MORALITY AND UNIVERSAL MORALITY

Morality can be expressed as a form of perception. Each person has his/her own moral construct. Is it right to spank a child for the purposes of discipline? Should parents take active and authoritative rolls in their child's education? What about a child that is not their own? People have wide ranging opinions on these matters, but what about kidnapping, rape and murder? Many more people would agree than disagree that these actions are wrong. **Whereas controlled spanking for the purposes of discipline is not illegal, murder is against the law in the US.** Is morality completely personal or is there a universal morality?

I will close this chapter by quoting the beginning portion of a speech presented by playwright, journalist, Connecticut Congresswoman, ambassador to Italy, winner of the Presidential Medal of Freedom, and wife to Time Magazine publisher Henry Luce - Clare Boothe Luce. It was presented in Honolulu, Hawaii, on May 28, 1978, to the Golden Circle of IBM Achievers and titled *"Is the New Morality Destroying America?"*.

It was a time when American women were transitioning from bread makers to bread winners, from wearing an apron to wearing a business suit. Cultural values and norms were shifting. Perceptions related to the roles of men and women were changing. She begins her discussion by describing the difference between traditional morality and this new cultural morality. She also asks if there is a universal morality that transcends people and cultures.

Is the New Morality Destroying America?
Clare Boothe Luce
May 28, 1978
Honolulu, Hawaii

"I was honored - as who would not be? - by the invitation to address this Golden Circle of remarkable IBM achievers. But I confess I was somewhat floored by the subject your program producer assigned to me. He asked me to hold forth for a half-hour on the condition of morality in the United States, with special reference to the differences between America's traditional moral values and the values of the so-called "New Morality." Now even a theologian or a philosopher might hesitate to tackle so vast and complex a subject in just 30 minutes. So I suggested that he let me talk instead about, well, politics or foreign affairs, or the Press. But he insisted that your convention wanted to talk on a subject related to morals.

Well, the invitation reminded me of a story about Archbishop Sheen, who received a telegram inviting him to deliver an address to a convention on "The World, Peace, War, and the Churches." He replied: "Gentlemen, I am honored to address your great convention, but I would not want my style to be cramped by so narrow a subject. However, I would be glad to accept if you will widen the subject to include `The Sun and the Moon and the Stars." So I finally agreed to talk if I could widen my subject to include, "The Traditional Morality, the New Morality, and the Universal Morality."

There's another trouble with talking about morals. It's a terribly serious subject. And a serious talk is just one step away from being a dull, not to say a soporific one. So I won't be offended if, before I finish, some of you leave. But please do so quietly, so as not to disturb those who may be sleeping.

The theme of this convention is "Involvement." Now there is one thing in which all Americans, including every one of us here, are already deeply involved. **Every day of our lives, every hour of our waking days, we are all inescapably involved in making America either a more moral or a more immoral country.**

So this morning, let's take a look at the direction in which we Americans are going. But first, we must begin by asking, "What are morals?" Morals, the dictionary tells us, are a set of principles of right action and behavior for the individual. The "traditional morality" of any given society is the set of moral principles to which the great majority of its members have subscribed over a good length of time. It is the consensus which any given society has reached on what right action and decent behavior are for everybody. It is the way that society expects a person to behave, even when the law - the civil law - does not require him to do so.

One example will have to suffice. There is no law that requires a person to speak the truth, unless he is under oath to do so in a court proceeding. A person can, with legal impunity, be an habitual liar. The traditional morality of our society, however, takes a dim view of the habitual liar. Accordingly, society punishes him in the only way it can - by social ostracism.

The person who believes in the traditional principles of his society, and who also succeeds in regulating his conduct by them, is recognized by society as a "moral person." But the person who believes in these principles - who knows the difference between "right and wrong" personal conduct, but who nevertheless habitually chooses to do what he himself believes to be wrong - is looked upon by his society as an "immoral person." But what about the person who does not believe in the traditional moral principles of his society, and who openly challenges them on grounds that he believes to be rational? Is such a person to be considered a moral or an immoral person?

Today there are many Americans who sincerely believe that many of our traditional moral values are "obsolete." They hold that some of them go against the laws of human nature, that others are no longer relevant to the economic and political condition of our society, that this or that so-called "traditional moral value" contravenes the individual's Constitutional freedoms and legitimate pursuit of happiness. Others believe that while a moral value system is necessary as a general guideline for societal behavior, it cannot, and should not, apply to everybody. Every person is unique; no two persons are ever in exactly the same situation or "moral bind"; circumstances alter moral cases. These persons believe, in other words, that all morals are "relative," and all ethics are "situational." They argue that what is wrong behavior for others is right behavior for me, because my circumstances are different. The new principles of right action and behavior which such persons have been advancing and practicing today have come to be called "the New Morality."

But before we undertake to discuss the differences between the traditional American morality and the so-called "New Morality," let us ask a most important question: Is there any such thing as a universal morality? Is there any set of moral principles which apply to everybody - everybody who has ever been born, and which has been accepted by the majority of mankind in all places and in all ages?

There is, indeed, a universal morality. It knows no race, no geographical boundaries, no time, and no particular religion. As John Ruskin, the English social reformer, wrote, "There are many religions, but there is only one morality." Immanuel Kant, the greatest of German philosophers, called it the Moral Law, which, he said, governs all mankind. Kant compared this Moral Law to the Sublime Law that rules the movement of the stars and the planets. "We are doomed to be moral and cannot help ourselves," said Dr. John Haynes Holmes, the Protestant theologian.

When we study the history of human thought, we discover a truly remarkable thing - all the great minds of the world have agreed on the marks of the moral person. In all civilizations, in all ages, they have hailed truthfulness as a mark of morality. "The aim of the superior man," said Confucius, "is Truth." **Plato, the Greek philosopher, held that "truth is the beginning of every good thing both in Heaven and on earth, and he who would be blessed and happy should be from the first a partaker of truth, for then he can be trusted."** "Veracity," said Thomas Huxley, the English scientist, "is the heart of morality." In Judeo-Christian lore, the Devil's other name is "The Liar."

Another mark of the moral person is honesty. "An honest man is the noblest work of God," wrote [Alexander] Pope in his Essay on Man. "Every honest man will suppose honest acts to flow from honest principles," said Thomas Jefferson. The moral person is just. "Justice is the firm and continuous desire to render to everyone that which is his due," wrote Justinian. Disraeli called Justice "Truth in action." The moral person is honorable. At whatever cost to himself - including, sometimes, his very life - he does his duty by his family, his job, his country. "To an honest man," wrote Plautus, the great Roman poet, "it is an honor to have minded his duty." Two thousand years later, Woodrow Wilson voiced the same conviction. "There is no question, what the Roll of Honor in America is." Wilson said: "The Roll of Honor consists of the names of men who have squared their conduct by ideals of duty."

If, in an hour of weakness, the moral man does a thing he knows to be wrong, he confesses it, and he "takes his punishment like a soldier." And, if he harms another, even inadvertently, he tries to make restitution. He takes responsibility for his own actions. And if they turn out badly for him, he does not put the blame on others. He does not, for example, yield to the post Freudian moral cop-out of blaming his follies and failures, his weaknesses and vices, on the way his parents treated him in childhood. Here I cannot resist mentioning the case of Tom Hansen, of Boulder, Colorado, a 24-year old youth who is living on welfare relief funds. He is presently suing his parents for 350,000 dollars damages because, he claims, they are to blame for lousing up his life, and turning him into a failure. Adam was, of course, the first man to try to shift responsibility for his behavior onto someone else. As there was no Jewish mom to blame, he laid it on to his wife Eve.

"Absolute morality," wrote the English philosopher, Herbert Spencer, "is the regulation of conduct in such a way that pain will not be inflicted." The moral person is kind to the weak and compassionate with those who suffer. Above all, he is courageous. Courage is the ladder on which all the other virtues mount. Plautus, a true nobleman of antiquity, wrote, **"Courage stands before everything. It is what preserves our liberty, our lives, our homes, and our parents, our children, and our country.** A man with courage has every blessing."

There is also one moral precept that is common to all the great religions of history. It is called the Golden Rule. **"Do unto others as you would have them do to you."** When Confucius was asked what he considered the single most important rule for right conduct, he replied, "Reciprocity." **The "universal morality" is based on these virtues - truthfulness, honesty, duty, responsibility, unselfishness, loyalty, honor, compassion and courage. As Americans, we can say proudly that the traditional moral values of our society have been a reflection, however imperfect, of this universal morality. All of our great men, all of our heroes, have been exemplars of some, if not all, of these virtues.**

To be sure, different cultures and civilizations have placed more emphasis on some of these virtues than on others. For example, the morality of the early Romans heavily stressed courage, honor, and duty. Even today we still call these the manly virtues, and we tend to associate them with another value we call "patriotism." In contrast, the morality of the Judeo-Christian cultures of the West have placed their heaviest emphasis on altruism, kindness, and compassion. "Though I speak with the tongue of men and angels, and have not charity," St. Paul wrote, "I am become as sounding brass or a tinkling cymbal." Americans, whose traditional morality reflects the Christian virtue of compassion, donated thirty billion dollars last year to charity. Americans also tend to consider compassion for the underprivileged a greater virtue in politicians than either honor or courage.

Now, if all these virtues do indeed represent the universal morality, then what do their opposites represent? Well, **lying, dishonesty, dereliction of duty, irresponsibility, dishonorable conduct, disloyalty, selfishness, cowardice, cruelty and hypocrisy represent, of course, the universal immorality.**

In passing, hypocrisy, which has been called "the compliment that vice pays to virtue," has been viewed as the height of immorality in all civilizations. "Of all villainy," cried Cicero, "there is none more base than that of the hypocrite, who at the moment he is most false, takes care to appear most virtuous." The English philosopher Henry Hazlitt called hypocrisy "the only vice that cannot be forgiven." Jesus cursed only one category of sinner, saying, "Oh woe to Ye, scribes and hypocrites!" Even the cynic and agnostic Voltaire, cried: "How inexpressible is the meanness of being a hypocrite!"

So now we are ready to ask: In what direction can we say that Americans are going? Are we, as a people, going on the high road of the universal morality or on the low road of the universal immorality? The question is a crucial one for the future of our country. All history bears witness to the fact that there can be no public virtue without private morality. There cannot be good government except in a good society. And there cannot be a good society unless the majority of individuals in it are at least trying to be good people. This is especially true in a democracy, where leaders and representatives are chosen from the people, by the people. The character of a democratic government will never be better than the character of the people it governs. A nation that is traveling the low road is a nation that is self-destructing. It is doomed, sooner or later, to collapse from within, or to be destroyed from without. And not all its wealth, science and technology will be able to save it. On the contrary, a decadent society will use, or rather, misuse and abuse, these very advantages in such a way as to hasten its own destruction."

SPOTLIGHT ON THEODORE ROOSEVELT

Theodore Roosevelt was an American author, naturalist, explorer, historian, Assistant Secretary of the Navy, leader of the

Republican Party, founder of the Progressive Party and 26th President of the United States. He is noted for his exuberant personality, range of interests and achievements and his "cowboy" persona. Born into a wealthy family in New York City, Roosevelt was a sickly child who suffered from asthma. To overcome his physical weakness, he embraced a strenuous life. Home schooled, he became an eager student of nature. He attended Harvard College where he studied biology, boxed and developed an interest in naval affairs. Roosevelt was a member of the Alpha Delta Phi literary society and the Delta Kappa Epsilon fraternity. He was an editor of The Harvard Advocate and graduated Phi Beta Kappa (22nd of 177) and magna cum laude from Harvard.

Theodore Roosevelt was known for politics and policies that crossed party lines. He held just as many conservative views as he did progressive views. He was the Republican nominee for Vice President with William McKinley, campaigning successfully against radicalism and for prosperity, national honor, imperialism (regarding the Philippines), high tariffs and the gold standard. Roosevelt became President after McKinley was assassinated. He attempted to move the GOP toward Progressivism, including trust busting and increased regulation of businesses. In November 1904 he was reelected in a landslide against conservative Democrat Alton Brooks Parker. Roosevelt called his domestic policies a "Square Deal", promising a fair deal to the average citizen while breaking up monopolistic corporations, holding down railroad rates, and guaranteeing pure food and drugs. He encouraged conservation, and he greatly expanded the system of national parks and national forests. His foreign policy focused on the Caribbean, where he built the Panama Canal and expanded the Navy. He negotiated an end to the Russo-Japanese War, for which he won the Nobel Peace Prize. At the end of his second term, Roosevelt supported his close friend William Howard Taft for the 1908 Republican nomination.

In 1910 he broke with President Taft on issues of progressivism and personalities. In the 1912 election Roosevelt tried but failed to block Taft's renomination. He then launched the Progressive ("Bull Moose") Party that called for progressive reforms, splitting the Republican vote. That allowed Democrat Woodrow Wilson to win the White House, while the Taft conservatives gained control of the GOP for decades. From 1914 to 1917 he campaigned for American entry into World War I, and reconciled with GOP leadership.

At the end of his second term in office, he set out to tour Africa and Europe, hoping to allow his successor to become his own man. After a safari in Africa, he traveled throughout Europe. While in France, he was invited to speak at the historic University of Paris. Roosevelt used the opportunity to deliver perhaps a long but nevertheless powerful speech on the requirements of citizenship, the characteristics which would keep democracies like France and the United States robust and strong. He makes two primary arguments. First, Americans must be active participants in protecting liberty and justice in our republic. Second, we should pull solutions from both philosophical ends of the political spectrum (namely individualism and socialism), but maintain a more moderate political stance.

Citizenship in a Republic
University of Paris
Paris, France
April 23, 1910

> "Strange and impressive associations rise in the mind of a man from the New World who speaks before this august body in this ancient institution of learning. Before his eyes pass the shadows of mighty kings and war-like nobles, of great masters of law and theology; through the shining dust of the dead centuries he sees crowded figures that tell of the power and learning and splendor of times gone by; and he sees also the innumerable host of humble students to whom

clerkship meant emancipation, to whom it was well-nigh the only outlet from the dark thraldom of the Middle Ages.

This was the most famous university of medieval Europe at a time when no one dreamed that there was a New World to discover. Its services to the cause of human knowledge already stretched far back into the remote past at a time when my forefathers, three centuries ago, were among the sparse bands of traders, ploughmen, wood-choppers, and fisherfolk who, in hard struggle with the iron unfriendliness of the Indian-haunted land, were laying the foundations of what has now become the giant republic of the West. To conquer a continent, to tame the shaggy roughness of wild nature, means grim warfare; and the generations engaged in it cannot keep, still less add to, the stores of garnered wisdom which where once theirs, and which are still in the hands of their brethren who dwell in the old land. To conquer the wilderness means to wrest victory from the same hostile forces with which mankind struggled on the immemorial infancy of our race. The primaeval conditions must be met by the primaeval qualities which are incompatible with the retention of much that has been painfully acquired by humanity as through the ages it has striven upward toward civilization. In conditions so primitive there can be but a primitive culture. At first only the rudest school can be established, for no others would meet the needs of the hard-driven, sinewy folk who thrust forward the frontier in the teeth of savage men and savage nature; and many years elapse before any of these schools can develop into seats of higher learning and broader culture.

The pioneer days pass; the stump-dotted clearings expand into vast stretches of fertile farm land; the stockaded clusters of log cabins change into towns; the hunters of game, the fellers of trees, the rude frontier traders and tillers of the soil, **the men who wander all their lives long through the wilderness as the heralds and harbingers of an oncoming civilization, themselves vanish before the civilization for which they have prepared the way.** The children of their successors and supplanters, and then their children and their children and children's children, change and develop with extraordinary rapidity. **The conditions accentuate vices and virtues, energy and ruthlessness, all the good qualities and all the defects of an intense individualism, self-reliant, self-centered, far more conscious of its rights than of its duties, and blind to its own shortcomings.** To the hard materialism of the frontier days succeeds the hard materialism of an industrialism even more intense and absorbing than that of the older nations; although these themselves have likewise already entered on the age of a complex and predominantly industrial civilization.

As the country grows, its people, who have won success in so many lines, turn back to try to recover the possessions of the mind and the spirit, which perforce their fathers threw aside in order better to wage the first rough battles for the continent their children inherit. **The leaders of thought and of action grope their way forward to a new life, realizing, sometimes dimly, sometimes clear-sightedly, that the life of material gain, whether for a nation or an individual, is of value only as a foundation, only as there is added to it the uplift that comes from devotion to loftier ideals.** The new life thus sought can in part be developed afresh from what is roundabout in the New World; but it can developed in full only by freely drawing upon the treasure-houses of the Old World, upon the treasures stored in the ancient abodes of wisdom and learning, such as this is where I speak to-day. **It is a mistake for any nation to merely copy another; but it is even a greater mistake, it is a proof of weakness in any nation, not to**

be anxious to learn from one another and willing and able to adapt that learning to the new national conditions and make it fruitful and productive therein. It is for us of the New World to sit at the feet of Gamaliel of the Old; then, if we have the right stuff in us, we can show that Paul in his turn can become a teacher as well as a scholar.

To-day I shall speak to you on the subject of individual citizenship, the one subject of vital importance to you, my hearers, and to me and my countrymen, because you and we a great citizens of great democratic republics. A democratic republic such as ours – an effort to realize its full sense government by, of, and for the people – represents the most gigantic of all possible social experiments, the one fraught with great responsibilities alike for good and evil. The success or republics like yours and like ours means the glory, and our failure of despair, of mankind; and for you and for us the question of the quality of the individual citizen is supreme. **Under other forms of government, under the rule of one man or very few men, the quality of the leaders is all-important.** If, under such governments, the quality of the rulers is high enough, then the nations for generations lead a brilliant career, and add substantially to the sum of world achievement, no matter how low the quality of average citizen; because the average citizen is an almost negligible quantity in working out the final results of that type of national greatness.

But with you and us the case is different. With you here, and with us in my own home, in the long run, **success or failure will be conditioned upon the way in which the average man, the average women, does his or her duty, first in the ordinary, every-day affairs of life, and next in those great occasional cries which call for heroic virtues. The average citizen must be a good citizen if our republics are to succeed. The stream will**

not permanently rise higher than the main source; and the main source of national power and national greatness is found in the average citizenship of the nation. Therefore it behooves us to do our best to see that the standard of the average citizen is kept high; and the average cannot be kept high unless the standard of the leaders is very much higher.

It is well if a large proportion of the leaders in any republic, in any democracy, are, as a matter of course, drawn from the classes represented in this audience to-day; but only provided that those classes possess the gifts of sympathy with plain people and of devotion to great ideals. You and those like you have received special advantages; you have all of you had the opportunity for mental training; many of you have had leisure; most of you have had a chance for enjoyment of life far greater than comes to the majority of your fellows. **To you and your kind much has been given, and from you much should be expected.** Yet there are certain failings against which it is especially incumbent that both men of trained and cultivated intellect, and men of inherited wealth and position should especially guard themselves, because to these failings they are especially liable; and if yielded to, their – your – chances of useful service are at an end.

Let the man of learning, the man of lettered leisure, beware of that queer and cheap temptation to pose to himself and to others as a cynic, as the man who has outgrown emotions and beliefs, the man to whom good and evil are as one. The poorest way to face life is to face it with a sneer. There are many men who feel a kind of twister pride in cynicism; **there are many who confine themselves to criticism of the way others do what they themselves dare not even attempt.** There is no more unhealthy being, no man less worthy of respect, than he who either really holds, or feigns to hold, an attitude of sneering disbelief toward all that is great and lofty, whether in achievement or in that noble effort which, even if it fails, comes to second achievement. A cynical habit of thought and speech, a readiness to criticize work which the critic himself never tries to perform, an intellectual aloofness which will not accept contact with life's realities – all these are marks, not as the possessor would fain to think, of superiority but of weakness. They mark the men unfit to bear their part painfully in the stern strife of living, who seek, in the affection of contempt for the achievements of others, to hide from others and from themselves in their own weakness. The rÃ´le is easy; there is none easier, save only the rÃ´le of the man who sneers alike at both criticism and performance.

It is not the critic who counts; not the man who points out how the strong man stumbles, or where the doer of deeds could have done them better. **The credit belongs to the man who is actually in the arena, whose face in marred by dust and sweat and blood; who strives valiantly; who errs, who comes short again and again, because there is no effort without error and shortcoming; but who does actually strive to do the deeds; who knows great enthusiasms, the great devotions; who spends himself in a worthy cause; who at the best knows in the end the triumph of high achievement, and who at the worst, if he fails, at least fails while daring greatly, so that his place shall never be with those cold and timid souls who neither know victory nor defeat.** Shame on the man of cultivated taste who permits refinement to develop into fastidiousness that unfits him for doing the rough work of a workaday world. Among the free peoples who govern themselves there is but a small field of usefulness open for the men of cloistered life who shrink from contact with their fellows. Still less room is there for those who deride of slight what is done by those who actually bear the brunt of the day; nor yet for those others who always profess that they would like to take action, if only the conditions of life were not exactly what they actually are. The man who does nothing cuts the same sordid figure in the pages of history, whether he be a cynic, or fop, or voluptuary. **There is little use for the being whose tepid soul knows nothing of great and generous emotion, of the high pride, the stern belief, the lofty enthusiasm, of the men who quell the storm and ride the thunder.** Well for these men if they succeed; well also, though not so well, if they fail, given only that they have nobly ventured, and have put forth all their heart and strength. It is war-worn Hotspur, spent with hard fighting, he of the many errors and valiant end, over whose memory we love to linger, not over the memory of the young lord who "but for the vile guns would have been a valiant soldier."

France has taught many lessons to other nations: surely one of the most important lesson is the lesson her whole history teaches, that a high artistic and literary development is compatible with notable leadership in arms and statecraft. The brilliant gallantry of the French soldier has for many centuries been proverbial; and during these same centuries at every court in Europe the "Freemasons of fashion" have treated the French tongue as their common speech; while every artist and man of letters, and every man of science able to appreciate that marvelous instrument of precision, French prose, had turned toward France for aid and inspiration. How long the leadership in arms and letters has lasted is curiously illustrated by the fact that the earliest masterpiece in a modern tongue is the splendid French epic which tells of Roland's doom and the vengeance of Charlemagne when the lords of the Frankish hosts where stricken at Roncesvalles.

Let those who have, keep, let those who have not, strive to attain, a high standard of cultivation and scholarship. Yet let us remember that these stand second to certain other things. There is need of a sound body, and even more of a sound mind. But above mind and above body stands character – the sum of those qualities which we mean when we speak of a man's force and courage, of his good faith and sense of honor. I believe in exercise for the body, always provided that we keep in mind that physical development is a means and not an end. I believe, of course, in giving to all the people a good education. But the education must contain much besides book-learning in order to be really good. We must ever remember that no keenness and subtleness of intellect, no polish, no cleverness, in any way make up for the lack of the great solid qualities. **Self restraint, self mastery, common sense, the power of accepting individual responsibility and yet of acting in conjunction with others, courage and resolution – these are the qualities which mark a masterful people.** Without them no people can control itself, or save itself from being controlled from the outside. I speak to brilliant assemblage; I speak in a great university which represents the flower of the highest intellectual development; I pay all homage to intellect and to elaborate and specialized training of the intellect; and yet I know I shall have the assent of all of you present when I add that more important still are the commonplace, every-day qualities and virtues.

Such ordinary, every-day qualities include the will and the power to work, to fight at need, and to have plenty of healthy children. The need that the average man shall work is so obvious as hardly to warrant insistence. There are a few people in every country so born that they can lead lives of leisure. These fill a useful function if they make it evident that leisure does not mean idleness; for some of the most valuable work needed by civilization is essentially non-remunerative in its character, and of course the people who do this work should in large part be drawn from those to whom remuneration is an object of indifference. But the average man must earn his own livelihood. He should be trained to do so, and he should be trained to feel that he occupies a contemptible position if he does not do so; that he is not an object of envy if he is idle, at whichever end of the social scale he stands, but an object of contempt, an object of derision.

In the next place, the good man should be both a strong and a brave man; that is, he should be able to fight, he should be able to serve his country as a soldier, if the need arises. There are well-meaning philosophers who declaim against the unrighteousness of war. They are right only if they lay all their emphasis upon the unrighteousness. War is a dreadful thing, and unjust war is a crime against humanity. But it is such a crime because it is unjust, not because it is a war. The choice must ever be in favor of righteousness, and this is whether the alternative be peace or whether the alternative be war. The question must not be merely, Is there to be peace or war? The question must be, Is it right to prevail? Are the great laws of righteousness once more to be fulfilled? And the answer from a strong and virile people must be "Yes," whatever the cost. **Every honorable effort should always be made to avoid war, just as every honorable effort should always be made by the individual in private life to keep out of a brawl, to keep out of trouble; but no self-respecting individual, no self-respecting nation, can or ought to submit to wrong.**

Finally, even more important than ability to work, even more important than ability to fight at need, is it to remember that chief of blessings for any nations is that it shall leave its seed to inherit the land. It was the crown of blessings in Biblical times and it is the crown of blessings now. The greatest of all curses in is the curse of sterility, and the severest of all condemnations should be that visited upon willful sterility. The first essential in any civilization is that the man and women shall be father and mother of healthy children, so that the race shall increase and not decrease. If that is not so, if through no fault of the society there is failure to increase, it is a great misfortune. If the failure is due to the deliberate and wilful fault, then it is not merely a misfortune, it is one of those crimes of ease and self-indulgence, of shrinking from pain and effort and risk, which in the long run Nature punishes more heavily than any other. If we of the great republics, if we, the free people who claim to have emancipated ourselves form the thraldom of wrong and error, bring down on our heads the curse that comes upon the willfully barren, then it will be an idle waste of breath to prattle of our achievements, to boast of all that we have done. No refinement of life, no delicacy of taste, no material progress, no sordid heaping up riches, no sensuous development of art and literature, can in any way compensate for the loss of the great fundamental virtues; and of these great fundamental virtues the greatest is the race's power to perpetuate the race.

Character must show itself in the man's performance both of the duty he owes himself and of the duty he owes the state. The man's foremast duty is owed to himself and his family; and he can do this duty only by earning money, by providing what is essential to material well-being; it is only after this has been done that he can hope to build a higher superstructure on the solid material foundation; it is only after this has been done that he can help in his movements for the general well-being. He must pull his own weight first, and only after this can his surplus strength be of use to the general public. It is not good to excite that bitter laughter which expresses contempt; and contempt is what we feel for the being whose enthusiasm to benefit mankind is such that he is a burden to those nearest him; who wishes to do great things for humanity in the abstract, but who cannot keep his wife in comfort or educate his children.

Nevertheless, while laying all stress on this point, while not merely acknowledging but insisting upon the fact that there must be a basis of material well-being for the individual as for the nation, let us with equal emphasis insist that this material well-being represents nothing but the foundation, and that the foundation, though indispensable, is worthless unless upon it is raised the superstructure of a higher life. That is why I decline to recognize the mere multimillionaire, the man of mere wealth, as an asset of value to any country; and especially as not an asset to my own country. If he has earned or uses his wealth in a way that makes him a real benefit, of real use – and such is often the case – why, then he does become an asset of real worth. But it is the way in which it has been earned or used, and not the mere fact of wealth, that entitles him to the credit. There is need in business, as in most other forms of human activity, of the great guiding intelligences. Their places cannot be supplied by any number of lesser intelligences. It is a good thing that they should have ample recognition, ample reward. But we must not transfer our admiration to the reward instead of to the deed rewarded; and if what should be the reward exists without the service having been rendered, then admiration will only come from those who are mean of soul. **The truth is that, after a certain measure of tangible material success or reward has been achieved, the question of increasing it becomes of constantly less importance compared to the other things that can be done in life.** It is a bad thing for a nation to raise and to admire a false standard of success; and their can be no falser standard

than that set by the deification of material well-being in
and for itself. But the man who, having far surpassed the
limits of providing for the wants; both of the body and
mind, of himself and of those depending upon him, then
piles up a great fortune, for the acquisition or retention of
which he returns no corresponding benefit to the nation as
a whole, should himself be made to feel that, so far from
being desirable, he is an unworthy, citizen of the community: that he is to be neither admired nor envied; that
his right-thinking fellow countrymen put him low in the
scale of citizenship, and leave him to be consoled by the
admiration of those whose level of purpose is even lower
than his own.

My position as regards the moneyed interests can be put
in a few words. In every civilized society property rights
must be carefully safeguarded; ordinarily, and in the great
majority of cases, human rights and property rights are
fundamentally and in the long run identical; but when it
clearly appears that there is a real conflict between them,
human rights must have the upper hand, for property belongs to man and not man to property.

In fact, it is essential to good citizenship clearly to understand that there are certain qualities which we in
a democracy are prone to admire in and of themselves,
which ought by rights to be judged admirable or the reverse solely from the standpoint of the use made of them.
Foremost among these I should include two very distinct
gifts – the gift of money-making and the gift of oratory.
Money-making, the money touch I have spoken of above.
It is a quality which in a moderate degree is essential. It
may be useful when developed to a very great degree, but
only if accompanied and controlled by other qualities; and
without such control the possessor tends to develop into
one of the least attractive types produced by a modern

industrial democracy. So it is with the orator. **It is highly desirable that a leader of opinion in democracy should be able to state his views clearly and convincingly. But all that the oratory can do of value to the community is enable the man thus to explain himself; if it enables the orator to put false values on things, it merely makes him power for mischief.** Some excellent public servants have not that gift at all, and must merely rely on their deeds to speak for them; and unless oratory does represent genuine conviction based on good common sense and able to be translated into efficient performance, then the better the oratory the greater the damage to the public it deceives. Indeed, **it is a sign of marked political weakness in any commonwealth if the people tend to be carried away by mere oratory, if they tend to value words in and for themselves, as divorced from the deeds for which they are supposed to stand. The phrase-maker, the phrase-monger, the ready talker, however great his power, whose speech does not make for courage, sobriety, and right understanding, is simply a noxious element in the body politic, and it speaks ill for the public if he has influence over them. To admire the gift of oratory without regard to the moral quality behind the gift is to do wrong to the republic.**

Of course all that I say of the orator applies with even greater force to the orator's latter-day and more influential brother, the journalist. The power of the journalist is great, but he is entitled neither to respect nor admiration because of that power unless it is used aright. He can do, and often does, great good. He can do, and he often does, infinite mischief. All journalists, all writers, for the very reason that they appreciate the vast possibilities of their profession, should bear testimony against those who deeply discredit it. Offenses against taste and morals, which are bad enough in a private citizen, are infinitely worse if made into instruments for debauching the community through a newspaper. **Mendacity, slander, sensationalism, inanity, vapid triviality, all are potent factors for the debauchery of the public mind and conscience.** The excuse advanced for vicious writing, that the public demands it and that demand must be supplied, can no more be admitted than if it were advanced by purveyors of food who sell poisonous adulterations.

In short, the good citizen in a republic must realize that the ought to possess two sets of qualities, and that neither avails without the other. He must have those qualities which make for efficiency; and that he also must have those qualities which direct the efficiency into channels for the public good. He is useless if he is inefficient. There is nothing to be done with that type of citizen of whom all that can be said is that he is harmless. Virtue which is dependent upon a sluggish circulation is not impressive. **There is little place in active life for the timid good man.** The man who is saved by weakness from robust wickedness is likewise rendered immune from robuster virtues. **The good citizen in a republic must first of all be able to hold his own. He is no good citizen unless he has the ability which will make him work hard and which at need will make him fight hard.** The good citizen is not a good citizen unless he is an efficient citizen.

But if a man's efficiency is not guided and regulated by a moral sense, then the more efficient he is the worse he is, the more dangerous to the body politic. Courage, intellect, all the masterful qualities, serve but to make a man more evil if they are merely used for that man's own advancement, with brutal indifference to the rights of others. It speaks ill for the community if the community worships these qualities and treats their possessors as heroes regardless of whether the qualities are used

rightly or wrongly. It makes no difference as to the precise way in which this sinister efficiency is shown. It makes no difference whether such a man's force and ability betray themselves in a career of money-maker or politician, soldier or orator, journalist or popular leader. If the man works for evil, then the more successful he is the more he should be despised and condemned by all upright and far-seeing men. **To judge a man merely by success is an abhorrent wrong; and if the people at large habitually so judge men, if they grow to condone wickedness because the wicked man triumphs, they show their inability to understand that in the last analysis free institutions rest upon the character of citizenship, and that by such admiration of evil they prove themselves unfit for liberty.**

The homely virtues of the household, the ordinary workaday virtues which make the woman a good housewife and housemother, which make the man a hard worker, a good husband and father, a good soldier at need, stand at the bottom of character. But of course many other must be added thereto if a state is to be not only free but great. Good citizenship is not good citizenship if only exhibited in the home. There remains the duties of the individual in relation to the State, and these duties are none too easy under the conditions which exist where the effort is made to carry on the free government in a complex industrial civilization. **Perhaps the most important thing the ordinary citizen, and, above all, the leader of ordinary citizens, has to remember in political life is that he must not be a sheer doctrinaire. The closest philosopher, the refined and cultured individual who from his library tells how men ought to be governed under ideal conditions, is of no use in actual governmental work; and the one-sided fanatic, and still more the mob-leader, and the insincere man who to achieve power promises what**

by no possibility can be performed, are not merely useless but noxious.

The citizen must have high ideals, and yet he must be able to achieve them in practical fashion. No permanent good comes from aspirations so lofty that they have grown fantastic and have become impossible and indeed undesirable to realize. The impractical visionary is far less often the guide and precursor than he is the embittered foe of the real reformer, of the man who, with stumblings and shortcoming, yet does in some shape, in practical fashion, give effect to the hopes and desires of those who strive for better things. **Woe to the empty phrasemaker, to the empty idealist, who, instead of making ready the ground for the man of action, turns against him when he appears and hampers him when he does work!** Moreover, the preacher of ideals must remember how sorry and contemptible is the figure which he will cut, how great the damage that he will do, if he does not himself, in his own life, strive measurably to realize the ideals that he preaches for others. Let him remember also that the worth of the ideal must be largely determined by the success with which it can in practice be realized. We should abhor the so-called "practical" men whose practicality assumes the shape of that peculiar baseness which finds its expression in disbelief in morality and decency, in disregard of high standards of living and conduct. Such a creature is the worst enemy of the body of politic. But only less desirable as a citizen is his nominal opponent and real ally, the man of fantastic vision who makes the impossible better forever the enemy of the possible good.

We can just as little afford to follow the doctrinaires of an extreme individualism as the doctrinaires of an extreme socialism. Individual initiative, so far from being discouraged, should be stimulated; and yet we should remember that, as society develops and grows more complex, we continually find that things which once it was desirable to leave to individual initiative can, under changed conditions, be performed with better results by common effort. It is quite impossible, and equally undesirable, to draw in theory a hard-and-fast line which shall always divide the two sets of cases. This every one who is not cursed with the pride of the closest philosopher will see, if he will only take the trouble to think about some of our closet phenomena. For instance, when people live on isolated farms or in little hamlets, each house can be left to attend to its own drainage and water-supply; but the mere multiplication of families in a given area produces new problems which, because they differ in size, are found to differ not only in degree, but in kind from the old; and the questions of drainage and water-supply have to be considered from the common standpoint. It is not a matter for abstract dogmatizing to decide when this point is reached; it is a matter to be tested by practical experiment. Much of the discussion about socialism and individualism is entirely pointless, because of the failure to agree on terminology. It is not good to be a slave of names. I am a strong individualist by personal habit, inheritance, and conviction; but **it is a mere matter of common sense to recognize that the State, the community, the citizens acting together, can do a number of things better than if they were left to individual action.** The individualism which finds its expression in the abuse of physical force is checked very early in the growth of civilization, and we of to-day should in our turn strive to shackle or destroy that individualism which triumphs by greed and cunning, which exploits the weak by craft instead of ruling them by brutality. We ought to go with any man in the effort to bring about justice and the equality of opportunity, to turn the tool-user more and more into the tool-owner, to shift burdens so that they can be more equitably borne. The deadening effect on any race of the adoption of a logical and extreme socialistic system could not be overstated; it would spell sheer destruction; it would produce grosser wrong and outrage, fouler immortality, than any existing system. But this does not mean that we may not with great advantage adopt certain of the principles professed by some given set of men who happen to call themselves Socialists; to be afraid to do so would be to make a mark of weakness on our part.

But we should not take part in acting a lie any more than in telling a lie. We should not say that men are equal where they are not equal, nor proceed upon the assumption that there is an equality where it does not exist; but we should strive to bring about a measurable equality, at least to the extent of preventing the inequality which is due to force or fraud. Abraham Lincoln, a man of the plain people, blood of their blood, and bone of their bone, who all his life toiled and wrought and suffered for them, at the end died for them, who always strove to represent them, who would never tell an untruth to or for them, spoke of the doctrine of equality with his usual mixture of idealism and sound common sense. He said (I omit what was of merely local significance):

"I think the authors of the Declaration of Independence intended to include all men, but they did not mean to declare all men equal in all respects. They did not mean to say all men were equal in color, size, intellect, moral development or social capacity. **They defined with tolerable distinctness in what they did consider all men created equal - equal in certain inalienable rights, among which are life, liberty and pursuit of happiness.** This they said, and this they meant. They did not mean to assert the obvious untruth that all were actually enjoying that equality, or yet that they were about to confer it immediately upon them. They meant to set up a standard maxim for free society which should be familiar to all – constantly looked to, constantly labored for, and, even though never perfectly attained, constantly approximated, and thereby constantly spreading and deepening its influence, and augmenting the happiness and value of life to all people, everywhere."

We are bound in honor to refuse to listen to those men who would make us desist from the effort to do away with the inequality which means injustice; the inequality of right, opportunity, of privilege. We are bound in honor to strive to bring ever nearer the day when, as far is humanly possible, we shall be able to realize the ideal that each man shall have an equal opportunity to show the stuff that is in him by the way in which he renders service. There should, so far as possible, be equal of opportunity to render service; but just so long as there is inequality of service there should and must be inequality of reward. We may be sorry for the general, the painter, the artists, the worker in any profession or of any kind, whose misfortune rather than whose fault it is that he does his work ill. But the reward must go to the man who does his work well; for any other course is to create a new kind of privilege, the privilege of folly and weakness; and special privilege is injustice, whatever form it takes.

To say that the thriftless, the lazy, the vicious, the incapable, ought to have reward given to those who are far-sighted, capable, and upright, is to say what is not true and cannot be true. **Let us try to level up, but let us beware of the evil of leveling down.** If a man stumbles, it is a good thing to help him to his feet. Every one of us needs a helping hand now and then. But **if a man lies down, it is a waste of time to try and carry him; and it is a very bad thing for every one if we make men feel that the same reward will come to those who shirk their work and those who do it.**

Let us, then, take into account the actual facts of life, and not be misled into following any proposal for achieving the millennium, for recreating the golden age, until we have subjected it to hardheaded examination. On the other hand, it is foolish to reject a proposal merely because it is advanced by visionaries. **If a given scheme is proposed, look at it on its merits, and, in considering it, disregard formulas. It does not matter in the least who proposes it, or why. If it seems good, try it. If it proves good, accept it; otherwise reject it.** There are plenty of good men calling themselves Socialists with whom, up to a certain point, it is quite possible to work. If the next step is one which both we and they wish to take, why of course take it, without any regard to the fact that our views as to the tenth step may differ. But, on the other hand, keep clearly in mind that, though it has been worth while to take one step, this does not in the least mean that it may not be highly disadvantageous to take the next. It is just as foolish to refuse all progress because people demanding it desire at some points to go to absurd extremes, as it would be to go to these absurd extremes simply because some of the measures advocated by the extremists were wise.

The good citizen will demand liberty for himself, and as a matter of pride he will see to it that others receive liberty which he thus claims as his own. Probably the best test of true love of liberty in any country in the way in which minorities are treated in that country. **Not only should there be complete liberty in matters of religion and opinion, but complete liberty for each man to lead his life as he desires, provided only that in so he does not wrong his neighbor.** Persecution is bad because it is persecution, and without reference to which side happens at the most to be the persecutor and which the persecuted. Class hatred is bad in just the same way, and without regard to the individual who, at a given time, substitutes loyalty to a class for loyalty to a nation, of substitutes hatred of men because they happen to come in a certain social category, for judgment awarded them according to their conduct. Remember always that the same measure of condemnation should be extended to the arrogance which would look down upon or crush any man because he is poor and to envy and hatred which would destroy a man because he is wealthy. The overbearing brutality of the man of wealth or power, and the envious and hateful malice directed against wealth or power, are really at root merely different manifestations of the same quality, merely two sides of the same shield. **The man who, if born to wealth and power, exploits and ruins his less fortunate brethren is at heart the same as the greedy and violent demagogue who excites those who have not property to plunder those who have.** The gravest wrong upon his country is inflicted by that man, whatever his station, who seeks to make his countrymen divide primarily in the line that separates class from class, occupation from occupation, men of more wealth from men of less wealth, instead of remembering that the only safe standard is that which judges each man on his worth as a man, whether he be rich or whether he be poor, without regard to his profession or to his station in life. Such is the only true democratic test, the only test that can with propriety be applied in a republic. **There have been many republics in the past, both in what we call antiquity and in what we call the Middle Ages. They fell, and the prime factor in their fall was the fact that the parties tended to divide along the wealth that separates wealth from poverty. It made no difference which side was successful; it made no difference whether the republic fell under the rule of and oligarchy or the rule of a mob. In either case, when once loyalty to a class had been substituted for loyalty to the republic, the end of the republic was at hand.** There is no greater need to-day than the need to keep ever in mind the fact that the cleavage between right and wrong, between good citizenship and bad citizenship, runs at right angles to, and not parallel with, the lines of cleavage between class and class, between occupation and occupation. Ruin looks us in the face if we judge a man by his position instead of judging him by his conduct in that position.

In a republic, to be successful we must learn to combine intensity of conviction with a broad tolerance of difference of conviction. Wide differences of opinion in matters of religious, political, and social belief must exist if conscience and intellect alike are not be stunted, if there is to be room for healthy growth. Bitter internecine hatreds, based on such differences, are signs, not of earnestness of belief, but of that fanaticism which, whether religious or antireligious, democratic or antidemocratic, it itself but a manifestation of the gloomy bigotry which has been the chief factor in the downfall of so many, many nations.

Of one man in especial, beyond any one else, the citizens of a republic should beware, and that is of the man who appeals to them to support him on the ground that he is hostile to other citizens of the republic, that he will secure for those who elect him, in one shape or another, profit at the expense of other citizens of the republic. It makes no difference whether he appeals to class hatred or class interest, to religious or antireligious prejudice. The man who makes such an appeal should always be presumed to make it for the sake of furthering his own interest. **The very last thing an intelligent and self-respecting member of a democratic community should do is to reward any public man because that public man says that he will get the private citizen something to which this private citizen is not entitled, or will gratify some emotion or animosity which this private citizen ought not to possess.** Let me illustrate this by one anecdote from my own experience. A number of years ago I was engaged in cattle-ranching on the great plains of the western Unite States. There were no fences. The cattle wandered free, the ownership of each one was determined by the brand; the calves were branded with the brand of the cows they followed. If on a round-up and animal was passed by, the following year it would appear as an unbranded yearling, and was then called a maverick. By the custom of the country these mavericks were branded with the brand of the man on whose range they were found. One day I was riding the range with a newly hired cowboy, and we came upon a maverick. We roped and threw it; then we built a fire, took out a cinch-ring, heated it in the fire; and then the cowboy started to put on the brand. I said to him, "It So-and-so's brand," naming the man on whose range we happened to be. He answered: "That's all right, boss; I know my business." In another moment I said to him: "Hold on, you are putting on my brand!" To which he answered: "That's all right; I always put on the boss's brand." I answered: "Oh, very well. Now you go straight back to the ranch and get whatever is owing to you; I don't need you any longer." He jumped up and said: "Why, what's the matter? I was putting on your brand." And I answered: "Yes, my friend, and if you will steal for me then you will steal from me."

Now, the same principle which applies in private life applies also in public life. **If a public man tries to get your vote by saying that he will do something wrong in your interest, you can be absolutely certain that if ever it becomes worth his while he will do something wrong against your interest.**

So much for the citizenship to the individual in his relations to his family, to his neighbor, to the State. There remain duties of citizenship which the State, the aggregation of all the individuals, owes in connection with other

States, with other nations. Let me say at once that I am no advocate of a foolish cosmopolitanism. I believe that a man must be a good patriot before he can be, and as the only possible way of being, a good citizen of the world. Experience teaches us that the average man who protests that his international feeling swamps his national feeling, that he does not care for his country because he cares so much for mankind, in actual practice proves himself the foe of mankind; that the man who says that he does not care to be a citizen of any one country, because he is the citizen of the world, is in fact usually and exceedingly undesirable citizen of whatever corner of the world he happens at the moment to be in. In the dim future all moral needs and moral standards may change; but at present, if a man can view his own country and all others countries from the same level with tepid indifference, it is wise to distrust him, just as it is wise to distrust the man who can take the same dispassionate view of his wife and mother. However broad and deep a man's sympathies, however intense his activities, he need have no fear that they will be cramped by love of his native land.

Now, this does not mean in the least that a man should not wish to do good outside of his native land. On the contrary, just as I think that the man who loves his family is more apt to be a good neighbor than the man who does not, so I think that the most useful member of the family of nations is normally a strongly patriotic nation. So far from patriotism being inconsistent with a proper regard for the rights of other nations, I hold that the true patriot, who is as jealous of the national honor as a gentleman of his own honor, will be careful to see that the nations neither inflicts nor suffers wrong, just as a gentleman scorns equally to wrong others or to suffer others to wrong him. I do not for one moment admit that a man should act deceitfully as a public servant in his dealing with other nations, any more than he should act deceitfully in his dealings as a private citizen with other private citizens. I do not for one moment admit that a nation should treat other nations in a different spirit from that in which an honorable man would treat other men.

In practically applying this principle to the two sets of cases there is, of course, a great practical difference to be taken into account. We speak of international law; but international law is something wholly different from private of municipal law, and the capital difference is that there is a sanction for the one and no sanction for the other; that there is an outside force which compels individuals to obey the one, while there is no such outside force to compel obedience as regards to the other. International law will, I believe, as the generations pass, grow stronger and stronger until in some way or other there develops the power to make it respected. But as yet it is only in the first formative period. As yet, as a rule, each nation is of necessity to judge for itself in matters of vital importance between it and its neighbors, and actions must be of necessity, where this is the case, be different from what they are where, as among private citizens, there is an outside force whose action is all-powerful and must be invoked in any crisis of importance. It is the duty of wise statesman, gifted with the power of looking ahead, to try to encourage and build up every movement which will substitute or tend to substitute some other agency for force in the settlement of international disputes. It is the duty of every honest statesman to try to guide the nation so that it shall not wrong any other nation. But as yet **the great civilized peoples, if they are to be true to themselves and to the cause of humanity and civilization, must keep in mind that in the last resort they must possess both the will and the power to resent wrong-doings from others.** The men who sanely believe in a lofty morality preach righteousness; but they do not preach weakness, whether among private citizens or among nations. We believe that our ideals should be so high, but not so high as to make it impossible measurably to realize them. We sincerely and earnestly believe in peace; but if peace and justice conflict, we scorn the man who would not stand for justice though the whole world came in arms against him.

And now, my hosts, a word in parting. You and I belong to the only two republics among the great powers of the world. The ancient friendship between France and the United States has been, on the whole, a sincere and disinterested friendship. A calamity to you would be a sorrow to us. But it would be more than that. In the seething turmoil of the history of humanity certain nations stand out as possessing a peculiar power or charm, some special gift of beauty or wisdom of strength, which puts them among the immortals, which makes them rank forever with the leaders of mankind. France is one of these nations. For her to sink would be a loss to all the world. There are certain lessons of brilliance and of generous gallantry that she can teach better than any of her sister nations. When the French peasantry sang of Malbrook, it was to tell how the soul of this warrior-foe took flight upward through the laurels he had won. Nearly seven centuries ago, Froisart, writing of the time of dire disaster, said that the realm of France was never so stricken that there were not left men who would valiantly fight for it. You have had a great past. I believe you will have a great future. Long may you carry yourselves proudly as citizens of a nation which bears a leading part in the teaching and uplifting of mankind."

Chapter 2

THE GREAT DIVIDE

"I thought I would dress in baggy pants, big shoes, a cane and a derby hat. everything a contradiction..."
— Charlie Chaplin

At the end of the last chapter, President Theodore Roosevelt described some differences in political ideals that exist in the US. He also said the following, *"It does not matter in the least who proposes it, or why. If it seems good, try it. If it proves good, accept it; otherwise reject it."* Similarly, the back cover of this book has a verse from the Holy Bible that states, "Prove all things; hold fast that which is good." Both statements essentially state the same truth. In this country we have hundreds of millions of residents and hundreds of millions of ideas on how to best use government to solve issues. There are those on the far right who believe in rugged individualism. It is up to that person to solve him own problems. Government should take a limited role. There are those on the far left who believe in complete socialism. It is up to the government to solve everyone's problems. Government should be involved in every aspect of our lives.

The primary focus of this chapter is to demonstrate the balancing act that many politicians may have to do in order to keep their myriad of constituents happy as they perform their Constitutional duties. This and the next four chapters describe conservatism (which leans towards individualism) and progressivism (which leans towards socialism) in more detail. An important point to mention is that these philosophies pertain more to American citizens than it does government officials. Later in this book I will discuss the differences in political thought between citizens and officials and how this affects our country.

GRADING SYSTEMS

Almost everyone has received grades from their teachers. This is a concept most people should be familiar with. Each teacher has his/her own philosophy towards grading a student's work. Part of the process is to provide constructive criticism in order to inform the student where improvements are necessary. The other element is to inform colleges and employers the academic potential of an individual. I want to show you a few examples of grading systems that you might be familiar with, and then I will use these examples to draw comparisons to broader social and political concepts that you might not be familiar with.

The Curve:

Grading on a curve is a statistical method of assigning grades designed to yield a predetermined distribution of grades among students in a class. For example, there are five grades given, A, B, C, D and F, where A is reserved for the top 10% of students, B for the next 20%, C for the next 40%, D for the next 20%, and F for the bottom 10%. If there are 100 students in the classroom, there will be 10 A's, 20 B's, 40 C's, 20 D's and 10 F's. Students have the option of dropping the class within the first few weeks. Those who think they might get a lower grade would be more apt to drop the class than those who think they might get an A. Now lets say that 50 people with the lowest grades drop the class, there will now be 5 A's, 10 B's, 20 C's, 10 D's and 5 F's. The person who had the

20th highest grade in a class of 100 now has the 20th highest grade out of 50. His grade went from a B to a C, even though nothing else changed.

This type of system is common with extremely competitive jobs that require a lot of skill and experience, such as a lawyer or doctor. Only those that are truly capable will be able to make a substantial living. Everyone else will either struggle with lower incomes or remove themselves from the system entirely. Is it a fair system? Of course it isn't, but would you want to have abdominal surgery by a doctor who does not know the difference between a spleen and pancreas?

Social Grades:

In the social system of grading, all the grades are combined together and all the students receive the same grade based on the class average. For example, let's assume the same class of 100 students received a variety of test scores ranging from 30% to 97% and the class average was 71%. So every individual student receives a C. In this scenario, the student at the bottom was pushed up from an F to a C and the student at the top was pushed down from an A to a C. A few weeks later, another test was given to the entire class. The scores ranged from 25% to 85% with a class average of 60%. Why did the scores drop? Because there was no incentive to put in extra effort. The people at the top did not put in that extra effort to try to get the top score, and the people at the bottom felt that everyone else could put in the effort so that he would not have to.

This is an example of a socialist way of thinking. Successful people are forced to pay large amounts of taxes that are redistributed to the poor. If the government implements a tax rate of 100% for anyone who makes over $500,000 per year, there is no incentive for a person to try to make $1 million a year. So they will either find a way around the tax or stop working once they made $500,000. For those at the bottom who receive large amounts of money for doing next to nothing, there is no incentive to work hard and achieve because they are already getting more than what they think they could get without any assistance. The end result of this system is mediocrity. Everyone is the same, and no one is encouraged to stand out above the crowd.

Assigned Grades:

In the assigned system of grading, everyone gets a predetermined grade. For example, a student is told that no matter how well he or anyone else in the class does, he will get a B. This is an example of a caste system. There is no incentive to improve oneself if that person will always get the same amount of money each month no matter what they do.

Straight Percentage:

In the straight percentage system, each person is graded based upon his/her own individual efforts and level of understanding. There is no preset grade. If a person gets a 97%, he will get an A in the class. If he gets a 30%, he will get an F. The difference is that each person is graded according to his/her own ability and effort. If a person works harder, he could potentially improve his grade in the future.

This is an example of free market capitalism (individualism) in which a person is judged by his efforts and abilities. People have the freedom to work as much or as little as they want, but there are consequences for inaction. Those who put in little effort will not be offered the better-paying jobs. They will have difficulty being successful.

These grading systems are generalized and only designed to illustrate the different economic systems. Each system has its strengths and weaknesses. If you want to be successful based on your own merits, you would want to be part of the capitalist system. If your desire is to be exactly the same as everyone else, you would want to be part of the socialist system. What is your vision for the future of the United States of America?

BALANCING ACT

On November 23, 1787, James Madison wrote the 10ᵗʰ essay released as part of the Federalist Papers, which were used to explain and promote the US Constitution. In it he argues that there needs to be a balance between liberty and government control. Too much liberty and individuality results in anarchy. Too much government control and socialism results in totalitarianism. It was true then and it is true today, for human nature has not changed. **For the US to survive as a free and just society, we must find the right balance between personal liberty and government control.**

Federalist Paper #10 (excerpt)
James Madison
November 22, 1787

"By a faction, I understand a number of citizens, whether amounting to a majority or a minority of the whole, who are united and actuated by some common impulse of passion, or of interest, adversed to the rights of other citizens, or to the permanent and aggregate interests of the community.

There are two methods of curing the mischiefs of faction: the one, by removing its causes; the other, by controlling its effects. There are again two methods of removing the causes of faction: the one, by destroying the liberty which is essential to its existence; the other, by giving to every citizen the same opinions, the same passions, and the same interests.

It could never be more truly said than of the first remedy, that it was worse than the disease. Liberty is to faction what air is to fire, an ailment without which it instantly expires. But it could not be less folly to abolish liberty, which is essential to political life, because it nourishes faction, than it would be to wish the annihilation of air, which is essential to animal life, because it imparts to fire its destructive agency.

The second expedient is as impracticable as the first would be unwise. As long as the reason of man continues fallible, and he is at liberty to exercise it, different opinions will be formed. As long as the connection subsists between his reason and his self-love, his opinions and his passions will have a reciprocal influence on each other; and the former will be objects to which the latter will attach themselves. The diversity in the faculties of men, from which the rights of property originate, is not less an insuperable obstacle to a uniformity of interests. The protection of these faculties is the first object of government. From the protection of different and unequal faculties of acquiring property, the possession of different degrees and kinds of property immediately results; and from the influence of these on the sentiments and views of the respective proprietors, ensues a division of the society into different interests and parties.

The latent causes of faction are thus sown in the nature of man; and we see them everywhere brought into different degrees of activity, according to the different circumstances of civil society. A zeal for different opinions concerning religion, concerning government, and many other points, as well of speculation as of practice; an attachment to different leaders ambitiously contending for pre-eminence and power; or to persons of other descriptions whose fortunes have been interesting to the human passions, have, in turn, divided mankind into parties, inflamed them with mutual animosity, and rendered them much more disposed to vex and oppress each other than to co-operate for their common good. So strong is this propensity of mankind to fall into mutual animosities, that where no substantial occasion presents itself, the most frivolous and fanciful distinctions have been sufficient to kindle their unfriendly passions and excite their most violent conflicts."

CONSERVATISM V. PROGRESSIVISM

Conservatives and progressives approach almost every issue with completely different philosophies and perspectives. Conservatives believe in American exceptionalism, freedom and personal responsibility. Progressives believe in social justice and mandate government to create solutions that improve the health and welfare of all Americans. It has been said by others that two heads are better than one and that two sticks stacked together are harder to break than one stick on its own. Are these two philosophical systems compatible enough that they can work together to create solutions that benefit all Americans, and even the world? Below is a description of some differences between conservatives and progressives. Keep in mind that these are broad generalizations being used to illustrate the differences.

1. Conservatives believe that the US Constitution and its amendments are the supreme law of the land. All other laws must be in compliance with these fundamental laws. Democrats believe that the US Constitution is often not enough to protect the rights of certain groups, and has in the past institutionalized various forms of social injustice, such as slavery and misogyny. Therefore it is necessary to add other laws and court decisions to make the United States *"a more perfect Union."*

2. Conservatives believe that judges should act like umpires rather than legislating from the bench. Judges should determine whether laws are permissible under the US Constitution and settle debates about the meaning of laws, not impose their will based on their ideology. Progressives believe that it is the role of a judge to create fairness & equity, and they should have the power and authority to fulfill these duties.

3. Conservatives believe that individual Americans have a right to defend themselves and their families with guns and that right cannot be taken away by any method short of a Constitutional Amendment, which conservatives would oppose. Progressives believe that taking guns away from most citizens would reduce violent crime because criminals would not have access to guns.

4. Conservatives believe that we should live in a color blind society where every individual is judged on the content of his/her character and the merits of his/her actions. Progressives believe that it is necessary to impose laws that improve social justice and equity, even if it hurts certain groups, because the end goal is more important than the method that was used to get there. In other words, the ends justify the means.

5. Conservatives are capitalists and believe that entrepreneurs who amass great wealth through their own efforts are good for the country because they create jobs and shouldn't be punished for being successful. Progressives view successful business owners as people who cheated the system and exploited others along the way. Their money should be taken away by the government and given to those more in need in order to improve social justice and equity.

6. Conservatives believe that abortion ends the life of an innocent child and that infanticide is wrong. Progressives believe that a mother's right to choose is much more important than the life of the fetus.

7. Conservatives believe in the uniqueness and greatness of the American culture and society. It is the reason why the United States of America is the most successful country in the history of the world. Progressives are internationalists who believe that other countries have great ideas as well and that in order to reduce

tension and increase international harmony, the US should be more like these other nations.

8. Conservatives believe that it is vitally important to the future of the country to reduce the size of government, keep taxes low, balance the budget, and get this country out of debt in order to promote capitalism and freedom. Progressives believe that government is the best agent to create social justice and equity. Higher taxes and more regulation are just the vehicles to accomplish these goals.

9. Conservatives believe that government, by its very nature, tends to be inefficient, incompetent, wasteful, and power hungry. They believe that the government that governs least, governs best. Progressives believe that the stronger and more well-funded the government is, the better it can accomplish its mission of social justice and improving the lives of those who do not have the ability to do it themselves.

10. Conservatives believe in God and believe that it is necessary, at least in a personal way, to follow certain guidelines and principles laid out within Holy Scriptures. Progressives believe that God should not be involved in government at all.

11. Conservatives believe that social inequities are part of life and that most of them are created by the character and actions of the individual. Progressives believe that social inequities are a scourge on this planet and should be addressed through governmental action.

12. Conservatives believe that enough energy, in the forms of gasoline, electricity, etc., should be available to meet our growing demands. The federal government should be focused on encouraging innovation. Progressives believe that traditional "fossil fuels" are harmful to the environment and that the government should enforce standards to reduce pollution.

13. Conservatives believe that this is a country of immigrants, but that uncontrolled immigration is harmful to our economy and our society. Progressives believe that anyone who wants to be here has the right to be here, have a job, and vote.

14. Conservatives believe that parents are ultimately responsible for the education of their children. They emphasize academic achievement. Progressives believe that a trained teacher is better suited to educate a child. They emphasize social awareness.

15. Conservatives believe that we are stewards of the environment and that we have dominion over it. It is important to pass on a functional and usable world to our children, as long as actions taken have a proven track record. Progressives believe that we must take an active role in preventing the loss of species, that animals have rights, and that the government must take steps to discourage certain behaviors that might harm the water, air, or other resources.

16. Conservatives encourage a strong local relationship between the doctor and the patient. The doctor, not the insurance agent or the government, should be making medical decisions. They believe that health care is too expensive because there are too many regulations and regulators. Progressives encourage free centralized healthcare to everyone in this country. They believe that healthcare is too expensive because of greedy doctors and insurance companies.

17. Conservatives believe that the best defense is a good offense. The best way to prevent harm to American citizens is a strong show of force. Progressives believe that enemies of the United States have as much right to their opinion as Americans have to theirs; that hatred towards the United States is caused by its social inequities; and that these enemies can be pacified through civilized discussion and debate.

As shown above, Americans are deeply divided by their most deeply held beliefs: access to wealth, the role of God in society, the role of government in society, a woman's right to choose, the preservation and care taking of other species, taxes, and personal liberty. As a result, individuals who represent the government, and the Nation as a whole, are pulled in many, often opposite directions. Compromise is a word commonly heard when different philosophies cannot agree on solutions to various issues, but is compromise the best solution? Does it make the country stronger, and is it possible?

As you read through the list of differences above, it becomes quite obvious that these two philosophies are not only significantly different, but polar opposites that generate much political conflict. President Theodore Roosevelt was one President who attempted throughout his entire Presidency to saddle both horses. He was as close to a progressive conservative as the US has had in the White House. On one hand he promoted bills that strongly regulated large corporations, created the National Park System, and signed the Pure Food and Drug Act of 1906. On the other hand, he encouraged the development of a strong Navy, forced the end of a labor strike, and governed the Philippines after the capture of President Aguinaldo in 1902. Many historians declare Theodore Roosevelt to be one of the best Presidents of all time, along with George Washington, Abraham Lincoln, Franklin Roosevelt and Thomas Jefferson. It is four out of five of these Presidents (the fifth actively serving during construction) that are immortalized in Mt. Rushmore National Monument in the Black Hills of South Dakota.

THREE LEGGED STOOLS

In order for conservative or progressive philosophies to have influence over government, each faction or political party must get people elected into state and federal offices. This requires a significant amount of funds and volunteers. The

major political parties, to increase the flow of money and volunteers, have unified various bases of power and influence. For
national elections, especially for the President of the United
States, it is important to have a clear and concise message that
reverberates within the community, enough money to ensure
that the message is heard, and a strong organization that has
the purpose to pull in voters on election day. That is why each
political party has developed a platform of issues that it campaigns on. These issues are based upon the needs and desires of
each of these factions within each political party.

Both the Republican and Democratic Parties have three
major sources of power and influence. The Republican Party is
composed of social conservatives, fiscal conservatives, and corporate industrialists. The 2008 Republican Party Presidential
primaries had top candidates from each group. Governor
Mike Huckabee represented the social conservatives who
want to make abortions illegal and promote prayer in schools.
Governor Mitt Romney represented the fiscal conservatives
who want less taxes and less government intrusion. Senator
John McCain represented the big business corporations and
industrialists that want to be able to spend government tax
money and create legislation in a way that favors them.

The Democratic Party is composed of labor unions, environmentalists, and progressives. Former Senator John Edwards
represented union leaders who want to make it easier for employees to join a union, support of fair trade initiatives that
sustain unionized jobs, and raise the minimum wage. Former
Vice President Al Gore represented environmentalists who
want to significantly reduce pollution and protect endangered
species. US Senator from Vermont, Bernie Sanders, represented progressives who want to promote civil rights for all and
reduce the influence of corporations.

If you have ever sat for an extended period of time on a
three legged stool, you will come to the inescapable conclusion that this chair is uncomfortable and unstable. Likewise,
these political factions often disagree with each other on what

social and political ideas to promote. For example, fiscal conservatives want to promote individual liberty, whereas social
conservatives want to enact legislation that promotes or bans
certain types of behavior, such as abortion, prayer in schools,
and drug use. Within the Democratic Party, unions want to
encourage the growth of a unionized labor force in manufacturing, whereas environmentalists want to restrict manufacturing and business expansion. These incompatible agendas
are just the beginning of the turmoil.

SPOTLIGHT ON WILLIAM GATES III

William "Bill" Gates III had become the wealthiest person
in the world through hard work, vision, and out-competing his
rivals – all leveraging individualism and free market capitalism.
Later in life, he donated a significant portion of his wealth to
improve the social injustices caused by individualism and free
market capitalism. He wrote, *"I hope you will judge yourselves
not on your professional accomplishments alone, but also on how
well you have addressed the world's deepest inequities."*
Bill Gates represents a potential outcome of the marriage
between individual achievement and social justice. Most of his
money has come from the sales of Microsoft products, which
he rigorously promoted to the world and aggressively protected against his competitors. It is this aggressive protectionism
that has created enemies along the way. Some respect him.
Others despise him. Regardless of what you think of him, he
has made a difference in the world.
William Henry "Bill" Gates III (born October 28, 1955),
has had a much different life than that of his friend and competitor Steve Jobs. Born in Seattle, Washington, his father was
a prominent lawyer, his mother served on the board of directors for First Interstate BancSystem and the United Way, and
her father, J. W. Maxwell, was a national bank president. At
13 he was enrolled in Lakeside School, an exclusive prepara-

tory school. It was here that he began to develop his love and understanding of the computer world. When he was in 8th grade, the Mothers Club at the school used proceeds from Lakeside School's rummage sale to buy an ASR-33 teletype terminal and a block of computer time on a General Electric (GE) computer for the school's students. Showing a passionate interest in computing, he was excused from math classes to pursue his passion. He wrote his first computer program (tic-tac-toe) that allowed users to play games against the computer. After the Mothers Club donation was exhausted, he and other students sought time on systems elsewhere. One of these systems was one belonging to Computer Center Corporation (CCC), which banned 4 Lakeside students: Bill Gates, Paul Allen, Ric Weiland, and Kent Evans after it caught them exploiting defects in the operating system to obtain free computer time. At the end of the ban, the 4 students offered to find bugs in CCC's software in exchange for computer time. Rather than using the system via a teletype terminal, Bill Gates went to CCC's offices and studied source code for various programs that ran on the system.

In 1973, Bill Gates graduated from Lakeside School, scored 1590 out of 1600 on the SAT, and enrolled at Harvard University. He remained in contact with Paul Allen, joining him at Honeywell during the summer of 1974. The following year saw the release of the MITS Altair 8800. Gates and Allen saw this as the opportunity to start their own computer software company. He had talked this decision over with his parents, who were supportive of him after seeing how passionate he was about starting a technology company. After reading the January 1975 issue of Popular Electronics that demonstrated the Altair 8800, Bill Gates contacted Micro Instrumentation and Telemetry Systems (MITS), the creators of the new microcomputer, to inform them that he and others were working on a BASIC interpreter for the platform. In reality, they did not have an Altair and had not written code for it. They just wanted to gauge MITS's interest. MITS president Ed Roberts agreed to meet with them for a demo, and over the course of a few weeks they developed an Altair emulator that ran on a minicomputer, and then the BASIC interpreter. The demonstration, held at MITS's offices in Albuquerque, was a success and resulted in a deal with MITS to distribute the interpreter as Altair BASIC. Paul Allen was hired into MITS, and Bill Gates took a leave of absence from Harvard to work with Allen at MITS in Albuquerque in November 1975. A year later, on November 26, 1976, the trade name "Microsoft" was registered with the Office of the Secretary of the State of New Mexico.

After nine years of hard work, Microsoft launched its first retail version of Microsoft Windows on November 20, 1985. From Microsoft's founding in 1975 until 2006, Bill Gates had primary responsibility for the company's product strategy. He aggressively broadened the company's range of products, and wherever Microsoft achieved a dominant position he vigorously defended it. Many decisions that led to antitrust litigation over Microsoft's business practices have had his approval. On April 3, 2000, Judge Thomas Penfield Jackson found Microsoft in violation of the Sherman Antitrust Act, stating that *"The Court concludes that Microsoft maintained its monopoly power by anti-competitive means."*

There are a number of reasons why some people do not like Bill Gates. Some of them may have merit. They range from him being socially awkward and overly competitive to over promising and under delivering. However, if you were a business owner that required advanced technology to improve communications and data management in order to remain competitive and reduce costs, you would be greatly appreciative of the products developed by Microsoft Corporation, such as: Windows, Bing, Office, Messenger, Internet Explorer, Hotmail, Movie Maker, Security Essentials, Media Player, and Xbox.

Bill Gates has changed the world and he has been rewarded for it. He was number one on the Forbes 400 list from 1993 through 2007 and number one on Forbes list of The World's Richest People from 1995 to 2007, 2009 and 2014. In 1999, his wealth briefly surpassed $101 billion, causing the media to call him a centibillionaire.

In 1994 he sold some of his Microsoft stock to create the William H. Gates Foundation, and in 2000, he and his wife combined three family foundations into one to create the charitable Bill & Melinda Gates Foundation, which is the largest transparently operated charitable foundation in the world. The generosity and extensive philanthropy of David Rockefeller has been credited as a major influence. He and his father have met with Rockefeller several times and have modeled their giving in part on the Rockefeller family's philanthropic focus, namely those global problems that are ignored by governments and other organizations. From its inception in 1994 to September 2011, the Bill and Melinda Gates Foundation has given over $26.2 billion to charity.

Bill Gates had the opportunity to present the commencement speech to the 2007 graduating class of Harvard University, the school he attended but never graduated from. His main focus is providing encouragement to go out and resolve issues related to social and economic inequities in the world. In the speech he states that the barrier to change is not too little caring but too much complexity.

Bill Gates
Harvard Commencement Speech
(Edited)
June 7, 2007

> "I've been waiting more than 30 years to say this: "Dad, I always told you I'd come back and get my degree." I want to thank Harvard for this timely honor. I'll be changing my job next year ... and it will be nice to finally have a college degree on my resume. I applaud the graduates today for taking a much more direct route to your degrees. For my part, I'm just happy that the Crimson has called me "Harvard's most successful dropout." I guess that makes

me valedictorian of my own special class ... I did the best of everyone who failed.

But I also want to be recognized as the guy who got Steve Ballmer to drop out of business school. I'm a bad influence. That's why I was invited to speak at your graduation. If I had spoken at your orientation, fewer of you might be here today. Harvard was a phenomenal experience for me. Academic life was fascinating. I used to sit in on lots of classes that I hadn't even signed up for.

One of my biggest memories of Harvard came in January 1975, when I made a call from Currier House to a company in Albuquerque, New Mexico, that had begun making the world's first personal computers. I offered to sell them software. I worried that they would realize I was just a student in a dorm and hang up on me. Instead they said: "We're not quite ready, come see us in a month," which was a good thing, because we hadn't written the software yet. From that moment, **I worked day and night on this little extra credit project that marked the end of my college education and the beginning of a remarkable journey with Microsoft.**

What I remember above all about Harvard was being in the midst of so much energy and intelligence. It could be exhilarating, intimidating, sometimes even discouraging, but always challenging. It was an amazing privilege – and though I left early, I was transformed by my years at Harvard, the friendships I made, and the ideas I worked on.

But taking a serious look back ... I do have one big regret. **I left Harvard with no real awareness of the awful inequities in the world – the appalling disparities of health, and wealth, and opportunity that condemn millions of people to lives of despair.** I learned a lot here at Harvard about new ideas in economics and politics. I got great exposure to the advances being made in the sciences. **But humanity's greatest advances are not in its discoveries – but in how those discoveries are applied to reduce inequity. Whether through democracy, strong public education, quality health care, or broad economic opportunity – reducing inequity is the highest human achievement.**

I left campus knowing little about the millions of young people cheated out of educational opportunities here in this country. And I knew nothing about the millions of people living in unspeakable poverty and disease in developing countries. It took me decades to find out.

You graduates came to Harvard at a different time. You know more about the world's inequities than the classes that came before. In your years here, I hope you've had a chance to think about how – in this age of accelerating technology – we can finally take on these inequities, and we can solve them.

Imagine, just for the sake of discussion, that you had a few hours a week and a few dollars a month to donate to a cause – and you wanted to spend that time and money where it would have the greatest impact in saving and improving lives. Where would you spend it?

For Melinda and I, the challenge is the same: how can we do the most good for the greatest number with the resources we have. During our discussions on this question, Melinda and I read an article about the millions of children who were dying every year in poor countries from diseases that we had long ago made harmless in this country. Measles, malaria, pneumonia, hepatitis B, yellow fever. One disease I had never even heard of, rotavirus, was killing half a million kids each year – none of them in the United States. We were shocked. We had assumed that if millions of children were dying and they could be saved, the world would make it a priority to discover and deliver the medicines to save them. But it did not. For under a dollar, there were interventions that could save lives that just weren't being delivered.

If you believe that every life has equal value, it's revolting to learn that some lives are seen as worth saving and others are not. We said to ourselves: "This can't be true. But if it is true, it deserves to be the priority of our giving." So we began our work in the same way anyone here would begin it. We asked: "How could the world let these children die?" **The answer is simple, and harsh. The market did not reward saving the lives of these children, and governments did not subsidize it. So the children died because their mothers and their fathers had no power in the market and no voice in the system.** But you and I have both.

We can make market forces work better for the poor if we can develop a more creative capitalism – if we can stretch the reach of market forces so that more people can make a profit, or at least earn a living, serving people who are suffering from the great inequities. We also can press governments around the world to spend taxpayer money in ways that better reflect the values of the people who pay the taxes.

If we can find approaches that meet the needs of the poor in ways that generate profits for business and votes for politicians, we will have found a sustainable way to reduce inequity in the world.

Now this task is open-ended. It can never be finished. But a conscious effort to answer this challenge can change the world. I am optimistic that we can do this, but I talk to skeptics who claim there is no hope. They say: "Inequity has been with us since the beginning, and will be with us until the end – because people just … don't … care." I completely disagree. I believe we have more caring than we know what to do with.

All of us here in this Yard, at one time or another, have seen human tragedies that broke our hearts, and yet we did nothing – not because we didn't care, but because we didn't know what to do. If we had known how to help, we would have acted. **The barrier to change is not too little caring; it is too much complexity. To turn caring into action, we need to see a problem, see a solution, and see the impact. But complexity blocks all three steps.**

Finding solutions is essential if we want to make the most of our caring. If we have clear and proven answers anytime an organization or individual asks "How can I help?," then we can get action – and we can make sure that none of the caring in the world is wasted. But complexity makes it hard to mark a path of action for everyone who cares — and that makes it hard for their caring to matter.

Cutting through complexity to find solutions runs through four predictable stages: determine a goal, find the highest-impact approach, deliver the technology ideal for that approach, and in the meantime, use the best application of technology you already have - whether it's something sophisticated, like a new drug, or something simple, like a bednet.

The final step – after seeing the problem and finding an approach – is to measure the impact of your work and share your successes and failures so that others learn from your efforts. You have to have the statistics, of course. You have to be able to show, for example, that a program is vaccinating millions more children. You have to be able to show a decline in the number of children dying from these diseases. This is essential not just to improve the program, but also to help draw more investment from business and government. **But if you want to inspire people to participate, you have to show more than numbers; you have to convey the human impact of the work – so people can feel what saving a life means to the families affected.**

Members of the Harvard Family: Here in the Yard is one of the great collections of intellectual talent in the world. For what purpose? There is no question that the faculty, the alumni, the students, and the benefactors of Harvard have used their power to improve the lives of people here and around the world. But can we do more? Can Harvard dedicate its intellect to improving the lives of people who will never even hear its name?

Let me make a request of the deans and the professors – the intellectual leaders here at Harvard: As you hire new faculty, award tenure, review curriculum, and determine degree requirements, please ask yourselves: Should our best minds be more dedicated to solving our biggest problems? Should Harvard encourage its faculty to take on the world's worst inequities? Should Harvard students know about the depth of global poverty … the prevalence of world hunger … the scarcity of clean water …the girls kept out of school … the children who die from diseases we can cure? Should the world's most privileged learn about the lives of the world's least privileged? These are not rhetorical questions – you will answer with your policies.

My mother, who was filled with pride the day I was admitted here – never stopped pressing me to do more for others. A few days before I was married, she hosted a bridal event, at which she read aloud a letter about marriage that she had written to Melinda. My mother was very ill with cancer at the time, but she saw one more opportunity to deliver her message, and at the close of the letter she said: "From those to whom much is given, much is expected."

When you consider what those of us here in this Yard have been given – in talent, privilege, and opportunity – there is almost no limit to what the world has a right to expect from us. In line with the promise of this age, I want to exhort each of the graduates here to take on an issue – a complex problem, a deep inequity, and become a specialist on it. If you make it the focus of your career, that would be phenomenal. But you don't have to do that to make an impact. **For a few hours every week, you can use the growing power of the Internet to get informed, find others with the same interests, see the barriers, and find ways to cut through them.**

Don't let complexity stop you. Be activists. Take on the big inequities. It will be one of the great experiences of your lives. You graduates are coming of age in an amazing time. As you leave Harvard, you have technology that members of my class never had. You have awareness of global inequity, which we did not have. And with that awareness, you likely also have an informed conscience that will torment you if you abandon these people whose lives you could change with modest effort. You have more than we had; you must start sooner, and carry on longer. And I hope you will come back here to Harvard 30 years from now and reflect on what you have done with your talent and your energy. I hope you will judge yourselves not on your professional accomplishments alone, but also on how well you have addressed the world's deepest inequities ... on how well you treated people a world away who have nothing in common with you but their humanity.

Good luck."

Chapter 3

ALL FOR ONE
AND ONE FOR ALL

*"My doctrine is this, that if we see cruelty or wrong that we
have the power to stop, and do nothing, we make
ourselves sharers in the guilt."*
— **Anna Sewell**

Now that you have read the Harvard commencement
speech by Bill Gates, you have just been in the mind of a
person with progressive tendencies. Progressivism is a political attitude advocating social justice directly through governmental action. It can be characterized by its promotion and
advancement of reformation and social engineering. It is a
political movement that seeks social and economic justice
above all else, most specifically with reference to the obstacles
imposed by large corporations and banks. Progressives advocate governance "of the people, by the people, for the people",
the phrase "the people" here standing in sharpest contrast to
governance by the corporation.

Characteristics of progressivism include a favorable attitude
toward urban-industrial society, belief in mankind's ability to improve the environment and conditions of life, in the obligation to
intervene in economic and social affairs, in the ability of experts,
and in the efficiency of and need for government intervention.

THE PROGRESSIVE ERA

Disturbed by the inefficiencies and injustices created by industrialists, such as Andrew Carnegie, John D. Rockefeller and J.P. Morgan, the progressives were committed to changing and reforming the country. Significant changes enacted at the national level included the imposition of an income tax (Sixteenth Amendment), direct election of Senators (Seventeenth Amendment), prohibition of alcohol manufacturing and distribution (Eighteenth Amendment), and women's right to vote (Nineteenth Amendment). Journalists exposed waste, corruption and scandal in the new media of national magazines. Upton Sinclair wrote his now famous novel, *The Jungle*, in 1906 describing the horrible details of how meat packing was done at that time. There was much grass root organizing during this period, which saw the establishment of labor unions, including: the Knights of Labor and the American Federation of Labor (led by Samuel Gompers). Progressives believed in science, technology, expertise and education as the solution to society's weaknesses.

W.E.B. Du Bois

William Edward Burghardt "W.E.B." Du Bois (February 23, 1868 – August 27, 1963) was an American sociologist, historian, civil rights activist, author and editor. He was a prominent African-American leader during the Progressive Era who had opposition from other prominent African-American leaders, such as Booker T. Washington and Frederick Douglass. Who is W.E.B. Du Bois, what was the opposition, and why should we know about him?

Born in Great Barrington, Massachusetts, Du Bois grew up in a relatively tolerant and integrated community. Du Bois received a B.A. degree in history from Fisk University, a historically black college in Nashville, Tennessee, from 1885 to 1888. His travel to, and residency in the South was Du Bois's first experience with Southern racism and the Jim Crow laws. Later, he completed some graduate courses at the University of Berlin in Germany and graduated from Harvard University, where he earned a PhD in history. As part of his studies, Du Bois presented a paper in which he rejected Frederick Douglass' plea for black Americans to integrate into white society. He wrote, *"We are Negroes, members of a vast historic race that from the very dawn of creation has slept, but half awakening in the dark forests of its African fatherland."* Du Bois, as seen through his many publications, believed that African-Americans should embrace their African heritage.

W.E.B. Du Bois worked in the fields of history, sociology and economics at Wilberforce University (Ohio), University of Pennsylvania (Philadelphia), and Atlanta University (Georgia). Du Bois rose to national prominence as the leader of the Niagara Movement, a group of African-American activists who wanted equal rights for blacks. Du Bois was one of the co-founders of the National Association for the Advancement of Colored People (NAACP) in 1909. Du Bois and his supporters opposed the Atlanta Compromise, an agreement crafted by Booker T. Washington (one of the most prominent black leaders) which provided that Southern blacks would work and submit to white political rule, while Southern whites guaranteed that blacks would receive basic educational and economic opportunities. Instead, Du Bois insisted on full civil rights and increased political representation, which he believed would be brought about by the African-American intellectual elite. He believed that African-Americans needed the chances for advanced education to develop its leadership. His cause included people of color everywhere, particularly Africans and Asians in their struggles against colonialism and imperialism. Du Bois made several trips to Europe, Africa and Asia. After World War I, he surveyed the experiences of American black soldiers in France and documented widespread bigotry in the United States military. Du Bois was a prolific author. In his role as editor of the NAACP's journal, The Crisis, he published many influential pieces. Du Bois believed that capitalism was a primary cause of racism, and he was generally sympathetic to socialist causes throughout his life. He was an ardent peace activist and advocated nuclear disarmament.

W.E.B. Du Bois was a member of the three-person delegation from the NAACP that attended the 1945 conference in San Francisco at which the United Nations was established. The NAACP delegation wanted the United Nations to endorse racial equality and to bring an end to the colonial era. To push the United Nations in that direction, Du Bois drafted a proposal that pronounced that the colonial system of government is undemocratic, socially dangerous and a main cause of wars. The NAACP proposal received support from China, Russia and India, but it was virtually ignored by the other major powers, and the NAACP proposals were not included in the United Nations charter. Du Bois helped to submit petitions to the UN concerning discrimination against African-Americans. He died on August 27, 1963, at the age of 95. Du Bois was buried in Accra near his home, which is now the Du Bois Memorial Centre. A day after his death, at the March on Washington, speaker Roy Wilkins asked the hundreds of thousands of marchers to honor Du Bois with a moment of silence. It was at this event that Martin Luther King, Jr, delivered his historic "I Have a Dream" speech. The United States' Civil Rights Act, embodying many of the reforms for which Du Bois had campaigned his entire life, was enacted a year after his death.

JOHN DEWEY, FRANK GOODNOW AND PROGRESSIVE EDUCATION

W.E.B. Du Bois and many other progressives complained about the inconsistency and inadequacy of the American education system. I am the product of the American education system. I am not just talking about graduating from a public school. Yes I did attend public schools for all but three years of my K-12 education. I also graduated from a California State University. I am an experienced school teacher, my father was a school teacher for most of his adult life until he retired, and my sister is a school teacher. There is more. My ancestors on my father's mother's side published a book in 1901 about our family genealogy dating back to 1634 when Thomas Boyden left Suffolk, England, and landed in the Massachusetts Bay Colony aboard the Francis. Within its pages are not only names and dates, but also job descriptions. A significant number of my family members have been civil servants, and at the top of the list are preachers and teachers. You can say that teaching is in my blood – literally.

In the American Colonies, the first formal schools appeared in the 1630s. The Boston Latin School opened in 1635. In 1647, the *"old Deluder Satan Act"* required that every Massachusetts town of at least 50 households hire a teacher of reading and writing. Towns with a hundred or more households had to operate a grammar school. The colonists were mainly concerned that children learned to read, write and learn the Holy Bible. In the middle colonies, such as Delaware, New Jersey, New York and Pennsylvania, education was left to the royal governor and various church groups. In the South, the children of rich planters were taught at home - usually by tutors from England. Poor children were usually apprenticed to craftsmen. Anyone who could read or write was allowed to teach, as long as he/she believed in the Church, was loyal to the Crown, and kept out of trouble.

In 1837, Horace Mann was appointed to a newly created position as Secretary of the Massachusetts Board of Education (the first of its kind in the US). Considered the father of the American education system, he followed six main principles:

1.   Education must not be religious in nature.

2.   The public should no longer remain ignorant.

3.   Education should be provided by well-trained, professional teachers.

4.   Education should be paid for, controlled, and sustained by an interested public.

5.   Education must be taught by the spirit, methods, and discipline of a free society.

6.   Education is best provided in schools that embrace children from a variety of backgrounds.

Some of these principles are still alive today in the modern American education system. However, its purpose and focus began to shift around the time of World War 1. One prominent leader of the Progressive Movement is Frank Johnson Goodnow. He was a teacher at Columbia University and President of Johns Hopkins University. Along with Woodrow Wilson (28th President of the United States), he was a pioneer in the field of administrative law. In a lecture given at Brown University in 1916, Goodnow stated:

> "Man is regarded now throughout Europe, contrary to the view expressed by Rousseau, as primarily a member of society and secondarily as an individual. The rights which he possesses are, it is believed, conferred upon him, not by his Creator, but rather by the society to which he belongs. What they are is to be determined by the legislative authority in view of the needs of that society. Social expediency, rather than natural right, is thus to determine the sphere of individual freedom of action. ...We teachers are in a measure responsible for the thoughts of the coming generation. This being the case, if under the conditions of modern life, it is the social group rather than the individual which is increasing in importance, if it is true that greater emphasis should be laid on social duties and less on individual rights, it is the duty of the University to call the attention of the student to this fact, and it is the duty of the student, when he goes out into the world, to do what in him lies to bring this truth home to his fellows."

His schooling at European universities in Paris and Berlin shaped his conceptualization of the relationship between government, society and individuals. In 1900, he released a book called *Politics and Administration* in which he states,

> "The concrete remedies proposed are first, a greater centralization of our state administrative system, following the model of the national administrative system, in the hope of taking from the vast mass of administrative authorities the power which they now have of obstructing the execution of state laws, and of thus making it possible to relieve such administrative authorities from political tests for holding office; and, second, the subjection of the political party, as a political organ recognized by law, to an effective public control, in the hope of making the party and its leaders more responsive to the public will."

While Goodnow was busy developing an administrative system that separates the federal government from the bonds of constitutional law, another progressive – John Dewey – was focused on shifting American education from teaching reading and writing to promoting the skills necessary to become socially adjusted adults that do their duty to society.

The term *"progressive education"* has been used to describe ideas and practices that aim to make schools more effective agencies of a democratic society. Although there are numerous differences of style and emphasis among progressive educators, they share the common conviction that democracy means active participation by all citizens in social, political and economic decisions that will affect their lives. The education of engaged citizens involves two essential elements, as developed by Dewey:

1. Respect for diversity, meaning that each individual should be recognized for his or her own abilities, interests, ideas, needs and cultural identity.

2. The development of critical, socially engaged intelligence, which enables individuals to understand and

participate effectively in the affairs of their community
in a collaborative effort to achieve a common good.

John Dewey saw that with the decline of local community
life and small scale enterprise, young people were losing valuable opportunities to learn the arts of democratic participation, and he concluded that education would need to make
up for this loss. In his Laboratory School at the University of
Chicago, Dewey tested ideas he shared with leading school
reformers such as Francis W. Parker and Ella Flagg Young.
Between 1899 and 1916 he circulated his ideas in works
such as *The School and Society*, *The Child and the Curriculum*,
Schools of Tomorrow, *Democracy and Education*, and numerous
lectures and articles. During these years other experimental
schools were established around the country, and in 1919 the
Progressive Education Association was founded, aiming at *"reforming the entire school system of America."*

Led by Dewey, progressive educators opposed a growing
national movement that sought to separate academic education for the few and narrow vocational training for the masses.
During the 1920s, when education turned increasingly to
scientific techniques such as intelligence testing and cost-
benefit management, progressive educators insisted on the
importance of the emotional, artistic, and creative aspects
of human development. After the Great Depression began,
a group of politically oriented progressive educators, led by
George Counts, dared schools to build a new social order and
published a provocative journal called *The Social Frontier* to
advance their reconstructionist critique of laissez-faire capitalism. At Teachers College, Columbia University, William H.
Kilpatrick and other students of Dewey taught the principles
of progressive education to thousands of teachers and school
leaders. A major research endeavor, the eight-year study demonstrated that students from progressive high schools were
capable, adaptable learners and excelled even in the finest
universities.

Today, scholars, educators and activists are rediscovering John Dewey's work and exploring its relevance to a postmodern age - an age of global capitalism, breathtaking cultural change, and major changes in the ecological health of the planet itself.

PUBLIC EMPLOYEE UNIONS

"It is essential that there should be organization of labor. This is an era of organization. Capital organizes and therefore labor must organize."

— Theodore Roosevelt

From railroad trains to light bulbs to all types of machinery, the 18th and 19th Centuries were witness to a significant lifestyle change that transformed the world and transferred numerous jobs from the farm to the factory. Before 1700 small family farms were the most common place to live and work. By the end of World War 2 only 16% of the total labor force worked in the agricultural industry, which accounted for only 6.8% of the nation's production annually. By the end of the millennium farming represented 1.9% of the labor force and 0.7% of the country's annual production.

The industrial revolution created both new opportunities and new problems. Communications vastly improved, wheres many lost easy access to food and shelter when they moved way from the farms. People were in search of increased personal security due to significant social and economic changes. One way some tried to improve their own personal security was to develop labor unions. A labor or trade union is an organization of workers that band together to achieve common goals such as increased salaries.

Some labor unions have moved away from their initial missions of improving the lives of their members and have recently moved towards spending over $500 million to influence certain political candidates that would use their position of power within the government to write and protect laws that protect themselves and their large donors. Between 1989 and 2011, of the Top 20 political donors seventeen are associations or unions that have contributed a combined total of $486 million to the Democratic Party and $70 million to the Republican Party. If you were to donate $10 to a political candidate, you might get a thank you letter. If you were to donate $1 million to that same political candidate, you would make yourself noticed and that politician would probably do a favor for you once in a while to make sure he/she has another large donation for the next campaign.

Labor unions have served a purpose in the past. In the 1830's workers at the federally operated Brooklyn navy yard fought for a ten-hour work day, and in 1840, President Martin Van Buren made the ten-hour work day standard for all federal workers.

In 1886, the American Federation of Labor (AFL) was organized by Samuel Gompers. In 1932 John L. Lewis organized the Congress of Industrial Organizations (CIO). These two unions merged in 1955 as the AFL-CIO and became the dominant labor union in the US. Currently there are about 16.1 million union members which account for about 12.4% of the workforce. About 68% (11 million) of these are AFL-CIO members. About 7.6% of the non-government work force is unionized, whereas about 36.8% of the government work force is unionized.

Labor unions generally have a progressive ideology in that they support a large well-financed federal government that plays an active role in regulating the labor force. The labor movement was a key supporter of President Franklin Delano Roosevelt's New Deal and President Lyndon B. Johnson's Great Society which included the creation of unemployment insurance, Social Security, Federal Housing Administration (FHA), Federal National Mortgage Association (Fannie Mae), minimum wage, Medicare and Medicaid. Something to think about related to federal government spending and Social Security. In 1940, for every 159.4 people paying Social Security taxes, one person was receiving benefits. By 2010, for every 2.9 people paying Social Security taxes, one person was receiving benefits. What would happen to the Social Security system if there was one recipient for every tax payer?

SPOTLIGHT ON SUSAN B. ANTHONY

Just before the American Revolution officially started, and three months before the Declaration of Independence was signed, Abigail Adams wrote a letter to John Adams (Second President of the US) on March 31, 1776. She wrote, *"I long to hear that you have declared an independency. And, by the way, in the new code of laws which I suppose it will be necessary for you to make, I desire you would remember the ladies and be more generous and favorable to them than your ancestors. Do not put such unlimited power into the hands of the husbands. Remember, all men would be tyrants if they could. If particular care and attention is not paid to the ladies, we are determined to foment a rebellion, and will not hold ourselves bound by any laws in which we have no voice or representation."*

Abigail Adams was a woman of great wisdom and influence. Her mother taught her and her sisters to read and write; her father's, uncle's and grandfather's large libraries enabled the sisters to study English, French literature, and many other subjects. She was descended from the Quincy family, a well-known political family in the Massachusetts Bay Colony (the same colony where my ancestors first landed in the Americas), wife of the second President of the United States (John Adams), mother of the sixth President of the United States (John Quincy Adams), second cousin through marriage to Massachusetts Governor Samuel Adams, and a cousin through marriage to Massachusetts Governor John Hancock. All but one of these men were involved in developing our founding documents (Declaration of Independence, Articles of Confederation, US Constitution).

Voting rights for American women, which was a political battle instigated by Abigail Adams, was a concept that took 144 years for it to become a reality. Even though many intellectually agreed with the idea, it took the hard work and dedication of many men and women for it to finally become a reality in the form of the 19th Amendment to the US Constitution which became law in 1920.

The beginning of the women's suffrage movement started at Seneca Falls, New York, in July 1848. It was there that Elizabeth Cady Stanton and Lucretia Mott organized the first convention regarding the woman's right to vote. Frederick Douglass, a prominent African-American pro-rights leader, was in attendance.

Susan B. Anthony's mother attended the Rochester women's rights convention which occurred two weeks after the Seneca Falls Convention, and was one of 68 women and 32 men (including Frederick Douglass) who signed the Rochester convention's Declaration of Sentiments. In late 1850, Susan read a detailed account in the New York Tribune of the first National Women's Rights Convention in Worcester, Massachusetts. In the article, she was introduced to a speech given by Lucy Stone. Her words catalyzed Susan to devote her life to a woman's right to vote.

> "We want to be something more than the appendages of Society; we want that Woman should be the coequal and help-meet of Man in all the interest and perils and enjoyments of human life. We want that she should attain to the development of her nature and womanhood; we want that when she dies, it may not be written on her gravestone that she was the 'relict' of somebody."

In 1851, Susan was introduced to Elizabeth Cady Stanton. They organized the first women's state temperance society in America, and traveled the United States giving speeches and attempting to persuade government officials and the populace that society should treat men and women equally.

In November 1872, Susan was arrested by a US Deputy Marshal for voting in the 1872 Presidential Election. She was tried and convicted seven months later, despite the eloquent presentation of her arguments using the recently adopted Fourteenth Amendment:

> "All persons born or naturalized in the United States, and subject to the jurisdiction thereof, are citizens of the United States and of the State wherein they reside. No State shall make or enforce any law which shall abridge the privileges or immunities of citizens of the United States; nor shall any State deprive any person of life, liberty, or property, without due process of law; nor deny to any person within its jurisdiction the equal protection of the laws."

Her trial took place at the Ontario County courthouse in Canandaigua, New York, before Supreme Court Associate Justice Ward Hunt. Found guilty, the sentence was a $100 fine. The trial gave her the opportunity to spread her message to a much wider audience than ever before as a direct result of her speaking tour of all 29 towns and villages of Monroe County where her trial was held. In her speeches she addressed the question *"Is it a Crime for a Citizen of the United States to Vote?"* and quoted the Declaration of Independence, the United States Constitution, the New York Constitution, James Madison, Thomas Paine, the Supreme Court and others to support her case that women as citizens have a right to vote.

The Nineteenth Amendment's text, which was formally introduced as a Constitutional amendment in January 1878, was drafted by Susan B. Anthony and Elizabeth Cady Stanton. The proposed amendment was formally introduced as a constitutional amendment in January 1878. The proposal sat in a committee until it was considered by the full Senate and rejected in a 16 to 34 vote in 1887. Another proposal was introduced to the House in January 1918. President Woodrow Wilson encouraged the House to pass the amendment. It was passed by the required two-thirds of the House with only one vote to spare. The vote was then carried into the Senate. It passed through the Senate in June 1919. 36 of 48 states ratified the amendment by August 18, 1920, making it law. Mississippi, the last of the 48 states to do so, ratified the 19th Amendment on March 22, 1984.

Susan B. Anthony was honored as the first American woman on circulating US coinage with her appearance on the Susan B. Anthony dollar. The Susan B. Anthony House in Rochester was declared a National Historic Landmark in 1966 and is operated as a museum. Along with Elizabeth Cady Stanton and Lucretia Mott, she is commemorated in The Woman Movement, a sculpture unveiled in 1921 at the United States Capitol.

Susan B. Anthony Speech

The following speech was given by Susan B. Anthony after her arrest for casting an illegal vote in the Presidential election of 1872. Her goal was to both define the issue and encourage others to support a woman's right to vote.

"Friends and fellow citizens: I stand before you tonight under indictment for the alleged crime of having voted at the last Presidential election, without having a lawful right to vote. It shall be my work this evening to prove to you that in thus voting, I not only committed no crime, but, instead, simply exercised my citizen's rights, guaranteed to me and all United States citizens by the National Constitution, beyond the power of any state to deny.

The preamble of the Federal Constitution says:

"We, the people of the United States, in order to form a more perfect union, establish justice, insure domestic tranquility, provide for the common defense, promote the general welfare, and secure the blessings of liberty to ourselves and our posterity, do ordain and establish this Constitution for the United States of America."

It was we, the people; not we, the white male citizens; nor yet we, the male citizens; but we, the whole people, who formed the Union. And we formed it, not to give the blessings of liberty, but to secure them; not to the half of ourselves and the half of our posterity, but to the whole people - women as well as men. And it is a downright mockery to talk to women of their enjoyment of the blessings of liberty while they are denied the use of the only means of securing them provided by this democratic-republican government - the ballot.

For any state to make sex a qualification that must ever result in the disfranchisement of one entire half of the people, is to pass a bill of attainder, or, an ex post facto law, and is therefore a violation of the supreme law of the land. By it the blessings of liberty are forever withheld from women and their female posterity.

To them this government has no just powers derived from the consent of the governed. To them this government is not a democracy. It is not a republic. It is an odious aristocracy; a hateful oligarchy of sex; the most hateful aristocracy ever established on the face of the globe; an oligarchy of wealth, where the rich govern the poor. An oligarchy of learning, where the educated govern the ignorant, or even an oligarchy of race, where the Saxon rules the African, might be endured; but this oligarchy of sex, which makes father, brothers, husband, sons, the oligarchs over the mother and sisters, the wife and daughters, of every household - which ordains all men sovereigns, all women subjects, carries dissension, discord, and rebellion into every home of the nation.

Webster, Worcester, and Bouvier all define a citizen to be a person in the United States, entitled to vote and hold office.

The only question left to be settled now is: Are women persons? And I hardly believe any of our opponents will have the hardihood to say they are not. Being persons, then, women are citizens; and no state has a right to make any law, or to enforce any old law, that shall abridge their privileges or immunities. Hence, every discrimination against women in the constitutions and laws of the several states is today null and void, precisely as is every one against Negroes."

Chapter 4

THE PATH OF THE JUST

Speeches are a part of the fabric of American culture. They are used to communicate ideas, but more importantly, they are used to motivate and encourage people to respond in a specified way. Many famous people, especially those who protect and exercise our Constitutional rights, have been involved in public lectures and seminars, have spoken at conventions and have penned manuscripts, such as books, magazines or letters. Even though thousands of quotes and speeches are available that illustrate a certain perspective or perception, only a few are able to integrate themselves into the American psyche. Let me explain this with an example:

"The only thing we have to fear is fear itself"

You may not know that President Franklin D. Roosevelt said this at his First Inaugural Address in 1933, but you probably recognize the quote and understand its meaning. Even more importantly, it provides clarity and focus towards a call to action.

The speeches in chapters 4 and 6 have been selected for the following reasons:

1.   It has become part of the American conversation.

2.   It provides clarity related to a specific perspective.

3.   There is a Call to Action.

4.   There is a clearly defined underlying philosophy.

You may not agree with the position of these speakers, but you do understand their purpose and their goals. Also, you may gain understanding as to why they believe the way they do.

ANNA HOWARD SHAW

Born on February 14, 1847, Anna Howard Shaw was a leader of the the women's suffrage movement, a physician, the first ordained female Methodist minister in the United States, and the first woman to receive the Distinguished Service Medal (Highest non-valorous military and civilian decoration of the US military which is issued for exceptionally meritorious service to the government in either a senior government service position or as a senior officer of the armed forces). In 2000, she was inducted into the National Women's Hall of Fame.

Shaw's personal and professional goal was to ensure voting rights for women. Her speech in New York had this singular goal in mind. With the consistent efforts of people like Susan B. Anthony, Frederick Douglass, Lucy Stone, and Anna Howard Shaw, the Nineteenth Amendment was finally passed in 1920 giving women the right to vote. Voting rights for women became a reality because suffragists like Anna Shaw had a clear singular message that others were willing to agree with: Granting women the right to vote will strengthen America and continue the goal of *"creating a more perfect Union."*

The Fundamental Principle of a Republic
June 21, 1915
Ogdenburg, New York

> "When I came into your hall tonight, I thought of the last time I was in your city. Twenty-one years ago I came here with Susan B. Anthony, and we came for exactly the same purpose as that for which we are here tonight. Boys have been born since that time and have become voters, and the women are still trying to persuade American men to

believe in the fundamental principles of democracy, and I never quite feel as if it was a fair field to argue this question with men, because in doing it you have to assume that a man who professes to believe in a Republican form of government does not believe in a Republican form of government, for the only thing that woman's enfranchisement means at all is that a government which claims to be a Republic should be a Republic, and not an aristocracy.

The difficulty with discussing this question with those who oppose us is that they make any number of arguments but none of them have anything to do with Woman's Suffrage; they always have something to do with something else, therefore the arguments which we have to make rarely ever have anything to do with the subject, because we have to answer our opponents who always escape the subject as far as possible in order to have any sort of reason in connection with what they say.

Now one of two things is true: either a Republic is a desirable form of government, or else it is not. If it is, then we should have it, if it is not then we ought not to pretend that we have it. We ought at least be true to our ideals, and the men of New York have for the first time in their lives, the rare opportunity on the second day of next November, of making the state truly a part of the Republic. It is the greatest opportunity which has ever come to the men of the state. They have never had so serious a problem to solve before, they will never have a more serious problem to solve in any future of our nation's life, and the thing that disturbs me more than anything else in connection with it is that so few people realize what a profound problem they have to solve on November 2. **It is not merely a trifling matter; it is not a little thing that does not concern the state, it is the most vital problem we could have, and any man who goes to the polls on**

the second day of next November without thoroughly informing himself in regard to this subject is unworthy to be a citizen of this state, and unfit to cast a ballot.

If woman's suffrage is wrong, it is a great wrong; if it is right, it is a profound and fundamental principle, and we all know, if we know what a Republic is, that it is the fundamental principle upon which a Republic must rise. Let us see where we are as a people; how we act here and what we think we are. The difficulty with the men of this country is that they are so consistent in their inconsistency that they are not aware of having been inconsistent; because their consistency has been so continuous and their inconsistency so consecutive that it has never been broken, from the beginning of our Nation's life to the present time.

If we trace our history back we will find that from the very dawn of our existence as a people, men have been imbued with a spirit and a vision more lofty than they have been able to live; they have been led by visions of the sublimest truth, both in regard to religion and in regard to government that ever inspired the souls of men from the time the Puritans left the old world to come to this country, led by the Divine ideal which is the sublimest and the supremest ideal in religious freedom which men have ever known, the theory that a man has a right to worship God according to the dictates of his own conscience, without the intervention of any other man or any other group of men. And it was this theory, this vision of the right of the human soul which led men first to the shores of this country.

Now, nobody can deny that they are sincere, honest, and earnest men. No one can deny that the Puritans were men of profound conviction, and yet these men who gave up everything in behalf of an ideal, hardly established their communities in this new country before they began to practice exactly the same sort of persecutions on other men which had been practiced upon them. They settled in their communities on the New England shores and when they formed their compacts by which they governed their local societies, they permitted no man to have a voice in the affairs unless he was a member of the church, and not a member of any church, but a member of the particular church which dominated the particular community in which he happened to be.

In Massachusetts they drove the Baptists down to Rhode Island; in Connecticut they drove the Presbyterians over to New Jersey; they burned the Quakers in Massachusetts and ducked the witches, and no colony, either Catholic or Protestant allowed a Jew to have a voice. And so a man must worship God according to the conscience of the particular community in which he was located, and yet they called that religious freedom, they were not able to live the ideal of religious liberty, and from that time to this the men of this government have been following along the same line of inconsistency, while they too have been following a vision of equal grandeur and power.

Never in the history of the world did it dawn upon the human mind as it dawned upon your ancestors, what it would mean for men to be free. They got the vision of a government in which the people would be the supreme power, and so inspired by this vision men wrote such documents as were went from the Massachusetts legislature, from the New York legislature and from the Pennsylvania group over to the Parliament of Great Britain, which rang with the profoundest measures of freedom and justice. They did not equivocate in a single word when they wrote the Declaration of Independence; no one can dream that these men had not got the sublimest ideal of democracy which had ever dawned upon the souls of men. **But as soon as the war was over and our government was formed, instead of asking the question, who shall be the governing force in this great new Republic, when they brought those thirteen little territories together, they began to eliminate instead of include the men who should be the great governing forces, and they said, who shall have the voice in this great new Republic, and you would have supposed that such men as fought the Revolutionary War would have been able to answer that every man who has fought, everyone who has given up all he has and all he has been able to accumulate shall be free, it never entered their minds.**

These excellent ancestors of yours had not been away from the old world long enough to realize that man is of more value than his purse, so they said every man who has an estate in the government shall have a voice; and they said what shall that estate be? And they answered that a man who had property valued at two hundred and fifty dollars will be able to cast a vote, and so they sang "The land of the free and the home of the brave." And they wrote into their Constitution, "All males who pay taxes on $250 shall cast a vote," and they called themselves a Republic, and we call ourselves a Republic, and they were not quite so much of a Republic that we should be called a Republic yet. We might call ourselves angels, but that wouldn't make us angels, you have got to be an angel before you are an angel, and you have got to be a Republic before you are a Republic. Now what did we do? Before the word "male" in the local compacts, they wrote the word "Church-members"; and they wrote in the word "taxpayer."

Then there arose a great Democrat, Thomas Jefferson, who looked down into the day when you and I are living and saw that the rapidly accumulated wealth in the hands of a few men would endanger the liberties of the people, and he knew what you and I know, that no power under heaven or among men is known in a Republic by which men can defend their liberties except by the power of the ballot, and so the Democratic Party took another step in the evolution of the Republic out of a monarchy and they rubbed out the word "taxpayer" and wrote in the word "white", and then the Democrats thought the millennium had come, and they sang " The land of the free and the home of the brave" as lustily as the Republicans had sung it before them and spoke of the divine right of mother-hood with the same thrill in their voices and at the same time they were selling mother's babies by the pound on the auction block - and mothers apart from their babies.

Another arose who said a man is not a good citizen because he is white, he is a good citizen because he is a man, and the Republican party took out that progressive evolution-ary eraser and rubbed out the word "white" from before the word "male' and could not think of another word to put in there - they were all in, black and white, rich and poor, wise and otherwise, drunk and sober; not a man left out to be put in, and so the Republicans could not write anything before the word "male", and they had to let the little word, "male" stay alone by itself.

And God said in the beginning, "It is not good for man to stand alone." That is why we are here tonight, and that is all that woman's suffrage means; just to repeat again and again that first declaration of the Divine, **"It is not good for man to stand alone," and so the women of this state are asking that the word "male" shall be stricken out of the Constitution altogether and that the Constitution stand as it ought to have stood in the beginning and as it must before this state is any part of a Republic. Every citizen possessing the necessary qualifications shall**

be entitled to cast one vote at every election, and have that vote counted. We are not asking as our Anti-Suffrage friends think we are, for any of awful things that we hear will happen if we are allowed to vote; **we are simply asking that that government which professes to be a Republic shall be a Republic and not pretend to be what it is not.**

Now what is a Republic? Take your dictionary, encyclopedia lexicon or anything else you like and look up the definition and you will find that a Republic is a form of government in which the laws are enacted by representatives elected by the people. Now when did the people of New York ever elect their own representatives? Never in the world. The men of New York have, and I grant you that men are people, admirable people, as far as they go, but they only go half way. There is still another half of the people who have not elected representatives, and you never read a definition of a Republic in which half of the people elect representatives to govern the whole of the people. That is an aristocracy and that is just what we are. We have been many kinds of aristocracies. We have been a hierarchy of church members, than an oligarchy of sex.

There are two old theories, which are dying today. Dying hard, but dying. One of them is dying on the plains of Flanders and the Mountains of Galicia and Austria, and that is the theory of the divine right of kings. The other is dying here in the state of New York and Massachusetts and New Jersey and Pennsylvania and that is the divine right of sex. Neither of them had a foundation in reason, or justice, or common sense.

Now I want to make this proposition, and I believe every man will accept it. Of course he will if he is intelligent. **Whenever a Republic prescribes the qualifications as applying equally to all the citizens of the Republic, when the Republic says in order to vote, a citizen must**

be twenty-one years of age, it applies to all alike, there is no discrimination against any race or sex. When the government says that a citizen must be a native-born citizen or a naturalized citizen that applies to all; we are either born or naturalized, somehow or other we are here. Whenever the government says that a citizen, in order to vote, must be a resident of a community a certain length of time, and of the state a certain length of time and of the nation a certain length of time, that applies to all equally. There is no discrimination.

We might go further and we might say that in order to vote the citizen must be able to read his ballot. We have not gone that far yet. We have been very careful of male ignorance in these United States.

I was much interested, as perhaps many of you, in reading the Congressional Record this last winter over the debate over the immigration bill, and when that illiteracy clause was introduced into the immigration bill, what fear there was in the souls of men for fear we would do injustice to some of the people who might want to come to our shores, and I was much interested in the language in which the President vetoed the bill, when he declared that by inserting the clause we would keep out of our shores a large body of very excellent people. I could not help wondering then how it happens that male ignorance is so much less ignorant than female ignorance. **When I hear people say that if women were permitted to vote a large body of ignorant people would vote, and therefore because an ignorant woman would vote, no intelligent women should be allowed to vote, I wonder why we have made it so easy for male ignorance and so hard for female ignorance.**

When I was a girl, years ago, I lived in the back woods and there the number of votes cast at each election depended entirely upon the size of the ballot box. We had what was known as the old-tissue ballots and the man who got the most tissue in was the man elected. Now the best part of our community was very much disturbed by this method, and they did not know what to do in order to get a ballot both safe and secret; but they heard that over in Australia, where the women voted, they had a ballot which was both safe and secret, so we went over there and we got the Australian ballot and we brought it here. But when we got it over we found it was not adapted to this country, because in Australia they have to be able to read their ballot. Now the question was how could we adapt it to our conditions? Someone discovered that if you should put a symbol at the head of each column, like a rooster, or an eagle, or a hand holding a hammer, that if a man has intelligence to know the difference between a rooster and an eagle he will know which political party to vote for, and when the ballot was adapted it was a very beautiful ballot, it looked like a page from Life.

Now almost any American could vote that ballot, or if she had not that intelligence to know the difference between an eagle and a rooster, we could take the eagle out and put in the hen. Now when we take so much pains to adapt the ballot to the male intelligence of the United States, we should be very humble when we talk about female ignorance. Now if we should take a vote and the men had to read their ballot in order to vote it, more women could vote than men. But **when the government says not only that you must be twenty-one years of age, a resident of the community and native born or naturalized, those are qualifications, but when it says that an elector must be a male, that is not a qualification for citizenship; that is an insurmountable barrier between one half of the people and the other half of the citizens and their rights as citizens. No such nation can call itself a Republic. It is only an aristocracy. That barrier must be removed**

before the government can become a Republic, and that is exactly what we are asking right now, that the last step in the evolutionary process be taken on November 2nd. and that this great state of New York shall become in fact as it is in theory, a part of a government of the people, by the people, and for the people.

Men know the inconsistencies themselves; they realize it in one way while they do not realize it in another, because you never heard a man make a political speech when he did not speak of this country as a whole as though the thing existed which does not exist and that is that the people were equally free, because you hear them declare over and over again on the Fourth of July "under God the people rule." They know it is not true, but they say it with a great hurrah, and they repeat over and over again that clause from the Declaration of Independence. "Governments derive their just powers from the consent of the governed," and they see how they can prevent half of us from giving our consent to anything, and then they give it to us on the Fourth of July in two languages, so if it is not true in one it will be in the other, "vox populi, vox Dei." "The voice of the people is the voice of God," and the orator forgets that in the people's voice there is a soprano as well as a bass.

If the voice of the people is the voice of God, how are we ever going to know what God's voice is when we are content to listen to a bass solo? Now if it is true that the voice of the people is the voice of God, we will never know what the Deity's voice in government is until the bass and soprano are mingled together, the result of which will be the divine harmony. Take any of the magnificent appeals for freedom, which men make, and rob them of their universal application and you take the very life and soul out of them.

Where is the difficulty? Just in one thing and one thing only, that men are so sentimental. We used to believe that women were the sentimental sex, but they can not hold a tallow candle compared with the arc light of the men. Men are so sentimental in their attitude about women that they cannot reason about them. Now men are usually very fair to each other. I think the average man recognizes that he has no more right to anything at the hands of the government than has every other man. He has no right at all to anything to which every other man has not an equal right with himself. He says why have I a right to certain things in the government; why have I a right to life and liberty; why have I a right to this or this? Does he say because I am a man? Not at all, because I am human, and being human I have a right to everything which belongs to humanity, and every right which any other human being has, I have. And then he says of his neighbor, and my neighbor he also is human, therefore every right which belongs to me as a human being, belongs to him as a human being, and I have no right to anything under the government to which he is not equally entitled.

And then up comes a woman, and then they say now she's a woman; she is not quite human, but she is my wife, or my sister, or my daughter, or an aunt, or my cousin. She is not quite human; she is only related to a human, and being related to a human a human will take care of her. So we have had that care-taking human being to look after us and they have not recognized that women too are equally human with men. Now if men could forget for a minute and believe the anti-suffragists say that we want men to forget that we are related to them, they don't know men, if for a minute they could forget our relationship and remember that **we are equally human with themselves, then they would say, yes, and this human being, not because she is a woman, but because she is human is entitled to every privilege and every right under the government which I, as a human being am entitled to.**

The only reason men do not see as fairly in regard to women as they do in regard to each other is because they have looked upon us from an altogether different plane than what they have looked at men; that is because women have been the homemakers while men have been the so-called protectors, in the period of the world's civilization when people needed to be protected. I know that they say that men protect us now and when we ask them what they are protecting us from the only answer they can give is from themselves. I do not think that men need any very great credit for protecting us from themselves. They are not protecting us from any special thing from which we could not protect ourselves except themselves. Now this old time idea of protection was all right when the world needed this protection, but today the protection in civilization comes from within and not from without.

What are the arguments, which our good Anti-friends give us? We know that lately they have stopped to argue and call suffragists all sorts of creatures. If there is anything we believe that we do not believe, we have not heard about them, so the cry goes out of this; the cry of the infant's mind; the cry of a little child. The anti-suffragists' cries are all the cries of little children who are afraid of the unborn and are forever crying, "The goblins will catch you if you don't watch out." So that anything that has not been should not be and all that is right, when as a matter of fact if the world believed that we would be in a static condition and never move, except back like a crab. And so the cry goes on.

When suffragists are feminists, and when I ask what that is no one is able to tell me. I would give anything to know what a feminist is. They say, would you like to be a feminist? If I could find out I would, you either have to be masculine or feminine and I prefer feminine. Then they cry that we are socialists, and anarchists. Just how a human can be both at the same time, I really do not know. If I know what socialism means it means absolute government and anarchism means no government at all. So we are feminists, socialists, anarchists, and Mormons or spinsters. Now that is about the list. I have not heard the last speech. Now as a matter of fact, as a unit we are nothing, as individuals we are like all other individuals.

We have our theories, our beliefs, **but as suffragists we have but one belief, but one principle, but one theory and that is the right of a human being to have a voice in the government,** under which he or she lives, on that we agree, if on nothing else. Whether we agree or not on religion or politics we are concerned. A clergyman asked me the other day, " By the way, what church does your official board belong to?" I said I don't know. He said, " Don't you know what religion your official board believes?" I said, "Really it never occurred to me, but I will [look] them up and see, they are not elected to my board because they believe in any particular church. We had no concern either as to what we believe as religionists or as to what we believe as women in regard to theories of government, except that one fundamental theory in the right of democracy. We do not believe in this fad or the other, but whenever any question is to be settled in any community, then the people of that community shall settle that question, the women people equally with the men people. That is all there is to it, and yet when it comes to arguing our case they bring up all sorts of arguments, and the beauty of it is they always answer all their own arguments. They never make an argument, but they answer it. When I was asked to answer one of their debates I said, " What is the use? Divide up their literature and let them destroy themselves."

I was followed up last year by a young, married woman from New Jersey. She left her husband home for three months to tell the women that their place was at home, and that they could not leave home long enough to go to the ballot box, and she brought all her arguments out in pairs and backed them up by statistics. The anti-suffragists can gather more statistics than any other person I ever saw, and there is nothing so sweet and calm as when they say, "You cannot deny this, because here are the figures, and figures never lie." Well they don't but some liars figure.

When they start out they always begin the same. She started by proving that it was no use to give the women the ballot because if they did have it they would not use it, and she had statistics to prove it. If we would not use it then I really can not see the harm of giving it to us, we would not hurt anybody with it and what an easy way for you men to get rid of us. No more suffrage meetings, never any nagging you again, no one could blame you for anything that went wrong with the town, if it did not run right, all you would have to say is, you have the power, why don't you go ahead and clean up.

Then the young lady, unfortunately for her first argument, proved by statistics, of which she had many, the awful results which happened where women did have the ballot; what awful laws have been brought about by women's vote; the conditions that prevail in the homes and how deeply women get interested in politics, because women are hysterical, and we can not think of anything else, we just forget our families, cease to care for our children, cease to love our husbands and just go to the polls and vote and keep on voting for ten hours a day 365 days in the year, never let up, if we ever get to the polls once you will never get us home, so that the women will not vote at all, and they will not do anything but vote. Now these are two very strong anti-suffrage arguments and they can prove them by figures. Then they will tell you that if women are permitted to vote it will be a great expense and no use because wives will vote just as their husbands do; even if we have no husbands, that would not effect the result because we would vote just as our husbands would vote if we had one. How I wish the anti-suffragists could make the men believe that; if they could make men believe that the women would vote just as they wanted them to do you think we would ever have to make another speech or hold another meeting, we would have to vote whether we wanted to or not.

And then the very one who will tell you that women will vote just as their husbands do will tell you in five minutes that they will not vote as their husbands will and then the discord in the homes, and the divorce. Why, **they have discovered that in Colorado there are more divorces than there were before women began to vote, but they have forgotten to tell you that there are four times as many people in Colorado today as there were when women began to vote, and that may have some effect, particularly as these people went from the East.** Then they will tell you all the trouble that happens in the home.

A gentleman told me that in California - and when he was talking I had a wonderful thing pass through my mind, because he said that he and his wife had lived together for twenty years and never had a difference in opinion in the whole twenty years and he was afraid if women began to vote that his wife would vote differently from him and then that beautiful harmony which they had had for twenty years would be broken, and all the time he was talking I could not help wondering which was the idiot because I knew that no intelligent human beings could live together for twenty years and not have differences of opinion.

All the time he was talking I looked at that splendid type of manhood and thought, how would a man feel being tagged up by a little woman for twenty years saying, "Me too, me too." I would not want to live in a house with a human being for twenty years who agreed with everything I said. The stagnation of a frog pond would be hilarious compared to that. What a reflection is that on men. If we should say that about men we would never hear the last of it. Now it may be that the kind of men being that the anti-suffragists live with is that kind, but they are not the kind we live with and we could not do it. Great big overgrown babies! Cannot be disputed without having a row! While we do not believe that men are saints, by any means, we do believe that the average American man is a fairly good sort of fellow.

In fact my theory of the whole matter is exactly opposite, because instead of believing that men and women will quarrel, I think just the opposite thing will happen. I think just about six weeks before election a sort of honeymoon will start and it will continue until they will think they are again hanging over the gate, all in order to get each other's votes. When men want each other's votes they do not go up and knock them down; they are very solicitous of each other, if they are thirsty or need a smoke or [missing text] well we don't worry about home. The husband and wife who are quarreling after the vote are quarreling now.

Then the other belief that the women would not vote if they had a vote and would not do anything else; and would vote just as their husbands vote, and would not vote like their husbands; that women have so many burdens that they cannot bear another burden, and that women are the leisure class.

I remember having Reverend Dr. Abbott speak before the anti-suffrage meeting in Brooklyn and he stated that if women were permitted to vote we would not have so much time for charity and philanthropy, and I would like to say,

"Thank God, there will not be so much need of charity and philanthropy." The end and aim of the suffrage is not to furnish an opportunity for excellent old ladies to be charitable. There are two words that we ought to be able to get along without, and they are charity and philanthropy. They are not needed in a Republic. If we put in the word "opportunity" instead, that is what Republics stand for.

Our doctrine is not to extend the length of our bread lines or the size of our soup kitchens, what we need is for men to have the opportunity to buy their own bread and eat their own soup. We women have used up our lives and strength in fool charities, and we have made more paupers than we have ever helped by the folly of our charities and philanthropies; the unorganized methods by which we deal with the conditions of society, and **instead of giving people charity we must learn to give them an opportunity to develop and make themselves capable of earning the bread; no human being has the right to live without toil;** toil of some kind, and that old theory that we used to hear **"The world owes a man a living" never was true and never will be true. This world does not owe anybody a living, what it does owe to every human being is the opportunity to earn a living.** We have a right to the opportunity and then the right to the living thereafter. We want it. **No woman, any more than a man, has the right to live an idle life in this world, we must learn to give back something for the space occupied and we must do our duty wherever duty calls, and the woman herself must decide where her duty calls, just as a man does.**

Now they tell us we should not vote because we have not the time, we are so burdened that we should not have any more burdens. Then, if that is so, I think we ought to allow the women to vote instead of the men, since we pay a man anywhere from a third to a half more than we do

women it would be better to use up the cheap time of the
women instead of the dear time of the men. And talking
about time you would think it took about a week to vote.

A dear, good friend of mine in Omaha said, "Now Miss.
Shaw," and she held up her child in her arms, "is not this
my job." I said it certainly is, and then she said, "How can
I go to the polls and vote and neglect my baby?" I said,
"Has your husband a job?" and she said, "Why you know
he has." I did know it; he was a banker and a very busy
one. I said, "Yet your husband said he was going to leave
husband and go down to the polls and vote," and she said,
"Oh yes, he is so very interested in election." Then I said,
"What an advantage you have over your husband, he has
to leave his job and you can take your job with you and
you do not need to neglect your job." Is it not strange that
the only time a woman might neglect her baby is on election day, and then the dear old Antis hold up their hands
and say, "You have neglected your baby." A woman can
belong to a whist club and go once a week and play whist,
she cannot take her baby to the whist club, and she has
to keep whist herself without trying to keep a baby whist.
She can go to the theatre, to church or a picnic and no one
is worrying about the baby, but to vote and everyone cries
out about the neglect.

You would think on Election Day that a woman grabbed
up her baby and started out and just dropped it somewhere and paid no attention to it. It used to be asked
when we had the question box, "Who will take care of the
babies?" I did not know what person could be got to take
care of all the babies, so I thought I would go out West
and find out. I went to Denver and I found that they took
care of their babies just the same on election day as they
did on every other day; they took their baby along with
them, when they went to put a letter in a box they took

their baby along and when they went to put their ballot in the box they took their baby along. If the mother had to stand in line and the baby got restless she would joggle the go-cart and when she went in to vote a neighbor would joggle the go-cart and if there was no neighbor there was the candidate and he would joggle the cart. That is one day in the year when you can get a hundred people to take care of any number of babies. I have never worried about the babies on Election Day since that time.

Then the people will tell you that women are so burdened with their duties that they can not vote, and they will tell you that women are the leisure class and the men are worked to death: but the funniest argument of the lady who followed me about in the West: Out there they were great in the temperance question, and she declared that we were not prohibition, or she declared that we were. Now in North Dakota which is one of the first prohibition states, and they are dry because they want to be dry. In that state she wanted to prove to them that if women were allowed to vote they would vote North Dakota wet and she had her figures; that women had not voted San Francisco dry, or Portland dry, or Chicago dry. Of course we had not voted on the question in Chicago, but that did not matter.

Then we went to Montana, which is wet. They have it wet there because they want it wet, so that any argument that she could bring to bear upon them to prove that we would make North Dakota wet and keep it wet would have given us the state, but that would not work, so she brought out the figures out of her pocket to prove to the men of Montana that if women were allowed to vote in Montana they would vote Montana dry. She proved that in two years in Illinois they had voted ninety-six towns dry, and that at that rate we would soon get over Montana and have it dry. Then I went to Nebraska and as soon as

I reached there a reporter came and asked me the question, "How are the women going to vote on the prohibition question?" I said, "I really don't know. I know how we will vote in North Dakota, we will vote wet in North Dakota; in Montana we will vote dry, but how we will vote in Nebraska, I don't know, but I will let you know just as soon as the lady from New Jersey comes."

We will either vote as our husbands vote or we will not vote as our husbands vote. We either have time to vote or we don't have time to vote. We will either not vote at all or we will vote all the time. It reminds me of the story of the old Irish woman who had twin boys and they were so much alike that the neighbors could not tell them apart, so one of the neighbors said, " Now Mrs. Mahoney, you have two of the finest twin boys I ever saw in all my life, but how do you know them apart." "Oh," she says, "That's easy enough any one could tell them apart. When I want to know which is which I just put my finger in Patsey's mouth and if he bites it is Mikey."

Now what does it matter whether the women will vote as their husbands do or will not vote; whether they have time or have not; or whether they will vote for prohibition or not. What has that to do with the fundamental question of democracy, no one has yet discovered. But they cannot argue on that; **they cannot argue on the fundamental basis of our existence so that they have to get off on all of these side tricks to get anything approaching an argument.** So they tell you that democracy is a form of government. It is not. It was before governments were; it will prevail when governments cease to be; it is more than a form of government; it is a great spiritual force emanating from the heart of the Infinite, transforming human character until some day, some day in the distant future, man by the power of the spirit of democracy, will be able to look back into the face of the Infinite and answer, as man can not answer today, " One is our Father, even God, and all we people are the children of one family."

And when democracy has taken possession of human lives no man will ask from him to grant to his neighbor, whether that neighbor be a man or woman; no man will then be willing to allow another man to rise to power on his shoulders, nor will he be willing to rise to power on the shoulders of another prostrate human being. But that has not yet taken possession of us, but some day we will be free, and we are getting nearer and nearer to it all the time; and never in the history of our country had the men and women of this nation a better right to approach it than they have today; never in the history of the nation did it stand out so splendidly as it stands today, and never ought we men and women to be more grateful for anything than that there presides in the White House today a man of peace.

As so our good friends go on with one thing after another and they say if women should vote they will have to sit on the jury and they ask whether we will like to see a woman sitting on a jury. I have seen some juries that ought to be sat on and I have seen some women that would be glad to sit on anything. When a woman stands up all day behind a counter, or when she stands all day doing a washing she is glad enough to sit; and when she stands for seventy-five cents she would like to sit for two dollars a day. But don't you think we need some women on juries in this country?

You read your paper and you read that one day last week or the week before or the week before a little girl went out to school and never came back; another little girl was sent on an errand and never came back; another little girl was left in charge of a little sister and her mother went out to work and when she returned the little girl was not there, and you read it over and over again, and the horror of it strikes you. You read that in these United States five thousand young girls go out and never come back, don't you think that the men and women the vampires of our country who fatten and grow rich on the ignorance and innocence of children would rather face Satan himself than a jury of mothers. I would like to see some juries of mothers. I lived in the slums of Boston for three years and I know the need of juries of mothers.

Then they tell us that if women were permitted to vote that they would take office, and you would suppose that we just took office in this country. There is a difference of getting an office in this country and in Europe. In England, a man stands for Parliament and in this country he runs for Congress, and so long as it is a question of running for office I don't think women have much chance, especially with our present hobbles. There are some women who want to hold office and I may as well own up.

I am one of them. I have been wanting to hold office for more than thirty-five years. Thirty-five years ago I lived in the slums of Boston and ever since then I have wanted to hold office. I have applied to the major to be made an officer; I wanted to be the greatest office holder in the world, I wanted the position of the man I think is to be the most envied, as far as the ability to do good is concerned, and that is a policeman. I have always wanted to be a policeman and I have applied to be appointed policeman and the very first question that was asked me was, "Could you knock a man down and take him to jail?"

That is some people's idea of the highest service that a policeman can render a community. Knock somebody down and take him to jail! My idea is not so much to arrest criminals as it is to prevent crime. That is what is needed in the police force of every community. When I lived for three years in the back alleys of Boston. I saw there that it was needed to prevent crime and from that day? This I believe there is no great public gathering of any sort whatever where we do not need women on the police force; we need them at every moving picture show, every dance house, every restaurant, every hotel, and every great store with a great bargain counter and every park and every resort where the vampires who fatten on the crimes and vices of men and women gather. We need women on the police force and we will have them there some day.

If women vote, will they go to war? They are great on having us fight. They tell you that the government rests on force, but there are a great many kinds of force in this world, and never in the history of man were the words of the Scriptures proved to the extent that they are today, that the men of the nation that lives by the sword shall die by the sword. When I was speaking in North Dakota from an automobile with a great crowd and a great number of men gathered around a man who had been sitting in front of a store whittling a stick called out to another man and asked if women get the vote will they go over to Germany and fight the Germans? I said, "Why no, why should we go over to Germany and fight Germans?" "If Germans come over here would you fight?" I said, "Why should we women fight men, but if Germany should send an army of women over here, then we would show you what we would do. We would go down and meet them and say, "Come on, let's go up to the opera house and talk this matter over." It might grow wearisome but it would not be death.

Would it not be better if the heads of the governments in Europe had talked things over? **What might have happened to the world if a dozen men had gotten together in Europe and settled the awful controversy, which is today discriminating the nations of Europe? We women got together there last year, over in Rome, the delegates**

from twenty-eight different nations of women, and for two weeks we discussed problems which had like interests to us all. They were all kinds of Protestants, both kinds of Catholics, Roman, and Greek, three were Jews and Mohamedans, but we were not there to discuss our different religious beliefs, but we were there to discuss the things that were of vital importance to us all, and at the end of the two weeks, after the discussions were over we passed a great number of resolutions.

We discussed white slavery, the immigration laws, we discussed the spread of contagious and infectious diseases; we discussed various forms of education, and various forms of juvenile criminals, every question which every nation has to meet, and at the end of two weeks we passed many resolutions, but two of them were passed unanimously. One was presented by myself as Chairman on the Committee on Suffrage and on that resolution we called upon all civilizations of the world to give to women equal rights with men and there was not a dissenting vote.

The other resolution was on peace. **We believed then and many of us believe today, notwithstanding all the discussion that is going on, we believe and we will continue to believe that preparedness for war is an incentive to war, and the only hope of permanent peace is the systematic and scientific disarmament of all the nations of the world, and we passed a resolution and passed it unanimously to that effect.**

A few days afterward I attended a large reception given by the American ambassador, and there was an Italian diplomat there and he spoke rather superciliously and said, " You women think you have been having a very remarkable convention, and I understand that a resolution on peace was offered by the Germans, the French women seconded it, and the British presiding presented it and it was carried unanimously." We none of us dreamed what was taking place at that time, but he knew and we learned it before we arrived home, that awful, awful thing that was about to sweep over the nations of the world. The American ambassador replied to the Italian diplomat and said, "Yes Prince, it was a remarkable convention, and it is a remarkable thing that the only people who can get together internationally and discuss their various problems without acrimony and without a sword at their side are the women of the world, but we men, even when we go to the Hague to discuss peace, we go with a sword dangling at our side." It is remarkable that even at this age men can not discuss international problems and discuss them in peace.

When I turned away from that place up in North Dakota that man in the crowd called out again, just as we were leaving, and said, "Well what does a woman know about war anyway?" I had read my paper that morning and I knew what the awful headline was, and I saw a gentleman standing in the crowd with a paper in his pocket, and I said, "Will that gentleman hold the paper up." And he held it up, and the headline read, "250,000 Men Killed Since the War Began". I said, "You ask me what a woman knows about war? No woman can read that line and comprehend the awful horror; no woman knows the significance of 250,000 dead men, but you tell me that one man lay dead and I might be able to tell you something of its awful meaning to one woman.

I would know that years before a woman whose heart beat in unison with her love and her desire for motherhood walked day by day with her face to an open grave, with courage, which no man has ever surpassed, and if she did not fill that grave, if she lived, and if there was laid in her arms a tiny little bit of helpless humanity, I would know that there went out from her soul such a cry of thankfulness as none save a mother could know. And then I would know, what men have not yet learned that women are human; that they have human hopes and human passions, aspirations and desires as men have, and I would know that that mother had laid aside all those hopes and aspirations for herself, laid them aside for her boy, and if after years had passed by she forgot her nights of sleeplessness and her days of fatiguing toil in her care of her growing boy, and when at last he became a man and she stood looking up into his eyes and beheld him, bone of her bone and flesh of her flesh, for out of her woman's life she had carved twenty beautiful years that went into the making of a man; and there he stands, the most wonderful thing in all the world; for in all the Universe of God there is nothing more sublimely wonderful than a strong limbed, clean hearted, keen brained, aggressive young man, standing as he does on the border line of life, ready to reach out and grapple with its problems.

O, how wonderful he is, and he is hers. She gave her life for him, and in an hour this country calls him out and in an hour he lies dead; that wonderful, wonderful thing lies dead; and sitting by his side, that mother looking into the dark years to come knows that when her son died her life's hope died with him, and in the face of that wretched motherhood, what man dare ask what a woman knows of war. And that is not all. Read your papers, you can not read it because it is not printable; you cannot tell it because it is not speakable, you cannot even think it because it is not thinkable, the horrible crimes perpetrated against women by the blood drunken men of the war.

You read your paper again and the second headlines read, "It Costs Twenty Millions of Dollars a Day," for what? To buy the material to slaughter the splendid results of civilization of the centuries. Men whom it has taken centuries to build up and make into great scientific forces of brain, the flower of the manhood of the great nations of Europe, and we spend twenty millions of dollars a day to blot out all the results of civilization of hundreds and hundreds of years. And what do we do? We lay a mortgage on every unborn child for a hundred and more years to come. Mortgage his brain, his brawn, and every pulse of his heart in order to pay the debt, to buy the material to slaughter the men of our country.

And that is not all, the greatest crime of war is the crime against the unborn. Read what they are doing. They are calling out every man, every young man, and every virile man from seventeen to forty-five or fifty years old; they are calling them out. All the splendid scientific force and energy of the splendid virile manhood are being called out to be food for the cannon, and they are leaving behind the degenerate, defective imbecile, the unfit, the criminals, the diseased to be the fathers of children yet to be born. The crime of crimes of the war is the crime against the unborn children, and in the face of the fact that women are driven out of the home shall men ask if women shall fight if they are permitted to vote.

No, we women do not want the ballot in order that we may fight, but we do want the ballot in order that we may help men to keep from fighting, whether it is in the home or in the state, just as the home is not without the man, so the state is not without the woman, and you can no more build up homes without men than you can build up the state without women. We are needed everywhere where human problems are to be solved. Men and women must go through this world together from the cradle to the grave; it is God's way and the fundamental principle of a Republican form of government."

FRANKLIN DELANO ROOSEVELT

Franklin Roosevelt was installed as President of the United States with 57.4% of the popular vote and 88.9% of the Electoral College vote during a time when the general population was worried about many different things. The stock market crash of October 29, 1929, was a major instigator of the Great Depression. In 1929, the US unemployment rate averaged 3.14%. Unemployment rates were 23.53% in 1932 and 24.75% in 1933. Millions of homeless people migrated across the United States. This was the backdrop for the 1932 Presidential elections.

Franklin Roosevelt had a strong mandate to stabilize the country. In his inaugural address, he set out to accomplish two goals: to quash the fears of Americans and to inform the population as to how he will get the country moving forward again. In his first 100 days in office, he was able to pass fifteen major pieces of legislation which were designed to stabilize the economy, put people to work and resolve many of the issues facing the Nation. He was the only person elected President four times. Many of his programs are still in place today. He dominated the American political scene, not only during the twelve years of his Presidency, but for decades afterward. He orchestrated the realignment of voters. FDR's New Deal Coalition united labor unions, big city liberals, African-Americans, seniors, Jews, Catholics, and rural white Southerners. Roosevelt was instrumental in the development of the United Nations. He is consistently rated by scholars as one of the top US Presidents.

First Inaugural Address
Washington, D.C.
March 4, 1933

"President Hoover, Mr. Chief Justice, my friends:

This is a day of national consecration. And I am certain that on this day my fellow Americans expect that on my induction into the Presidency, I will address them with a candor and a decision which the present situation of our people impels.

This is preeminently the time to speak the truth, the whole truth, frankly and boldly. Nor need we shrink from honestly facing conditions in our country today. **This great Nation will endure, as it has endured, will revive and will prosper.**

So, first of all, let me assert my firm belief that the only thing we have to fear is fear itself - nameless, unreasoning, unjustified terror which paralyzes needed efforts to convert retreat into advance. In every dark hour of our national life, a leadership of frankness and of vigor has met with that understanding and support of the people themselves which is essential to victory. And I am convinced that you will again give that support to leadership in these critical days.

In such a spirit on my part and on yours we face our common difficulties. They concern, thank God, only material things. Values have shrunk to fantastic levels; taxes have risen; our ability to pay has fallen; government of all kinds is faced by serious curtailment of income; the means of exchange are frozen in the currents of trade; the withered leaves of industrial enterprise lie on every side; farmers find no markets for their produce; and the savings of many years in thousands of families are gone. More important, a host of unemployed citizens face the grim problem of existence, and an equally great number toil with little return. Only a foolish optimist can deny the dark realities of the moment.

And yet our distress comes from no failure of substance. We are stricken by no plague of locusts. Compared with the perils which our forefathers conquered, because they believed and were not afraid, we have still much to be thankful for. Nature still offers her bounty and human efforts have multiplied it. Plenty is at our doorstep, but a generous use of it languishes in the very sight of the supply. Primarily, this is because the rulers of the exchange of mankind's goods have failed, through their own stubbornness and their own incompetence, have admitted their failure, and have abdicated. Practices of the unscrupulous money changers stand indicted in the court of public opinion, rejected by the hearts and minds of men.

True, they have tried. But their efforts have been cast in the pattern of an outworn tradition. Faced by failure of credit, they have proposed only the lending of more money. Stripped of the lure of profit by which to induce our people to follow their false leadership, they have resorted to exhortations, pleading tearfully for restored confidence. They only know the rules of a generation of self-seekers. **They have no vision, and when there is no vision the people perish.**

Yes, the money changers have fled from their high seats in the temple of our civilization. We may now restore that temple to the ancient truths. The measure of that restoration lies in the extent to which we apply social values more noble than mere monetary profit.

Happiness lies not in the mere possession of money; it lies in the joy of achievement, in the thrill of creative effort. The joy, the moral stimulation of work no longer must be forgotten in the mad chase of evanescent profits. **These dark days, my friends, will be worth all they cost us if they teach us that our true destiny is not to**

be ministered unto but to minister to ourselves, to our fellow men.

Recognition of that falsity of material wealth as the standard of success goes hand in hand with the abandonment of the false belief that public office and high political position are to be valued only by the standards of pride of place and personal profit; and there must be an end to a conduct in banking and in business which too often has given to a sacred trust the likeness of callous and selfish wrongdoing. **Small wonder that confidence languishes, for it thrives only on honesty, on honor, on the sacredness of obligations, on faithful protection, and on unselfish performance; without them it cannot live.** Restoration calls, however, not for changes in ethics alone. This Nation is asking for action, and action now.

Our greatest primary task is to put people to work. This is no unsolvable problem if we face it wisely and courageously. It can be accomplished in part by direct recruiting by the Government itself, treating the task as we would treat the emergency of a war, but at the same time, through this employment, accomplishing great - greatly needed projects to stimulate and reorganize the use of our great natural resources.

Hand in hand with that we must frankly recognize the overbalance of population in our industrial centers and, by engaging on a national scale in a redistribution, endeavor to provide a better use of the land for those best fitted for the land.

Yes, the task can be helped by definite efforts to raise the values of agricultural products, and with this the power to purchase the output of our cities. It can be helped by preventing realistically the tragedy of the growing loss through foreclosure of our small homes and our farms.

It can be helped by insistence that the Federal, the State, and the local governments act forthwith on the demand that their cost be drastically reduced. It can be helped by the unifying of relief activities which today are often scattered, uneconomical, unequal. It can be helped by national planning for and supervision of all forms of transportation and of communications and other utilities that have a definitely public character. There are many ways in which it can be helped, but it can never be helped by merely talking about it. We must act. We must act quickly.

And finally, in our progress towards a resumption of work, we require two safeguards against a return of the evils of the old order. There must be a strict supervision of all banking and credits and investments. There must be an end to speculation with other people's money. And there must be provision for an adequate but sound currency.

These, my friends, are the lines of attack. I shall presently urge upon a new Congress in special session detailed measures for their fulfillment, and I shall seek the immediate assistance of the 48 States.

Through this program of action we address ourselves to putting our own national house in order and making income balance outgo. Our international trade relations, though vastly important, are in point of time, and necessity, secondary to the establishment of a sound national economy. I favor, as a practical policy, the putting of first things first. I shall spare no effort to restore world trade by international economic readjustment; but the emergency at home cannot wait on that accomplishment.

The basic thought that guides these specific means of national recovery is not nationally - narrowly nationalistic. It is the insistence, as a first consideration, upon the interdependence of the various elements in and parts of the United States of America - a recognition of the old and permanently important manifestation of the American spirit of the pioneer. It is the way to recovery. It is the immediate way. It is the strongest assurance that recovery will endure.

In the field of world policy, I would dedicate this Nation to the policy of the good neighbor: the neighbor who resolutely respects himself and, because he does so, respects the rights of others; the neighbor who respects his obligations and respects the sanctity of his agreements in and with a world of neighbors.

If I read the temper of our people correctly, we now realize, as we have never realized before, our interdependence on each other; that we can not merely take, but we must give as well; that if we are to go forward, we must move as a trained and loyal army willing to sacrifice for the good of a common discipline, because without such discipline no progress can be made, no leadership becomes effective.

We are, I know, ready and willing to submit our lives and our property to such discipline, because it makes possible a leadership which aims at the larger good. This, I propose to offer, pledging that the larger purposes will bind upon us, bind upon us all as a sacred obligation with a unity of duty hitherto evoked only in times of armed strife. With this pledge taken, I assume unhesitatingly the leadership of this great army of our people dedicated to a disciplined attack upon our common problems.

Action in this image, action to this end is feasible under the form of government which we have inherited from our ancestors. **Our Constitution is so simple, so practical that it is possible always to meet extraordinary needs by changes in emphasis and arrangement without loss**

of essential form. That is why our constitutional system has proved itself the most superbly enduring political mechanism the modern world has ever seen.

It has met every stress of vast expansion of territory, of foreign wars, of bitter internal strife, of world relations. And it is to be hoped that the normal balance of executive and legislative authority may be wholly equal, wholly adequate to meet the unprecedented task before us. But it may be that an unprecedented demand and need for undelayed action may call for temporary departure from that normal balance of public procedure.

I am prepared under my constitutional duty to recommend the measures that a stricken nation in the midst of a stricken world may require. These measures, or such other measures as the Congress may build out of its experience and wisdom, I shall seek, within my constitutional authority, to bring to speedy adoption.

But, in the event that the Congress shall fail to take one of these two courses, in the event that the national emergency is still critical, I shall not evade the clear course of duty that will then confront me. **I shall ask the Congress for the one remaining instrument to meet the crisis - broad Executive power to wage a war against the emergency, as great as the power that would be given to me if we were in fact invaded by a foreign foe.**

For the trust reposed in me, I will return the courage and the devotion that befit the time. I can do no less. We face the arduous days that lie before us in the warm courage of national unity; with the clear consciousness of seeking old and precious moral values; with the clean satisfaction that comes from the stern performance of duty by old and young alike. We aim at the assurance of a rounded, a permanent national life.

We do not distrust the - the future of essential democracy. The people of the United States have not failed. In their need they have registered a mandate that they want direct, vigorous action. They have asked for discipline and direction under leadership. They have made me the present instrument of their wishes. In the spirit of the gift I take it. In this dedication - In this dedication of a Nation, we humbly ask the blessing of God. May He protect each and every one of us. May He guide me in the days to come."

LYNDON BAINES JOHNSON

Lyndon Baines Johnson is one of only four people who served in all four elected federal offices of the United States: Representative, Senator, Vice President and President; including six years as Senate Majority Leader, two as Senate Minority Leader and two as Senate Majority Whip. He took over as President when John F. Kennedy was assassinated and was a major personality with power and influence during the many violent civil rights activities that took place during the 1960s. Johnson was greatly supported by the Democratic Party and, as President, was responsible for designing the "Great Society" legislation that included laws that upheld civil rights, a public broadcasting system, Medicare, Medicaid, environmental protection, aid to education, and "War on Poverty." He also escalated direct American involvement in the Vietnam War.

Address to a Joint Session of Congress on Voting Legislation
We Shall Overcome
March 15, 1965
Washington, D.C.

"Mr. Speaker, Mr. President, Members of the Congress:

I speak tonight for the dignity of man and the destiny of democracy. I urge every member of both parties,

Americans of all religions and of all colors, from every section of this country, to join me in that cause.

At times history and fate meet at a single time in a single place to shape a turning point in man's unending search for freedom. So it was at Lexington and Concord. So it was a century ago at Appomattox. So it was last week in Selma, Alabama. There, long-suffering men and women peacefully protested the denial of their rights as Americans. Many were brutally assaulted. One good man, a man of God, was killed.

There is no cause for pride in what has happened in Selma. **There is no cause for self-satisfaction in the long denial of equal rights of millions of Americans. But there is cause for hope and for faith in our democracy in what is happening here tonight. For the cries of pain and the hymns and protests of oppressed people have summoned into convocation all the majesty of this great government - the government of the greatest nation on earth. Our mission is at once the oldest and the most basic of this country: to right wrong, to do justice, to serve man.**

In our time we have come to live with the moments of great crisis. Our lives have been marked with debate about great issues - issues of war and peace, issues of prosperity and depression. But rarely in any time does an issue lay bare the secret heart of America itself. **Rarely are we met with a challenge, not to our growth or abundance, or our welfare or our security, but rather to the values, and the purposes, and the meaning of our beloved nation.**

The issue of equal rights for American Negroes is such an issue. And should we defeat every enemy, and should we double our wealth and conquer the stars, and still be unequal to this issue, then we will have failed as

a people and as a nation. For with a country as with a person, "What is a man profited, if he shall gain the whole world, and lose his own soul?"

There is no Negro problem. There is no Southern problem. There is no Northern problem. There is only an American problem. And we are met here tonight as Americans - not as Democrats or Republicans. We are met here as Americans to solve that problem.

This was the first nation in the history of the world to be founded with a purpose. The great phrases of that purpose still sound in every American heart, North and South: "All men are created equal," "government by consent of the governed," "give me liberty or give me death." Well, those are not just clever words, or those are not just empty theories. In their name Americans have fought and died for two centuries, and tonight around the world they stand there as guardians of our liberty, risking their lives.

Those words are a promise to every citizen that he shall share in the dignity of man. This dignity cannot be found in a man's possessions; it cannot be found in his power, or in his position. It really rests on his right to be treated as a man equal in opportunity to all others. It says that he shall share in freedom, he shall choose his leaders, educate his children, provide for his family according to his ability and his merits as a human being. To apply any other test **- to deny a man his hopes because of his color, or race, or his religion, or the place of his birth is not only to do injustice, it is to deny America and to dishonor the dead who gave their lives for American freedom.**

Our fathers believed that if this noble view of the rights of man was to flourish, it must be rooted in democracy. The most basic right of all was the right to choose your own leaders. The history of this country, in large measure, is the history of the expansion of that right to all of our people. Many of the issues of civil rights are very complex and most difficult. But about this there can and should be no argument.

Every American citizen must have an equal right to vote. There is no reason which can excuse the denial of that right. There is no duty which weighs more heavily on us than the duty we have to ensure that right. Yet the harsh fact is that in many places in this country men and women are kept from voting simply because they are Negroes. Every device of which human ingenuity is capable has been used to deny this right. The Negro citizen may go to register only to be told that the day is wrong, or the hour is late, or the official in charge is absent. And if he persists, and if he manages to present himself to the registrar, he may be disqualified because he did not spell out his middle name or because he abbreviated a word on the application. And if he manages to fill out an application, he is given a test. The registrar is the sole judge of whether he passes this test. He may be asked to recite the entire Constitution, or explain the most complex provisions of State law. And even a college degree cannot be used to prove that he can read and write.

For the fact is that the only way to pass these barriers is to show a white skin. Experience has clearly shown that the existing process of law cannot overcome systematic and ingenious discrimination. No law that we now have on the books - and I have helped to put three of them there - can ensure the right to vote when local officials are determined to deny it. In such a case our duty must be clear to all of us. **The Constitution says that no person shall be kept from voting because of his race or his color. We have all**

sworn an oath before God to support and to defend that Constitution. We must now act in obedience to that oath.

Wednesday, I will send to Congress a law designed to eliminate illegal barriers to the right to vote. The broad principles of that bill will be in the hands of the Democratic and Republican leaders tomorrow. After they have reviewed it, it will come here formally as a bill. I am grateful for this opportunity to come here tonight at the invitation of the leadership to reason with my friends, to give them my views, and to visit with my former colleagues. I've had prepared a more comprehensive analysis of the legislation which I had intended to transmit to the clerk tomorrow, but which I will submit to the clerks tonight. But I want to really discuss with you now, briefly, the main proposals of this legislation.

This bill will strike down restrictions to voting in all elections - Federal, State, and local - which have been used to deny Negroes the right to vote. This bill will establish a simple, uniform standard which cannot be used, however ingenious the effort, to flout our Constitution. It will provide for citizens to be registered by officials of the United States Government, if the State officials refuse to register them. It will eliminate tedious, unnecessary lawsuits which delay the right to vote. Finally, this legislation will ensure that properly registered individuals are not prohibited from voting.

I will welcome the suggestions from all of the Members of Congress - I have no doubt that I will get some - on ways and means to strengthen this law and to make it effective. But **experience has plainly shown that this is the only path to carry out the command of the Constitution.**

To those who seek to avoid action by their National Government in their own communities, who want to and who seek to maintain purely local control over elections, the answer is simple: open your polling places to all your people. Allow men and women to register and vote whatever the color of their skin. Extend the rights of citizenship to every citizen of this land.

There is no constitutional issue here. The command of the Constitution is plain. There is no moral issue. It is wrong - deadly wrong - to deny any of your fellow Americans the right to vote in this country. There is no issue of States' rights or national rights. There is only the struggle for human rights. I have not the slightest doubt what will be your answer.

But the last time a President sent a civil rights bill to the Congress, it contained a provision to protect voting rights in Federal elections. That civil rights bill was passed after eight long months of debate. And when that bill came to my desk from the Congress for my signature, the heart of the voting provision had been eliminated. This time, on this issue, there must be no delay, or no hesitation, or no compromise with our purpose.

We cannot, we must not, refuse to protect the right of every American to vote in every election that he may desire to participate in. And we ought not, and we cannot, and we must not wait another eight months before we get a bill. We have already waited a hundred years and more, and the time for waiting is gone.

So I ask you to join me in working long hours - nights and weekends, if necessary - to pass this bill. And I don't make that request lightly. For from the window where I sit with the problems of our country, I recognize that from outside this chamber is the outraged conscience of a nation, the grave concern of many nations, and the harsh judgment of history on our acts.

But even if we pass this bill, the battle will not be over. What happened in Selma is part of a far larger movement which reaches into every section and State of America. It is the effort of American Negroes to secure for themselves the full blessings of American life. Their cause must be our cause too. Because **it's not just Negroes, but really it's all of us, who must overcome the crippling legacy of bigotry and injustice. And we shall overcome.**

As a man whose roots go deeply into Southern soil, I know how agonizing racial feelings are. I know how difficult it is to reshape the attitudes and the structure of our society. But a century has passed, more than a hundred years since the Negro was freed. And he is not fully free tonight.

It was more than a hundred years ago that Abraham Lincoln, a great President of another party, signed the Emancipation Proclamation; but emancipation is a proclamation, and not a fact. A century has passed, more than a hundred years, since equality was promised. And yet the Negro is not equal. A century has passed since the day of promise. And the promise is un-kept.

The time of justice has now come. I tell you that I believe sincerely that no force can hold it back. It is right in the eyes of man and God that it should come. And when it does, I think that day will brighten the lives of every American. For Negroes are not the only victims. How many white children have gone uneducated? How many white families have lived in stark poverty? How many white lives have been scarred by fear, because we've wasted our energy and our substance to maintain the barriers of hatred and terror? And so I say to all of you here, and to all in the nation tonight, that **those who appeal to you to hold on to the past do so at the cost of denying you your future.**

This great, rich, restless country can offer opportunity and education and hope to all, all black and white, all North and South, sharecropper and city dweller. These are the enemies: poverty, ignorance, disease. They're our enemies, not our fellow man, not our neighbor. And these enemies too - poverty, disease, and ignorance: we shall overcome.

Now let none of us in any section look with prideful righteousness on the troubles in another section, or the problems of our neighbors. **There's really no part of America where the promise of equality has been fully kept.** In Buffalo as well as in Birmingham, in Philadelphia as well as Selma, Americans are struggling for the fruits of freedom. **This is one nation. What happens in Selma or in Cincinnati is a matter of legitimate concern to every American. But let each of us look within our own hearts and our own communities, and let each of us put our shoulder to the wheel to root out injustice wherever it exists.**

As we meet here in this peaceful, historic chamber tonight, men from the South, some of whom were at Iwo Jima, men from the North who have carried Old Glory to far corners of the world and brought it back without a stain on it, men from the East and from the West, are all fighting together without regard to religion, or color, or region, in Vietnam. Men from every region fought for us across the world twenty years ago. And now in these common dangers and these common sacrifices, the South made its contribution of honor and gallantry no less than any other region in the Great Republic - and in some instances, a great many of them, more. And I have not the slightest doubt that good men from everywhere in this country, from the Great Lakes to the Gulf of Mexico, from the Golden Gate to the harbors along the Atlantic, will rally now together in this cause to vindicate the freedom of all Americans. For all of us owe this duty; and I believe that all of us will respond to it. Your President makes that request of every American.

The real hero of this struggle is the American Negro. His actions and protests, his courage to risk safety and even to risk his life, have awakened the conscience of this nation. His demonstrations have been designed to call attention to injustice, designed to provoke change, designed to stir reform. He has called upon us to make good the promise of America. And who among us can say that we would have made the same progress were it not for his persistent bravery, and his faith in American democracy.

For at the real heart of battle for equality is a deep seated belief in the democratic process. Equality depends not on the force of arms or tear gas but depends upon the force of moral right; not on recourse to violence but on respect for law and order. And there have been many pressures upon your President and there will be others as the days come and go. But I pledge you tonight that we intend to fight this battle where it should be fought - in the courts, and in the Congress, and in the hearts of men.

We must preserve the right of free speech and the right of free assembly. But the right of free speech does not carry with it, as has been said, the right to holler fire in a crowded theater. We must preserve the right to free assembly. But free assembly does not carry with it the right to block public thoroughfares to traffic. We do have a right to protest, and a right to march under conditions that do not infringe the constitutional rights of our neighbors. And I intend to protect all those rights as long as I am permitted to serve in this office. We will guard against violence, knowing it strikes from our hands the very weapons which we seek: progress, obedience to law, and belief in American values.

In Selma, as elsewhere, we seek and pray for peace. We seek order. We seek unity. But we will not accept the peace of stifled rights, or the order imposed by fear, or the unity that stifles protest. For **peace cannot be purchased at the cost of liberty.** In Selma tonight - and we had a good day there - as in every city, we are working for a just and peaceful settlement And we must all remember that after this speech I am making tonight, after the police and the FBI and the Marshals have all gone, and after you have promptly passed this bill, the people of Selma and the other cities of the Nation must still live and work together. And when the attention of the nation has gone elsewhere, they must try to heal the wounds and to build a new community. This cannot be easily done on a battleground of violence, as the history of the South itself shows. It is in recognition of this that men of both races have shown such an outstandingly impressive responsibility in recent days - last Tuesday, again today.

The bill that I am presenting to you will be known as a civil rights bill. But, in a larger sense, most of the program I am recommending is a civil rights program. Its object is to open the city of hope to all people of all races. **Because all Americans just must have the right to vote. And we are going to give them that right. All Americans must have the privileges of citizenship - regardless of race. And they are going to have those privileges of citizenship - regardless of race. But I would like to caution you and remind you that to exercise these privileges takes much more than just legal right. It requires a trained mind and a healthy body. It requires a decent home, and the chance to find a job, and the opportunity to escape from the clutches of poverty.**

Of course, people cannot contribute to the nation if they are never taught to read or write, if their bodies are stunted from hunger, if their sickness goes untended, if their life is spent in hopeless poverty just drawing a welfare check. So we want to open the gates to opportunity. But we're also going to give all our people, black and white, the help that they need to walk through those gates.

My first job after college was as a teacher in Cotulla, Texas, in a small Mexican-American school. Few of them could speak English, and I couldn't speak much Spanish. My students were poor and they often came to class without breakfast, hungry. And they knew, even in their youth, the pain of prejudice. They never seemed to know why people disliked them. But they knew it was so, because I saw it in their eyes. I often walked home late in the afternoon, after the classes were finished, wishing there was more that I could do. But all I knew was to teach them the little that I knew, hoping that it might help them against the hardships that lay ahead.

And somehow you never forget what poverty and hatred can do when you see its scars on the hopeful face of a young child. I never thought then, in 1928, that I would be standing here in 1965. It never even occurred to me in my fondest dreams that I might have the chance to help the sons and daughters of those students and to help people like them all over this country. But now I do have that chance - and I'll let you in on a secret - I mean to use it. And I hope that you will use it with me.

This is the richest and the most powerful country which ever occupied this globe. The might of past empires is little compared to ours. But I do not want to be the President

who built empires, or sought grandeur, or extended dominion. I want to be the President who educated young children to the wonders of their world. I want to be the President who helped to feed the hungry and to prepare them to be tax-payers instead of tax-eaters. I want to be the President who helped the poor to find their own way and who protected the right of every citizen to vote in every election. I want to be the President who helped to end hatred among his fellow men, and who promoted love among the people of all races and all regions and all parties. I want to be the President who helped to end war among the brothers of this earth.

And so, at the request of your beloved Speaker, and the Senator from Montana, the majority leader, the Senator from Illinois, the minority leader, Mr. McCulloch, and other Members of both parties, I came here tonight - not as President Roosevelt came down one time, in person, to veto a bonus bill, not as President Truman came down one time to urge the passage of a railroad bill - but I came down here to ask you to share this task with me, and to share it with the people that we both work for. I want this to be the Congress, Republicans and Democrats alike, which did all these things for all these people.

Beyond this great chamber, out yonder in fifty States, are the people that we serve. Who can tell what deep and unspoken hopes are in their hearts tonight as they sit there and listen. We all can guess, from our own lives, how difficult they often find their own pursuit of happiness, how many problems each little family has. They look most of all to themselves for their futures. But I think that they also look to each of us.

Above the pyramid on the great seal of the United States it says in Latin: "[Annuit cœptis] God has favored our undertaking." God will not favor everything that we do. It is rather our duty to divine His will. But I cannot help believing that He truly understands and that He really favors the undertaking that we begin here tonight."

BARACK OBAMA

Barack Hussein Obama II (August 4, 1961 -) was a community organizer in Chicago, graduated from Columbia University & Harvard Law School, president of the Harvard Law Review, civil rights attorney, and teacher of constitutional law at the University of Chicago Law School. He represented the 13th District in the Illinois Senate from 1997 to 2004, campaigned unsuccessfully for the 1st District of the United States House of Representatives in 2000, and became the 44th President of the United States in which he was the first African-American to hold that office.

During his term in office, Obama, a leader with a strong progressive ideology, signed into law or supported: economic stimulus legislation (American Recovery and Reinvestment Act of 2009), the Tax Relief, Unemployment Insurance Reauthorization, and Job Creation Act of 2010, Patient Protection and Affordable Care Act (Obamacare), Dodd–Frank Wall Street Reform and Consumer Protection Act, Don't Ask, Don't Tell Repeal Act of 2010, the end of US military involvement in Iraq, increased US troop levels in Afghanistan, US military involvement in Libya, the military operation that resulted in the death of Osama bin Laden, the Budget Control Act of 2011, the American Taxpayer Relief Act of 2012, policies related to gun control, full equality for LGBT Americans, and a court strike down of the Defense of Marriage Act of 1996 & California's Proposition 8.

In 2004, Obama received national attention during his campaign to represent Illinois in the United States Senate with his victory in the March Democratic Party primary, his keynote address at the Democratic National Convention in July, and his election to the Senate in November. He has been known as a great orator with the ability to persuade the masses. It was his 2004 Democratic National Convention speech, known as the "Audacity of Hope," that helped propel him into the White House.

Audacity of Hope
2004 Democratic Party National Convention
July 27, 2004
Boston, Massachusetts

"Thank you so much. Thank you. Thank you. Thank you so much. Thank you so much. Thank you, Dick Durbin. You make us all proud.

On behalf of the great state of Illinois, crossroads of a nation, land of Lincoln, let me express my deep gratitude for the privilege of addressing this convention. Tonight is a particular honor for me because, let's face it, my presence on this stage is pretty unlikely.

My father was a foreign student, born and raised in a small village in Kenya. He grew up herding goats, went to school in a tin- roof shack. His father, my grandfather, was a cook, a domestic servant to the British. But my grandfather had larger dreams for his son. **Through hard work and perseverance my father got a scholarship to study in a magical place, America, that's shown as a beacon of freedom and opportunity to so many who had come before him.**

While studying here my father met my mother. She was born in a town on the other side of the world, in Kansas.

Her father worked on oil rigs and farms through most of the Depression. The day after Pearl Harbor, my grandfather signed up for duty, joined Patton's army, marched across Europe. Back home my grandmother raised a baby and went to work on a bomber assembly line. After the war, they studied on the GI Bill, bought a house through FHA and later moved west, all the way to Hawaii, in search of opportunity. And they too had big dreams for their daughter, a common dream born of two continents.

My parents shared not only an improbable love; they shared an abiding faith in the possibilities of this nation. They would give me an African name, Barack, or "blessed," believing that in a tolerant America, your name is no barrier to success. They imagined me going to the best schools in the land, even though they weren't rich, because **in a generous America you don't have to be rich to achieve your potential.**

They're both passed away now. And yet I know that, on this night, they look down on me with great pride. And I stand here today grateful for the diversity of my heritage, aware that my parents' dreams live on in my two precious daughters. I stand here knowing that my story is part of the larger American story, that I owe a debt to all of those who came before me, and that in no other country on Earth is my story even possible.

Tonight, we gather to affirm the greatness of our nation not because of the height of our skyscrapers, or the power of our military, or the size of our economy; our pride is based on a very simple premise, summed up in a declaration made over two hundred years ago: "We hold these truths to be self-evident, that all men are created equal, that they are endowed by their Creator with certain inalienable rights, that among these are life, liberty and the pursuit of happiness."

That is the true genius of America, a faith - a faith in simple dreams, an insistence on small miracles; that we can tuck in our children at night and know that they are fed and clothed and safe from harm; that we can say what we think, write what we think, without hearing a sudden knock on the door; that we can have an idea and start our own business without paying a bribe; that we can participate in the political process without fear of retribution; and that our votes will be counted - or at least, most of the time.

This year, in this election, we are called to reaffirm our values and our commitments, to hold them against a hard reality and see how we are measuring up, to the legacy of our forebearers and the promise of future generations. And fellow Americans, Democrats, Republicans, independents, I say to you, tonight, we have more work to do - more work to do, for the workers I met in Galesburg, Illinois, who are losing their union jobs at the Maytag plant that's moving to Mexico, and now they're having to compete with their own children for jobs that pay 7 bucks an hour; more to do for the father I met who was losing his job and chocking back the tears wondering how he would pay $4,500 a months for the drugs his son needs without the health benefits that he counted on; more to do for the young woman in East St. Louis, and thousands more like her who have the grades, have the drive, have the will, but doesn't have the money to go to college.

Now, don't get me wrong, the people I meet in small towns and big cities and diners and office parks, they don't expect government to solves all of their problems. They know they have to work hard to get ahead. And they want to. Go into the collar counties around Chicago, and people will tell you: They don't want their tax money wasted by a welfare agency or by the Pentagon. Go into any inner-city neighborhood, and folks will tell you that government alone can't teach kids to learn. They know that parents have to teach, that children can't achieve unless we raise their expectations and turn off the television sets and eradicate the slander that says a black youth with a book is acting white. They know those things.

People don't expect - people don't expect government to solve all their problems. But they sense, deep in their bones, that with just a slight change in priorities, we can make sure that every child in America has a decent shot at life and that the doors of opportunity remain open to all. They know we can do better. And they want that choice. In this election, we offer that choice. Our party has chosen a man to lead us who embodies the best this country has to offer. And that man is John Kerry.

John Kerry understands the ideals of community, faith and service because they've defined his life. From his heroic service to Vietnam to his years as prosecutor and lieutenant governor, through two decades in the United States Senate, he has devoted himself to this country. Again and again, we've seen him make tough choices when easier ones were available. His values and his record affirm what is best in us. John Kerry believes in an America where hard work is rewarded. So **instead of offering tax breaks to companies shipping jobs overseas, he offers them to companies creating jobs here at home. John Kerry believes in an America where all Americans can afford the same health coverage our politicians in Washington have for themselves.** John Kerry believes in energy independence, so we aren't held hostage to the profits of oil companies or the sabotage of foreign oil fields. **John Kerry believes in the constitutional freedoms that have made our country the envy of the world, and he will never sacrifice our basic liberties nor use faith as a wedge to divide us.**

And John Kerry believes that in a dangerous world, war must be an option sometimes, but it should never be the first option.

You know, a while back, I met a young man named Seamus in a VFW hall in East Moline, Illinois. He was a good-looking kid, 6'2", 6'3", clear eyed, with an easy smile. He told me he'd joined the Marines and was heading to Iraq the following week. And as I listened to him explain why he had enlisted - the absolute faith he had in our country and its leaders, his devotion to duty and service - I thought, this young man was all that any of us might ever hope for in a child. But then I asked myself: Are we serving Seamus as well as he's serving us?

I thought of the 900 men and women, sons and daughters, husbands and wives, friends and neighbors who won't be returning to their own hometowns. I thought of the families I had met who were struggling to get by without a loved one's full income or whose loved ones had returned with a limb missing or nerves shattered, but still lacked long-term health benefits because they were Reservists.

When we send our young men and women into harm's way, we have a solemn obligation not to fudge the numbers or shade the truth about why they are going, to care for their families while they're gone, to tend to the soldiers upon their return and to never, ever go to war without enough troops to win the war, secure the peace and earn the respect of the world.

Now, let me be clear. Let me be clear. We have real enemies in the world. These enemies must be found. They must be pursued. And they must be defeated. John Kerry knows this. And just as Lieutenant Kerry did not hesitate to risk his life to protect the men who served with him in Vietnam, President Kerry will not hesitate one moment to use our military might to keep America safe and secure. John Kerry believes in America. And he knows that it's not enough for just some of us to prosper. **For alongside our famous individualism, there's another ingredient in the American saga, a belief that we are all connected as one people.**

If there's a child on the south side of Chicago who can't read, that matters to me, even if it's not my child. If there's a senior citizen somewhere who can't pay for their prescription and having to choose between medicine and the rent, that makes my life poorer, even if it's not my grandparent. If there's an Arab-American family being rounded up without benefit of an attorney or due process, that threatens my civil liberties. **It is that fundamental belief - it is that fundamental belief - I am my brother's keeper, I am my sisters' keeper - that makes this country work.** It's what allows us to pursue our individual dreams, yet still come together as a single American family: "E pluribus unum," out of many, one.

Now even as we speak, there are those who are preparing to divide us, the spin masters and negative ad peddlers who embrace the politics of anything goes. Well, I say to them tonight, there's not a liberal America and a conservative America; there's the United States of America. There's not a black America and white America and Latino America and Asian America; there's the United States of America.

The pundits, the pundits like to slice and dice our country into red states and blue States: red states for Republicans, blue States for Democrats. But I've got news for them, too. We worship an awesome God in the blue states, and we don't like federal agents poking around our libraries in the red states. We coach little league in the blue states and, yes, we've got some gay friends in the red states. There are patriots who opposed the war in Iraq, and there are patriots who supported the war in Iraq. We are one people, all of us pledging allegiance to the stars and stripes, all of us defending the United States of America.

In the end, that's what this election is about. **Do we participate in a politics of cynicism, or do we participate in a politics of hope?** John Kerry calls on us to hope. John Edwards calls on us to hope. I'm not talking about blind optimism here, the almost willful ignorance that thinks unemployment will go away if we just don't think about it, or health care crisis will solve itself if we just ignore it. That's not what I'm talking. I'm talking about something more substantial. It's the hope of slaves sitting around a fire singing freedom songs; the hope of immigrants setting out for distant shores; the hope of a young naval lieutenant bravely patrolling the Mekong Delta; the hope of a millworker's son who dares to defy the odds; the hope of a skinny kid with a funny name who believes that America has a place for him, too.

Hope in the face of difficulty, hope in the face of uncertainty, the audacity of hope: In the end, that is God's greatest gift to us, the bedrock of this nation, a belief in things not seen, a belief that there are better days ahead.

I believe that we can give our middle class relief and provide working families with a road to opportunity. I believe we can provide jobs for the jobless, homes to the homeless, and reclaim young people in cities across America from violence and despair. I believe that we have a righteous wind at our backs, and that as we stand on the crossroads of history, we can make the right choices and meet the challenges that face us.

America, tonight, if you feel the same energy that I do, if you feel the same urgency that I do, if you feel the same passion that I do, if you feel the same hopefulness that I do, if we do what we must do, then I have no doubt that all across the country, from Florida to Oregon, from Washington to Maine, the people will rise up in November, and John Kerry will be sworn in as President. And John Edwards will be sworn in as Vice President. And this country will reclaim it's promise. And out of this long political darkness a brighter day will come.

Thank you very much, everybody. God bless you. Thank you."

Chapter 5

A SHINING CITY
UPON A HILL

"The basis of conservatism is a desire for less government interference or less centralized authority or more individual freedom."
— **President Ronald Reagan**

The last two chapters discussed various aspects of progressivism. Its primary tenet is government intervention to ensure social justice. It strongly leans towards socialism. The next two chapters discuss conservatism, which strongly leans towards individualism, personal liberty, and limited government.

On October 27, 1964, Ronald Reagan, who was the General Electric Theater host for eight years, released a pre-recorded television program: *Rendezvous with Destiny*. His impassioned speech for lower taxes, less government and more personal liberty resonated with the American population to such an extent that he was elected to serve as Governor of California just two years later.

President Ronald Reagan personifies conservatism. He was born a few months before my grandmother was. I have asked myself in the past, which generation has seen more change than any other? I have but one conclusion: It is those who were born around 1900. Before 1900, people were primarily using horses and trains for transportation and the telephone was just starting to become a common household item. My grandmother, during her lifetime from 1911 to 2002, was part of a generation that saw the advancement of travel from trains to automobiles and airplanes, the improvement of communications from rudimentary telephones to cell phones and the Internet, the completion of five wars (although Congress never officially declared some of these as wars: WWI, WWII, Korea, Vietnam, Cold) and the beginning of a sixth (Terror), the Great Depression, the enactment of twelve Amendments to the Constitution, the landing of a man on the Moon, and the successful man-made satellite missions to seven other planets.

Of all the major accomplishments that have occurred in the 20th Century, American ingenuity and effort have been the driving force for a large proportion of them. Ronald Reagan remembered what life was like before the New Deal and the Great Society. Through his speeches and actions, he took an active role in preserving what is great about America.

AMERICAN EXCEPTIONALISM

There is something that Ronald Reagan truly believed in, and that was the concept of American Exceptionalism. There is something special about the United States of America that does not exist in any other culture, past or present, in the history of the world. There are a confluence of ideas that, when put together, begin to explain why America is not just great, but exceptional and unique. **The United States has stood out as a place to live one's own life with a high degree of liberty and freedom, and to pursue happiness in order to fulfill one's own dreams. The concepts of self-determination and individualism are celebrated in our founding documents, our national anthem and our pledge of allegiance.** Do any of these quotes sound familiar?

"We hold these truths to be self-evident, that all men are created equal, that they are endowed by their Creator with certain unalienable Rights, that among these are Life, Liberty and the pursuit of Happiness."

— Declaration of Independence

"We the People of the United States, in Order to form a more perfect Union, establish Justice, insure domestic Tranquility, provide for the common defense, promote the general Welfare, and secure the Blessings of Liberty to ourselves and our Posterity, do ordain and establish this Constitution for the United States of America."

— Preamble to the U.S. Constitution

"O say does that star-spangled banner yet wave, O'er the land of the free and the home of the brave?"

— United States National Anthem

"I pledge allegiance to the Flag of the United States of America, and to the Republic for which it stands, one Nation under God, indivisible, with liberty and justice for all."

— Pledge of Allegiance

You may have them memorized, but have you truly asked yourself about their significance? They all demonstrate that the Nation's prime focus is liberty, justice and freedom. No other nation can compete with us when we organize and set our efforts towards achieving specific goals and objectives, such as when we helped defeat the Axis powers during World War II or landed a person on the Moon. The United States was the first to: invent the single-wire telegraph system (1837), invent rubber (1839), invent the telephone (1876), patent the roller coaster (1898), achieve flight (1903), demonstrate the first talking motion picture (1910), invent television (1927), fly solo across the Atlantic Ocean (1927), invent the computer (1942), develop the atomic bomb (1945), break the sound barrier (1947), develop the Internet (1969), land a man on the Moon (1969), and develop online social networking (1997) to name a few. The United States has distinguished itself in many ways, such as: winning 93 of 168 (55%) Nobel prizes in medicine and physiology from 1933 to 2011, producing over 21% of the world's GDP in 2005, and winning more Olympic medals (2681) than the second (Russia), third (Great Britain), and sixth (Italy) place countries combined (2673).

What makes the United States of America exceptional and unique?

1. America is the most culturally potent Nation in the world.

   American music, television, movies, and other forms of cultural enrichment are one of the country's biggest exports. According to the US Census Bureau, the category of arts, entertainment and recreation generated approximately $193 billion in revenues in 2008.

2. America has one of the most relaxed immigration policies in the world.

   There are some steps a person must take in order to become a citizen of the United States. Until recently, those steps were minimal. My grandfather immigrated through Ellis Island prior to World War I. There was minimal screening for health and security concerns. Once he passed, he was eligible to live and work in the United States. In comparison, it is much more difficult to become a naturalized citizen of Switzerland. To even start the process, you have to have already been a resident for twelve years. One must pass a series of examinations to determine if that person is integrated into the Swiss way of life, is familiar with Swiss customs and traditions, complies with the Swiss rule of law, and does not endanger Switzerland's security. According to the US Census Bureau, there are about 337 languages spoken in the United States. The Nation's motto is *e pluribus umum* (out of many one). Each person has a specific set of talents and skills. The American system is designed to leverage those skills for the betterment of that individual and society as a whole regardless of his/her ethnicity or faith.

3. America is the most technologically advanced nation in the world.

    Steam engine, submarine, typewriter, refrigerator, revolver, telegraph, rubber, sewing machine, plastic, barbed wire, phonograph, roller coaster, air conditioner, airplane, tractor, motion picture, electric shaver, photocopier, Teflon, computer, and cell phone – All American inventions.

4. America encourages capitalism and free trade.

    According to Forbes Magazine, 20 out of 50 of the wealthiest individuals in the world live in the US. This is only part of the picture. There is a type of merit based social mobility in the US that does not exist in most other places in the world. If a person has the right set of skills, the right personality and a strong work ethic, a person in the US can become extremely successful.

5. America is the most generous country in the world.

    If you were to look at the combined totals of foreign aid given to other countries, donations given to non-profit organizations, and tithes given to religious centers, Americans gave away over $315 billion in 2008 alone. This is about the same as the annual Gross

Domestic Production (GDP) of Venezuela, which had the 31st highest GDP in the world in 2008.

6.	Americans celebrate and encourage human achievement.

	From the first flight in Kittyhawk, NC, to the first robot on Mars, Americans are motivated to not just show up and do their job, but to be a part of something extraordinary.

7.	America is one of a small handful of countries that uses its power and might to liberate others.

	From slavery in the Southern states, to Nazi control in Europe, to communism in Korea, to terrorism in the Middle East, America is not just able to, but is willing to spill blood and spend treasure to set others free from tyranny.

8.	Americans value human life.

	One example of this is in the field of medicine. A doctor must take an oath to do no harm, but it goes well beyond that. Americans have developed cures for some of the worst biological hazards known, including: polio, tuberculosis, yellow fever, and hepatitis B. Americans have won 93 of 168 (55%) Nobel prizes in medicine or physiology from 1933 to 2011.

9.	Americans elect their representatives.

	Because officials are placed into office through elections and not by appointment, they are held accountable to serve the people that reside within their district. Voters have the ability to remove a person from office. Many states also allow non-government people to create legislation through an initiative or referendum process.

10.	America values a belief in a Creator.

	The First Amendment to the Constitution states that government cannot establish or restrict religion. Also, the Declaration of Independence states, *"We hold these truths to be self-evident, that all men are created equal, that they are endowed by their Creator with certain unalienable rights, that among these are life, liberty and the pursuit of happiness. "*

11. America values freedom.

America was established on the ideas of social mobility, limited government, government accountability, and above all else, personal liberty. The purpose and design of the Bill of Rights was not for government to grant freedoms to society, which could later be taken away. It was designed to prevent government from taking preexisting freedoms away from the individual. It is the establishment of the *"unalienable rights"* within the American psyche and culture that truly makes the United States of America the most unique, the most productive, and the most inspired Nation in the history of the world.

These eleven attributes join together into a matrix that is American culture. If just one of these foundations is removed, America would cease to be the great Nation that it is. That is why these attributes and values have to be protected, nurtured, and unleashed upon the world.

The American conservative believes that America is unique and rare. Many conservative also believe in:

- Death penalty
- Minimal taxation
- Balanced budgets
- Limited government
- Respect for human life
- Strong national defense
- American exceptionalism
- Capitalism and free markets
- Parental control of education
- Unrestricted prayer in schools
- Respect for our military and police

- Restricted use or prohibition of abortion
- Private medical care and retirement plans
- Strict interpretation of the US Constitution
- Personal liberty and personal responsibility
- Traditional marriage between a man and a woman
- Respect for differences between males and females
- Science is based on unbiased analysis of data not consensus
- Canceling ineffective and/or inefficient government programs
- US Constitution and Bill of Rights are the lawful foundations of American governance
- Favoring states' rights over federal power, while accepting the Constitutional role of the federal government

SHELBY STEELE ON AMERICAN EXCEPTIONALISM

Shelby Steele, who is well-versed in American politics, wrote an article in the Wall Street Journal on September 1, 2011, that accurately describes the difficulties a President faces should he not accept the premise that America is unique in the world. Shelby Steele was born on January 1, 1946, and is an African-American author, columnist, documentary film maker, and a Senior Fellow at Stanford University's Hoover Institution (a public policy think tank started by Stanford alumnus Herbert Hoover) since 1994 specializing in the study of race relations, American social culture and identity politics. In 1990, he received the National Book Critics Circle Award for his book *The Content of Our Character*. In 1991, he received the Emmy, Writer's Guild, and San Francisco Film Festival Awards for his work on the documentary *Seven Days in Bensonhurst*. He won the National Humanities Medal in 2004, and the Bradley Prize in 2006.

Shelby Steele is a contributor to the New York Times and Wall Street Journal, an editor at Harper's magazine, and appeared on many national current affairs programs - including Nightline and 60 Minutes. Steele is a member of the National Association of Scholars, national board of the American Academy for Liberal Education, University Accreditation Association, and national board at the Center for the New American Community at the Manhattan Institute. He has a PhD in English from the University of Utah, an MA in sociology from Southern Illinois University, and a BA in political science from Coe College, Cedar Rapids, Iowa. It could be safe to state that Shelby Steele understands the concept of American Exceptionalism.

Obama and the Burden of Exceptionalism
Shelby Steele
Wall Street Journal
September 1, 2011

"If I've heard it once, I've heard it a hundred times: President Obama is destroying the country. Some say this destructiveness is intended; most say it is inadvertent, an outgrowth of inexperience, ideological wrong-headedness and an oddly undefined character. Indeed, on the matter of Mr. Obama's character, today's left now sounds like the right of three years ago. They have begun to see through the man and are surprised at how little is there.

Yet **there is something more than inexperience or lack of character that defines this Presidency: Mr. Obama came of age in a bubble of post-'60s liberalism that conditioned him to be an adversary of American exceptionalism.** In this liberalism, America's exceptional status in the world follows from a bargain with the devil - an indulgence in militarism, racism, sexism, corporate greed, and environmental disregard as the means to a broad economic, military, and even cultural supremacy in the world. And therefore America's greatness is as much the fruit of evil as of a devotion to freedom.

Mr. Obama did not explicitly run on an anti-exception-alism platform. Yet once he was elected it became clear that his idea of how and where to apply Presidential power was shaped precisely by this brand of liberalism. There was his devotion to big government, his passion for redistribution, and his scolding and scapegoating of Wall Street - as if his mandate was somehow to overcome, or at least subdue, American capitalism itself.

Anti-exceptionalism has clearly shaped his "leading from behind" profile abroad - an offer of self-effacement to offset the presumed American evil of swaggering cowboyism. **Once in office, his "hope and change" campaign slogan came to look like the "hope" of overcoming American exceptionalism and "change" away from it. So, in Mr. Obama, America gained a President with ambivalence, if not some antipathy, toward the singular greatness of the Nation he had been elected to lead.** But then again, the American people did elect him. Clearly Americans were looking for a new kind of exceptionalism in him (a black President would show America to have achieved near perfect social mobility). But were they also looking for - in Mr. Obama - an assault on America's bedrock exceptional-ism of military, economic and cultural pre-eminence?

American exceptionalism is, among other things, the result of a difficult rigor: the use of individual initia-tive as the engine of development within a society that strives to ensure individual freedom through the rule of law. Over time a society like this will become great. This is how - despite all our flagrant shortcomings and self-betrayals - America evolved into an exceptional nation. Yet today America is fighting in a number of Muslim coun-tries, and that number is as likely to rise as to fall. **Our exceptionalism saddles us with overwhelming burdens. The entire world comes to our door when there is real**

trouble, and every day we spill blood and treasure in foreign lands - even as anti-Americanism plays around the world like a hit record.

At home the values that made us exceptional have been smeared with derision. Individual initiative and individual responsibility - the very engines of our exceptionalism - now carry a stigma of hypocrisy. For centuries America made sure that no amount of initiative would lift minorities and women. So in liberal quarters today - where historical shames are made to define the present - these values are seen as little more than the cynical remnants of a bygone era. Talk of "merit" or "a competition of excellence" in the admissions office of any Ivy League university today, and then stand by for the howls of incredulous laughter.

Our national exceptionalism both burdens and defames us, yet it remains our fate. We make others anxious, envious, resentful, admiring and sometimes hate-driven. There's a reason al Qaeda operatives targeted the U.S. on 9/11 and not, say, Buenos Aires. They wanted to enrich their act of evil with the gravitas of American exceptionalism. They wanted to steal our thunder.

So we Americans cannot help but feel some ambivalence toward our singularity in the world - with its draining entanglements abroad, the selfless demands it makes on both our military and our taxpayers, and all the false charges of imperial hubris it incurs. Therefore **it is not surprising that America developed a liberalism - a political left - that took issue with our exceptionalism. It is a left that has no more fervent mission than to recast our greatness as the product of racism, imperialism and unbridled capitalism. But this leaves the left mired in an absurdity: It seeks to trade the burdens of greatness for the relief of mediocrity.** When greatness fades, when a nation contracts to a middling place in the world, then the world in fact no longer knocks on its door. (Think of England or France after empire.) To civilize America, to redeem the nation from its supposed avarice and hubris, the American left effectively makes a virtue of decline - as if we can redeem America only by making her indistinguishable from lesser nations.

Since the '60s we have enfeebled our public education system even as our wealth has expanded. **Moral and cultural relativism now obscure individual responsibility.** We are uninspired in the wars we fight, calculating our withdrawal even before we begin - and then we fight with a self-conscious, almost bureaucratic minimalism that makes the wars interminable.

America seems to be facing a pivotal moment: Do we move ahead by advancing or by receding - by reaffirming the values that made us exceptional or by letting go of those values, so that a creeping mediocrity begins to spare us the burdens of greatness?

As a President, Barack Obama has been a force for mediocrity. He has banked more on the hopeless interventions of government than on the exceptionalism of the people. His greatest weakness as a President is a limp confidence in his countrymen. He is afraid to ask difficult things of them.

Like me, he is black, and it was the government that in part saved us from the ignorances of the people. So the concept of the exceptionalism - the genius for freedom - of the American people may still be a stretch for him. But in fact he was elected to make that stretch. It should be held against him that he has failed to do so."

HISTORY OF AMERICAN CONSERVATISM

Many conservatives believe that college-level teaching about conservatism has been distorted by a *"liberal state paradigm"* in that textbooks usually interpret recent American history in terms of the origins and successes of political liberalism, especially the New Deal, rise of labor unions, women's suffrage and the Civil Rights movement. Conservative politics is usually defined as a reaction: as a free market reply to the growth of big government; as an expression of outrage against declining support for tradition and Christian morality. Where the violent Wobblies (Industrial Workers of the World) and illegal sit down strikes of the 1930s are seen as heroic, exposing Communist subversion by Joe McCarthy is denounced as the all-time low point of political morality. Therefore, I want to provide a history lesson from the conservative perspective.

Founding Fathers

Political thought in the early years of our country could be grouped into three main groups personified by Alexander Hamilton, George Mason and Thomas Jefferson.

Alexander Hamilton:

Alexander Hamilton was Secretary of the Treasury under President George Washington, signer of the US Constitution and one of the most influential interpreters and promoters of the US Constitution. As Secretary of the Treasury, Hamilton was the primary author of the economic policies of the George Washington administration, especially the funding of the state debts by the Federal government, the establishment of a national bank, a system of tariffs, and friendly trade relations with Britain. He was the founder of the Federalist Party (which included George Washington, John Adams and John Jay) and was directly opposed by the Democratic-Republican Party which was organized by Thomas Jefferson and James Madison. Hamilton was among those dissatisfied with the Articles of Confederation - the first attempt at a national governing document - because it lacked an executive, courts, and taxing powers. He led the Annapolis Convention, which successfully influenced Congress to issue a call for the Philadelphia Convention in order to create a new constitution. He was an active participant at Philadelphia and helped achieve ratification by writing 51 of the 85 Federalist Papers, which supported the new Constitution. Hamilton was a nationalist who emphasized a strong central government and argued that the implied powers of the US Constitution could be used to fund the national debt, assume state debts, and create the government-owned Bank of the United States. These programs were funded primarily by a tariff on imports and later also by a highly controversial excise tax on whiskey. As a side note, Senator Henry Clay was in agreement with many of Alexander Hamilton's policies, and an apprentice and admirer of Henry Clay was none other than President Abraham Lincoln.

George Mason:

George Mason was an American patriot, statesman and a delegate from Virginia to the US Constitutional Convention. Along with James Madison, he is called the "Father of the United States Bill of Rights." Mason was a leader of those who pressed for the addition of explicit States rights and individual rights to the US Constitution as a balance to the increased federal powers, and did not sign the document in part because it lacked such a statement. On December 15, 1791, the US Bill of Rights, based primarily on George Mason's Virginia Declaration of Rights (written in 1776), was ratified in response to the agitation of George Mason and other Anti-Federalists, including: Patrick Henry, Samuel Adams, Richard Henry Lee, Robert Yates and James Monroe. The Anti-Federalists were composed of diverse elements, including those opposed to the US Constitution because they thought that a stronger government threatened the sovereignty and prestige of the states, localities, or individuals; those that claimed a new centralized power would only replace the despotism of Great Britain; and those who simply feared that the new government threatened their personal liberties. Some of the opposition believed that the central government under the Articles of Confederation was sufficient. Still others believed that while the national government under the Articles was too weak, the national government under the US Constitution would be too strong. With the passage of the US Constitution and the Bill of Rights, the Anti-Federalist movement was exhausted. Some Anti-Federalists joined the Democratic-Republican party that James Madison and Thomas Jefferson founded.

Thomas Jefferson:

Thomas Jefferson was the principal author of the Declaration of Independence, Secretary of State under President George Washington and third President of the United States. He embraced the principles of republicanism, federalism, separation of powers and the rights of man. Republicanism is the governing of a society or state where the head of state is elected by the people. Federalism is a political system in which some powers are given to a government that has jurisdiction over the entire nation and other powers are given to this nation's subordinate states. Separation of powers is much more than the horizontal distribution of governmental powers between the judicial, executive and legislative branches within the federal government. There is also a vertical distribution (as expressed by the Tenth Amendment) in which governmental powers are distributed between the federal government, state governments and the people. The Act Prohibiting Importation of Slaves of 1807 is a United States federal law - drafted and signed by President Thomas Jefferson - that stated that no new slaves were permitted to be imported into the United States.

The Democratic-Republican Party was organized by Thomas Jefferson and James Madison and opposed the

Federalist Party. It formed to oppose the programs of Secretary of the Treasury Alexander Hamilton. The party denounced many of Hamilton's measures (especially the national bank) as unconstitutional. It favored states' rights and farmers. It was deeply committed to the principles of republicanism and federalism. The Federalists totally collapsed after 1815. The Democratic-Republican Party split after the 1824 Presidential election into two parties: the Democratic Party and the National Republican Party. By 1824 the party was split 4 ways and lacked a center. One remnant followed Andrew Jackson and Martin Van Buren into the new Democratic Party. That party still exists. Another remnant led by John Quincy Adams and Henry Clay formed the National Republican Party which morphed into the Whig Party.

Whig Party (1834 – 1854)

Organized by opponents of President Andrew Jackson (1829 – 1837). The Whigs favored a program of national development. Jackson's opposition to the Second Bank of the United States and nullification in South Carolina allowed Henry Clay to bring fiscal conservatives and Southern states' rights proponents together in a coalition with those who still believed in protective tariffs and federally financed internal improvements. The Whig's candidate, William H. Harrison, won the 1840 Presidential election and the party gained control of Congress, but Harrison's premature death halted enactment of the Whig program (his Vice President and successor, John Tyler, vetoed much of the Whig's agenda). Clay was the party's unsuccessful candidate in the 1844 election. In 1848 it nominated Zachary Taylor, who won the Presidency. The party began to divide on the topic of slavery and was further divided by the Compromise of 1850, which was brokered by Henry Clay and Democrat Stephen Douglas to maintain equal federal representation of slave states and free states. The Party's nominee in the 1852 election, Winfield Scott, failed to win wide support as most Southern Whigs joined the Democratic Party. In 1854 most Northern Whigs joined the new Republican Party.

Abraham Lincoln to Benjamin Harrison (1860 – 1892)

From 1860 to 1928, the Republican Party dominated American politics and won 14 of 18 Presidential elections. In the 1860 election, prior to the Civil War, Abraham Lincoln did not win any Electoral College votes from any Southern states. Lincoln did, however, win in California and Oregon. He won 180 of the 303 (59.4%) Electoral College votes. This victory allowed him to become President from a position of strength. Violence broke out and the Civil War began. After the war, liberals and Southern Democrats were unable to gain a large enough coalition to provide any resistance to the Republican Party. Since 1865 the Republican Party has identified itself with President Abraham Lincoln, who was the ideological heir of the Whigs and Thomas Jefferson. As the Gettysburg Address indicates, Lincoln cast himself as a second Jefferson bringing a second birth of freedom to the nation that had been born in Jefferson's Declaration of Independence.

Depression and Post-Depression Era

The Depression brought liberals to power under President Franklin D. Roosevelt (1933). The term "liberal" now came to mean a supporter of the New Deal. In 1934 Al Smith and pro-business Democrats formed the American Liberty League to fight the new liberalism, but failed to stop Roosevelt from shifting the Democratic party to the left. When Roosevelt tried to pack the US Supreme Court in 1937 the conservatives finally cooperated across party lines and defeated it with help from Vice President John Nance Garner. Roosevelt unsuccessfully tried to purge the conservative Democrats in the 1938 election. The conservatives in Congress then formed a bipartisan informal Conservative Coalition of Republicans and Southern Democrats. It largely controlled Congress from 1937 to 1964. Its most prominent leaders were Senator Robert Taft, a Republican from Ohio, and Senator Richard Russell, Democrat from Georgia.

By 1950, American liberalism was so dominant intellectually that liberal critic Lionel Trilling could dismiss contemporary conservatism as *"irritable mental gestures which seek to resemble ideas."* But a revival was underway. In the 1950s, principles for a conservative political movement were hashed out in books like Russell Kirk's *The Conservative Mind* (1953) and in the highly influential new magazine *National Review*, founded by William F. Buckley in 1955.

The new conservatism favored American intervention overseas to oppose communism. It looked to the Founding Fathers for historical inspiration. The success of the Civil Rights movement came in the Civil Rights Act of 1964 and the Voting Rights Act of 1965. Most conservatives supported both. Until then Southern whites (both liberal and conservative) had been locked into the Democratic party. That lock was now broken and Southern conservatives started voting for Republican candidates for President in 1964, and by the 1990s they were also voting for GOP candidates for state and local office. The Southern blacks now began to vote in large numbers, and they became Democrats, moving that party in the South to the left. By 2000, for the first time, all Southern states had a conservative Republican and a liberal Democratic party. The region favored the GOP heavily in Presidential elections, but split in state contests.

Ronald Reagan (1981 – 1989)

In the eight years of Ronald Reagan's Presidency the American conservative movement achieved ascendancy. In 1980 the GOP took control of the Senate for the first time since 1954, and conservative principles dominated Reagan's economic and for-

eign policies, with supply side economics as well as a strict opposition to Soviet Communism. Reagan promised to cut welfare spending but failed to do so. He did cut taxes, but raised
military spending and created large federal deficits that turned
out working to our advantage, because the Soviet Union was defeated in 1989 as symbolized by the falling of the Berlin Wall. It
should be known that the Republicans also balanced the budget
in the late 1990s. An icon of the American conservative movement, Reagan is credited by his supporters with transforming
American politics, galvanizing the Republican Party, uniting a
coalition of economic conservatives who supported his supply
side economic policies, foreign policy conservatives who favored
his success in stopping and rolling back Communism, and
social conservatives who identified with Reagan's conservative
religious and social ideals.

VARIOUS FLAVORS OF CONSERVATISM

President Ronald Reagan is celebrated amongst modern
conservatives because he clearly defined what a conservative is
and actively promoted it. Modern conservatism and conservatism during the Colonial period are very different. To better
comprehend these differences, it is necessary to understand its
more diverse elements and how it developed over time.

Neoconservativism

A neoconservative (or neocon) in American politics is
someone presented as a conservative but who actually favors
big government, interventionalism, and a hostility to religion
in politics and government. The word means "newly conservative," and thus formerly liberal. Neoconservatives tend to
oppose the appointment of social conservatives to high governmental positions, such as nomination to the US Supreme
Court. They tend to support candidates who are liberal on
social issues. The defining position of a neoconservative is

advocacy of an American foreign policy that seeks to install democracy in other nations. The neoconservative movement emerged in the mid 1970s, played a limited role in the Ronald Reagan Administration, and then had a voice in the Defense Department under the George W. Bush Administration after 9/11. In contrast to traditional conservatives, neoconservatives favor globalism, downplay religious issues and differences, and are unlikely to actively oppose abortion and homosexuality. Neocons disagree with conservatives on issues such as classroom prayer, the separation of powers, cultural unity and immigration. Neocons favor a strong active state in world affairs. Neoconservatism is popular in the New England states.

Paleoconservativism

Paleoconservative is a term that describes an academic or scholarly conservative who emphasizes religious heritage, national and Western identity, tradition, civil society, classical federalism, the importance of demographics, and an anti-interventionist policy. Paleoconservatives oppose immigration, communism, authoritarianism, social democracy and entitlement programs. Many paleoconservatives identify themselves as "classical conservatives" and trace their philosophy to the Old Right Republicans of the interwar period, which helped keep the US out of the League of Nations, reduced immigration with the passage of the Immigration Act of 1924, and opposed Franklin Roosevelt's New Deal. They were isolationists who opposed entry into World War II. Paleoconservatism is popular in Southern and Lower Midwestern states.

Fiscal Conservatism

Fiscal conservatism is a political position that calls for lower levels of public spending, lower taxes and lower government debt. It is concerned with economic rather than social issues. Fiscal conservatives oppose unnecessary government expenditures, deficits and government debt. They support balanced budgets. Fiscal conservatism may also support limited periods of higher taxes in order to lower the public debt. It assumes the private sector is more efficient than the public sector in achieving most objectives. High spending, budget deficits, and high debt are seen as indicators of corruption. Fiscal conservatism rejects the Keynesian policy of deficit spending, which is an economic theory stating that active government intervention in the marketplace and monetary policy is the best method of ensuring economic growth and stability.

Social Conservatism

Social conservatism refers to conservative values on social matters, such as promoting marriage between a man and a woman, opposition to abortion, opposition to homosexuality, promotion of prayer in schools, and opposition to teaching evolution in schools. The views of social conservatives and religious conservatives often overlap.

SPOTLIGHT ON WILLIAM F. BUCKLEY

William F. Buckley Jr., considered the Godfather of modern American conservatism, was born in New York. Ronald Reagan said of Buckley, *"Bill Buckley is perhaps the most influential journalist and intellectual in our era – he changed our country, indeed our century."* His father was a lawyer and wealthy oil magnate. The sixth of ten children, he was schooled as a child in Paris, London and New York, and attended Millbrook School (a private preparatory school). While at Millbrook, Buckley founded and edited the school's yearbook, *The Tamarack*, and was introduced to Albert Jay Nock's (libertarian author, educational theorist and social critic of the early 20th Century) writings by his father.

Upon graduation in 1943 from the US Army Officer Candidate School in Fort Benning, Georgia, he was commissioned as a second lieutenant in the US Army. At the end of World War II, he enrolled in Yale University. While there he became a member of the secret Skull and Bones society, was an active member of the Conservative Party and Yale Political Union, was captain of the Yale Debate Team, served as Chairman of the *Yale Daily News*, studied political science, history and economics, and graduated with honors in 1950. After graduation, he worked for the Central Intelligence Agency for two years.

Buckley became a prolific writer with over 50 titles to his name that were related to writing, speaking, history, politics, and sailing. His first book, *God and Man at Yale*, argued that Yale University had strayed from its original educational mission. The introduction of the book was written by famous *Life* magazine editorial writer John Chamberlain.

Buckley worked as an editor for *The American Mercury* in 1951 and 1952, but left after perceiving anti-Semitic tendencies in the magazine. He founded the *National Review* in 1955, serving as editor-in-chief until 1990. It has now released over 1300 issues.

In the late 1950s, Buckley believed in white supremacy and segregation in the South. James Kilpatrick, who supported segregation and lived in Richmond, Virginia, was *National Review*'s voice on the civil rights movement and the Constitution. However, by the end of the 1960s, he claimed that it was a mistake for *National Review* to have opposed civil rights legislation in 1964 and grew to admire Dr. Martin Luther King, Jr. Also, in 1962, Buckley denounced Robert W. Welch, Jr. and the John Birch Society, stating that they are *"far removed from common sense."* His style of writing has been called *"flashy and combative, filled with sound bites, and leads to an inflammatory drama."*

In 1960, Buckley helped form Young Americans for Freedom (YAF). YAF was guided by principles Buckley called, "The Sharon Statement". Written by M. Stanton Evans with the assistance of Annette Kirk, wife of Russell Kirk (author of *The Conservative Mind*), the statement reads:

IN THIS TIME of moral and political crisis, it is the responsibility of the youth of America to affirm certain eternal truths.

WE, as young conservatives, believe:

THAT foremost among the transcendent values is the individual's use of his God-given free will, whence derives his right to be free from the restrictions of arbitrary force;

THAT liberty is indivisible, and that political freedom cannot long exist without economic freedom;

THAT the purpose of government is to protect those freedoms through the preservation of internal order, the provision of national defense, and the administration of justice;

THAT when government ventures beyond these rightful functions, it accumulates power, which tends to diminish order and liberty;

THAT the Constitution of the United States is the best arrangement yet devised for empowering government to fulfill its proper role, while restraining it from the concentration and abuse of power;

THAT the genius of the Constitution - the division of powers - is summed up in the clause that reserves primacy to the several states, or to the people in those spheres not specifically delegated to the Federal government;

THAT the market economy, allocating resources by the free play of supply and demand, is the single economic system compatible with the requirements of personal freedom and constitutional government, and that it is at the same time the most productive supplier of human needs;

THAT when government interferes with the work of the market economy, it tends to reduce the moral and physical strength of the nation, that when it takes from one to bestow on another, it diminishes the incentive of the first, the integrity of the second, and the moral autonomy of both;

THAT we will be free only so long as the national sovereignty of the United States is secure; that history shows periods of freedom are rare, and can exist only when free citizens concertedly defend their rights against all enemies. . .

THAT the forces of international Communism are, at present, the greatest single threat to these liberties;

THAT the United States should stress victory over, rather than coexistence with this menace; and

THAT American foreign policy must be judged by this criterion: does it serve the just interests of the United States?"

YAF alumni include a Vice President, US Congressmen, US Circuit Court Judges and conservative activists.

In 1963-64, William F. Buckley Jr., helped mobilize support for Arizona Senator Barry Goldwater in his run for President of the United States. In 1965, Buckley ran for mayor of New York City. He ran to restore momentum to the conservative cause in the wake of Goldwater's defeat. In 1970, he helped get his brother James elected as US Senator from New York. James Buckley was a one term US Senator who lost his re-election to Daniel Patrick Moynihan. In 1973, Buckley served as a delegate to the United Nations. In 1981, Buckley informed President-elect (and personal friend) Ronald Reagan that he would decline any official position offered to him. Reagan jokingly replied that that was too bad, because he had wanted to make Buckley ambassador to (then Soviet-occupied) Afghanistan. Buckley replied that he was willing to take the job but only if he were to be supplied with 10 divisions of bodyguards.

In 1953–1954, Buckley was an occasional panelist on the conservative public affairs program, *Answers for Americans*, broadcast on ABC. In 1966, Buckley founded *Firing Line* on PBS. Hosted by Buckley, its 1,504 episodes over 33 years made *Firing Line* the longest-running public affairs show in television history with a single host. It featured many of the most prominent intellectuals and public figures in the United States and won an Emmy Award in 1969. In 1991, he was awarded the Presidential Medal of Freedom (award for meritorious contribution to the security or national interests of the United States).

At a time when most liberals thought that conservatism was weak and almost non-existent, the 1950s saw a resurgence in the conservative movement. Russell Kirk released his book *The Conservative Mind* in 1953, and William F. Buckley, Jr. stood atop the podium at the 1950 Yale commencement ceremony and warned against accepting the monolithic voice of the American left. He encouraged people to embrace the diversity of ideas.

Today We Are Educated Men
William F. Buckley
Yale Commencement Ceremony
New Haven, Connecticut
June 11, 1950

> "A year ago, the orator for the class of 1949 stood here and told his classmates that the troubles of the United States in particular and of Western democracy in general were attributable to the negativism of our front against Communism. His was not a lone voice jarring smug opinion in mid-twentieth-century America. Rather he is part of the swelling forefront of men and women who are raising a hue and a cry for what they loosely call positivism, by which they mean bold new measures, audacious steps forward, a reorientation towards those great new horizons and that Brave New World.

It is natural at this point to realize that (although we must be very careful how we put it) we are, as Yale men, privileged members of our society, and to us falls the responsibility of leadership in this great new positivist movement. For we had had a great education, and our caps and gowns weigh heavy upon us as we face our responsibilities to mankind.

All of us here have been exposed to four years' education in one of the most enlightened and advanced liberal-arts colleges in the world. Here we can absorb the last word in most fields of academic endeavor. Here we find the headquarters of a magazine devoted exclusively to metaphysics, and another devoted entirely to an analysis of French existentialism. And here, for better or worse, we have been jolted forcefully away from any preconceived judgments we may have had when we come. Here we can find men who will tell us that Jesus Christ was the greatest fraud that history has known. Here we can find men who will tell us that morality is an anachronistic conception, rendered obsolete by the advances of human thought. From neo-Benthamines at Yale we can learn that laws are a sociological institution, to be wielded to facilitate the sacrosanct will of the enlightened minority.

Communism is a real force to cope with only because of the deficiencies of democracy. Our fathers, who worked to send us to Yale, their fathers and their fathers, who made Yale and the United States, were hardworking men, shrewd men, and performed a certain economic service, but they were dreadfully irresponsible, y'know, in view of today's enlightenment.

And it so goes: two and two make three, the shortest distance between two points is a crooked line, good is bad and bad is good, and from this morass we are to extract a workable, enlightened synthesis to govern our thoughts and our actions, for today we are educated men.

Nothing, it is true, is healthier than honest scrutiny, with maybe even a little debunking thrown in. When a dean tells us that our task is to go out and ennoble mankind, we nod our heads and wonder whether the opening in the putty-knife factory or in the ball-bearing works will pay more. When we are told that Lincoln was totally unconcerned with politics, we might ponder the occasion in 1863 when he could not focus his attention on the questions of a distinguished visitor because he was terribly worried over what Republican to appoint postmaster of Chicago. In 1913 Charles Beard wrote his Economic Interpretation of the Constitution. It was banned in seven state universities and brought almost nationwide ostracism for the author. Today a study of this analysis is a prerequisite to a doctoral degree in American history.

Certainly civilization cannot advance without freedom of inquiry. The fact is self-evident. What seems equally self-evident is that in the process of history certain immutable truths have been revealed and discovered and that their value is not subject to the limitations of time and space. The probing, the relentless debunking, has engendered a skepticism that threatens to pervade and atrophy all our values. In apologizing for our beliefs and our traditions we have bent over backwards so far that we have lost our balance, and we see a topsy-turvy world and we say topsy-turvy things, such as that the way to beat Communism is by making our democracy better. What a curious self-examination! Beat the Union of Soviet Socialist Republics by making America socialistic. Beat atheism by denying God. Uphold individual freedom by denying natural rights. We neglect to say to the Communist, "In the name of heaven look at what we now have. Your standards don't interest us." As Emerson threatened to say to the obstreperous government tax collector, "If you pursue, I will slit your throat, sir"

The credo of the so-called positivists is characterized by the advocacy of change. Republicanism, on the other hand, is negativism because conservatives believe that America has grown and has prospered, has put muscle on her bones, by rewarding initiative and industry, by conceding to her citizens not only the right and responsibilities of self-government, but also the right and responsibilities of self-care, of individually earned security. The role of the so-called conservative is a difficult one. A starry-eyed young man, nevertheless aggressive in his wisdom, flaunting the badge of custodian of the common man, approaches our neat, sturdy white house and tells us we must destroy it, rebuild it of crystallized cold cream, and paint it purple. "But we like it the way it is," we retort feebly. "Rip 'er down! This is a changing world."

Is our effort to achieve perspective all the more difficult by virtue of our having gone to Yale? In many respects it is, because the university does not actively aid us in forming an enlightened synthesis. That job is for us to perform: to reject those notions that do not square with the enlightenment that should be ours as moral, educated men, beneficiaries of centuries of historical experience. Yale has given us much. Not least is an awesome responsibility to withstand her barrage, to emerge from her halls with both feet on the ground, with a sane head and a reinforced set of values. If our landing is accomplished, we are stronger men for our flight.

Keenly aware, then, of the vast deficiencies in American life today – the suffering, the injustice, the want – we must nevertheless spend our greatest efforts, it seems to me, in preserving the framework that supports the vaster boun-

ties that make our country an oasis of freedom and prosperity. **Our concern for deficiencies in America must
not cause us to indict the principles that have allowed
our country, its faults notwithstanding, to tower over
the nations of the world as a citadel of freedom and
wealth. With what severity and strength we can muster,
we must punch the gasbag of cynicism and skepticism, and thank providence for what we have and must
retain.** Our distillation of the ideas, concepts, and theories
expounded at Yale must serve to enhance our devolution
to the good in what we have, to reinforce our allegiance to
our principles, to convince us that our outlook is positive:
that the retention of the best features of our way of life is
the most enlightened and noble of goals. Insofar as the
phrase "For God, for Country, and for Yale" is meaningful, we need not be embarrassed to mean "For God as we
know him, for country as we know it, and for Yale as we
have known her."

Chapter 6

TEAR DOWN THIS WALL

Just a quick note. Chapter 4 and chapter 6 are opposite sides of the same coin. Where chapter 4 contains relevant progressive speeches from Anna Howard Shaw, Franklin Delano Roosevelt, Lyndon Baines Johnson and Barack Obama, chapter 6 contains relevant conservative speeches from Ronald Reagan, Marco Rubio, Mitt Romney and Newt Gingrich. Both sets of speeches are designed to give you incite into the ideals and values of conservatives and progressives.

RONALD REAGAN

Ronald Reagan was one of the most influential Presidents of the 20th Century. During the 1980 Presidential election he received 50.7% of the popular vote compared to Jimmy Carter's 41.0%, and he received 91% of the Electoral College votes. He was so popular four years later that in 1984 he received 58.8% of the popular vote and 98% of the Electoral College votes. There have only been two elections that have had a larger margin of victory than that of Reagan v. Mondale (Monroe v. Adams (1820) and Roosevelt v. Landon (1936)).

On the day that Reagan took office, after 444 days as hostages of Islamic students in Iran, 52 Americans were released. Just over two months later, John Hinckley, Jr. shot six rounds at Reagan and almost killed him. Over the next eight years, Reagan improved the business climate leading to an unprecedented rise in wealth and a decrease in unemployment. What

I will remember him best for is that he ended the Cold War with the Soviet Union. I remember when he addressed Mikhail Gorbachev at the Brandenburg Gate on June 12, 1987, and told Mr. Gorbachev directly to *"tear down this wall."* Two and half years later, the Berlin Wall came down and reunification between East and West began. One of my favorite pictures from this time period was that of Ronald Reagan, George H.W. Bush and Mikhail Gorbachev standing in front of the Statue of Liberty. In the years following, HW Bush and Gorbachev have developed a friendly relationship. In 2008 Gorbachev received the US Medal of Freedom, and it was George H.W. Bush that presented it to him. Also, Mrs. Raisa Gorbachev was present at First Lady Barbara Bush's commencement speech at Wellesley College on June 1, 1990. All this started with his now famous speech in 1964 called *A Time for Choosing.* The speech signifies a shift in the Republican Party from moderate to conservative.

A Time for Choosing
Ronald Reagan Barry Goldwater Speech
October 27, 1964

> "Thank you. Thank you very much. Thank you and good evening. The sponsor has been identified, but unlike most television programs, the performer hasn't been provided with a script. As a matter of fact, I have been permitted to choose my own words and discuss my own ideas regarding the choice that we face in the next few weeks.

> I have spent most of my life as a Democrat. I recently have seen fit to follow another course. I believe that the issues confronting us cross party lines. Now, one side in this campaign has been telling us that the issues of this election are the maintenance of peace and prosperity. The line has been used, "We've never had it so good."

But I have an uncomfortable feeling that this prosperity isn't something on which we can base our hopes for the future. No nation in history has ever survived a tax burden that reached a third of its national income. Today, 37 cents out of every dollar earned in this country is the tax collector's share, and yet our government continues to spend 17 million dollars a day more than the government takes in. We haven't balanced our budget 28 out of the last 34 years. We've raised our debt limit three times in the last twelve months, and now our national debt is one and a half times bigger than all the combined debts of all the nations of the world. We have 15 billion dollars in gold in our treasury; we don't own an ounce. Foreign dollar claims are 27.3 billion dollars. And we've just had announced that the dollar of 1939 will now purchase 45 cents in its total value.

As for the peace that we would preserve, I wonder who among us would like to approach the wife or mother whose husband or son has died in South Vietnam and ask them if they think this is a peace that should be maintained indefinitely. Do they mean peace, or do they mean we just want to be left in peace? **There can be no real peace while one American is dying some place in the world for the rest of us. We're at war with the most dangerous enemy that has ever faced mankind in his long climb from the swamp to the stars, and it's been said if we lose that war, and in so doing lose this way of freedom of ours, history will record with the greatest astonishment that those who had the most to lose did the least to prevent its happening. Well I think it's time we ask ourselves if we still know the freedoms that were intended for us by the Founding Fathers.**

Not too long ago, two friends of mine were talking to a Cuban refugee, a businessman who had escaped from

Castro, and in the midst of his story one of my friends turned to the other and said, "We don't know how lucky we are." And the Cuban stopped and said, "How lucky you are? I had someplace to escape to." And in that sentence he told us the entire story. **If we lose freedom here, there's no place to escape to. This is the last stand on earth. And this idea that government is beholden to the people, that it has no other source of power except the sovereign people, is still the newest and the most unique idea in all the long history of man's relation to man. This is the issue of this election: whether we believe in our capacity for self-government or whether we abandon the American revolution and confess that a little intellectual elite in a far-distant capitol can plan our lives for us better than we can plan them ourselves.**

You and I are told increasingly we have to choose between a left or right. Well I'd like to suggest there is no such thing as a left or right. There's only an up or down: [up] man's old - old-aged dream, the ultimate in individual freedom consistent with law and order, or down to the ant heap of totalitarianism. And **regardless of their sincerity, their humanitarian motives, those who would trade our freedom for security have embarked on this downward course.**

In this vote-harvesting time, they use terms like the "Great Society," or as we were told a few days ago by the President, we must accept a greater government activity in the affairs of the people. But they've been a little more explicit in the past and among themselves; and all of the things I now will quote have appeared in print. These are not Republican accusations. For example, they have voices that say, "The cold war will end through our acceptance of a not undemocratic socialism." Another voice says, "The profit motive has become outmoded. It must be replaced by the incentives of the welfare state." Or, "Our traditional system of individual freedom is incapable of solving the complex problems of the 20th century." Senator Fulbright has said at Stanford University that the Constitution is outmoded. He referred to the President as "our moral teacher and our leader," and he says he is "hobbled in his task by the restrictions of power imposed on him by this antiquated document." He must "be freed," so that he "can do for us" what he knows "is best." And Senator Clark of Pennsylvania, another articulate spokesman, defines liberalism as "meeting the material needs of the masses through the full power of centralized government."

Well, I, for one, resent it when a representative of the people refers to you and me, the free men and women of this country, as "the masses." This is a term we haven't applied to ourselves in America. But **beyond that, "the full power of centralized government" - this was the very thing the Founding Fathers sought to minimize. They knew that governments don't control things. A government can't control the economy without controlling people. And they know when a government sets out to do that, it must use force and coercion to achieve its purpose. They also knew, those Founding Fathers, that outside of its legitimate functions, government does nothing as well or as economically as the private sector of the economy.**

Now, we have no better example of this than government's involvement in the farm economy over the last 30 years. Since 1955, the cost of this program has nearly doubled. One-fourth of farming in America is responsible for 85% of the farm surplus. Three-fourths of farming is out on the free market and has known a 21% increase in the per capita consumption of all its produce. You see, that one-fourth of farming - that's regulated and controlled by the federal government. In the last three years we've spent 43 dollars in the feed grain program for every dollar bushel of corn we don't grow.

Senator Humphrey last week charged that Barry Goldwater, as President, would seek to eliminate farmers. He should do his homework a little better, because he'll find out that we've had a decline of 5 million in the farm population under these government programs. He'll also find that the Democratic administration has sought to get from Congress [an] extension of the farm program to include that three-fourths that is now free. He'll find that they've also asked for the right to imprison farmers who wouldn't keep books as prescribed by the federal government. The Secretary of Agriculture asked for the right to seize farms through condemnation and resell them to other individuals. And contained in that same program was a provision that would have allowed the federal government to remove 2 million farmers from the soil.

At the same time, there's been an increase in the Department of Agriculture employees. There's now one for every 30 farms in the United States, and still they can't tell us how 66 shiploads of grain headed for Austria disappeared without a trace and Billie Sol Estes never left shore.

Every responsible farmer and farm organization has repeatedly asked the government to free the farm economy, but how - who are farmers to know what's best for them? The wheat farmers voted against a wheat program. The government passed it anyway. Now the price of bread goes up; the price of wheat to the farmer goes down.

Meanwhile, back in the city, under urban renewal the assault on freedom carries on. Private property rights [are] so diluted that public interest is almost anything a few government planners decide it should be. In a program that takes from the needy and gives to the greedy, we see such spectacles as in Cleveland, Ohio, a million-and-a-half-dollar building completed only three years ago must be destroyed to make way for what government officials call a "more compatible use of the land." The President tells us he's now going to start building public housing units in the thousands, where heretofore we've only built them in the hundreds. But FHA [Federal Housing Authority] and the Veterans Administration tell us they have 120,000 housing units they've taken back through mortgage foreclosure. **For three decades, we've sought to solve the problems of unemployment through government planning, and the more the plans fail, the more the planners plan.** The latest is the Area Redevelopment Agency. They've just declared Rice County, Kansas, a depressed area. Rice County, Kansas, has two hundred oil wells, and the 14,000 people there have over 30 million dollars on deposit in personal savings in their banks. And when the government tells you you're depressed, lie down and be depressed.

We have so many people who can't see a fat man standing beside a thin one without coming to the conclusion the fat man got that way by taking advantage of the thin one. **So they're going to solve all the problems of human misery through government and government planning. Well, now, if government planning and welfare had the answer - and they've had almost 30 years of it - shouldn't we expect government to read the score to us once in a while? Shouldn't they be telling us about the decline each year in the number of people needing help? The reduction in the need for public housing? But the reverse is true. Each year the need grows greater; the program grows greater.** We were told four years ago that 17 million people went to bed hungry each night. Well that was probably true. They were all on a diet. But now we're told that 9.3 million families in this country are poverty-stricken on the basis of earning less than 3,000 dollars a year. Welfare spending [is] 10 times greater than in the dark depths of the Depression. We're spending 45 billion dollars on welfare. Now do a little arithmetic, and you'll find that if we divided the 45 billion dollars up equally among those 9 million poor families, we'd be able to give each family 4,600 dollars a year. And this added to their present income should eliminate poverty. Direct aid to the poor, however, is only running only about 600 dollars per family. It would seem that someplace there must be some overhead.

Now - so now we declare "war on poverty," or "You, too, can be a Bobby Baker." Now do they honestly expect us to believe that if we add 1 billion dollars to the 45 billion we're spending, one more program to the 30-odd we have - and remember, this new program doesn't replace any, it just duplicates existing programs - do they believe that poverty is suddenly going to disappear by magic? Well, in all fairness I should explain there is one part of the new program that isn't duplicated. This is the youth feature. We're now going to solve the dropout problem, juvenile delinquency, by reinstituting something like the old CCC camps [Civilian Conservation Corps], and we're going to put our young people in these camps. But again we do some arithmetic, and we find that we're going to spend each year just on room and board for each young person we help 4,700 dollars a year. We can send them to Harvard for 2,700! Course, don't get me wrong. I'm not suggesting Harvard is the answer to juvenile delinquency. But seriously, what are we doing to those we seek to help? **Not too long ago, a judge called me here in Los Angeles. He told me of a young woman who'd come before him for a divorce. She had six children, was pregnant with her seventh. Under his questioning, she revealed her husband was a laborer earning 250 dollars a month.**

She wanted a divorce to get an 80 dollar raise. She's eligible for 330 dollars a month in the Aid to Dependent Children Program. She got the idea from two women in her neighborhood who'd already done that very thing. Yet anytime you and I question the schemes of the do-gooders, we're denounced as being against their humanitarian goals. They say we're always "against" things - we're never "for" anything. Well, the trouble with our liberal friends is not that they're ignorant; it's just that they know so much that isn't so.

Now - we're for a provision that destitution should not follow unemployment by reason of old age, and to that end we've accepted Social Security as a step toward meeting the problem. But we're against those entrusted with this program when they practice deception regarding its fiscal shortcomings, when they charge that any criticism of the program means that we want to end payments to those people who depend on them for a livelihood. **They've called it "insurance" to us in a hundred million pieces of literature. But then they appeared before the Supreme Court and they testified it was a welfare program. They only use the term "insurance" to sell it to the people. And they said Social Security dues are a tax for the general use of the government, and the government has used that tax. There is no fund, because Robert Byers, the actuarial head, appeared before a congressional committee and admitted that Social Security as of this moment is 298 billion dollars in the hole. But he said there should be no cause for worry because as long as they have the power to tax, they could always take away from the people whatever they needed to bail them out of trouble.** And they're doing just that.

A young man, 21 years of age, working at an average salary - his Social Security contribution would, in the open market, buy him an insurance policy that would guarantee 220 dollars a month at age 65. The government promises 127. He could live it up until he's 31 and then take out a policy that would pay more than Social Security. Now are we so lacking in business sense that we can't put this program on a sound basis, so that people who do require those payments will find they can get them when they're due — that the cupboard isn't bare? Barry Goldwater thinks we can.

At the same time, can't we introduce voluntary features that would permit a citizen who can do better on his own to be excused upon presentation of evidence that he had made provision for the non-earning years? Should we not allow a widow with children to work, and not lose the benefits supposedly paid for by her deceased husband? Shouldn't you and I be allowed to declare who our beneficiaries will be under this program, which we cannot do? **I think we're for telling our senior citizens that no one in this country should be denied medical care because of a lack of funds. But I think we're against forcing all citizens, regardless of need, into a compulsory government program**, especially when we have such examples, as was announced last week, when France admitted that their Medicare program is now bankrupt. They've come to the end of the road. In addition, was Barry Goldwater so irresponsible when he suggested that our government give up its program of deliberate, planned inflation, so that when you do get your Social Security pension, a dollar will buy a dollar's worth, and not 45 cents worth?

I think we're for an international organization, where the nations of the world can seek peace. But I think we're against subordinating American interests to an organization that has become so structurally unsound that today you can muster a two-thirds vote on the floor of the General Assembly among nations that rep-

resent less than 10 percent of the world's population. I think we're against the hypocrisy of assailing our allies because here and there they cling to a colony, while we engage in a conspiracy of silence and never open our mouths about the millions of people enslaved in the Soviet colonies in the satellite nations.

I think we're for aiding our allies by sharing of our material blessings with those nations which share in our fundamental beliefs, but we're against doling out money government to government, creating bureaucracy, if not socialism, all over the world. We set out to help 19 countries. We're helping 107. We've spent 146 billion dollars. With that money, we bought a 2 million dollar yacht for Haile Selassie. We bought dress suits for Greek undertakers, extra wives for Kenya[n] government officials. We bought a thousand TV sets for a place where they have no electricity. In the last six years, 52 nations have bought 7 billion dollars worth of our gold, and all 52 are receiving foreign aid from this country.

No government ever voluntarily reduces itself in size. So, governments' programs, once launched, never disappear. Actually, a government bureau is the nearest thing to eternal life we'll ever see on this earth. Federal employees - federal employees number two and a half million; and federal, state, and local, one out of six of the nation's work force employed by government. These proliferating bureaus with their thousands of regulations have cost us many of our constitutional safeguards. How many of us realize that today federal agents can invade a man's property without a warrant? They can impose a fine without a formal hearing, let alone a trial by jury? And they can seize and sell his property at auction to enforce the payment of that fine. In Chico County, Arkansas, James Wier over-planted his rice allotment. The government obtained a 17,000 dollar judgment. And a U.S. marshal sold his 960-acre farm at auction. The government said it was necessary as a warning to others to make the system work.

Last February 19th at the University of Minnesota, Norman Thomas, six-times candidate for President on the Socialist Party ticket, said, "If Barry Goldwater became President, he would stop the advance of socialism in the United States." I think that's exactly what he will do. But as a former Democrat, I can tell you Norman Thomas isn't the only man who has drawn this parallel to socialism with the present administration, because back in 1936, Mr. Democrat himself, Al Smith, the great American, came before the American people and charged that the leadership of his Party was taking the Party of Jefferson, Jackson, and Cleveland down the road under the banners of Marx, Lenin, and Stalin. And he walked away from his Party, and he never returned til the day he died - because to this day, the leadership of that Party has been taking that Party, that honorable Party, down the road in the image of the labor Socialist Party of England.

Now it doesn't require expropriation or confiscation of private property or business to impose socialism on a people. What does it mean whether you hold the deed to the - or the title to your business or property if the government holds the power of life and death over that business or property? And such machinery already exists. The government can find some charge to bring against any concern it chooses to prosecute. Every businessman has his own tale of harassment. Somewhere a perversion has taken place. **Our natural, unalienable rights are now considered to be a dispensation of government, and freedom has never been so fragile, so close to slipping from our grasp as it is at this moment.**

Our Democratic opponents seem unwilling to debate these issues. They want to make you and I believe that this is a contest between two men - that we're to choose just between two personalities. Well what of this man that they would destroy - and in destroying, they would destroy that which he represents, the ideas that you and I hold dear? Is he the brash and shallow and trigger-happy man they say he is? Well I've been privileged to know him "when." I knew him long before he ever dreamed of trying for high office, and I can tell you personally I've never known a man in my life I believed so incapable of doing a dishonest or dishonorable thing. This is a man who, in his own business before he entered politics, instituted a profit-sharing plan before unions had ever thought of it. He put in health and medical insurance for all his employees. He took 50 percent of the profits before taxes and set up a retirement program, a pension plan for all his employees. He sent monthly checks for life to an employee who was ill and couldn't work. He provides nursing care for the children of mothers who work in the stores. When Mexico was ravaged by the floods in the Rio Grande, he climbed in his airplane and flew medicine and supplies down there.

An ex-GI told me how he met him. It was the week before Christmas during the Korean War, and he was at the Los Angeles airport trying to get a ride home to Arizona for Christmas. And he said that [there were] a lot of servicemen there and no seats available on the planes. And then a voice came over the loudspeaker and said, "Any men in uniform wanting a ride to Arizona, go to runway such-and-such," and they went down there, and there was a fellow named Barry Goldwater sitting in his plane. Every day in those weeks before Christmas, all day long, he'd load up the plane, fly it to Arizona, fly them to their homes, fly back over to get another load.

During the hectic split-second timing of a campaign, this is a man who took time out to sit beside an old friend who was dying of cancer. His campaign managers were understandably impatient, but he said, "There aren't many left who care what happens to her. I'd like her to know I care." This is a man who said to his 19-year-old son, **"There is no foundation like the rock of honesty and fairness, and when you begin to build your life on that rock, with the cement of the faith in God that you have, then you have a real start."** This is not a man who could carelessly send other people's sons to war. And that is the issue of this campaign that makes all the other problems I've discussed academic, unless we realize we're in a war that must be won.

Those who would trade our freedom for the soup kitchen of the welfare state have told us they have a utopian solution of peace without victory. They call their policy "accommodation." And they say if we'll only avoid any direct confrontation with the enemy, he'll forget his evil ways and learn to love us. All who oppose them are indicted as warmongers. They say we offer simple answers to complex problems. Well, perhaps there is a simple answer - not an easy answer - but simple: If you and I have the courage to tell our elected officials that we want our national policy based on what we know in our hearts is morally right.

We cannot buy our security, our freedom from the threat of the bomb by committing an immorality so great as saying to a billion human beings now enslaved behind the Iron Curtain, "Give up your dreams of freedom because to save our own skins, we're willing to make a deal with your slave masters." Alexander Hamilton said, "A nation which can prefer disgrace to danger is prepared for a master, and deserves one." Now let's set the record straight. There's no argument over the choice between peace and war, but there's only one guaranteed way you can have peace - and you can have it in the next second - surrender.

Admittedly, there's a risk in any course we follow other than this, but every lesson of history tells us that the greater risk lies in appeasement, and this is the specter our well-meaning liberal friends refuse to face - that their policy of accommodation is appeasement, and it gives no choice between peace and war, only between fight or surrender. If we continue to accommodate, continue to back and retreat, eventually we have to face the final demand - the ultimatum. And what then - when Nikita Khrushchev has told his people he knows what our answer will be? He has told them that we're retreating under the pressure of the Cold War, and someday when the time comes to deliver the final ultimatum, our surrender will be voluntary, because by that time we will have been weakened from within spiritually, morally, and economically. He believes this because from our side he's heard voices pleading for "peace at any price" or "better Red than dead," or as one commentator put it, he'd rather "live on his knees than die on his feet." And therein lies the road to war, because those voices don't speak for the rest of us.

You and I know and do not believe that life is so dear and peace so sweet as to be purchased at the price of chains and slavery. If nothing in life is worth dying for, when did this begin - just in the face of this enemy? Or should Moses have told the children of Israel to live in slavery under the pharaohs? Should Christ have refused the cross? Should the patriots at Concord Bridge have thrown down their guns and refused to fire the shot heard 'round the world? The martyrs of history were not fools, and our honored dead who gave their lives to stop the advance of the Nazis didn't die in vain. Where, then, is the road to peace? Well it's a simple answer after all.

You and I have the courage to say to our enemies, "There is a price we will not pay." "There is a point beyond which they must not advance." And this - this is the meaning in the phrase of Barry Goldwater's "peace through strength." Winston Churchill said, "The destiny of man is not measured by material computations. When great forces are on the move in the world, we learn we're spirits - not animals." And he said, "There's something going on in time and space, and beyond time and space, which, whether we like it or not, spells duty."

You and I have a rendezvous with destiny. We'll preserve for our children this, the last best hope of man on earth, or we'll sentence them to take the last step into a thousand years of darkness. We will keep in mind and remember that Barry Goldwater has faith in us. He has faith that you and I have the ability and the dignity and the right to make our own decisions and determine our own destiny.

Thank you very much."

MARCO RUBIO

Born in 1971 to Cuban exiles, Marco Rubio has only begun his political career. He attended Tarkio College in Missouri on a football scholarship for one year. He graduated from University of Florida with a BS in political science, and he obtained his Juris Doctorate graduating *cum laude* from the University of Miami School of Law in 1996. He was elected to the Florida House of Representatives in 2000, and in 2006, he was elected Speaker of the Florida House of Representatives. In 2010, he soundly defeated Florida Governor Charlie Crist for US Senator from Florida. He is a conservative that values reduced government spending, lower taxes, a strong military, and less government action in the lives of individuals.

On August 24, 2011, Rubio and other Republicans held an event at the Ronald Reagan Library in Simi Valley, CA. It was here that Rubio speaks about American exceptionalism, prosperity and compassion.

Prosperity and Compassion
Florida Senator Marco Rubio
Reagan Library
August 24, 2011

"Thank you very much for this opportunity. Gerald, let me thank you for that introduction, you talking about my communications skills, or so called communications skills, I appreciate you not setting the bar too high. Thanks so much. Mrs. Reagan, thank you for this opportunity. And in a moment I'll talk a little about what this opportunity means to me in general, but let me just say it is one of the highest privileges and honors I've ever had to be able to come here and speak in this place. And **earlier today I was able to walk through here, and not just to see the exhibits, but to meet the people, some from all over the world, that were touched by the extraordinary life of an extraordinary man. The contributions that he made to this country were tremendous, but the contributions he made to the world were even greater.** And in just an hour and a half of walking through here and meeting people who had been touched by those contributions, it reminded me what a privilege it is that I would get to stand here today and speak to all of you from a place like this and I am honored beyond any words that I could use to describe it and I thank you for this invitation. Thank you.

In fact I have a distinct honor because, not many people can say, that the only two people I have ever walked down the aisle with are here today. One is my wife Jeanette and the other is Mrs. Reagan that we just walked down here, so I tell people all the time that I was born and raised in Ronald Reagan's America. I was raised in Ronald Reagan's America. He was elected when I was in fourth grade and he left - he left office when I was in high school. Those are very important years, fourth grade through high school, they were the years that formed so much of what today what I believe and know to be true about the world and about our nation.

Ronald Reagan's era can be defined, number one in most people's minds, by the Cold War and by the end of it - and by the strong principles he stood for. **Ronald Reagan didn't just believe that the Soviet Union and communism could fail, he believed it was inevitably destined to fail. And that it was our obligation to accelerate that process, that all we had to do was be America and that that would happen.** And that defined his Presidency. And that defined Ronald Reagan's America in the time that I lived. The time that I grew up during that era.

There was something else though that defined the Reagan Presidency and that was defining the proper role of government. He did that better than any American has done ever before. And I stand before you, it has always been important for Americans and America to do that, but I stand here before you today all of us gathered here today at a time when defining the proper role of government is as important as it has ever been.

The answer to what the proper role of government is really lies in what kind of country we want to have. And I think the vast majority of Americans share a common

vision for what they want our nation to be. They want our nation to be two things at the same time.

Number one: they want it to be free and prosperous, a place where your economic hopes and dreams can be accomplished and brought up to fruition. That through hard work and sacrifice you can be who God meant you to be. No matter who your parents were, no matter where you were born, no matter how much misfortune you may have met in your life, if you have a good idea, you can be anything if you work hard and play by the rules. Most, if not all, Americans share that vision of a free and prosperous America. But **they also want us to be a compassionate America, a place where people are not left behind. We are a nation that is not going to tolerate those who cannot take care of themselves being left to fend for themselves.** We're not going to tolerate our children being punished for the errors of their parents and society. **So, we are a nation that aspires to two things – prosperity and compassion. And Ronald Reagan understood that. Perhaps better, again, than any voice I've ever heard speak on it.**

Now America's leaders during the last century set out to accomplish that, but they reached a conclusion that has placed us on this path, except for the Reagan Administration to be quite frank. **Both Republicans and Democrats established a role for government in America that said, yes, we'll have a free economy, but we will also have a strong government, who through regulations and taxes will control the free economy and through a series of government programs, will take care of those in our society who are falling behind. That was a vision crafted in the twentieth century by our leaders and though it was well intentioned, it was doomed to fail from the start. It was doomed to fail from the start**

first and foremost because it forgot that the strength of our nation begins with its people and that these programs actually weakened us as a people.

You see, almost in forever, it was institutions and society that assumed the role of taking care of one another. If someone was sick in your family, you took care of them. If a neighbor met misfortune, you took care of them. You saved for your retirement and your future because you had to. **We took these things upon ourselves and our communities and our families and our homes and our churches and our synagogues. But all that changed when the government began to assume those responsibilities. All of the sudden, for an increasing number of people in our nation, it was no longer necessary to worry about saving for security because that was the government's job.**

For those who met misfortune, that wasn't our obligation to take care of them, that was the government's job. And as government crowded out the institutions in our society that did these things traditionally, it weakened our people in a way that undermined our ability to maintain our prosperity.

The other thing is that **we built a government and its programs without any account whatsoever for how we were going to pay for it.** There was not thought given into how this was going to be sustained. When Social Security first started, there was 16 workers for every retiree. Today there are only three for every retiree and soon there will only be two for every retiree.

Program after program was crafted without any thought as to how they will be funded in future years or the impact it would have on future Americans. **They were done with the best of intentions, but because it weakened our people and didn't take account the simple math of not**

being able to spend more money than you have, it was destined to fail and brought us to the point at which we are at today.

It is a startling place to be, because the 20th Century was not a time of decline for America, it was the American Century. Americans in the 20th Century built here - we built here - the richest, most prosperous nation in the history of the world. And yet today we have built for ourselves a government that not even the richest and most prosperous nation in the face of the Earth can fund or afford to pay for. An extraordinary tragic accomplishment, if you can call it that. And that is where we stand today. And so, if defining the proper role of government was one of the central issues of the Reagan era, it remains that now. The truth is that people are going around saying that, well, we're worried about – let me just add something to this because I think this is an important forum for candor.

I know that it is popular in my party to blame the President, the current President. But the truth is the only thing this President has done is accelerate policies that were already in place and were doomed to fail. All he is doing through his policies is making the day of reckoning come faster, but it was coming nonetheless.

What we have now is not sustainable. The role of government and the role that government plays now in America cannot be sustained the way it is. Now some are worried about how it has to change, we have to change it. The good news is it is going to change. It has to change. That's not the issue.

The issue is not whether the role that government now plays in America will change. **The question is how will it change. Will it change because we make the changes necessary? Or, will it change because our creditors force**

us to make these changes? And over the next few moments I hope to advocate to you - I don't think that I have to given the make up of the crowd - but I hope to advocate to you that, in fact, what we have before us is a golden opportunity afforded to few Americans.

We have the opportunity - within our lifetime - to actually craft a proper role for government in our nation that will allow us to come closer than any Americans have ever come to our collective vision of a nation where both prosperity and compassion exist side-by-side. To do that, we must begin by embracing certain principles that are absolutely true. Number one: the free enterprise system does not create poverty. The free enterprise system does not leave people behind. People are poor and people are left behind because they do not have access to the free enterprise system because something in their lives or in their community has denied them access to the free enterprise system. All over the world this truism is expressing itself every single day. Every nation on the Earth that embraces market economics and the free enterprise system is pulling millions of its people out of poverty. **The free enterprise system creates prosperity, not denies it.**

The second truism that we must understand is that poverty does not create our social problems, our social problems create our poverty. Let me give you an example. All across this country, at this very moment, there are children who are born into and are living with five strikes against them, already, through no fault of their own. They're born into substandard housing in dangerous neighborhoods, to broken families, being raised by their grandmothers because they never knew their father and their mom is either working two jobs to make ends meet or just not home. These kids are going to struggle to succeed unless something dramatic happens in their life.

These truisms are important because they lead the public policies that define the proper role of government. **On the prosperity side, the number one objective of our economic policy, in fact the singular objective of our economic policy from a government perspective is simple - it's growth. It's not distribution of wealth; it's not picking winners and losers. The goal of our public policy should be growth. Growth in our economy, the creation of jobs and of opportunity, of equality of opportunity through our governmental policies.**

Now often when I give these speeches, members of the media and others get frustrated because there is nothing new or novel in it. We don't have to reinvent this. It's worked before and it will work again and they are simple things. Like a tax code that's fair, predictable, easy to comply with. Like a regulatory framework that doesn't exist to justify the existence of the regulators, that doesn't exist to accomplish through regulation and rule-making what they couldn't accomplish through the Congress. And **it is the proper role of government to invest in infrastructure. Yes, government should build roads and bridges, but it should do so as part of economic development as part of infrastructure. Not as a jobs program.** And **government should invest in our people at the state level.** Education is important, critically important. **We must educate and train our children to compete and succeed in the 21st century.** Our kids are not going to grow up to compete with children in Alabama or Mississippi. They're going to grow up to compete with kids in India, and China, all over the world; children who are learning to compete and succeed in the 21st century themselves.

These are proper roles of government within the framework of creating an environment where economic security and prosperity is possible. And on the compassion side of the ledger, which is also important to Americans, and it's important that we remind ourselves of that. I don't really like labels in politics, but I will gladly accept the label of conservatism. Conservatism is not about leaving people behind. **Conservatism is about empowering people to catch up, to give them the tools at their disposable that make it possible for them to access all the hope, all the promise, all the opportunity that America offers. And our programs to help them should reflect that.**

Now, yes, there are people that cannot help themselves. And those folks we will always help. We are too rich and prosperous a nation to leave them to fend for themselves. But all the others that can work should be given the means of empowering themselves to enter the marketplace and the workforce. And our programs and our policies should reflect that. We do need a safety net, but it cannot be a way of life. It must be there to help those who have fallen, to stand up and try again. And by the way, **I believe in America's retirement programs. But I recognize that these programs as they are currently structured are not sustainable for future generations. And so we must embrace public policy changes to these programs.** Now, I personally believe that you cannot make changes to these programs for the people that are currently in them right now. My mother just – well she gets mad when I say this. She is in her eighth decade of life and she is on both of these programs. I can't ask my mom to go out and get another job. She paid into the system. But the truth is that Social Security and Medicare, as important as they are, cannot look for me how they look for her.

My generation must fully accept, the sooner the better, that if we want there to be a Social Security and a Medicare when we retire, and if we want America as we know it to continue when we retire, then we must accept and begin to make changes to those programs now, for us. These changes will not be easy. **Speeches are easy. Actually going out and doing them will be difficult.** It's never easy to go to people and say what you've always known we have to change. It isn't. It will be hard. It will actually really call upon a specific generation of Americans, those of us, like myself, decades away from retirement, to assume certain realities - that we will continue to pay into and fund for a system that we will never fully access - that we are prepared to do whatever it takes in our lives and in our generation so that our parents and grandparents can enjoy the fruits of their labor and so that our children and our grandchildren can inherit the fullness of America's promise. But you see, **every generation of Americans has been called to do their part to ensure that the American promise continues.** We're not alone; we're not unique; we're not the only ones. In fact, I would argue to you that we have it pretty good. And yet I think it's fully appropriate that those of us raised in Ronald Reagan's America are actually the ones who are being asked to stand up and respond to the issues of the day. For we, perhaps better than any other people who have ever lived in this nation, should understand how special and unique America truly is.

When I was a boy, the world looked very different than it does now. I remember vividly how many assumed and believed that Soviet-style communism was destined to at least rule half the world, and they urged our public policy leaders to accept that and to understand that America would have to share this planet with a godless, oppressive form of government that perhaps was destined to overtake us one day as well.

There were many who discouraged our leaders from talking about the inevitability of decline for communism and how it was destined to fail. There were many who encouraged us to simply accept this as the way it has to be, and who told us that America could no longer continue to be what America had been – the world was just too complicated and too difficult, it had changed too much. Sounds familiar, but that's what they told us. But one person at least didn't believe them, and he happened to be the President of the United States. **He actually believed that all we had to do is be America, that our example alone would one day lead to the decline and fall of a system that was unsustainable, because he understood that the desire to be free, prosperous and compassionate, although shared by all Americans, was universal. The desire to leave your children better off than yourself is something we hold as Americans, but so do people all over the world.** *Because* **he understood that the principles that this nation was founded upon was not that we are all people in North America are endowed by their creator with inalienable rights, but that all people are endowed by their creator with certain inalienable rights, that transcribed in our hearts is the desire to live in freedom and in liberty, that it is our natural right, and that government's job is to protect those rights, not to grant them to us. This is the natural state of man, and anything that prevents it is unnatural and doomed to fail and that all we had to do was be America, that all we had to do was be prosperous and be free. All we had to do was live our republic. All we had to do was be a voice for these principles anywhere in the world where these principles were challenged and oppressed, and eventually time was on our side.** And how right he was.

When I was in fourth grade, the Soviet Union was a co-equal power to the United States. Before I finished college, the Soviet Union didn't even exist. And so many people born since then have no idea what it even was. To me, this is extremely special, and I'll tell you why. During the '80s, politically especially, there were two people that deeply influenced me. One clearly was Ronald Reagan, the other was my grandfather, who lived with us most of the time in our home. We lived part of our life, especially the key years, '80-'84, in Las Vegas, Nevada. And my grandfather loved to sit on the porch of our home and smoke cigars. He was Cuban. Three cigars a day, he lived to be 84. This is not an advertisement for cigar smoking, I'm just saying to you that . . .

He loved to talk about politics. My grandfather was born in 1899. He was born to an agricultural family in Cuba. He was stricken with polio when he was a very young man, he couldn't work the fields, so they sent him to school. He was the only member of his family that could read. And because he could read, he got a job at the local cigar rolling factory. They didn't have radio or television, so they would hire someone to sit at the front of the cigar factory and read to the workers while they worked. So, the first thing he would read every day, of course, was the daily newspaper. Then he would read some novel to entertain them. And then, when he was done reading things he actually went out and rolled the cigars because he needed the extra money. But through all of those years of reading, he became extremely knowledgeable about history, not to mention all the classics. He loved to talk about history. My grandfather loved being Cuban. He loved being from Cuba. He never would have left Cuba if he didn't have to. But he knew America was special. He knew that without America, Cuba would still be a Spanish colony. He knew that without America, the Nazis and Imperial Japan would have won World War II. When he was born in 1899 there weren't even airplanes. By the time I was born, an American had walked on the surface of the moon. And he knew something else. He knew that he had lost his country. And that the only thing from preventing other people in the world from losing theirs to communism was this country – this nation.

It is easy for us who are born here - like me - and so many of you, to take for granted how special and unique this place is. But when you come from somewhere else, when what you always knew and loved, you lost, you don't have that luxury. My grandfather didn't know America was exceptional because he read about it in a book. He knew about it because he lived it and saw it with his eyes. That powerful lesson is the story of Ronald Reagan's Presidency. **It's our legacy as a people. And it's who we have a chance to be again. And I think that's important for all of us because being an American is not just a blessing, it's a responsibility.** As we were commanded to do long ago, "Let your light shine before men, that they may see your good works and glorify your Father in heaven." Well, as we gather here today in this place, that pays homage and tribute to the greatest American of the twentieth century, we are reminded that for him and for our nation, **being a light to the world, that's not just our common history, it remains our common destiny.** Thank you."

MITT ROMNEY

Willard Mitt Romney was born on March 12, 1947, to George W. Romney (former Governor of Michigan) and Lenore Romney. Mitt Romney was raised in Bloomfield Hills, Michigan, and later served as a Mormon missionary in France. He received his undergraduate degree from Brigham Young University, and earned Juris Doctor/Master of Business Administration joint degrees from Harvard's law and business schools. He entered the management consulting business, which led to a position at Bain & Company, where he eventually served as CEO and brought the company out of crisis. He was also co-founder and head of the spin-off company Bain Capital, a private equity investment firm that became highly profitable and one of the largest such firms in the nation. The wealth Romney accumulated there would help fund his future political campaigns. He ran as the Republican candidate in the 1994 US Senate election in Massachusetts, losing to incumbent Ted Kennedy. He organized and steered the 2002 Winter Olympics as head of the Salt Lake Organizing Committee, and helped turn the troubled games into a financial success. Mitt Romney was elected Governor of Massachusetts in 2002, but did not seek reelection in 2006. He presided over a series of spending cuts and increases in fees that eliminated a projected $3 billion deficit. He also signed into law the Massachusetts health care reform legislation, which provided near-universal health insurance access via subsidies and state-level mandates and was the first of its kind in the nation. During the course of his political career, his positions or rhetorical emphasis have shifted more towards American conservatism in several areas. He ran for the Republican nomination in the 2008 US Presidential election and was the Republican nominee for the 2012 US Presidential election. The following speech was given after winning the 2012 New Hampshire Primary.

Mitt Romney
New Hampshire Victory Speech
Tonight We Made History
January 10, 2012

"Thank you, New Hampshire! Tonight, we made history! This state has always been a very special place for our family. Ann and I made a home here and we've filled it with great memories of our children and grandchildren. And this Granite State moment we just enjoyed is one we will always remember. Tonight, we celebrate. Tomorrow, we go back to work.

We do remember when Barack Obama came to New Hampshire four years ago. He promised to bring people together. He promised to change the broken system in Washington. He promised to improve our nation. Those were the days of lofty promises made by a hopeful candidate. Today, we are faced with the disappointing record of a failed President. The last three years have held a lot of change, but they haven't offered much hope.

The middle class has been crushed. Nearly 24 million of our fellow Americans are still out of work, struggling to find work, or have just stopped looking. The median income in America has dropped 10% in the last four years. Soldiers returning from the front lines are waiting now in unemployment lines. **Our debt is too high and our opportunities too few.** And this President wakes up every morning, looks out across America and is proud to announce, "It could be worse." It could be worse? That is not what it means to be an American. It could be worse? Of course not.

What defines us as Americans is our unwavering conviction that we know it must be better, and it will be better. That conviction guides our campaign. It has rallied millions of Americans in every corner of this country to our cause. Over the last six months, I've listened to anxious voices in town meetings and visited with students and soldiers. In break rooms and living rooms, I've heard stories of families getting by on less, of carefully planned retirements now replaced by jobs at minimum wage. But even now, amidst the worst recovery since the Great Depression, I've rarely heard any speech of hopelessness.

Americans know that our future is brighter and better than these troubled times. We still believe in the hope, the promise, and the dream of America. We still believe in that shining city on a hill. We know that the future of this country is better than 8 or 9% unemployment. It is better than $15 trillion in debt. It is better than the misguided policies and broken promises of the last three years – and the failed leadership of one man. The President has run out of ideas. Now, he's running out of excuses. And tonight, we are asking the good people of South Carolina to join the citizens of New Hampshire and make 2012 the year he runs out of time.

President Obama wants to put free enterprise on trial. In the last few days, we have seen some desperate Republicans join forces with him. This is such a mistake for our Party and for our nation. This country already has a leader who divides us with the bitter politics of envy. We have to offer an alternative vision. **I stand ready to lead us down a different path, where we are lifted up by our desire to succeed, not dragged down by a resentment of success. In these difficult times, we cannot abandon the core values that define us as a unique Nation – We are One Nation, Under God.**

Make no mistake, in this campaign, I will offer the American ideals of economic freedom a clear and unapologetic defense. And we're going to win with that message. But you know that **our campaign is about more than replacing a President; it is about saving the soul of America. This election is a choice between two very different destinies.**

President Obama wants to fundamentally transform America. We want to restore America to the founding principles that made this country great. He wants to turn America into a European-style social welfare state. We want to ensure that we remain a free and prosperous land of opportunity. This President takes his inspiration from the capitals of Europe; we look to the cities and towns across America for our inspiration. This President puts his faith in government. We put our faith in the American people. This President is making the federal government bigger, burdensome, and bloated. I will make the federal government simpler, smaller, and smarter. He raised the national debt. I will cut, cap, and balance the federal budget. He has enacted job-killing regulations; I'll eliminate them. He lost our AAA credit rating; I'll restore it. He passed Obamacare; I'll repeal it.

When it comes to the economy, my highest priority as President will be worrying about your job, not about saving my own. Internationally, President Obama has adopted an appeasement strategy. He believes America's role as leader in the world is a thing of the past. I believe a strong America must – and will – lead the future. He doesn't see the need for overwhelming American military superiority. I will insist on a military so powerful no one would ever think of challenging it. He criticizes our friends like Israel; I will always stand with our friends. He apologizes for America; I will never apologize for the greatest nation in the history of the Earth.

Our plans protect freedom and opportunity, and our blueprint is the Constitution of the United States. Now the path I lay out is not one paved with ever increasing government checks and cradle-to-grave assurances that government will always be the solution. If this election is a bidding war for those who can promise the most benefits, then I'm not your President. You already have that President. **If you want to make this election about restoring American greatness, then I hope you will join us.** If you believe that the disappointments of the last few years are a detour, not our destiny, then I am asking for your vote.

I'm asking each of you to remember how special it is to be an American. I want you to remember what it was like to be hopeful and excited about the future, not to dread each new headline. I want you to remember when you spent more time dreaming about where to send your kids to college than wondering how to make it to the next paycheck. I want you to remember when you weren't afraid to look at your retirement savings or the price at the pump. I want you to remember when our White House reflected the best of who we are, not the worst of what Europe has become. That America is still out there. We still believe in that America. **We still believe in the America that is a land of opportunity and a beacon of freedom. We believe in the America that challenges each of us to be better and bigger than ourselves.**

This election, let's go on to fight for the America we love. Because we believe in America. Thank you so much. God bless America."

NEWT GINGRICH

Newt Gingrich was born to Newton McPherson and Kathleen Daugherty on June 17, 1943, at the height of World War 2. His parents married nine months earlier in September 1942, but the marriage quickly fell apart. After the war ended, his mother married Army officer Robert Gingrich in 1946. Because his father was active in the military, they moved often, including Pennsylvania, Georgia and France. In 1965 he graduated from Emory University in Atlanta, GA, with a B.A. in history. Over the next six years, he earned a masters degree and finally a Ph.D. in modern European history from Tulane University in New Orleans. Shortly before he finished his doctorate degree, he was appointed an assistant professor in the history department of West Georgia College. While there he was instrumental in establishing an inter-disciplinary Environmental Studies program.

In 1974 and 1976, Gingrich ran twice unsuccessfully for US House of Representatives. 1974 was the time of the Watergate scandal and 1976 was the time that Georgia Democrat Governor Jimmy Carter was running for President of the United States. In 1978, the Democrat incumbent, Jack Flynt, who had served in office since 1955, chose not to run for another term. This paved the way for a strong victory against the new Democrat challenger, Georgia State Senator Virginia Shapard. He remained in office until 1999. He campaigned for President of the United States in 2012.

In May 1988, Gingrich, along with 77 other House members, brought ethics charges against the Democrat Speaker of the House Jim Wright. Wright eventually resigned as a result, and Gingrich was credited for it. This event increased his influence within the Republican Party. About ten months later, when House Minority Whip Dick Cheney was appointed as Secretary of Defense for the President George H. W. Bush Administration, Gingrich was elected by his peers to succeed him.

In the 1994 campaign season, in an effort to unite various factions of the Republican Party and offer a clear alternative to Democratic policies, Gingrich and others crafted the *Contract with America*. It laid out ten policies that Republicans promised to bring to the House floor if they were to regain control of the House of Representatives after forty years of Democratic Party rule. In January 1995, they regained control of both the House and Senate, made Newt Gingrich Speaker of the House, and began to act on many of their promises. Most of the legislation passed by the House was eventually quashed by either the Senate or President Bill Clinton. However, there were a couple bills that were eventually enacted. The end result of the *Contract with America* was that it legitimized the Republican Party and created a distinct choice between them and the Democratic Party.

Contract With America
Newt Gingrich Inaugural Address Opening of the 1995
Congress
January 4, 1995

"Let me say first of all that I am very deeply grateful to my good friend, Dick Gephardt. I couldn't help but - when my side maybe overreacted to your statement ending 40 years of Democratic rule - that I couldn't help but look over at Bob Michel, who has often been up here and who knows that everything Dick said was true - that this is difficult and painful to lose, and on my side of the aisle, we have for 20 elections been on the losing side. And yet **there is something so wonderful about the process by which a free people decides things** - that, in my own case, I lost two elections, and with the good help of my friend Vic Fazio, came close to losing two others. And I'm sorry, guys, it just didn't quite work out. And **yet I can tell you that every time when the polls closed and I waited for the votes to come in, I felt good, because win or lose, we've been part of this process.** In a little while, I'm going to ask the dean of the House, John Dingell, to swear me in, to insist on the bipartisan nature of the way in which we together work in this House. John's father was one of the great stalwarts of the New Deal, a man who, as an FDR Democrat, created modern America. And I think that John and his father represent a tradition that we all have to recognize and respect, and recognize that the America we are now going to try to lead grew from that tradition and is part of that great heritage.

I also want to take just a moment to thank Speaker Foley, who was extraordinarily generous, both in his public utterances and in everything that he and Mrs. Foley did to help Marianne and me, and to help our staff make the transition. I think that he worked very hard to reestablish the dignity of the House. And I think that we can all be proud of the reputation that he takes and of the spirit with which he led the speakership. And our best wishes go to Speaker and Mrs. Foley. I also want to thank the various House officers, who have been just extraordinary. And **I want to say for the public record that faced with a result none of them wanted, in a situation I suspect none of them expected, but within 48 hours every officer of this House reacted as a patriot, worked overtime, bent over backwards, and in every way helped us.** And I am very grateful, and this House I think owes a debt of gratitude to every officer that the Democrats elected two years ago. Thank you.

This is a historic moment. I was asked over and over, how did it feel, and the only word thats [sic] comes close to adequate is "overwhelming." I feel overwhelmed in every way, overwhelmed by all the Georgians who came up, overwhelmed by my extended family that is here, over-whelmed by the historic moment. I walked out and stood on the balcony just outside the Speaker's office, looking down the Mall this morning, very early. And I was just overwhelmed by the view, which two men I've introduced and know very, very well - [indecipherable] of us know very, very well. Just the sense of being part of America, being part of this - this great tradition.

I have two gavels, actually. Dick happened to use one that - maybe this was appropriate. This is a Georgia gavel I just got this morning, done by Dorsey Newman of Tallapoosa, who decided that the gavels he saw on TV weren't big enough or strong enough, so he cut down a walnut tree in his backyard, made a gavel, put a commemorative item [on it] and sent it up here. So this is a genuine Georgia gavel. I'm the first Georgia Speaker in over a hundred years. The last one, by the way, had a weird accent, too. Speaker [Charles] Crisp was born in Britain. His parents were actors and they came to the U.S. - a good word, by the way, for the value we get from immigration. And secondly, this is the gavel that Speaker [Joseph] Martin used [1947-1949, 1953-1955]. Now I'm not sure what it says about the inflation of Government, if you put them side by side, but this was the gavel used by the last Republican Speaker. And - And I want to comment for a minute on two men who served as my leader, and from whom I learned so much and who are here today.

When I arrived as a freshman, the Republican Party, deeply dispirited by Watergate and by the loss of the Presidency, banded together and worked with a leader who helped pave the way for our great Party victory of 1980, and a man who just did a marvelous job. And I can't speak too highly of what I learned about integrity and leadership and courage from serving with him in my freshman term. And he's here with us again today. Hope all of you will recognize Congressman John Rhodes of Arizona. Let me say also that at our request, he wasn't sure he should be here at all, then he thought he was going to hide in the back of the room. And then I insisted that he come down front, somebody who I regard as a mentor. I think virtually every Democrat in the House will say is a man who genuinely cares about and loves the House and who represents the best spirit of the House, a man who I've under and who I hope as Speaker I can always rely on for advice; and who I hope frankly I can emulate in his commitment to this institution and in his willingness to try to reach beyond his personal interest and his personal partisanship. I hope all of you will join me in thanking for his years of service, Congressman Bob Michel of Illinois.

I'm - I'm very fortunate today. I have my Mom and my Dad are here. They're right up there - Bob and Kit Gingrich.

And I am so delighted that they were both able to be here. You know, sometimes when you get to my age, you can't have everyone near you you'd like to. I can't say how much I learned from my Dad and his years of serving the U.S. Army and how much I learned from my Mother, who is clearly my most enthusiastic cheerleader. My daughters are here up there [in the gallery] - Kathy Lovewith and her husband Paul, and Jackie and her husband Mark Zyler. And the person who clearly is my closest friend and my best adviser and who, if I listened to about 20 percent more, I'd get in less trouble, my wife Marianne, is there.

I have a very large extended family between Marianne and me. And they're virtually all in town, and we've done our part for the Washington tourist season. But I couldn't help - 'cause when I first came on the floor earlier, I went around and saw a number of the young people who are here - a number of the children who are on the floor, the young adults, who are close to 12 years of age. And I couldn't help but think that sitting in the back rail near the center of the House are my - one of my nephews, Kevin McPherson, who is five; and Susan Brown, who is six; and Emily Brown, who is eight; and Laura McPherson, who is nine. And they're all back there - I think probably more than allowed to bring on, but they're my nieces and my nephew. And I have two other nephews who are a little older who are actually up in the gallery.

I couldn't help but think, as a way I wanted to start the Speakership and to talk with every Member, that in a sense these young people you see around you are really what, at its best, this is all about. Much more than the - the negative advertising and the interest groups and the - all the different things that make politics all too often cynical and nasty and sometimes frankly just plain miserable. What makes politics worthwhile is

that the choice, as Dick Gephardt said, between what we see so tragically on the evening news and the way we try to do it is to work very hard to make this system of free, representative self-government work. And the ultimate reason for doing that is these children, and the country they will inherit, and the world they will live in. I - we're starting the 104th Congress. I don't know if you've ever thought about the concept, but for 208 years, we gather together - the most diverse country in the history of the world. We send all sorts of people. Each of us could find at least one Member we thought was weird. And I'll tell you, if you went around the room the person chosen to be weird would be different for virtually every one of us. Because **we do allow and insist upon the right of a free people to send an extraordinary diversity of people here.**

Brian Lamb of C-SPAN read to me Friday a phrase from de Tocqueville that was so central to the House. I've been reading Remini's biography of Henry Clay. And Henry Clay always preferred the House. He was the first strong Speaker. And he preferred the House to the Senate, although he served in both. Well he said **the House is more vital, more active, more dynamic, more common.** And this is what de Tocqueville wrote (quote):

"Often there is not a distinguished man in the whole number. Its members are almost all obscure individuals whose names bring no associations to mind. They are mostly village lawyers, men in trade, or even persons belonging to the lower classes of society."

Now, if you put women in with men, I don't know that we'd change much. But the word "vulgar" in de Tocqueville's time had a very particular meaning. And it's a meaning the world would do well to study in this room. You see, de Tocqueville was an aristocrat. He lived in a world of kings and princes. And **the folks who come here come here by the one single act that their citizens freely chose them.** And I don't care what your ethnic background - what your ideology. I don't care whether you're younger or older. I don't care whether you were born in America or you're a naturalized citizen. **Every one of the 435 people have equal standing because their citizens freely sent them, and their voice should be heard, and they should have a right to participate. And it is the most marvelous act of a complex, giant country trying to argue and talk - and, as Dick [Gephardt] said, to have a great debate, to reach great decisions, not through a civil war, not by bombing one of our regional capitals, not by kill- ing a half million people, not by having snipers - and let me say unequivocally I condemn all acts of violence against the law by all people for all reasons. This is a society of law and a society of civil behavior.**

Here we are as commoners together, to some extent Democrats and Republicans, to some extent liberals and conservatives, but Americans all. Steve Gunderson today gave me a copy of the "Portable Abraham Lincoln." He suggested there is much for me to learn about our party, but I would also say that it does not hurt to have a copy of the portable F.D.R. This is a great country of great people. If there is any one factor or acts of my life that strikes me as I stand up here as the first Republican in 40 years to do so. When I first became whip in 1989, Russia was beginning to change, the Soviet Union as it was then. Into my whip's office one day came eight Russians and a Lithuanian, members of the Communist Party, newspaper editors. They asked me, "What does a whip do?" They said, "In Russia we have never had a free parliament since 1917 and that was only for a few months, so what do you do?" I tried to explain, as Dave Bonior or Tom DeLay might now. It is a little strange if you are from a dictatorship to explain you are called the whip but you do not really have a whip, you are elected by the people you are supposed to pressure - other members. If you pressure them too much they will not reelect you. On the other hand If you do not pressure them enough they will not reelect you.

Democracy is hard. It is frustrating. So our group came into the Chamber. The Lithuanian was a man in his late sixties, and I allowed him to come up here and sit and be Speaker, something many of us have done with constituents. Remember, this is the very beginning of perestroika and glasnost. When he came out of the chair, he was physically trembling. He was almost in tears. He said, "Ever since World War II, I have remembered what the Americans did and I have never believed the propaganda. But I have to tell you, I did not think in my life that I would be able to sit at the center of freedom." It was one of the most overwhelming, compelling moments of my life. It struck me that something I could not help but think of when we were here with President Mandela. I went over and saw Ron Dellums and thought of the great work Ron had done to extend freedom across the planet. You get that sense of emotion when you see something so totally different than you had expected. Here was a man who reminded me first of all that while Presidents are important, they are in effect an elected kingship, that this and the other body across the way are where freedom has to be fought out. That is the tradition I hope that we will take with us as we go to work.

Today we had a bipartisan prayer service. Frank Wolf made some very important points. He said, **"We have to recognize that many of our most painful problems as a country are moral problems, problems of dealing with ourselves and with life." He said character is the key to leadership and we have to deal with that.** He preached a little bit. I do not think he thought he was preaching, but he was. It was about a spirit of reconciliation. He talked about caring about our spouses and our children and our families. **If we are not prepared to model our own family life beyond just having them here for 1 day, if we are not prepared to care about our children and we are not prepared to care about our families, then by what arrogance do we think we will transcend our behavior to care about others?**

That is why with Congressman Gephardt's help we have established a bipartisan task force on the family. We have established the principle that we are going to set schedules we stick to so families can count on time to be together, built around school schedules so that families can get to know each other, and not just by seeing us on C-SPAN. I will also say that means one of the strongest recommendations of the bipartisan committee, is that we have 17 minutes to vote. This is the bipartisan committee's recommendations, not just mine. They pointed out that if we take the time we spent in the last Congress where we waited for one more Member, and one more, and one more, that we literally can shorten the business and get people home if we will be strict and firm. At one point this year we had a 45-minute vote. I hope all of my colleagues are paying attention because we are in fact going to work very hard to have 17 minute votes and it is over. So, leave on the first bell, not the second bell. Okay?

This may seem particularly inappropriate to say on the first day because this will be the busiest day on opening day in congressional history. I want to read just a part of the Contract With America. I don't mean this as a partisan act, but rather to remind all of us what we are about to go through and why. Those of us who ended up in the majority stood on these steps and signed a contract, and here is part of what it says: **On the first day of the 104th Congress the new Republican majority will immediately pass the following reforms aimed at restoring the faith and trust of the American people in their government:**

First, require all laws that apply to the rest of the country also to apply equally to the Congress. Second, select a major, independent auditing firm to conduct a comprehensive audit of the Congress for waste, fraud or abuse. Third, cut the number of House committees and cut committee staffs by a third. Fourth, limit the terms of all committee chairs. Fifth, ban the casting of proxy votes in committees. Sixth, require committee meetings to be open to the public. Seven, require a three-fifths majority vote to pass a tax increase. Eight, guarantee an honest accounting of our federal budget by implementing zero baseline budgeting.

Now, I told Dick Gephardt last night that if I had to do it over again we would have pledged within 3 days that we will do these things, but that is not what we said. So we have ourselves in a little bit of a box here. Then we go a step further. I carry the TV Guide version of the contract with me at all times. We then say that within the first 100 days of the 104th Congress we shall bring to the House floor the following bills, each to be given full and open debate, each to be given a full and clear vote, and each to be immediately available for inspection. We made it available that day. We listed 10 items.

A balanced budget amendment and line-item veto, A bill to stop violent criminals, emphasizing among other things an effective and enforceable death penalty. Third was welfare reform. Fourth, legislation protecting our kids. Fifth was to provide tax cuts for families. Sixth was a bill to strengthen our national defense. Seventh was a bill to raise the senior citizens` earning limit. Eighth

was legislation rolling back Government regulations. Ninth was a commonsense legal reform bill, and Tenth was congressional term limits legislation.

Our commitment on our side, and this is an absolute obligation, is first of all to work today until we are done. I know that is going to inconvenience people who have families and supporters. But we were hired to do a job, and we have to start today to prove we will do it. Second, I would say to our friends in the Democratic Party that we are going to work with you, and we are really laying out a schedule working with the minority leader to make sure that we can set dates certain to go home. That does mean that if 2 or 3 weeks out we are running short we will, frankly, have longer sessions on Tuesday, Wednesday, and Thursday. We will try to work this out on a bipartisan basis to, in a workmanlike way, get it done. It is going to mean the busiest early months since 1933.

Beyond the Contract I think there are two giant challenges. I know I am a partisan figure. But I really hope today that I can speak for a minute to my friends in the Democratic Party as well as my own colleagues, and speak to the country about these two challenges so that I hope we can have a real dialog. **One challenge is to achieve a balanced budget by 2002.** I think both Democratic and Republican Governors will say we can do that but it is hard. I do not think we can do it in a year or two. I do not think we ought to lie to the American people. This is a huge, complicated job. **The second challenge is to find a way to truly replace the current welfare state with an opportunity society.** Let me talk very briefly about both challenges. First, on the balanced budget I think we can get it done. I think the baby boomers are now old enough that we can have an honest dialog about priorities, about resources, about what works, and what does not work. Let me say I have already told Vice President Gore that we are going to invite him to address a Republican conference. We would have invited him in December but he had to go to Moscow, I believe there are grounds for us to talk together and to work together, to have hearings together, and to have task forces together.

If we set priorities, if we apply the principles of Edwards, Deming and of Peter Drucker we can build on the Vice President's reinventing government effort and **we can focus on transforming, not just cutting. The choice becomes not just do you want more or do you want less, but are there ways to do it better?** Can we learn from the private sector, can we learn from Ford, IBM, from Microsoft, from what General Motors has had to go through? **I think on a bipartisan basis we owe it to our children and grandchildren to get this Government in order and to be able to actually pay our way.** I think 2002 is a reasonable time frame. I would hope that together we could open a dialog with the American people.

I have said that I think Social Security ought to be off limits, at least for the first 4 to 6 years of the process, because I think it will just destroy us if we try to bring it into the game. But let me say about everything else, whether it is Medicare, or it is agricultural subsidies, or it is defense or anything that I think the greatest Democratic President of the 20th century, and in my judgment the greatest President of the 20th century, said it right.

On March 4, 1933, he stood in braces as a man who had polio at a time when nobody who had that kind of disability could be anything in public life. He was President of the United States, and he stood in front of this Capitol on a rainy March day and he said, 'We have nothing to fear but fear itself.' I want every one of us to reach out in that spirit and pledge to live up to that spirit, and I think frankly on a bipartisan basis. I would say to Members of the Black and Hispanic Caucuses that I would hope we could arrange by late spring to genuinely share districts.

You could have a Republican who frankly may not know a thing about your district agree to come for a long weekend with you, and you will agree to go for a long weekend with them. We begin a dialog and an openness that is totally different than people are used to seeing in politics in America. I believe if we do that we can then create a dialog that can lead to a balanced budget. But I think we have a greater challenge. I do want to pick up directly on what Dick Gephardt said, because he said it right. No Republican here should kid themselves about it. The greatest leaders in fighting for an integrated America in the 20th century were in the Democratic Party. The fact is, it was the liberal wing of the Democratic Party that ended segregation. The fact is that it was Franklin Delano Roosevelt who gave hope to a Nation that was in distress and could have slid into dictatorship. **Every Republican has much to learn from studying what the Democrats did right. But I would say to my friends in the Democratic Party that there is much to what Ronald Reagan was trying to get done.** There's much to what is being done today by Republicans like Bill Weld, and John Engler, and Tommy Thompson, and George Allen, and Christy Whitman, and Pete Wilson. There is much we can share with each other.

We must replace the welfare state with an opportunity society. The balanced budget is the right thing to do. But it does not in my mind have the moral urgency of coming to grips with what is happening to the poorest Americans. I commend to all Marvin Olasky's "The Tragedy of American Compassion." Olasky goes back for 300 years and looked at what has worked in America, how we have helped people rise beyond poverty, and how we

have reached out to save people. He may not have the answers, but he has the right sense of where we have to go as
Americans. I do not believe that there is a single American
who can see a news report of a 4-year-old thrown off of a
public housing project in Chicago by other children and
killed and not feel that a part of your heart went, too.

I think of my nephew in the back, Kevin, and how all of
us feel about our children. How can any American read
about an 11-year-old buried with his Teddy bear because
he killed a 14-year-old, and then another 14-year-old
killed him, and not have some sense of "My God, where
has this country gone?" How can we not decide that this
is a moral crisis equal to segregation, equal to slavery?
How can we not insist that every day we take steps to do
something? I have seldom been more shaken than I was
after the election when I had breakfast with two members
of the Black Caucus. One of them said to me, "Can you
imagine what it is like to visit a first-grade class and realize
that every fourth or fifth young boy in that class may be
dead or in jail within 15 years? And they are your constituents and you are helpless to change it?"

For some reason, I do not know why, maybe because I
visit a lot of schools, that got through. I mean, that per-
sonalized it. That made it real, not just statistics, but real
people. Then I tried to explain part of my thoughts by
talking about the need for alternatives to the bureaucracy,
and we got into what I think frankly has been a pretty distorted and cheap debate over orphanages. Let me say, first
of all, my father, who is here today, was a foster child. He
was adopted as a teenager. I am adopted. We have relatives
who were adopted. We are not talking out of some vague
impersonal Dickens "Bleak House" middle-class intellectual model. We have lived the alternatives. I believe when
we are told that children are so lost in the city bureau-

cracies that there are children who end up in dumpsters, when we are told that there are children doomed to go to schools where 70 or 80 percent of them will not graduate, when we are told of public housing projects that are so dangerous that if any private sector ran them they would be put in jail, and the only solution we are given is, `Well, we will study it, we will get around to it,` my only point is that this is unacceptable.

We can find ways immediately to do things better, to reach out, break through the bureaucracy and give every young American child a better chance. Let me suggest to you Morris Schectman's new book. I do not agree with all of it, but it is fascinating. It is entitled "Working Without a Net." It is an effort to argue that in the 21st century we have to create our own safety nets. He draws a distinction between caring and caretaking. It is worth every American reading. He said caretaking is when you bother me a little bit, and I do enough, I feel better because I think I took care of you. That is not any good to you at all. You may be in fact an alcoholic and I just gave you the money to buy the bottle that kills you, but I feel better and go home. He said **caring is actually stopping and dealing with the human being, trying to understand enough about them to genuinely make sure you improve their life**, even if you have to start with a conversation like, "If you will quit drinking, I will help you get a job." This is a lot harder conversation than, "I feel better. I gave him a buck or 5 bucks."

I want to commend every Member on both sides to look carefully. I say to those Republicans who believe in total privatization, you cannot believe in the Good Samaritan and explain that as long as business is making money we can walk by a fellow American who is hurt and not do something. I would say to my

friends on the left who believe there has never been a government program that was not worth keeping, you cannot look at some of the results we now have and not want to reach out to the humans and forget the bureaucracies. If we could build that attitude on both sides of this aisle, we would be an amazingly different place, and the country would begin to be a different place. We have to create a partnership. We have to reach out to the American people. We are going to do a lot of important things.

Thanks to the House Information System and Congressman Vern Ehlers, as of today we are going to be on line for the whole country, every amendment, every conference report. We are working with C-SPAN and others, and Congressman Gephardt has agreed to help on a bipartisan basis to make the building more open to television, more accessible to the American people. We have talk radio hosts here today for the first time. I hope to have a bipartisan effort to make the place accessible for all talk radio hosts of all backgrounds, no matter their ideology. The House Historian's office is going to be more aggressively run on a bipartisan basis to reach out to Close Up, and to other groups to teach what the legislative struggle is about. I think over time we can and will this Spring rethink campaign reform and lobbying reform and review all ethics, including the gift rule. But that isn't enough. **Our challenge shouldn't be just to balance the budget or to pass the Contract. Our challenge should not be anything that is just legislative. We are supposed to, each one of us, be leaders.** I think our challenge has to be to set as our goal, and maybe we are not going to get there in 2 years. This ought to be the goal that we go home and we tell people we believe in: that there will be a Monday morning when for the entire weekend not a single child was killed anywhere in America; that there will be a Monday morning when every child in the country went to a school that they and their parents thought prepared them as citizens and prepared them to compete in the world market; that there will be a Monday morning where it was easy to find a job or create a job, and your own Government did not punish you if you tried. We should not be happy just with the language of politicians and the language of legislation.

We should insist that our success for America is felt in the neighborhoods, in the communities, is felt by real people living real lives who can say, "Yes, we are safer, we are healthier, we are better educated, America succeeds." This morning's closing hymn at the prayer service was the Battle Hymn of the Republic. It is hard to be in this building, look down past Grant to the Lincoln Memorial and not realize how painful and how difficult that battle hymn is. The key phrase is, "As he died to make men holy, let us live to make men free."

It is not just political freedom, although I agree with everything Congressman Gephardt said earlier. If you cannot afford to leave the public housing project, you are not free. If you do not know how to find a job and do not know how to create a job, you are not free. If you cannot find a place that will educate you, you are not free. If you are afraid to walk to the store because you could get killed, you are not free. So as all of us over the coming months sing that song, "As he died to make men holy, let us live to make men free."

I want us to dedicate ourselves to reach out in a genuinely nonpartisan way to be honest with each other. I promise each of you that without regard to party my door is going to be open. I will listen to each of you. I will try to work with each of you. I will put in long hours, and I will guarantee that I will listen to you first. I will let you get it all out before I give you my version, because you have been patient with me today, and you have given me a chance to set the stage. But I want to close by reminding all of us of how much bigger this is than us. Because beyond talking with the American people, beyond working together, I think we can only be successful if we start with our limits.

I was very struck this morning with something Bill Emerson used, a very famous quote of Benjamin Franklin, at the point where the Constitutional Convention was deadlocked. People were tired, and there was a real possibility that the Convention was going to break up. Franklin, who was quite old and had been relatively quiet for the entire Convention, suddenly stood up and was angry, and he said: "I have lived, sir, a long time, and the longer I live the more convincing proofs I see of this truth, that God governs in the affairs of men, and if a sparrow cannot fall to the ground without His notice, is it possible that an empire can rise without His aid?" At that point the Constitutional Convention stopped. They took a day off for fasting and prayer. Then, having stopped and come together, they went back, and they solved the great question of large and small States. They wrote the Constitution, and the United States was created.

All I can do is pledge to you that, if each of us will reach out prayerfully and try to genuinely understand each other, if we will recognize that in this building we symbolize America, and that we have an obligation to talk with each other, then I think a year from now we can look on the 104th Congress as a truly amazing institution without regard to party, without regard to ideology. We can say, "Here America comes to work, and here we are preparing for those children a better future." Thank you. Good luck and God bless you."

Chapter 7

THE OBLITERATION
OF REASON

"Experience hath shewn, that even under the best forms of government those entrusted with power have, in time, and by slow operations, perverted it into tyranny."

— **Thomas Jefferson**

You have now completed reading through the first section of the book. Its primary focus was to describe how you and I as Americans view our social and political environment. The next two chapters discuss how many government officials view power, politics, and social reformation. Government officials follow a very different agenda than that of the American citizen. Many officials, once they are bestowed with power and authority have one primary goal in mind – to increase his/her power and authority. It is specifically for this reason that our Founders wrote a constitution with separation of powers and a federal government with specific defined authority. It is also the reason why state governments and American citizens were given powers and authority to keep the federal government accountable (Tenth Amendment). **What happens when the federal or national government is allowed to perform its tasks unencumbered by accountability?** The next two chapters discuss that specific issue.

1876 PRESIDENTIAL ELECTION

In the 2000 Presidential election between Vice President Al Gore and Texas Governor George W. Bush, Gore received 544 thousand more votes out of 105.4 million votes counted or a difference of about half a percent. The Electoral College vote, which is what is used to determine who won the Presidency, was indecisive as well. There were five states that were too close to call, having less than 0.5% difference: New Mexico (5 electoral votes), Oregon (7 electoral votes), Iowa (7 electoral votes), Wisconsin (11 electoral votes) and Florida (25 electoral votes). For either candidate to win the Presidency, he would have to win Florida. The margin of victory in Florida was less than 0.01%. A deal was reached: the candidate who won Florida won the Presidency. Recounts ensued and on November 26, 2000, George W. Bush was declared the winner in Florida by 537 votes.

I remember how angry Democrats were when Republican George W. Bush was declared the winner. As contentious as this transition was, the Presidential election of 1876 was significantly more controversial. **The Presidential election of 1876 set the stage for future dramatic changes to the political process and to the American culture.**

There were very few momentous events that occurred during the mid 1870s. The Civil War had been over for a decade, battles with Native Americans were occurring far away from New York and Boston in lands west of the Mississippi River, and the War with Spain was still another two decades into the future. The major event of this time period was the Battle of Little Big Horn (Custer's Last Stand) on June 25-26, 1876.

During the US Civil War and Reconstruction, there was no significant opposition to the Republican Party which allowed for much abuse of power by federal government officials. Ulysses S. Grant, the national hero who defeated General Robert E. Lee and was in control of Reconstruction, became President of the United States in 1868. The equestrian statue on the front cover of this book is that of Ulysses S. Grant on a horse. The Republic Party had full control of both houses of Congress from 1865-1874, which set the stage for numerous scandals.

Black Friday (September 24, 1869): Speculators recruited Grant's brother-in-law, a financier named Abel Corbin, to get close to Grant where they would manipulate the government sale of gold. Although Grant was not directly involved in the scandal, his personal association with these speculators gave clout to their attempt to manipulate the gold market.

New York Custom House (1871): New York Custom House collected more tax revenue from imports than any other port in the US. Future President Chester A. Arthur implemented the Treasury Office's reforms.

Star Route Frauds (1872, 1876): The Star Route Frauds scandal involved a lucrative scheme whereby US postal officials received bribes in exchange for awarding postal delivery contracts in southern and western areas. The 1872 investigation results had been tainted by bribery, while the 1876 investigation managed to shut down the Star Route frauds temporarily. Those involved in the scandals included some of the large contractors, ex-US Representative Bradley Barlow of Vermont, Second Assistant Postmaster-General, and Arkansas Senator Stephen W. Dorsey. A federal trial took place in 1882, which was finally able to shut down the postal ring.

Salary Grab Act (March 3, 1873): The day before the second-term inauguration of President Ulysses S. Grant, the salary of the President and the of Supreme Court Justices were doubled. Hidden in the salary increases was also a 50% retroactive increase for members of Congress. Public outcry caused Congress to rescind its increase.

Sanborn Incident (1874): The Secretary of the Treasury hired John D. Sanborn (a private citizen) to collect $427,000 in unpaid taxes. The Secretary allowed Sanborn to keep half of what he collected.

Delano Affair (1875): Interior Secretary Columbus Delano took bribes for fraudulent land grants. Delano had also given lucrative contracts to his son John Delano and Grant's brother, Orvil Grant.

Pratt & Boyd (1875): Attorney General George H. Williams (head of the US Department of Justice) took bribes in exchange for declining to prosecute pending cases. The Senate Judiciary Committee had found that Williams had dropped the merchant house Pratt & Boyd case after his wife received a $30,000 payoff.

Whiskey Ring (1875): The Whiskey Ring was a scandal involving diversion of tax revenues in a conspiracy among government agents, politicians, whiskey distillers, and distributors.

Trading Post Scandal (1876): Secretary of War William W. Belknap received payments from a clandestine contract related to Fort Sill (a US Army post in Lawton, Oklahoma). During the investigation Colonel George A. Custer wrote anonymous articles for the New York Herald that exposed trader post kickback rings and implied that Secretary Belknap was the leader. Custer testified on hearsay evidence that President Grant's brother, Orvil, was involved. While attempting to restore his military prestige in the US Army, Custer was killed in action at the Battle of the Little Big Horn.

Catellism (1876): A congressional committee discovered that $15 million of the $56 million allotted to Secretary George M. Robeson's Department of the Navy for construction programs was unaccounted for. The committee suspected that Robeson, who was responsible for naval spending, embezzled some of the missing money and laundered it in real estate transactions.

Nepotism: President Grant's cousin, Silas A. Hudson, was appointed minister to Guatemala. His brother-in-law, Reverend M.J. Cramer, was appointed as counsel to Leipzig. His brother-in-law, James F. Casey, was in charge of customs in New Orleans, Louisiana, where he made money by stealing fees. Frederick Dent, another brother-in-law, was the White

House usher, and made money giving out insider information. In all, it is estimated that 40 relatives gained financially while Grant was President.

The purpose of describing these scandals is not to say that Republicans are bad and Democrats are good. Its purpose is to show, regardless of political affiliation, that too much unchecked power and authority is bad for American citizens and taxpayers. Ulysses S. Grant's Presidency was wrought with numerous scandals. As a direct result, he became extremely unpopular. Reform Republican leaders met privately and nominated Ohio Governor Rutherford B. Hayes, who eventually became the Republican nominee. Democratic Party leaders could feel victory after twenty years of straight losses. There was a national desire for reform due to Presidential scandals and the growth in power of industrialists such as Andrew Carnegie, J.P. Morgan and John D. Rockefeller.

New York Governor Samuel Tilden was to lead the Democratic Party to victory. He studied law at both Yale and New York Universities. As chairman of the Democratic State Committee, he had conflict with "Boss" William M. Tweed. Tweed was the third-largest landowner in New York City, director of the Erie Railway, the Tenth National Bank & the New-York Printing Company, and proprietor of the Metropolitan Hotel. He used his money and prominence to influence politicians. Martin Scorsese's 2002 *Gangs of New York* (2002) depicted Boss Tweed in charge of New York in 1862.

Samuel Tilden gained a reputation as a reformer when he took on Tweed by participating in the impeachment of judges that were favorable to Tweed. Tweed was eventually convicted of stealing money from taxpayers in excess of $25 million. He also brought down the "Canal Ring" based in Albany, in which New York State Democrat Senator Jarvis Lord was one of the key participants. The Canal Ring was a group of corrupt contractors and their political supporters who conspired to defraud the State of New York by overcharging for repairs and improvement of the state's canal system. With the reform credentials, Governor Samuel Tilden won the Democrat Presidential nomination in a landslide. On November 7, 1876 (exactly 124 years before Bush v. Gore), the national Presidential election occurred. Tilden won 51.0% of the popular vote, whereas Hayes won 47.9% of the vote. There was a difference of 254 thousand votes with a total of 8.3 million votes counted – or a difference of about 3%. Just to remind you, as a comparison Bush v. Gore had a difference of 0.5%.

How does a candidate, who lost by more than 3% of the popular vote, become President? Republicans claimed fraud and voter intimidation in the following states: Oregon (3 electoral votes), Florida (4 electoral votes), South Carolina (7 electoral votes), and Louisiana (8 electoral votes). The closest margin of victory was in South Carolina at 0.49% - which is significantly greater than the 0.01% for Florida in Bush v. Gore. Putting these four states aside for a moment, Tilden had 184 out of the 185 electoral votes needed to become President. He just needed one single electoral vote to put him over the top.

There were a total of twelve states that had a margin of victory less than 3.6%. Why were these four specifically mentioned and not all twelve? It seems convenient that with these four states in contention, the margin of victory was only 1 electoral college vote. The dispute went on for months, until finally on January 29, 1877, Congress passed a bill that created a 15 person panel to settle the issue. There was also an informal compromise stating that if Hayes was elected, the federal government would pull troops out of the former Confederate states and end Reconstruction. The issue was finally settled along a party-line vote to elect Hayes as the next President. In this situation it was the federal government in the form of the US Congress that appointed the President thus ignoring the electoral process (established by the US Constitution) and the wishes of American citizens. With either Bush v. Gore or Hayes v. Tilden, it should matter less what candidate you supported than that the US Constitution and the Rule of Law were followed. In my opinion, and those of tens of millions of others, the US Constitution has more authority than any political party.

OLIGARCHY

The example above, namely the Presidential election of 1876, is an example of a government that places party politics and selfish desires above the US Constitution and the Rule of Law. In this situation, the Republicans, except for a couple rare instances (Grover Cleveland and Woodrow Wilson), held onto the top executive office in the land until early 1933 when Franklin D Roosevelt became the 32nd President of the United States. **Do the ends justified the means?** When government officials ignore laws agreed to by the general population and do what is in their own self interest, that government begins to write & execute laws that benefit themselves and convert into an oligarchy. What is an oligarchy?

Many of us have been taught incorrectly in school that communism and fascism are very different forms of government. Both forms of government are very similar in nature. In both cases, a small group of people are in direct control of the national government. Communism is a form of government in which the elite ruling class has absolute power and control over almost every aspect of daily living, including housing, food, medical care, job creation, and the military. Fascism seeks a powerful single-party totalitarian state in order to further its own ideological agenda. These are both examples of an oligarchy. Under both communism and fascism, the average person has no real power or control over what they are taught in school, where they live, what they eat or where they go to church. People are often put in jail or killed for saying something bad against the government.

James Madison stated in a speech at the Virginia Constitutional Convention, *"The essence of Government is power; and power, lodged as it must be in human hands, will ever be liable to abuse."* He and many other authors of the US Constitution understood this and the concept of the quote by Lord Acton, *"Power corrupts, and absolute power corrupts absolutely."* There is also another quote of his related to concentration of power. *"Where you have a concentration of power in a few hands, all too frequently men with the mentality of gangsters get control. History has proven that."* **If you were to look at government based not on ideology, but upon how power is exerted through government, it becomes obvious that the most common form of government in the world (past and present) is that of an oligarchy.**

Let me ask you a question. **If you were granted a wish, what would you wish for? Money? Love? Power?** Abraham Maslow, an American professor of psychology at Columbia University, studied people like Albert Einstein, Eleanor Roosevelt and Frederick Douglass to determine what drove them to become the people they were. Through his studies he developed three primary groups of activities: physical, psychological and self-fulfillment. Physical activities relate to eating, sleeping and breathing. Once a person has tended to those absolute needs of life, he/she can tend to his/her psychological needs, such as love, friendship and family. Now that these requirements have been resolved, a person is now free to develop self-fulfillment activities, such as a career and hobbies.

The pursuit of power, in its essential form, resides in Abraham Maslow's third level of self-fulfillment activities in that some pursue power purely because they crave power. You can think of the acquisition of power as a career choice. Some choose to become doctors to cure disease. Some choose to be part of a non-profit organization because they are driven to help others. Some desire to be the leader of a country because they seek power. There is a passage in George Orwell's *1984* which partially explains this thirst for power. *"The Party seeks power entirely for its own sake. We are not interested in the* *good of others; we are interested solely in power. Not wealth or luxury or long life or happiness: only power, pure power. What pure power means you will understand presently. We are different from all the oligarchies of the past, in that we know what we are doing. All the others, even those who resembled ourselves, were cowards and hypocrites. The German Nazis and the Russian Communists came very close to us in their methods, but they never had the courage to recognize their own motives. They pretended, perhaps they even believed, that they had seized power unwillingly and for a limited time, and that just round the corner there lay a paradise where human beings would be free and equal. We are not like that. We know that no one ever seizes power with the intention of relinquishing it. Power is not a means, it is an end. One does not establish a dictatorship in order to safeguard a revolution; one makes the revolution in order to establish the dictatorship. The object of persecution is persecution. The object of torture is torture. The object of power is power. "*

There is a significant difference between an oligarchy and a republic as to how it distributes and exerts power, and how it protects the rights of the individual. The combination of republicanism and federalism are systems of governance in which power is decentralized, a balance of power is established and the rule of law is followed. An oligarchy in its simplest form is a governance in which those in power set the rules, and these rules protect those in power. In an oligarchy, schools are more focused on teaching proper behavior than reading, writing, arithmetic and history. Oligarchs often remove freedoms, such as freedom of speech, freedom of religion, freedom of assembly and the right to carry a gun. The end result of an oligarchy is that those in charge become wealthier and more powerful at the expense of the common person. Government is in control of most aspects of an individual's life, and the average person lives in fear of its government.

DEBT & DEFICIT SPENDING

"Mr. Obama denounced the $2.3 trillion added to the national debt on Mr. Bush's watch as 'deficits as far as the eye can see.' But Mr. Obama's budget adds $9.3 trillion to the debt over the next 10 years. What happened to Obama the deficit hawk?"

— Karl Rove

According to this quote by Karl Rove (advisor to President George W. Bush), the national debt has and will significantly increase. **What is debt and deficit spending, what are their significance, and why do they matter?** Deficit spending means that the government spends more money than it takes in as tax revenue on an annual basis. Over the years, these deficits turn into debts. The first time the federal government's debt rose above 40% of Gross Domestic Product (GDP) was in 1933 during the Great Depression. Just like we have annual salaries, the government has one as well. If spending is greater than income, debt is created. Between 1792 and 1910, the average federal debt was between 10 and 15 percent of GDP. Between 1930 and 2000, the average federal debt was about 50 percent of GDP where it peaked over 100% at the end of World War 2. Between 1901 and 1930, the government did not run a deficit for 21 out of the 30 years (70%). Between 1931 and 2014, the government did not run a deficit for 12 out of the 84 years (14%). Just as with us in our personal lives, the larger the federal debt the more intrusive and obstructive it becomes. For example, if we have a low debt to income ratio, it would be relatively easy for us to buy a nice car. If we owe more than we make in a year – in other words a debt ratio greater than 100% - it would be difficult to qualify for any type of loan.

Federal Deficits Since The Founding
US from FY 1792 to FY 2019

percent GDP

30

20

10

0

-10

1800 1820 1840 1860 1880 1900 1920 1940 1960 1980 2000

jpgraph   usgovernmentspending.com

Federal Debt Since The Founding
US from FY 1792 to FY 2019

percent GDP

120

100

80

60

40

20

0

1800 1820 1840 1860 1880 1900 1920 1940 1960 1980 2000

jpgraph   usgovernmentspending.com

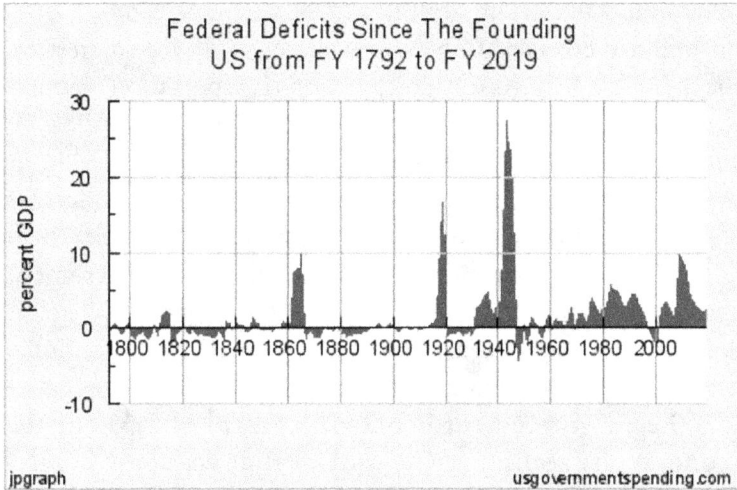

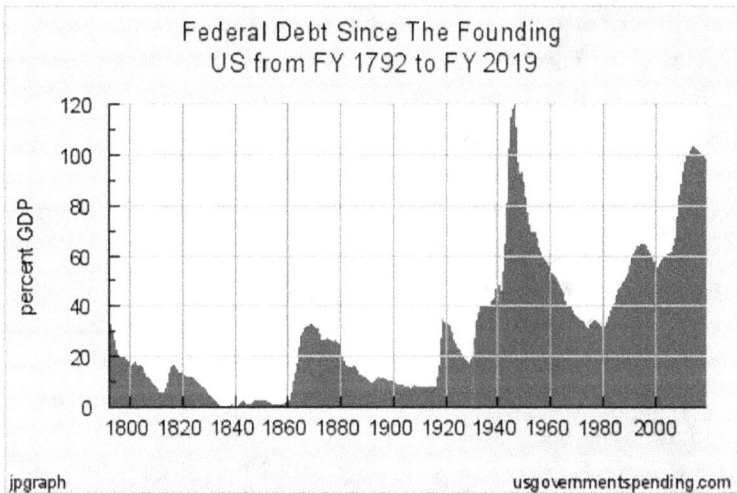

One of the primary differences between the early 20th Century and the early 21st Century is what the federal government spent the money on. In 1910, the federal government spent 26% of its annual budget on military defense, 26% on communications, 7% on transportation, 3% for interest on the debt, and less than 1% for welfare, education, health care, and foreign economic aid for a grand total of $840 million or 2.5% of GDP. In 2010, the federal government spent 23.7%

of its annual budget on health care, 21.7% on pensions, 20.1% on military defense, 14.5% on welfare, 5.7% for interest on the debt, 4.0% on education, 2.7% on transportation, and less than 1% for foreign economic aid for a grand total of $3.46 trillion or 23.8% of GDP. These numbers show a significant shift in spending from basic functions, such as military defense and communications, to government sponsored benefits, such as health care and welfare. Not only is the federal government spending significantly more money in terms of real dollars, it is in direct control of a much larger portion of the national economy – from 2.5% in 1910 to 23.8% in 2010.

When a government is only in control of 2.5% of the economy, its real power to control that economy is relatively insignificant. However, when that same government has direct control over a large proportion of the economy, its power to control that economy has increased exponentially. The federal government is in direct control of an ever increasing proportion of the economy which leads to an increase in power towards the federal government and a reduction in power away from the states and the people, which reduces the power and authority of the Tenth Amendment and the entire US Constitution. This is why we should pay attention to how much money the federal government spends.

In Section I of this book we discussed the differences in priorities between those who want to promote social justice and those who want to promote individual liberty. We also mentioned the importance of finding a balance between individual liberty and government control. Each person has a different idea of how much the government should spend and where it should go. The answer, if you value the US Constitution, the Rule of Law, justice and freedom, is that we must find solutions that promote these values - neither allowing the national government to have ultimate power and authority nor forcing all individuals to fend for themselves without any assistance. We as Americans who

love freedom, justice and liberty must work together, properly leverage our varied political perspectives & strengths, and create solutions that benefit all who work and play in these United States of America.

Robert Welch is one with his own perspective on priorities for government spending. In 1958 Robert Welch, founder of the John Birch Society, made some predictions about the death of American liberty. He believed there was a group of insiders intent on *"the surrender of American sovereignty piece by piece and step by step to various international organizations."* He described the death of Constitutional sovereignty with ten predictions:

1. Greatly expanded government spending for every conceivable means of getting rid of ever larger sums of American money, as wastefully as possible.

2. Higher and then much higher taxes.

3. An increasingly unbalanced budget despite the higher taxes.

4. Wild inflation of our currency.

5. Government controls of prices, wages, and materials, supposedly to combat inflation.

6. Greatly increased socialistic controls over every operation of our economy and every activity of our daily lives. This is to be accompanied naturally and automatically by a correspondingly huge increase in the size of our bureaucracy and in both the cost and reach of our domestic government.

7. Far more centralization of power in Washington and the practical elimination of our state lines. There is a many faceted drive at work to have our state lines eventually mean no more within the nation than our county lines do now within the states.

8. They study advance of federal aide to, and control over, our educational system leading to complete federalization of our public education.

9.   A constant hammering into the American conscious-
     ness of the horror of modern warfare. The beauties
     and the absolute necessity of peace.

10. The consequent willingness of the American people
     to allow the steps of appeasement by our government
     which amount to a piecemeal surrender of the rest of
     the free world and of the United States itself.

As I read through this list, I could not help feeling helpless
and hopeless. To understand the veracity of these predictions,
I looked at some facts. In 1910, total federal, state and local
government spending was $2.68 billion (8.0% of GDP) with
an annual surplus of 0.1% of GDP and a total debt of 18.7%
of GDP. In 2010, total government spending was $5.87 tril-
lion (40.3% of GDP) with an annual deficit of 8.89% of
GDP and a total debt of 111.4% of GDP. Let me explain
these numbers this way. Assuming no taxes were taken out, if
everybody in 1910 were to give all their monthly wages to the
government to pay down its debt, it would take just under 10
weeks to pay off the debt completely. If everyone in 2010 did
the same thing, it would take about 58 weeks to pay off the
debt completely.

As stated earlier, the higher the debt, the more difficult it is
to accomplish your financial goals. It is true that the federal government can print an unlimited amount of money, but with it
would arise unlimited inflation (see Chapter 8). How high can
the national debt go before it starts causing problems. Actually,
the problems are already here. Because of the high debt, loans
are more difficult to get, financial institutions are more regulated, interest rates are higher (unless they are artificially kept
low by federal government intervention), and banks are consoli-
dating to reduce the risk to large amounts of bad debt. We just
have to look at countries like Spain, Portugal, Italy, Greece and
Ireland to see the effects of a high national debt.

REGULATORY ENVIRONMENT

This section on the regulatory environment represents the initial rumblings of an idea I had that eventually became this book. Regulations are rules designed to enforce certain types of behavior. The more regulations are enforced, the more government intervention is involved. For a while now I have heard about government corruption and over regulation. For most of my life, I lived in the heart of Southern California. I didn't have to travel too far to find examples of a government possibly overreaching in its power and authority. From the millions stolen from residents by the City of Bell representatives, to the murder of a schizophrenic homeless man by Fullerton police officers and its subsequent cover up, to the California Air Resources Board that wants to eliminate all industrial activity within the state, I was irritated. When is someone going to do something to fix these problems? I realized that in order to have HOPE for a better tomorrow, the CHANGE has to start with me today.

I wanted to do more than generate a list of complaints. I wanted to educate people on how to understand the problems, and more importantly how to fix them because information is power, and the right information in the right hands can generate positive results of epic proportions.

The following stories are true. They are representative of how easy it can become for any form of government (from local to federal) to trample the liberties of an individual. These stories were selected not only because they show how arrogant government agents can become, they also show real solutions to real problems.

Donald Shoenholt v. City of New York

Donald Shoenholt and Hy Chabbott, owners of Gillies Coffee Company, had a coffee bean roasting plant on 19th St in New York City. The coffee company was established in 1840. This is the year that Antarctica was discovered by Charles Wilkes, Samuel Morse patented the telegraph and William H. Harrison was elected President of the United States. In 2002, a city inspector dropped by on an anonymous tip. The inspector issued a $400 fine for fugitive odors in an industrial area. The business was ordered to eliminate all coffee odors in the future. At the city's Environmental Control Board administrative hearing, Donald stated, *"Research has shown that coffee smells like coffee. There is nothing that can reasonably be done to separate the natural smell of already roasted coffee from a coffee business."* Under the current interpretation of the New York City Air Pollution Control Code, shoe stores, barber shops, doctor's offices and flower shops are all in violation of the law. Gillies Coffee Company was convicted of the violation on April 2, 2003, and the company accrued $30,000 in legal bills. According to the Philadelphia Inquirer, NYC's Department of Environmental Protection has also fined pickle companies, bagel bakeries and doughnut shops for air quality violations. Today, Gillies Coffee Company operates a website where consumers can order its coffees, but more than 95% of its $3 million in annual revenue is from wholesale. Most of the coffee business has since left New York City - shipments come in through Newark and are warehoused in New Jersey near the Holland Tunnel. Since Gillies Coffee Company is no longer based in New York City, it has lost a stream of tax revenue. The good news is that New York City has one less coffee company polluting its air.

Amazon v. State of California

On June 29, 2011, California Governor Jerry Brown signed CA State Bill AB 28X into law. This law, also known as the California Affiliate Nexus Tax, *"imposes a tax on retailers... from the sale of tangible personal property sold at retail in this state."* The law specifically includes Internet activity performed by a person who is in the State of California. Brown signed the measure into law as part of his plan to reduce the state's budget gap. The California State Board of Equalization expected to increase government revenue by $200 million a year. Brown and some lawmakers responded to critics by saying the measure levels the playing field for California's brick-and-mortar retailers, which are required to collect sales taxes. Amazon.com, Overstock.com and other online retailers responded to this new law by terminating all relationships with all affiliates who work in California. An official letter sent by Amazon to its California affiliates stated: *"We oppose this bill because it is unconstitutional and counterproductive... Similar legislation in other states has led to job and income losses, and little, if any, new tax revenue."* Other states that have passed the so-called "Amazon tax" in recent years include Connecticut, Illinois, New York, North Carolina, Arkansas and Rhode Island. Amazon has dropped the affiliate program in all these states, except New York, where it has filed a lawsuit against the state. The business environment is an always changing obstacle course. Experienced business leaders, and, in this case, successful Amazon affiliates have already reacted to this government created problem. Instead of getting mad or breaking the law, they simply closed their businesses in California and some relocated to a more business friendly state, like Texas, Nevada or Arizona. As a result of this new tax law, California-based online entrepreneur, Nick Loper, relocated to Nevada. Loper has been quoted to say that 70 other affiliates had already left. Another online entrepreneur, Erica Douglass, posted a mock "It's Over" letter to California on her blog. Douglass, who sold an internet company she had built for $1.1 million in 2007 when she was just 26, cited multiple reasons for moving to Austin, Texas. Among them were unnecessary paperwork requirements mandated by the state and high taxes. However, the straw that broke the camel's back was Brown signing the Amazon Tax into law. In September 2012, the State of California and Amazon.com came to an agreement. Amazon will collect sales taxes on items it sells to California residents. Orders fulfilled by but not purchased from Amazon are exempt from tax payments by Amazon. In this broker relationship Amazon has with its affiliates, Amazon is just providing a service. Amazon is not the official retailer of many of the products being processed through its warehouses. Only if the retailer has a physical presence in California and sells to Californians is Amazon required to pay California sales tax.

Online retailers have to deal with an inconsistent patchwork of local laws that require sales tax in some states but not in others. Amazon has fought hard against local levies but says it would support a simple, nationwide system of state and local sales tax collection. If you have ever developed a business that sells products across the nation, you will quickly encounter how complicated this process is. There are literally thousands of different sales tax rates across the country. The state will have one tax rate, each county will often add to it, and each city may or may not add to it as well. I am not convinced that a single national sales tax rate for online purchases is the best answer either. How will it work? My best guess based on other government tax distribution systems is that the money would go to the federal treasury first and then get redistributed down the line. Who's to say that the federal government would properly distribute tax revenue down the line? This is a complicated problem in which there is probably not a simple answer. I work with many companies that sell products online. I have been, and will continue to follow this closely.

Americans with Disabilities Act

The Americans with Disabilities Act (ADA) was passed July 26, 1990, as Public Law 101-336 and became effective on January 26, 1992. The ADA is federal legislation that opens up services and employment opportunities to Americans with disabilities. The law was written to strike a balance between the reasonable accommodation of citizens' needs and the capacity of private and public entities to respond. It is intended to elim-

inate discrimination and level the playing field for disabled individuals. California Citizens Against Lawsuit Abuse reports,
*"the Americans with Disabilities Act was meant to increase access
for disabled people, but a few unscrupulous personal injury lawyers and professional plaintiffs have made fortunes by targeting
businesses for shake down lawsuits. These lawsuits don't ask for any
accessibility improvements to be made, they ask for money to make
the lawsuit go away."* California, along with Hawaii, Illinois
and Florida, is a particular hotbed for ADA lawsuits and the
law firms that bring them to court. California has one of the
largest amount of ADA lawsuits in the country, citing several
factors for potential abuse, chief among them two California
statutes that provide $1,000 or $4,000 in minimum damages,
plus attorney fees, per each successful claimant. Many claimants multiply these damage amounts by the number of conditions they observe at a property. This frequently results in
$50,000 or more in damage demands. Some serial claimants
will file for damages against dozens of businesses. Jarek Molski
was disabled in a 1985 motorcycle accident that left him a
paraplegic. He has filed 400 lawsuits against businesses under
the Americans with Disabilities Act, alleging access violations.
He was dubbed a "hit-and-run plaintiff" in 2004 by a federal
judge and barred from filing any more lawsuits. Molski's attorney, Thomas Frankovich, says his client and the dozen or
so serial ADA plaintiffs his firm has represented are activists
and crusaders. Frankovich dubbed Molski (who does not have
a criminal record) "the sheriff" because *"he started going into
town to clean it up."* Frankovich says he has filed 223 ADA lawsuits on behalf of Molski. Frankovich says Molski began suing
only after his letters to offending businesses were ignored. Says
Frankovich: *"Letters don't work. Only the hammer of litigation
gets them to do what they need,"* but Frankovich himself is being
charged by the state bar of California on three counts of misconduct, stemming from ADA lawsuits he filed on behalf of
Molski. One count alleges that Frankovich's litigation strategy
amounted to a scheme to extort money from defendants. Says

Frankovich of the charge: *"It's an absolute fabrication based on absolutely no supportive facts. Using the fact that he filed 223 lawsuits as evidence of a scheme is absurd. His rights were violated in 223 cases where significant architectural barriers existed."* Disabled plaintiffs in cases like this will team up with a trial attorney. The disabled person will go out to restaurants and other public facilities to specifically look for access violations. The trial attorney will file a lawsuit on his behalf. The location owner may then be looking at over $100,000 in repair costs and legal fees. After the suit has been filed, the attorney in league with the disabled person would call up the owner and arrange for a $5000 to $10,000 out of court settlement to make the lawsuit go away. It would often cost much more to fight the lawsuit than to pay the settlement, so the location owner will often pay the money to make the lawsuit go away.

In September 2012, California Governor Jerry Brown signed into law Senate Bill 1186, a bipartisan bill sponsored by State Senators Bob Dutton and Darrell Steinberg, which is an effort to curb the high number of predatory ADA lawsuits being brought against property and small business owners in California. SB 1186 significantly limits certain tactics often used by the attorneys behind these types of lawsuits, adds additional requirements aimed at deterring frivolous lawsuits, and implements certain lease disclosure requirements for commercial landlords. Some of the highlights of SB 1186 include:

- The requirement that demand letters or complaints sent to property or business owners include a written advisory detailing certain obligations and rights available to such owners. The advisory, among other things, includes resources for property and business owners to obtain information regarding their ADA obligations and compliance requirements. The advisory also clarifies that owners at the receiving end of such demand letters or complaints are not required to pay any money in connection with such letters or complaints unless and until a court has found the property or business owners liable.

- The requirement that demand letters or complaints sent to property or business owners describe in plain language the basis for the ADA claim.
- A prohibition against including specific demands for money in demand letters based on ADA claims. The demand letters may, however, include a generic statement stating that the property or business owner "may be civilly liable for actual and statutory damages for a violation of a construction-related accessibility requirement."
- The requirement that all demand letters include the State Bar license number of the attorneys drafting the letters.
- The requirement that copies of all demand letters be submitted to both the California Commission on Disability Access ("CCDA") and, until January 1, 2016, the California State Bar. A copy of any complaint would also be required to be sent to the CCDA.
- A significant reduction in the minimum liability for properties in violation of construction-related accessibility standards to: $1,000 for each offense if the owner has corrected all construction-related violations that are the basis of the claim within 60 days after being served with the complaint; and $2,000 for each offense if the defendant is a small business and has corrected all construction-related violations that are the basis of the claim within 30 days after being served with the complaint.

Redevelopment: The Unknown Government

Municipal Officers for Redevelopment Reform, headed by Orange County Supervisor Chris Norby released a report in September 2007 discussing the legal underground government that has arisen through redevelopment agencies. The following is edited from that report. *"There is an unknown government in California. This unknown government currently consumes 10% of all property taxes statewide - $2.8 billion in 2003. It has a total indebtedness of over $56 billion. It is supported by* *a powerful Sacramento lobby, backed by an army of lawyers, consultants, bond brokers and land developers. Unlike new counties, cities and school districts, it can be created without a vote of the citizens affected. Unlike other governments, it can incur bonded indebtedness without voter approval. Unlike other governments, it may use the power of eminent domain to benefit private interests. This unknown government provides no public services. It does not educate our children, maintain our streets, protect us from crime, nor stock our libraries. It claims to eliminate blight and promote economic development, yet there is no evidence it has done so in the half century since it was created. Indeed, it has become a rapidly growing drain on California's public resources, amassing enormous power with little public awareness or oversight. This unknown government is Redevelopment. It is time Californians knew more about it. State law allows a city council to create a redevelopment agency to administer one or more "project areas" within its boundaries. An area may be small, or it can encompass the entire city. These project areas are governed by a redevelopment agency with its own staff and governing board, appointed by the city council. Thus, an agency and city may appear to be one entity. Usually city councils appoint themselves as agency board members, with council meetings doubling as redevelopment meetings. Legally, however, a redevelopment agency is an entirely separate government authority, with its own revenue, budget, staff and expanded powers to issue debt and condemn private property. Out of California's 477 cities, 381 have active redevelopment agencies. No vote of the residents affected was required. No review by the Local Agency Formation Commission (LAFCO) was done. (Only 21 of 58 counties have active redevelopment agencies, and with unincorporated areas shrinking, counties constitute barely 4% of all redevelopment expenditures.) Californians often confuse redevelopment with federal "urban renewal" projects typical of large eastern cities of the 1940's-60's. Sadly, the methods and results are often similar. Yet redevelopment is a state-authorized layer of government without federal funds, rules or requirements. It is entirely within the power of the California legislature and voters to control,* *reform, amend or abolish. The only thing a city need do to create or expand a redevelopment area is to declare it "blighted". This is easily done. State law is so vague that most anything has been designated as "blight". Parkland, new residential areas, professional baseball stadiums, oil fields, shopping centers, orange groves, open desert and dry riverbeds have all been designated as "blight" for redevelopment purposes. To make a finding of blight, a consultant is hired to conduct a study. New redevelopment areas are largely driven by city staff, who choose the consultant with the approval of the city council. Consultants know their job is not to determine if there is blight, but to declare blighted whatever community conditions may be. "Cities adopted very loose and very creative definitions of blight," writes syndicated Sacramento Bee columnist Dan Walters, author and long-time state policy analyst. "Often, vacant, never-developed land is branded as blighted to allow its inclusion in a redevelopment zone." A city park in Lancaster has been declared blighted to justify paving over 19 acres of parkland and axing 100 trees for a new Costco. Raw desert acreage in California City was declared blighted to justify its seizure for a Hyundai test track. An Orange County public health facility was declared blighted by the Santa Ana Redevelopment Agency in order to condemn it and turn the property over to a BMW dealer. Blight has been proclaimed in some of California's most affluent cities. Indian Wells, a guard-gated community with an average $210,000 household income, has two separate redevelopment areas. Understandably, many homeowners fear an official designation of blight will hurt property values. Small property owners fear redevelopment's use of eminent domain. Building permits can also be denied if an applicant does not conform precisely to the redevelopment plan. So, local citizen groups often challenge the blight findings in court. Judges overturned blight findings in Mammoth Lakes, Diamond Bar and Temecula, invalidating their redevelopment plans. Others are challenged by counties and school districts that stand to lose major property tax revenue if a new redevelopment area is created. Recent state legislation has tightened definitions of blight, particularly those involving open* *and agricultural land. Still, enforcement is lax, legal challenges costly, and most agencies were already created long before recent reform attempts. Once the consultant's blight findings are ratified, a city may create or expand a redevelopment area. Voter approval is never asked. Citizens can force a vote by gathering 10% of the signatures of all registered voters within 30 days of the council action. Where this has occurred, redevelopment nearly always lose by wide margins (rejected in Montebello by 82%, La Puente by 67%, Ventura by 57%, Los Alamitos by 55%, Half Moon Bay by 76%, for example). The requirements to force a vote are difficult to meet, however. In the vast majority of cases, a popular vote is never held. Rather, the consultant's findings of blight are quickly certified. A law firm is then retained to draw up the paperwork and defend against legal challenges. A growing number of law firms specialize in redevelopment. Like the consultants, they are members of the California Redevelopment Association, a Sacramento-based lobby. They are listed in the CRA's directory and advertise in its newsletter. Their livelihood depends on the aggressive use of redevelopment and increasingly imaginative definitions of blight. To eliminate alleged blight, a redevelopment agency, once created, has four extraordinary powers held by no other government authority:*

1. Tax Increment: A redevelopment agency has the exclusive use of all increases in property tax revenues ("tax increment") generated in its designated project areas.

2. Bonded Debt: An agency has the power to sell bonds secured against future tax increment, and may do so without voter approval.

3. Business Subsidies: An agency has the power to give public money directly to developers and other private businesses in the form of cash grants, tax rebates, free land or public improvements.

4.   <u>Eminent Domain</u>: An agency has expanded powers to condemn private property, not just for public use, but to transfer to other private owners.

These four powers represent an enormous expansion of government intrusion into our traditional system of private property and free enterprise. Let us carefully consider the costs of this power and if it has done anything to eliminate real blight."

INTERPRETATION OF LAW

Adopted initially on September 17, 1787, the US Constitution and its twenty-seven amendments enacted between 1791 and 1992 are the supreme law of the land. They create balance of power between three co-equal branches of government (Executive, Legislative, and Judicial), limit the power of the federal government, empower states and individual citizen to maintain control of federal government officials (Tenth Amendment), and inscribe a series of individual rights.

Some laws are quite explanatory without any interpretation. The 26th Amendment states: *"Section 1. The right of citizens of the United States, who are eighteen years of age or older, to vote shall not be denied or abridged by the United States or by any State on account of age. Section 2. The Congress shall have the power to enforce this article by appropriate legislation."* Basically, any citizen over 18 years cannot be denied the right to vote simply because that person is 18 years old. Alternatively, the Patient Protection and Affordable Care Act signed into law by President Barack Obama is thousands of pages. This type of law leaves the door wide open for a significant amount of interpretation. When laws are more open to interpretation, individual perceptions and political preferences play much more of a role in how the law is enforced.

As I discussed in chapter 1, perception is reality. Each individual will interpret laws and the role of government differently, depending on his/her political goals. The progressive focuses on "establish justice" and encourages equal rights for all individuals. The conservative focuses on "provide for the common defence" and "powers not delegated to the United States... are reserved to the States... or to the people (10th Amendment)." I will irritate many people with this next statement. Both interpretations are correct. Over the years we have given voting rights to all races and both genders, and we have been victorious in many armed conflicts, including: War of 1812, Spanish-American War, World War I and World War II.

The US Constitution is a flexible design that allows for various interpretations. As a matter of fact, the US Constitution is a direct result of compromise. During the Constitutional Convention of 1787, there was a dispute between large states and small as to how many representatives a state should have. Large states wanted proportional representation in which larger states would have more representation. Small states wanted equal representation in which all states have the same number of representatives. A compromise was reached and the House of Representatives and Senate were born. The House conforms to proportional governance whereas the Senate conforms to equal governance. For a bill to pass the legislative body and be advanced to the President for a signature, both houses have to agree on a final version.

Individuals vote for the President and Congressional members. It is through this method that government officials stay in tune with their constituencies. If a government official does something that citizens disagree with, that person runs the risk of losing his/her position. This, in theory, is partly what encourages government officials to improve the lives of Americans. **What happens when government officials stop representing their constituents and attempt to by-pass the US Constitution?** Some of this is addressed in the next chapter.

SPOTLIGHT ON ANDREW NAPOLITANO

Andrew Napolitano was born in Newark, New Jersey. He is a graduate of Princeton University and Notre Dame Law School. He was a founding member of the Concerned Alumni of Princeton. Napolitano was a New Jersey judge from 1987 to 1995, becoming the state's youngest Superior Court judge. He also served as an adjunct professor at Seton Hall University School of Law for 11 years. Napolitano resigned his judgeship in 1995 for private practice but later pursued a writing and television career.

Before joining Fox as a news analyst, Napolitano was the presiding judge on the television show, Power of Attorney, in which people brought small-claims disputes to a televised courtroom. Differing from similar formats, the plaintiffs and defendants were represented pro bono by famous attorneys. The show ran in syndication during the 2000–2001 season. From 2006 to 2010, Napolitano co-hosted a talk radio show on Fox News Radio with Brian Kilmeade titled Brian and the Judge. Napolitano hosted a libertarian talk show called Freedom Watch that aired daily on Fox Business Channel. Frequent guests on Freedom Watch were Representative Ron Paul, financial commentator Peter Schiff and libertarian Lew Rockwell. Napolitano regularly substituted for television host Glenn Beck when Beck was absent from his program. After Beck announced that he would be leaving Fox News, he asked Napolitano to replace him.

Napolitano is pro-life, opposes capital punishment, believes that the protections within the US Constitution are not limited to Americans citizens, and has called Presidential hopeful Ralph Nader a hero. In February, 2014, Napolitano expressed sympathy with the Confederacy on Fox News. He explained that "I am a contrarian on Abraham Lincoln," because, according to Napolitano, "Lincoln set about the most murderous war in American history." Slavery in the US would have "died a natural death." In February 2012, Napolitano was fired from Fox News for a candid speech on the American political system. Fox had every right to fire Napolitano. Fox is a private business and not a government agency. As such the First Amendment does not apply. Fox management did this primarily because they thought that more people would be upset if they did not do anything regarding how he presented his controversial opinions versus if they terminated Napolitano. The following is his speech in its entirety. Make your own conclusions.

5-Minute Speech that Got Judge Andrew Napolitano Fired from Fox News
February 13, 2012

"What if Democrats and Republicans were two wings of the same bird of prey?

What if elections were actually useful tools of social control? What if they just provided the populace with meaningless participation in a process that validates an establishment that never meaningfully changes? What if that establishment doesn't want and doesn't have the consent of the governed? What if the two-party system were actually a mechanism used to limit so-called public opinion? What if there were more than two sides to every issue, but the two parties wanted to box you in to one of their corners?

What if there's no such thing as public opinion, because every thinking person has opinions that are uniquely his own? What if public opinion were just a manufactured narrative that makes it easier to convince people that if their views are different, there's something wrong with that – or something wrong with them?

What if the whole purpose of the Democratic and Republican parties was not to expand voters' choices, but to limit them? What if the widely perceived differences between the two parties were just an illusion? What if the heart of government policy remains the same, no matter who's in the White House? What if the heart of government policy remains the same, no matter what the people want?

What if those vaunted differences between Democrat and Republican were actually just minor disagreements? What if both parties just want power and are willing to have young people fight meaningless wars to enhance that power? What if both parties continue to fight the war on drugs just to give bureaucrats and cops bigger budgets and more jobs?

What if government policies didn't change when government's leaders did? What if no matter who won an election, government stayed the same? What if government were really a revolving door of political hacks, bent on exploiting the people while they're in charge?

What if both parties supported welfare, war, debt, bailouts and big government? What if the rhetoric candidates displayed on the campaign trail was dumped after electoral victory? What if Barack Obama campaigned as an antiwar, pro-civil liberties candidate, then waged senseless wars while assaulting your rights that the Constitution is supposed to protect? What if George W. Bush campaigned on a platform of nonintervention and small government, then waged a foreign policy of muscular military intervention and a domestic policy of vast government borrowing and growth?

What if Bill Clinton declared the era of big government to be over, but actually just convinced Republicans like Newt Gingrich that they can get what they want out of big government, too? What if the Republicans went along with it?

What if Ronald Reagan spent six years running for president promising to shrink government, but then the gov-

ernment grew while he was in office? What if, notwithstanding Reagan's ideas and cheerfulness and libertarian
rhetoric, there really was no Reagan Revolution?

What if all this is happening again? What if Rick Santorum
is being embraced by voters who want small government
even though he voted for the Patriot Act, for an expansion
of Medicare and for raising the debt ceiling by trillions
of dollars? What if Mitt Romney is being embraced by
voters who want anyone but Obama, but don't realize that
Romney might as well be Obama on everything from warfare to welfare?

What if Ron Paul is being ignored by the media not
because they claim he's unappealing or unelectable, but
because he doesn't fit into the pre-manufactured public-
opinion mold used by the establishment to pigeonhole
the electorate and create the so-called narrative that drives
media coverage of elections?

What if the biggest difference between most candidates was
not substance but style? What if those stylistic differences
were packaged as substantive ones to reinforce the illusion of a difference between Democrats and Republicans?
What if Romney wins and ends up continuing most of the
same policies Obama promoted? What if Obama's policies, too, are merely extensions of Bush's?

What if a government that manipulated us could be fired?
What if a government that lacked the true and knowing
consent of the governed could be dismissed? What if it
were possible to have a game-changer? What if we need a
Ron Paul to preserve and protect our freedoms from assault by the government?

What if we could make elections matter again? What if we
could do something about this?"

Chapter 8

DUPLICITY IN THE GOVERNMENT PROCESS

"There's nothing that makes people hungry like being out of power and out of government. When you're in government, all of the big operatives have good jobs or they're working for some lobbying firm and making $3 million a year, while the other guys don't have anything to do."

— James Carville

The Founders of our country were well-versed in world history. They came in direct contact with some national governments, including Spain, France and Great Britain. They were also aware of ancient powers, such as the Babylonian, Roman, and Greek empires. They wanted to create a system that had the best chance of preserving liberty and freedom, and the end result was the US Constitution and the Bill of Rights.

Benjamin Franklin wrote, *"The deliberations of the Constitutional Convention of 1787 were held in strict secrecy. Consequently, anxious citizens gathered outside Independence Hall when the proceedings ended in order to learn what had been produced behind closed doors. The answer was provided immediately. A Mrs. Powel of Philadelphia asked Benjamin Franklin, 'Well, Doctor, what have we got, a republic or a monarchy?' With no hesitation whatsoever, Franklin responded, 'A republic, if you can keep it.'"*

Franklin understood that in order to maintain a free republic, Americans must take an active participation in protecting freedom, otherwise the end result will be an oligarchy, which has been the most common form of government in world history. **How do we as Americans identify government corruption? Is there anything we can do to fix government corruption?**

STATISM

Statism is a philosophy and practice of government self-preservation. One can define statism as a political and philosophical viewpoint in which the government is a homogeneous institution capable of using its political power to force policy on a society to protect and even enlarge itself. This depends on an elitist or oligarchical form of power rather than a pluralistic one.

As I described previously in chapter 3, Frank Goodnow and President Woodrow Wilson are some of these elitist statists. They purposely and methodically removed the bonds of constitutional government and developed a system that favors the betterment of the government. Let me explain this in terms of the Democratic and Republican parties.

The Democratic Party is guilty of abusing the American education system for its own gain. Over the last 20 years, the American Federation of Teachers (AFT) has given more than $28 million in campaign contributions and the National Education Association (NEA) has given almost $31 million. Of that almost $60 million, more than $56 million went to Democrats. Unions have spent almost three times as much money on campaign ads as all corporations combined. In fiscal year 2007, the NEA spent more than 20% of its budget (~$80.5 million) on gifts and grants to non-educational progressive leaning organizations, such as: ACORN, Center for Policy Alternatives, Children's Defense Fund, Congressional Black Caucus Foundation, Congressional Hispanic Caucus

Institute, Democratic GAIN, Democratic Leadership Council and NAACP. To complete the cycle, most teachers around the country are required to pay union dues. So this is how the whole financial/political machine works. Teachers are hired by the states to teach our children. These teachers must pay union dues. These union dues are used to fund people and bills that will increase school spending. They provide large amounts of campaign contributions to Democrats and bills that increase school spending. The Democrats, in turn, pass bills that increase school spending and increase the number of teachers. Teachers will continue to pay these union dues and participate in union activities in order to ensure that they get pay raises, increased benefits, and job security. A Wall Street Journal editorial noted, the NEA is a honey pot for left-wing political causes that have nothing to do with teachers, much less students.

The Republicans are just as guilty of this as well. Lobbying jobs have become the foundation of a powerful new Republican political machine in Washington politics. This one is built upon patronage and contracts. The GOP is building its machine outside government, among Washington's thousands of trade associations and corporate offices, with their tens of thousands of employees, and the hundreds of millions of dollars in political money at their disposal. The emerging Republican machine is the mirror image of that built by the Democratic Party under Franklin D. Roosevelt and his successors. The "K Street Project" is a database intended to track the party affiliation, Washington, DC, experience, and political giving of every lobbyist in town. Slowly, the GOP is marginalizing Democratic lobbyists and populating K Street with loyal Republicans. Increasingly, the trade associations and their corporate representatives - those firms run by Republicans - are the beneficiaries of Washington's new spoils system, and they are expected to display total loyalty. The most trusted lobbyists provide the leadership with eyes and ears as well as valuable advice and feedback. Placing party surrogates atop trade associations make them more responsive to the party's needs. The K Street strategy also provides the GOP with a number of specific advantages. Political machines thrive on closed-door secret decision-making. There are no rules against whom you can meet with, no reporters armed with Freedom of Information Act requests. These jobs also make for better patronage. Whereas a deputy undersecretary might earn $140,000, a top oil lobbyist can make $400,000 or more. Controlling K Street also helps Republicans accumulate political talent. The GOP, able to dole out the most desirable jobs, has kept more of its best people in Washington, where they can be hauled out for government or campaign work like clubs in a golf bag.

Political patronage is one of the primary tools used by both political parties to remain in power. Another similar name to this is crony capitalism. Government officials pick winners and losers and give the best connected the most financially lucrative jobs. Government has trillions of dollars at their disposal and many laws to protect them.

SECRECY

There is one tool statists and elitists value above most others, and that is the tool of secrecy. They have private meetings, make private deals, and quickly pass large amounts of legislation without allowing the time to truly understand their repercussions.

In chapter 7, I discussed the backroom deal that was the 1876 Presidential election. It was one of the most contentious Presidential elections in US history. Instead of listening to the voters (who made it clear by a 3.1% margin that they wanted Democrat Samuel Tilden), secrecy and manipulation were used to elect Republican Rutherford B. Hayes as President. It was so contentious, that Hayes took the oath of office in a private ceremony and did not run for re-election. However, an argument could be made that because of this Republican win, the Republican party was able to maintain large amounts of power in Washington, DC, until 1933. So the end result may have justified the means in which to get there. However, was it good for the country? I have allegiance to the United States of America, not to the Democratic or Republican Party. One party rule – either party – leads to secrecy, corruption, and unrestrained power. These are not in the best interest of the American electorate.

Federal Reserve System

Those who control a nation's currency are among the most powerful people in the world. The current Chairman of the Federal Reserve is considered the seventh most powerful person in the world - ahead of leaders of the United Kingdom, France and India. How could this be? What makes the head of the US Federal Reserve System so powerful and influential? What is the Federal Reserve ("Fed"), and why should we pay attention to what it does?

When you look at the top-front of a one-dollar bill and you read, "FEDERAL RESERVE NOTE." The Fed, as the central bank of the United States, was granted a monopoly over the US banking system and had three objectives for monetary policy: "maximum employment, stable prices and moderate long-term interest rates." What that means for you, is that the Fed has the power and authority as a private organization to determine how much a dollar bill can buy based upon the monetary policies it adopts. The Fed's policies can cause prices to rise (or fall), affecting what you pay for items. For example, if you made the median income of $12,050 per year in 1973 when the median house price in April of 1973 was $32,800, you would have to make about $94,400 in 2006 just to afford that same house which now has the median value of $257,000 in April 2006. The problem is that 2006 median income was nowhere near

$94,400. It was about half of that at $48,450. This essentially means that the cost of housing has outpaced income.

There has been an ongoing debate over monetary policy in the United States since its birth. Some, like Alexander Hamilton (first US Secretary of the Treasury), believed that a central bank was necessary to ensure a stable money supply. Others, like Thomas Jefferson (first US Secretary of State), were strongly opposed, believing that giving the federal government the ability to control the money supply would concentrate too much power and wealth into the hands of too few people. Jefferson once wrote, *"I sincerely believe, with you, that banking establishments are more dangerous than standing armies; and that the principle of spending money to be paid by posterity, under the name of funding, is but swindling futurity on a large scale."*

As a direct result of the Panic of 1907, a government-sponsored banking system became part of the national dialogue in order to stabilize the national economy and prevent major bank runs. The large banking institutions saw this as their opportunity to gain control of America's money supply. In 1908, President Theodore Roosevelt signed the National Monetary Commission, which was responsible for developing a plan to reform the nation's monetary system. In 1910, Senator Nelson Aldrich (who was related to J.D. Rockefeller through marriage) held a secret meeting on Jekyll Island with some of the wealthiest and most influential bankers in the world: Abram Piatt Andrew (Assistant Secretary of the Treasury), Frank Vanderlip (President of the National City Bank of New York), Henry P. Davison (senior partner of J.P. Morgan Company), Benjamin Strong (J.P. Morgan's emissary), Charles D. Norton (President of the First National Bank of New York), Paul Warburg (Director of Wells Fargo & Company), and Jacob Schiff (Director of National City Bank of New York & Wells Fargo, brother-in-law of Paul Warburg, and affiliated with the wealthy Rothschild banking family in Germany). About 25% of the world's wealth was represented at this secret meeting. Those in attendance had five objectives for any proposed legislation: 1) to reduce competition; 2) to obtain the ability to create money, 3) to gain control of all bank reserves, 4) to shift losses to taxpayers, and 5) to convince Congress that its purpose is to protect the public.

In the Presidential election of 1912, due to Theodore Roosevelt campaigning as a third party candidate, Thomas Woodrow Wilson received only 41.9% of the popular vote and yet became the 28th President of the United States. Some have reported that his Presidential campaign was financed and staffed by members of large banking institutions, and yet he pursued banking reforms. If this is true, this created a scenario in which he was to reform the very industry that helped get him elected. So was Wilson's allegiance to the US Constitution & the American people or to those who financed and operated his Presidential campaign? The Glass-Owen Bill (Federal Reserve Act) was sneaked through Congress during the Christmas holiday, and Wilson quickly signed it into law.

After passage of the Federal Reserve Act, Congressman Charles Lindbergh said,

> "To cause high prices, all the Federal Reserve Board will do will be to lower the rediscount rate... producing an expansion of credit and a rising stock market; then when... men are adjusted to these conditions, it can check... prosperity in mid-career by arbitrarily raising the rate of interest. It can cause the pendulum of a rising and falling market to swing gently back and forth by slight changes... or cause violent fluctuations by a greater rate variation, and in either case it will possess inside information as to financial conditions and advanced knowledge of the coming change, either up or down... The system is private, conducted for the sole purpose of obtaining the greatest possible profits from the use of other people's money. They know in advance when to create panics to their advantage. They also know when to stop panic. Inflation and deflation work equally well for them when they control finance."

The Fed generates profits through the creation and destruction of debt and transfers a fixed percentage of its profits to the US Treasury. As the Fed makes more money, the federal government makes more money. In 2008 (which marks the end of GW Bush's Presidency), it transferred about $34.9 billion. It transferred $46.1 billion in 2009, $78.4 billion in 2010, $76.9 billion in 2011, $88.9 billion in 2012, and $77.7 billion in 2013. While the nation was fighting a recession, and many were unemployed, the Federal Reserve substantially increased its profits. Who benefits most from the existence of the Federal Reserve? It is the federal government and the large banks that control the Federal Reserve System.

Who owns the Federal Reserve?

The following has been edited from the Federal Reserve Bank of Atlanta's website:

> "What institutions are members of the Federal Reserve System, and what does membership entail? . . . Those chartered by the federal government (through the Office of the Comptroller of the Currency in the Department of the Treasury) are national banks; by law, they are members of the Federal Reserve System. Banks chartered by the states are divided into those that are members of the Federal Reserve System (state member banks) and those that are not (state nonmember banks). . . . As of March 2004, of the nation's approximately 7,700 commercial banks approximately 2,900 were members of the Federal Reserve System - approximately 2,000 national banks and 900 state banks. Member banks must subscribe to stock in their regional Federal Reserve Bank in an amount equal to 6 percent of their capital and surplus. . . . Member banks receive a 6 percent dividend annually on their stock, as specified by law."

The largest holders of the common stock as described above would be the largest national banks: Bank of America, JP Morgan Chase, Citigroup, Wells Fargo, Goldman Sachs and

Morgan Stanley. Also, the assets within the Federal Reserve System are not distributed evenly. As of January 2009, the Federal Reserve Bank of New York was in control of 53.3% of all the assets within the twelve federal reserves. This means that the remaining eleven reserves each controlled an average of 4.2% of the remaining assets. These statistics show that wealth is concentrated into the hands of a few national banks and the Federal Reserve of New York - all of which are privately owned and act in secret to make monetary policy for the entire Nation.

JFK and the Secret Society

Three months after taking the oath of office, President John F. Kennedy delivered his "Secret Society" speech at the Waldorf-Astoria Hotel in New York. In it he expresses his discontent with, but need for limited government secrecy, and that the solution is the liberal almost unrestricted use of the First Amendment, freedom of speech and freedom of the press. He encourages the press to use their best judgment when it comes to certain types of information related to national security. There are numerous contentious government actions in which citizens complain that the government is awarding themselves too much power. Some of these actions include: creation of the Department of Homeland Security, the Patriot Act, the Omnibus spending bills, and President Barack Obama's healthcare bill.

Speaker of the House Nancy Pelosi, during Obama's healthcare debate said, *"...We have to pass the bill so that you can find out what is in it, away from the fog of the controversy."* This is like buying a house without even stepping foot on the property. Shouldn't the general public know what the content of legislation is before it is signed by the President? This is just bad policy, especially if the citizens of the country wish to remain a free representative republic.

We must fight against censorship. We must fight against secrecy, and we must fight to preserve the Constitution of the United States. We as American voters still hold the trump card. We can remove people from office. **Our main weapons are our understanding of the facts and our willingness to hold our public officials accountable to our needs and wants.**

President John F. Kennedy encouraged us to fight this fight. I do not dwell on conspiracy theories, but I want to quickly mention the assassination of President JFK, because it is relevant to this discussion. JFK was shot to death in Dallas on November 22, 1963. Some say it was a lone gunman. Others say it was a well orchestrated plan developed by dozens of people. Regardless of who killed him, his life was abruptly terminated because he made at least one too many enemies. I am sure that when President JFK advocated for a more open and responsive government, many who would be harmed by this openness did not appreciate it.

There are people who do not want to live within the constraints of a constitutional government - elitists, statists, call them what you may. The underlying point to all of this is that if we the citizens do not actively participate in and protect our current form of representative government, we will lose it. Kennedy spoke of this, and it may have been a contributing factor to his early death.

The President and the Press
aka *"Secret Society Speech"*
John F. Kennedy
April 27, 1961
American Newspaper Publishers Association
Waldorf-Astoria Hotel, New York

"Mr. Chairman, ladies and gentlemen:

I appreciate very much your generous invitation to be here tonight. You bear heavy responsibilities these days and an article I read some time ago reminded me of how particularly heavily the burdens of present day events bear upon your profession. You may remember that in 1851 the New York Herald Tribune under the sponsorship and publishing of Horace Greeley, employed as its London correspondent an obscure journalist by the name of Karl Marx.

We are told that foreign correspondent Marx, stone broke, and with a family ill and undernourished, constantly appealed to Greeley and managing editor Charles Dana for an increase in his munificent salary of $5 per installment, a salary which he and Engels ungratefully labeled as the "lousiest petty bourgeois cheating." But when all his financial appeals were refused, Marx looked around for other means of livelihood and fame, eventually terminating his relationship with the Tribune and devoting his talents full time to the cause that would bequeath to the world the seeds of Leninism, Stalinism, revolution and the cold war.

If only this capitalistic New York newspaper had treated him more kindly; if only Marx had remained a foreign correspondent, history might have been different. And I hope all publishers will bear this lesson in mind the next time they receive a poverty-stricken appeal for a small increase in the expense account from an obscure newspaper man.

I have selected as the title of my remarks tonight "The President and the Press." Some may suggest that this would be more naturally worded "The President Versus the Press." But those are not my sentiments tonight. It is true, however, that when a well-known diplomat from another country demanded recently that our State Department repudiate certain newspaper attacks on his colleague it was unnecessary for us to reply that this Administration was not responsible for the press, for the press had already made it clear that it was not responsible for this Administration.

Nevertheless, my purpose here tonight is not to deliver the usual assault on the so-called one party press. On the contrary, in recent months I have rarely heard any complaints about political bias in the press except from a few Republicans. Nor is it my purpose tonight to discuss or defend the televising of Presidential press conferences. I think it is highly beneficial to have some 20,000,000 Americans regularly sit in on these conferences to observe, if I may say so, the incisive, the intelligent and the courteous qualities displayed by your Washington correspondents. Nor, finally, are these remarks intended to examine the proper degree of privacy which the press should allow to any President and his family. If in the last few months your White House reporters and photographers have been attending church services with regularity, that has surely done them no harm.

On the other hand, I realize that your staff and wire service photographers may be complaining that they do not enjoy the same green privileges at the local golf courses which they once did. It is true that my predecessor did not object as I do to pictures of one's golfing skill in action. But neither on the other hand did he ever bean a Secret Service man.

My topic tonight is a more sober one of concern to publishers as well as editors. **I want to talk about our common responsibilities in the face of a common danger.** The events of recent weeks may have helped to illuminate that challenge for some; but the dimensions of its threat have loomed large on the horizon for many years. Whatever our hopes may be for the future - for reducing this threat or living with it - there is no escaping either the gravity or the totality of its challenge to our survival and to our security - a challenge that confronts us in unaccustomed ways in every sphere of human activity.

This deadly challenge imposes upon our society two requirements of direct concern both to the press and to the President - two requirements that may seem almost contradictory in tone, but which must be reconciled and fulfilled if we are to meet this national peril. I refer, first, to the need for far greater public information; and, second, to the need for far greater official secrecy.

The very word "secrecy" is repugnant in a free and open society; and we are as a people inherently and historically opposed to secret societies, to secret oaths and to secret proceedings. We decided long ago that the dangers of excessive and unwarranted concealment of pertinent facts far outweighed the dangers which are cited to justify it. Even today, there is little value in opposing the threat of a closed society by imitating its arbitrary restrictions. Even today, **there is little value in insuring the survival of our nation if our traditions do not survive with it. And there is very grave danger that an announced need for increased security will be seized upon by those anxious to expand its meaning to the very limits of official censorship and concealment.** That I do not intend to permit to the extent that it's in my control. And no official of my Administration, whether his rank is high or low, civilian or military, should interpret my words here tonight as an excuse to censor the news, to stifle dissent, to cover up our mistakes or to withhold from the press and the public the facts they deserve to know. But I do ask every publisher, every editor, and every newsman in the nation to reexamine his own standards, and to recognize the nature of our country's peril. In time of war, the government and the press have customarily joined in an effort based largely on self-discipline, to prevent unauthorized disclosures to the enemy. In times of "clear and present danger," the courts have held that even the privileged rights of the First Amendment must yield to the public's need for national security.

Today no war has been declared and however fierce the struggle may be, it may never be declared in the traditional fashion. Our way of life is under attack. Those who make themselves our enemy are advancing around the globe. The survival of our friends is in danger. And yet no war has been declared, no borders have been crossed by marching troops, no missiles have been fired.

If the press is awaiting a declaration of war before it imposes the self-discipline of combat conditions, then I can only say that no war ever posed a greater threat to our security. If you are awaiting a finding of "clear and present danger," then I can only say that the danger has never been more clear and its presence has never been more imminent.

It requires a change in outlook, a change in tactics, a change in missions - by the government, by the people, by every businessman or labor leader, and by every newspaper. For we are opposed around the world by a monolithic and ruthless conspiracy that relies primarily on covert means for expanding its sphere of influence - on infiltration instead of invasion, on subversion instead of elections, on intimidation instead of free choice, on guerrillas by night instead of armies by day. It is a system which has conscripted vast human and material resources into the building of a tightly knit, highly efficient machine that combines military, diplomatic, intelligence, economic, scientific and political operations. Its preparations are concealed, not published. Its mistakes are buried, not headlined. Its dissenters are silenced, not praised. No expenditure is questioned, no rumor is printed, no secret is revealed. It conducts the Cold War, in short, with a war-time discipline no democracy would ever hope or wish to match.

Nevertheless, every democracy recognizes the necessary restraints of national security - and the question remains whether those restraints need to be more strictly observed if we are to oppose this kind of attack as well as outright invasion. For the facts of the matter are that this nation's foes have openly boasted of acquiring through our newspapers information they would otherwise hire agents to acquire through theft, bribery or espionage; that details of this nation's covert preparations to counter the enemy's covert operations have been available to every newspaper reader, friend and foe alike; that the size, the strength, the location and the nature of our forces and weapons, and our plans and strategy for their use, have all been pinpointed in the press and other news media to a degree sufficient to satisfy any foreign power; and that, in at least in one case, the publication of details concerning a secret mechanism whereby satellites were followed required its alteration at the expense of considerable time and money.

The newspapers which printed these stories were loyal, patriotic, responsible and well-meaning. Had we been engaged in open warfare, they undoubtedly would not have published such items. But in the absence of open warfare, they recognized only the tests of journalism and not the tests of national security. And my question tonight is whether additional tests should not now be adopted. That question is for you alone to answer. No public official should answer it for you. No governmental plan should impose its restraints against your will. But I would be failing in my duty to the nation, in considering all of the responsibilities that we now bear and all of the means at hand to meet those responsibilities, if I did not commend this problem to your attention, and urge its thoughtful consideration.

On many earlier occasions, I have said - and your newspapers have constantly said - that these are times that appeal to every citizen's sense of sacrifice and self-discipline. They call out to every citizen to weigh his rights and comforts against his obligations to the common good. I cannot now believe that those citizens who serve in the newspaper business consider themselves exempt from that appeal.

I have no intention of establishing a new Office of War Information to govern the flow of news. I am not suggesting any new forms of censorship or new types of security classifications. **I have no easy answer to the dilemma that I have posed, and would not seek to impose it if I had one. But I am asking the members of the newspaper profession and the industry in this country to reexamine their own responsibilities, to consider the degree and the nature of the present danger, and to heed the duty of self-restraint which that danger imposes upon us all.**

Every newspaper now asks itself, with respect to every story: "Is it news?" All I suggest is that you add the question: "Is it in the interest of the national security?" And I hope that every group in America - unions and businessmen and public officials at every level will ask the same question of their endeavors, and subject their actions to the same exacting tests. And should the press of America consider and recommend the voluntary assumption of specific new steps or machinery, I can assure you that we will cooperate whole-heartedly with those recommendations.

Perhaps there will be no recommendations. Perhaps there is no answer to the dilemma faced by a free and open society in a cold and secret war. In times of peace, any discussion of this subject, and any action that results, are both painful and without precedent. But this is a time of peace and peril which knows no precedent in history. **It is the unprecedented nature of this challenge that also gives rise to your second obligation - an obligation which I share and that is our obligation to inform and**

alert the American people to make certain that they possess all the facts that they need, and understand them as well - the perils, the prospects, the purposes of our program and the choices that we face.

No President should fear public scrutiny of his program. For from that scrutiny comes understanding; and from that understanding comes support or opposition and both are necessary. I am not asking your newspapers to support the Administration, but **I am asking your help in the tremendous task of informing and alerting the American people. For I have complete confidence in the response and dedication of our citizens whenever they are fully informed.**

I not only could not stifle controversy among your readers - I welcome it. This Administration intends to be candid about its errors; for as a wise man once said: "An error does not become a mistake until you refuse to correct it." We intend to accept full responsibility for our errors and we expect you to point them out when we miss them.

Without debate, without criticism, no Administration and no country can succeed and no republic can survive. That is why the Athenian lawmaker Solon decreed it a crime for any citizen to shrink from controversy. And **that is why our press was protected by the First Amendment - the only business in America specifically protected by the Constitution - not primarily to amuse and entertain, not to emphasize the trivial and the sentimental, not to simply "give the public what it wants" - but to inform, to arouse, to reflect, to state our dangers and our opportunities, to indicate our crises and our choices, to lead, mold, educate and sometimes even anger public opinion.** This means greater coverage and analysis of international news - for it is no longer far away and foreign but close at hand and local. It means greater attention to improved understanding of the news as well as improved transmission. And it means, finally, that **government at all levels, must meet its obligation to provide you with the fullest possible information outside the narrowest limits of national security - and we intend to do it.**

It was early in the Seventeenth Century that Francis Bacon remarked on three recent inventions already transforming the world: the compass, gunpowder and the printing press. Now the links between the nations first forged by the compass have made us all citizens of the world, the hopes and threats of one becoming the hopes and threats of us all. In that one world's efforts to live together, the evolution of gunpowder to its ultimate limit has warned mankind of the terrible consequences of failure. And so **it is to the printing press - to the recorder of man's deeds, the keeper of his conscience, the courier of his news - that we look for strength and assistance, confident that with your help man will be what he was born to be: free and independent."**

WINNERS AND LOSERS

"It is hard to argue that the current economic malaise was in any way produced by anything resembling pure capitalism. But it is fairly easy to conclude that interventionism was, in fact, the culprit."

— **Marc A. Thiessen**

A new era of government intervention has emerged from the ashes of personal liberty, justice and freedom. Time and time again the federal government has enacted laws that go against the grain of the US Constitution as it simultaneously erodes our abilities to hold our government officials accountable to the Rule of Law. States and American citizens have but a weak voice remaining in the edifices of Washington, DC, even though it was Americans like you and me that established our state and federal governments. **Politicians and government officials have convinced many of us that we are happier when the federal government has the money, power and authority to tend to us from cradle to grave.** As the American public embraces federal government spending on everything from apples to zoos, we encourage and even cause the federal government to race towards becoming an oligarchy in which we lose all our freedoms and cannot hold our government officials accountable to the Rule of Law.

I do not blame the government or its officials. They are only fulfilling their own selfish wants and desires. So how do they do this? Government taxes in order to raise revenue and approves budgets in order to determine where that money is spent. In reality, the system is much more complicated than that. Special interest groups have a voice in who pays taxes and who receives government funding, such as corporations, organizations, government agencies, politicians, and individuals. The way the system is setup, and has always been so, is that government officials pick winners and losers. The winners are those who receive government money and are protected by law. The losers are those who have to pay the taxes and are punished by law. Lobbyists work on behalf of special interests to ensure government funding for their own pet projects.

If you receive government funds, such as a federal pension, Social Security, welfare, or Medicare, you have an incentive to make sure that money keeps rolling in. You may even vote for the person that offers you the most money. If you are one who pays a large share of the taxes, you have an incentive to decrease the amount that the government takes from you. You might vote for the person who promises to reduce your taxes. The fundamental problem is that some politicians encourage class warfare. They want the poor to be angry at the wealthy. They want the uneducated to be angry at the educated. They want people to feel helpless and hopeless. The government wants the population to look towards the government for answers. The government's ultimate goal is to be in charge of everything. That is what all governments want to do. That is the natural state of government.

Let us take a brief look at how our own federal officials have increased the size of their piggy banks. First, the Federal Reserve (a private organization operated by people not elected by the public) is in control of the money supply. Of the total gold reserves held in the United States (~261.5 million ounces) by the federal government or the Federal Reserve as of March 2014, the Federal Reserve of New York's vaults contained about 99.98% of its own gold reserves (~13.45 million ounces) and Fort Knox, KY, stores about 147.3 million ounces. There is a little over 1 billion ounces of gold in circulation. Second, the Sixteenth Amendment gives the federal government the power to tax the individual without setting any upper limits as to how high those taxes could go. The top income tax rate went from 7% in 1913 to over 78% from 1936- 1963.

So what have these government officials done with all this tax revenue? Pork spending or earmarks are a type of spending not related to general government functions that are awards or incentives for political support. There are numerous examples of earmarks. In 2010, Democratic Senator Tom Harkin from Iowa received $7.2 million for his Harkin Grant Program in which some of the funds go to Iowa's public schools. In 2010, the Robert C. Byrd (Democratic Senator from West Virginia) Institute of Advanced Flexible Manufacturing (a statewide facility that provides manufacturers with advanced CNC equipment, workforce development and technical training programs to develop new business and jobs in West Virginia) received $7 million. In 2010, Republican Harold Rogers from Kentucky received $50,000 for the Pulaski County Sheriff Department for helicopter improvements. In 2010, Republican Chris

Shays from Connecticut received $1.9 million for the Pleasure Beach, CT, water taxi service project. Both Republican and Democratic government officials are guilty of pork barrel spending. In these examples, those that won include Iowa's public school system, West Virginia's technical trainees, the Pulaski County Kentucky Sheriff, and the Pleasure Beach water taxi service.

I do not live in any of these states, so when are my representatives going to get money for me and my state? This response will not resolve the underlying problem. It merely empowers government officials to create more earmarks. Since you are paying for these services, would you consider it to be money well spent? The argument is not where the money is going. The fundamental question is whether or not it is the federal government's responsibility to pay for these things. If we let them get away with one earmark, they will simply create more earmarks. Earmarks only benefit those who receive them. It is the government choosing the winners. What if you owned a fleet of boats and were willing to provide water taxi services in Pleasure Beach, CT? You now have to try to out compete the federal government with the law, lawyers, and substantial funding on its side. You are the loser in this scenario.

These are just small samples of how involved government (whether federal, state or local) is in the economy. Government enforces its own goals and agendas, and the more you fund it and not hold it accountable, the more you allow it to pick winners and losers, despite your wishes.

PRESIDENT DWIGHT D. EISENHOWER ON THE MILITARY-INDUSTRIAL COMPLEX

On January 17, 1961, outgoing President Dwight D. Eisenhower delivers his farewell speech to the Nation. The importance of this particular speech is that he warns against the military-industrial complex which selects its own winners and losers, and that as its power increases, the number of personal liberties decrease. He encourages us to be *"an alert and knowledgeable citizenry"* that *"can compel the proper meshing of the huge industrial and military machinery of defense with our peaceful methods and goals, so that security and liberty may prosper together."*

Military spending, corporate welfare, energy subsidies, and bank bailouts are just some examples of how an uncontrolled government reduces the freedoms and liberties of the masses in exchange for financial support from select individuals. This is not healthy for a democratic society, and both Democrats and Republicans are guilty of this. There are solutions to this problem. The 34th President of the United States stated, *"Now this conjunction of an immense military establishment and a large arms industry is new in the American experience. The total influence - economic, political, even spiritual - is felt in every city, every Statehouse, every office of the Federal government. We recognize the imperative need for this development. Yet, we must not fail to comprehend its grave implications. Our toil, resources, and livelihood are all involved. So is the very structure of our society."* He warns us to remain vigilant and wise in order to protect our freedoms, values and livelihoods.

Farewell Address
Dwight D. Eisenhower
January 17, 1961

"Good evening, my fellow Americans.

First, I should like to express my gratitude to the radio and television networks for the opportunities they have given me over the years to bring reports and messages to our nation. My special thanks go to them for the opportunity of addressing you this evening.

Three days from now, after half century in the service of our country, I shall lay down the responsibilities of office as, in traditional and solemn ceremony, the authority of the Presidency is vested in my successor. This evening, I come to you with a message of leave-taking and farewell, and to share a few final thoughts with you, my countrymen.

Like every other citizen, I wish the new President, and all who will labor with him, Godspeed. I pray that the coming years will be blessed with peace and prosperity for all.

Our people expect their President and the Congress to find essential agreement on issues of great moment, the wise resolution of which will better shape the future of the nation. My own relations with the Congress, which began on a remote and tenuous basis when, long ago, a member of the Senate appointed me to West Point, have since ranged to the intimate during the war and immediate post-war period, and finally to the mutually interdependent during these past eight years. In this final relationship, the Congress and the Administration have, on most vital issues, cooperated well, to serve the nation good, rather than mere partisanship, and so have assured that the business of the nation should go forward. So, my official relationship with the Congress ends in a feeling - on my part - of gratitude that we have been able to do so much together.

We now stand ten years past the midpoint of a century that has witnessed four major wars among great nations. Three of these involved our own country. Despite these holocausts, America is today the strongest, the most influential, and most productive nation in the world. Understandably proud of this pre-eminence, we yet realize that America's leadership and prestige depend, not merely upon our unmatched material progress, riches, and military strength, but on how we use our power in the interests of world peace and human betterment.

Throughout America's adventure in free government, our basic purposes have been to keep the peace, to foster progress in human achievement, and to enhance liberty, dignity, and integrity among peoples and among nations. To strive for less would be unworthy of a free and religious people. Any failure traceable to arrogance, or our lack of comprehension, or readiness to sacrifice would inflict upon us grievous hurt, both at home and abroad.

Progress toward these noble goals is persistently threatened by the conflict now engulfing the world. It commands our whole attention, absorbs our very beings. We face a hostile ideology global in scope, atheistic in character, ruthless in purpose, and insidious in method. Unhappily, the danger it poses promises to be of indefinite duration. To meet it successfully, there is called for, not so much the emotional and transitory sacrifices of crisis, but rather those which enable us to carry forward steadily, surely, and without complaint the burdens of a prolonged and complex struggle with liberty the stake. Only thus shall we remain, despite every provocation, on our charted course toward permanent peace and human betterment.

Crises there will continue to be. In meeting them, whether foreign or domestic, great or small, there is a recurring temptation to feel that some spectacular and costly action could become the miraculous solution to all current difficulties. A huge increase in newer elements of our defenses; development of unrealistic programs to cure every ill in agriculture; a dramatic expansion in basic and applied research - these and many other possibilities, each possibly promising in itself, may be suggested as the only way to the road we wish to travel. *But* **each proposal must be weighed in the light of a broader consideration: the need to maintain balance in and among national**

programs, balance between the private and the public economy, balance between the cost and hoped for advantages, balance between the clearly necessary and the comfortably desirable, balance between our essential requirements as a nation and the duties imposed by the nation upon the individual, balance between actions of the moment and the national welfare of the future. Good judgment seeks balance and progress. Lack of it eventually finds imbalance and frustration. The record of many decades stands as proof that our people and their Government have, in the main, understood these truths and have responded to them well, in the face of threat and stress. But threats, new in kind or degree, constantly arise. Of these, I mention two only.

A vital element in keeping the peace is our military establishment. Our arms must be mighty, ready for instant action, so that no potential aggressor may be tempted to risk his own destruction. Our military organization today bears little relation to that known of any of my predecessors in peacetime, or, indeed, by the fighting men of World War II or Korea.

Until the latest of our world conflicts, the United States had no armaments industry. American makers of plowshares could, with time and as required, make swords as well. But we can no longer risk emergency improvisation of national defense. We have been compelled to create a permanent armaments industry of vast proportions. Added to this, three and a half million men and women are directly engaged in the defense establishment. We annually spend on military security alone more than the net income of all United States corporations.

Now this conjunction of an immense military establishment and a large arms industry is new in the American experience. The total influence - economic, political, even spiritual - is felt in every city, every Statehouse, every office of the Federal government. We recognize the imperative need for this development. Yet, we must not fail to comprehend its grave implications. Our toil, resources, and livelihood are all involved. So is the very structure of our society.

In the councils of government, we must guard against the acquisition of unwarranted influence, whether sought or unsought, by the military-industrial complex. The potential for the disastrous rise of misplaced power exists and will persist. We must never let the weight of this combination endanger our liberties or democratic processes. We should take nothing for granted. Only an alert and knowledgeable citizenry can compel the proper meshing of the huge industrial and military machinery of defense with our peaceful methods and goals, so that security and liberty may prosper together.

Akin to, and largely responsible for the sweeping changes in our industrial-military posture, has been the technological revolution during recent decades. In this revolution, research has become central; it also becomes more formalized, complex, and costly. A steadily increasing share is conducted for, by, or at the direction of, the Federal government.

Today, the solitary inventor, tinkering in his shop, has been overshadowed by task forces of scientists in laboratories and testing fields. In the same fashion, the free university, historically the fountainhead of free ideas and scientific discovery, has experienced a revolution in the conduct of research. Partly because of the huge costs involved, a government contract becomes virtually a substitute for intellectual curiosity. For every old blackboard there are now hundreds of new electronic computers. The prospect of domination of the nation's scholars by Federal employment, project allocations, and the power of money is ever present - and is gravely to be regarded.

Yet, in holding scientific research and discovery in respect, as we should, **we must also be alert to the equal and opposite danger that public policy could itself become the captive of a scientific-technological elite. It is the task of statesmanship to mold, to balance, and to integrate these and other forces, new and old, within the principles of our democratic system - ever aiming toward the supreme goals of our free society.**

Another factor in maintaining balance involves the element of time. As we peer into society's future, **we - you and I, and our government - must avoid the impulse to live only for today, plundering for our own ease and convenience the precious resources of tomorrow. We cannot mortgage the material assets of our grandchildren without risking the loss also of their political and spiritual heritage. We want democracy to survive for all generations to come, not to become the insolvent phantom of tomorrow.**

During the long lane of the history yet to be written, America knows that this world of ours, ever growing smaller, must avoid becoming a community of dreadful fear and hate, and be, instead, a proud confederation of mutual trust and respect. Such a confederation must be one of equals. The weakest must come to the conference table with the same confidence as do we, protected as we are by our moral, economic, and military strength. That table, though scarred by many past frustrations - past frustrations, cannot be abandoned for the certain agony of disarmament - of the battlefield.

Disarmament, with mutual honor and confidence, is a continuing imperative. Together we must learn how to compose differences, not with arms, but with intellect and decent purpose. Because this need is so sharp and apparent, I confess that I lay down my official responsibilities in this field with a definite sense of disappointment. As one who has witnessed the horror and the lingering sadness of war, as one who knows that another war could utterly destroy this civilization which has been so slowly and painfully built over thousands of years, I wish I could say tonight that a lasting peace is in sight.

Happily, I can say that war has been avoided. Steady progress toward our ultimate goal has been made. But so much remains to be done. As a private citizen, I shall never cease to do what little I can to help the world advance along that road. So, in this, my last good night to you as your President, I thank you for the many opportunities you have given me for public service in war and in peace. I trust in that - in that - in that service you find some things worthy. As for the rest of it, I know you will find ways to improve performance in the future.

You and I, my fellow citizens, need to be strong in our faith that all nations, under God, will reach the goal of peace with justice. May we be ever unswerving in devotion to principle, confident but humble with power, diligent in pursuit of the Nations' great goals.

To all the peoples of the world, I once more give expression to America's prayerful and continuing aspiration: We pray that peoples of all faiths, all races, all nations, may have their great human needs satisfied; that those now denied opportunity shall come to enjoy it to the full; that all who yearn for freedom may experience its few spiritual blessings. Those who have freedom will understand, also, its heavy responsibility; that all who are insensitive to the needs of others will learn charity; and that the sources - scourges of poverty, disease, and ignorance will be made [to] disappear from the earth; and that in the goodness of time, all peoples will come to live together in a peace guaranteed by the binding force of mutual respect and love.

Now, on Friday noon, I am to become a private citizen. I am proud to do so. I look forward to it. Thank you, and good night."

ZIMBABWE

"It may be necessary to use methods other than constitutional ones."

— Robert Mugabe (President of Zimbabwe)

Zimbabwe is an extreme example of an oligarchy destroying a nation. On April 18, 1980, Zimbabwe (aka Rhodesia) gained its independence from Britain. It is land-locked and is located in southeastern Africa just north of South Africa. Robert Mugabe became the Prime Minister and used part of the $15 million it received from Nigeria to purchase newspaper companies owned by South Africans which increased the government's control and influence over the local news reporting agencies. The national government kept in force a "state of emergency" due to continuing anti-government dissension. This gave the government widespread powers under the "Law and Order Maintenance Act," including the right to detain persons without charge, which it used quite frequently.

In January 1988, following changes to the constitution abolishing the Prime Minister position, Mugabe became President. In 1990 the government abolished the Senate and increased the House of Assembly's membership to include members nominated by and loyal to Mugabe. Elections in March 1990 resulted in another overwhelming victory for Mugabe in which his party won 117 of the 120 election seats. The government began further amending the constitution and the laws of the country. In the months leading up to the Presidential elections of March 2002, Mugabe supporters used voter intimidation and suppression of the opposition to get re-elected. In September 2005 Mugabe nationalized all land which removed all private land ownership rights, which caused severe food shortages and mass hunger.

Zimbabwe had the second highest monthly inflation rate in history, second only to Hungary in 1946. In 1996, the yearly inflation rate was 16%. In 2006, it was 1281%. In 2007, it was 66,212%. In July 2008, the monthly inflation rate was 231 million percent. At its peak in November 2008, the monthly inflation rate was 79.6 billion percent. As a direct result of this hyperinflation, Zimbabwe currency was no longer used or accepted by most people. It became more worthless than the Confederate dollar after the US Civil War. Anyone who owned property, investments or currency in Zimbabwe saw their assets lose all their value. The unemployment rate in January 2009 was 94%. So many people fled the country that the population fell from 12.7 million in 2005 to 11.3 million in 2008. Agricultural production of soybeans and corn decreased 42% between 1999 and 2008.

Robert Mugabe's supporters used voter intimidation and voter suppression to ensure victory, and under the Mugabe regime, land was nationalized, poverty significantly increased, and monetary inflation was one of the worst in history. Robert Mugabe is in complete control over the country's rich mineral resources, which are significant and include: gold, diamonds, asbestos, chrome, coal, platinum, nickel, copper and methane gas. While the overwhelming majority of the population lives in poverty, Robert Mugabe and those that are part of his inner circle enjoy the bounties of that country's harvest.

SPOTLIGHT ON KARL ROVE

Karl Rove is one of the most influential people of the 21st Century. He was critical in getting George W. Bush elected as President in 2000 and re-elected in 2004. Born on Christmas

Day 1950 in Denver, Colorado, he was the second of five children. His mother was a gift shop manager and his adoptive father was a geologist. The family moved to Salt Lake City in 1965 where Rove entered high school and became a skilled debater. He was the quintessential scrawny nerd complete with briefcase and pocket protector. He was encouraged by a teacher to run for class senate. As part of his campaign strategy he rode in the back of a convertible inside the school gym sitting between two attractive girls before his election speech. He won the election.

In 1968 he was part of the re-election campaign for US Senator Wallace Bennett. He was elected to a third term, and his son Bob Bennett became Rove's friend and eventually US Senator from Utah. In the fall of 1970, Rove used a false identity to enter the campaign office of Democrat Alan J. Dixon, who was running for Treasurer of Illinois. He stole a thousand sheets of paper with campaign letterhead, printed fake campaign rally fliers promising "free beer, free food, girls and a good time", and distributed them at rock concerts and homeless shelters, with the effect of disrupting Dixon's rally. (Dixon eventually won the election). Rove's role would not become publicly known until August 1973. Rove told the Dallas Morning News in 1999, "It was a youthful prank at the age of 19 and I regret it." Rove later wrote that when he was nominated to the Board for International Broadcasting by President George H.W. Bush, Senator Dixon did not kill his nomination. In Rove's account, "Dixon displayed more grace than I had shown and kindly excused this youthful prank."

In June 1971, Rove took a paid position as Executive Director of the College Republican National Committee. Joe Abate, who was National Chairman of the College Republicans at the time, became a mentor to Rove. Rove traveled extensively, participating as an instructor at weekend seminars for campus conservatives across the country. He was an active participant in Richard Nixon's 1972 Presidential campaign. Rove held the position of executive director of the College Republicans until early 1973. He left the job to spend five months, without pay, campaigning full time for the position of national chairman of the organization, for the 1973-1975 term.

The College Republicans summer 1973 convention at the Lake of the Ozarks resort in Missouri was quite contentious. Rove's opponent was Robert Edgeworth of Michigan. In the end, there were two votes conducted by two convention chairs, and two winners - Rove and Edgeworth - each of whom delivered an acceptance speech. After the convention, both Edgeworth and Rove appealed to Republican National Committee Chairman George H. W. Bush, each contending that he was the new College Republican chairman.

George H. W. Bush chose Rove to be chairman of the College Republicans. Bush then wrote Edgeworth a letter saying that he had concluded that Rove had fairly won the vote at the convention. As National Chairman, Rove introduced Bush to Atwater, who had taken Rove's job as the College Republican's executive director, and who would become Bush's main campaign strategist in future years. Bush hired Rove as a special assistant in the Republican National Committee, a job Rove left in 1974 to become executive assistant to the co-chair of the RNC, Richard D. Obenshain.

In recent years, Karl Rove served as Senior Advisor to President George W. Bush from 2000–2007 and Deputy Chief of Staff from 2004–2007. At the White House he oversaw the Offices of Strategic Initiatives, Political Affairs, Public Liaison, and Intergovernmental Affairs and was Deputy Chief of Staff for Policy, coordinating the White House policy-making process.

Before he became known as "The Architect" of President Bush's 2000 and 2004 campaigns, he was president of Karl Rove & Company, an Austin-based public affairs firm that worked for Republican candidates, non-partisan causes, and non-profit groups. His clients included over 75 Republican US Senate, Congressional, and gubernatorial candidates in 24 states, as well as the Moderate Party of Sweden.

Rove writes weekly for the Wall Street Journal and is the author of the New York Times Bestseller, "Courage and Consequence: My Life as a Conservative in the Fight." He has written for various publications, including The Daily Beast, Financial Times, Forbes, FoxNews.com, HumanEvents.com, Newsweek, The Times, Washington Post, and The Weekly Standard.

He has taught graduate students at UT Austin's Lyndon B. Johnson School of Public Affairs and undergraduates in a joint appointment from the Journalism and Government departments at the university. He was also a faculty member at the Salzburg Seminar. He was previously a member of the Board of International Broadcasting, which oversaw the operations of Radio Free Europe and Radio Liberty, and served on the White House Fellows regional selection panel. He was also a member of the Boards of Regents at Texas Women's Union and East Texas State University. Rove served on the University of Texas Chancellor's Council Executive Committee and on the Board of Trustees for the Texas Parks and Wildlife Foundation and the Texas State History Museum Foundation. He was a member of the McDonald Observatory Board of Visitors and the Texas Philosophical Society.

Rove has been described by columnist Michael Barone in U.S. News & World Report as "unique... no Presidential appointee has ever had such a strong influence on politics and policy, and none is likely to do so again anytime soon." Washington Post columnist David Broder has called Rove a master political strategist whose "game has always been long term... and he plays it with an intensity and attention to detail that few can match." Fred Barnes, executive editor of The Weekly Standard, has called Rove "the greatest political mind of his generation... He knows history, understands the moods of the public, and is a visionary on matters of public policy." The following is an article posted on the Wall Street Journal by Karl Rove discussing the importance of moderate / independent voters in getting elected to office. As a political strategist, he provides incite into the voting and electoral process.

Karl Rove
Independents Will Decide The 2014 Elections
Wall Street Journal
January 16, 2014

"Independents Will Decide The 2014 Elections - Debunking the myth that turning out the base alone is enough to win.

Among political urban legends, one of the more persistent is "base elections" - the notion that successful campaigns can rely simply on turning out a party's hard-core supporters. Nonsense. The party that wins independents wins Congress. Energizing core supporters is necessary but insufficient.

Democrats took control of the House in 2006 by winning independents 57% to 39%, according to national exit polls. They kept control in 2008 by carrying independents 51% to 43%. In 2010, Republicans won back the House by sweeping independents 56% to 37% and retained their majority two years later by taking independents 51% to 44%. Independents made up between 26% and 29% of voters in those elections while constituting between 34% and 40% of the electorate.

The independent voter will be even more important in this year's midterm. Last week Gallup announced that in 2013 the percentage of the electorate that self-identified as independent rose to 42%, the highest share since it began conducting surveys by phone a quarter century ago. The percentage of the electorate that was independent was 40% in 2012 and 36% in 2008.

The alarming news for Republicans in the Gallup survey is that the percentage of voters who identify with the GOP is the lowest since 1983 - 25%, a drop of three points from 2012. The Democratic share of the electorate is 31%, where it's been since 2010 (down from a quarter-century high of 36% in 2008).

While President Obama's approval rating took a dive last year, the GOP didn't gain as much of an advantage as it might have. Independents strongly disapproved of last October's government shutdown and blamed Republicans. The more dysfunctional Washington appears, the more independents blame everyone.

The Republican-controlled House appears unlikely to provoke another shutdown; to do so would be insanity. But avoiding disaster isn't enough. Strengthening their House majority and taking control of the Senate will require Republicans to present a constructive conservative agenda on big issues that win over independents. Fortunately for Republicans, independents this year look more like Republicans than Democrats on those issues and are therefore more "gettable" by GOP candidates.

A Jan. 7 Quinnipiac University poll underscores this. Forty-seven percent of Democrats are very or somewhat "satisfied with the way things are going in the nation today." But only 19% of independents and 12% of Republicans say the same. On Mr. Obama's "handling his job as president," 81% of Democrats approve while only 35% of independents and 9% of Republicans do. Among Democrats, 86% believe Mr. Obama is honest and trustworthy and 10% don't. Fifty-three percent of independents and 84% of Republicans say he is not.

More than three-quarters of Democrats (76%) approve of the president's handling of the economy, compared with only 36% of independents and 7% of Republicans. Quinnipiac found 71% of Democrats approve of the president's handling of the federal budget while 66% of independents and 89% of Republicans don't.

Then there's ObamaCare. Seventy-one percent of Democrats approve of the president's handling of health care and 80% support his Affordable Care Act. Independents give Mr. Obama a miserable 31% approval on handling the issue and 35% approve of ObamaCare. Only 6% of Republicans approve of Mr. Obama's handling of health care while 9% approve of ObamaCare.

The Quinnipiac Poll found that independents would be less likely to vote for "a candidate for Congress" who "supports Mr. Obama" by a better than 2-1 margin (44% to 20%). It is likely that independents look even more like Republicans in the seven red and half dozen purple states with Democratic senators where control of the upper chamber will be decided.

The reason? Independents are not parked in the middle between the two parties. They are spread out across the political spectrum. Independents tend to look like the rest of the voters in their state or district but with much less party loyalty, political interest or civic engagement and, compared with partisans, lack a cohesive, organized belief system.

This could be a Republican year if the GOP understands how important independents are to deciding elections and cultivates them. Criticizing Democrats who have loyally backed Mr. Obama is part of what's needed. But criticism comes naturally and easily. A comprehensive agenda focused on the economy, spending, deficits, health care and energy is more difficult. And more important."

Chapter 9

YOUR PERSONAL JOURNEY

"Those who stand for nothing fall for anything."
— **Alexander Hamilton**

Now that we have provided some basic information as to the character of the modern political framework within our nation, it is now time to develop your own social and political philosophies. This chapter is dedicated to those people who are confused about the issues; who should I vote for, or on which side of the political spectrum should I lean toward. During many of my speeches I give around the country, I am often confronted by people asking the same question: "Which politician is right and which one is wrong?"

Young adults still in school find themselves with this same dilemma as the adults in this country. In my early days with a large business association, I would look at a particular legislative issue and weigh out both sides to see what was best for the United States. It was very informative and thought provoking to be able to look at both sides of a piece of legislation and make up my own mind. Making up one's own mind on what you believe takes knowing what your personal philosophy is. What will affect you and America as a country can come down to your personal perspective and philosophy.

PERSONAL PHILOSOPHY

Your personal philosophy is related to how you conduct yourself when no one else is watching. What are you like and what do you think about when you are by yourself? Your personal philosophy is your personal guidance system in life. What do you stand for? What do you desire to accomplish with your life? And more importantly, what you don't want. How many people do you want controlling your outcome and looking over your shoulder?

I truly get a kick out of people trying to sell me on what their personal belief system is. (Fill in the blank) _____ is the most important issue of our time. Can you have a separate personal and political philosophy? Yes you can. I have seen it many times before. But there are things that affect both, such as integrity. If you do not have personal integrity you will not have political integrity. They are difficult to separate.

In his autobiography, Benjamin Franklin wrote, *"In order to secure my credit and character as a tradesmen, I took care not only to be in reality industrious & frugal, but to avoid all appearances of the contrary."* Franklin is well-respected for his many accomplishments as a colonel in the Pennsylvania militia, printer of the *Pennsylvania Gazette*, publisher of *Poor Richard's Almanack*, member of the Continental Congress representing Pennsylvania and ambassador to both England and France. But according to Franklin, integrity has more value to him than any of his accomplishments.

Also, Leonard Roberts, former CEO of Arby's (1985-1990) – a fast food restaurant chain - became CEO of Shoney's – a family dining restaurant chain - in 1990. He made Arby's profitable, but then resigned from the board of directors when Arby's owner threatened to withhold bonuses for Robert's staff, and not to give promised help to Arby's franchisees in order to further increase profits. In retaliation for his stand, Arby's owner fired Roberts.

Roberts was then hired as CEO of Shoney's. He found that Shoney's was the subject of a large racial discrimination lawsuit by the National Association for the Advancement of Colored People (NAACP). Shoney's owner not only would not hire African-Americans, but also fired any restaurant manager who did. Roberts promised that the suit would be settled fairly. Shoney's owner agreed to pay up and settle, but only if Roberts would resign. Roberts said, *"My stand on integrity was getting a little hard on my wife and kids. However, I knew it had to be done. There was no other way."* Ultimately, Roberts became CEO of RadioShack, and a year after that, CEO of Tandy's, which owned RadioShack.

In 1987, President Ronald Reagan presented Leonard Roberts with the Presidential Private Sector Initiative Award. In 1991, Roberts was honored with the annual Business Leadership Award presented by *Restaurant Business* magazine. He also received the B'nai B'rith International Distinguished Achievement Award and the 1991 Multi-Unit Foodservice Chain Operator's Award. In 1992, Roberts received the Wall Street Bronze Critics Award. Roberts was named *Brandweek* magazine's Retailing Marketer of the Year in 1996. In 1997, Roberts was named Sales & Marketing Executive of the Year by the Sales & Marketing Executives of Fort Worth, Texas. Roberts says, *"You cannot fake it. You must stand up for what is right regardless. You cannot maintain your integrity 90 percent and be a leader. It's got to be 100 percent."*

Having a personal philosophy will help you decide your political positions, such as: who to vote for, what to vote on, and how to keep America moving forward as a strong country. You cannot have a republic when the people who vote are not educated. As Alexander Hamilton said in the beginning of this chapter, *"Those who stand for nothing fall for anything."*

POLITICAL PHILOSOPHY

Your political philosophy is about what you value within a society or culture. What would you like the American society to do or be like? It is often based upon what you value related to these main concepts:

1. The US Constitution as the supreme law of the land

2. The role of judges

3. How much gun control should there be

4. Whether to value a person based upon their merit and character or because of their gender and ethnicity

5. The role of business in society

6. Which a person values more: an unborn child or his/her mother

7. US position in the world

8. The role of taxation in society

9. The size of government

10. The role of God (or superior being) in society and government

11. The level of tolerance towards social inequity

12. How should we produce and distribute energy

13. Who do we allow into the country

14. Who should make the final decisions related to the education of our children

15. What is our role in protecting the environment

16. The role of government related to health care

17. The role of the country's military and police force

Each political party has their own solutions to these and other issues. As of 2011, there are five political parties with over 200,000 registered voters within their ranks: Democratic, Republican, Constitution, Green and Libertarian.

Democratic Party

Despite the long historical legacy of the Democratic Party in US political history, only a few Americans can state the basic facts about its history. Democrats dominated US politics in two distinct time periods: 1828-1860 and 1932-1994. The Democratic Party was established in 1829 when Andrew Jackson became the 7th President of the Unites States. In those days, Democrats were in favor of slavery and had widespread support in the Southern states where slavery was part of everyday life.

After the Civil War, the Democratic party was the party of big business. They were able to perfect the urban political machine long before the Civil War by getting loyal votes from immigrants and others who were given jobs and services. The combination of large urban support in the North and unwavering support in the South, paved the way for the Democrats to often win the Presidency or control of Congress. Between the Civil War and the Great Depression, Democrats stood primarily for the oppression of African Americans.

It all changed when, Franklin D. Roosevelt was elected in 1932 and immediately began to work on the New Deal. It was designed to bring the US closer to the European countries in providing social safety nets for those *"unfortunate victims of the ruthless side effects of the industrial economy."* Southern African Americans were aligned with the Republican Party until the 1960s when the Democrats under President Lyndon Johnson finally enacted and enforced a meaningful civil rights act. Johnson also led the Democrats to extend the New Deal.

The modern Democratic Party believes that *"every American, whatever their background or station in life, should have the chance to get a good education, to work at a good job with good wages, to raise and provide for a family, to live in safe surroundings, and to retire with dignity and security. Democrats believe that quality and affordable health care is a basic right, and that each succeeding generation should have the opportunity, through hard work, service and sacrifice, to enjoy a brighter future than the last."*

Republican Party

Founded in Northern states in 1854 by antislavery activists, modernizers, ex-Whigs and ex-Free Soldiers, the Republican Party quickly became the principal opposition to the Democratic Party. It first came to power in 1860 with the election of Abraham Lincoln to the Presidency and oversaw the US Civil War and Reconstruction. The first official party convention was held on July 6, 1854, in Jackson, Michigan. The Republican's initial base was in the Northeast and the upper Midwest. Early Republican ideology was reflected in the 1856 slogan *"free labor, free land, free men."* Free labor referred to the Republican opposition to slave labor and a belief in independent artisans and businessmen. Free land referred to Republican opposition to a plantation system whereby the rich could buy up all the good farm land and work it with slaves, leaving the yeoman independent farmers the leftovers. The early Republican Party had the primary goal of restricting the expansion of slavery.

The Republican Party's success created factions within the party in the 1870s. Those who felt that Reconstruction had been accomplished and was continued mostly to promote the large-scale corruption tolerated by President Ulysses S. Grant nominated Horace Greeley for the Presidency. The main issue that divided the Stalwarts and the Half-Breeds was political patronage. The Stalwarts (which included Chester A. Arthur) were in favor of political patronage, while the Half-Breeds (led by Maine Senator James G. Blaine) were against it.

The Republican Party supported business, the gold standard, high tariffs to promote economic growth, high wages and high profits, generous pensions for Union veterans, and (after 1893) the annexation of Hawaii. They supported the Protestants who demanded Prohibition (the ban on production, sale and distribution of alcohol).

After the two terms of Democrat Grover Cleveland, the election of William McKinley in 1896 is widely seen as a resurgence of Republican dominance and is sometimes cited as a realigning election. McKinley promised that high tariffs would end the severe hardship caused by the Panic of 1893, and that the Republican Party would guarantee a sort of pluralism in which all groups would benefit. The Republicans were cemented as the party of business. Theodore Roosevelt was the 26th President of the United States (1901–1909). Republicans controlled the Presidency throughout the 1920s, running on a platform of opposition to the League of Nations, high tariffs, and promotion of business interests. Warren G. Harding, Calvin Coolidge and Herbert Hoover were resoundingly elected in 1920, 1924, and 1928 respectively. The pro-business policies of the decade seemed to produce an unprecedented prosperity until the Wall Street Crash of 1929 heralded the Great Depression.

The New Deal coalition of Democrat Franklin D. Roosevelt controlled American politics for most of the next three decades, excepting the two-term Presidency of Republican Dwight D. Eisenhower. African Americans began moving toward favoring the Democratic Party during Roosevelt's time. After Roosevelt took office in 1933, New Deal legislation sailed through Congress at lightning speed. In the 1934 midterm elections, 10 Republican senators went down to defeat, leaving them with only 25 against 71 Democrats. The House of Representatives was split in a similar ratio. Republicans in Congress heavily criticized the "Second New Deal" and likened it to class warfare and socialism, but they did not have the votes to block any legislation.

The volume of legislation, and the inability of the Republicans to block it, soon elevated the level of opposition to Roosevelt. Conservative Democrats, mostly from the South, joined with Republicans led by Senator Robert Taft to create the conservative coalition, which dominated domestic issues in Congress until 1964. The Republicans recaptured Congress in 1946 after gaining 13 seats in the Senate and 55 seats in the House.

The second half of the 20th Century saw election or succession of Republican Presidents Dwight D. Eisenhower, Richard Nixon, Gerald Ford, Ronald Reagan, George H. W. Bush and George W. Bush. The Republican Party, led by House Republican Minority Whip Newt Gingrich campaigning on a *Contract with America*, was elected to majorities to both houses of Congress in the Republican Revolution of 1994. The Senate majority lasted until 2001, when the Senate became split evenly but was regained in the 2002 elections. Republican majorities in both the House and Senate were held until the Democrats regained control in the mid-term elections of 2006. In the 21st Century, the Republican Party has been defined by social conservatism, a preemptive war foreign policy intended to defeat terrorism and promote global democracy, supply-side economics, support for gun ownership, and deregulation.

Constitution Party

The Constitution Party is a conservative political party founded as the US Taxpayers Party in 1992. The party's official name was changed to the Constitution Party in 1999. It ranks third nationally amongst all United States political parties in registered voters, with 438,222 registered members as of October 2008. The Constitution Party advocates a platform that they believe reflects the Founding Fathers' original intent of the US Constitution, principles found in the Declaration of Independence, and morals taken from the Bible.

Green Party

The Green Party has been active as a third party since the 1980s. The party first gained widespread public attention during Ralph Nader's second Presidential run in 2000. The Green Party has won elected office mostly at the local level, such as city council members. In 2005, the Green Party had

305,000 registered members. During the 2006 elections the party had ballot access in 31 states. The Green Party emphasizes environmentalism, social justice, respect for diversity, and nonviolence.

Libertarian Party

The Libertarian Party was founded on December 11, 1971. It claims more than 200,000 registered voters and more than 600 people in public office, including mayors, county executives, county-council members, school-board members, and other local officials. It has more people in office than all other minor parties combined. The political platform of the Libertarian Party reflects its particular brand of libertarianism, favoring minimally regulated, laissez-faire markets, strong civil liberties, minimally regulated migration across borders, and non-interventionism in foreign policy that respects freedom of trade and travel to all foreign countries.

YOUR PARTY, YOUR DECISION

Have you ever thought about why you're a Democrat, or a Republican, or a Libertarian, or a Green? If someone asked you what party you belonged to and why, would you be prepared enough to respond, assuming you consider yourself to be of a certain party? If someone asked you if you believe in everything the Democratic Party stands for, as an example, would you be able to say yes with absolute certainty? Do you even know all of the platforms that the Democratic Party even pursues? What about the Republican Party; are you absolutely sure that you know about all of the positions they represent? Sometimes it's baffling that someone would pick one or two issues and then go with a party on those issues alone, as if there are no independents or other parties that take the same exact stances on those issues. I have also heard the opposite excuse as well. I do not vote because I don't like any of them. They are all corrupt.

The reasons that explain these occurrences simply do not satisfy me, such as aligning yourself with the same political party as your parents, friends, or coworkers. You need to take a step back, and analyze their positions carefully. Do you know why they vote for a certain party? Are you of the same alignment because their ideas are firmly engraved into your brain?

It does not have to be this way, but it happens a lot. Otherwise, it's due to ignorance, I mean how many people can claim that they know all of the party's platforms and their stances. My guess would be not many, and I would be right.

The two big shots, the Democrats and the Republicans, are backed by the people as well as corporate interest. It's true. They pull in a lot of money from donations, it's simply not fair. People often vote for only these two because people feel like voting for anyone else outside of these two parties is a waste of a vote. No one should ever feel like their vote is being wasted, ever. Why should there only ever be two candidates we can vote on and not feel like the other candidates are a waste of time? The world is not in black and white. The world is not one way or the other, it's simply not true. There are not only two opinions on any matter. Let's not argue about the different colors within each party; we all know that these two parties are virtually in the center when you look at the grand scheme of political alignments. So the question becomes, will these two parties be from now until forever the only two "choices" that America really has, or is the public eventually going to do its research and vote for their truly best match?

With the development of the Internet, it's simply inexcusable not to know what the major party platforms are, as well as the platforms of independent candidates and the minor parties. So many hours of the day are spent, wasted away from unproductive tasks, such as posting selfies, reading Facebook walls, and Twittering what you had for dinner. Why not do a

Google search on Ralph Nader? Don't take a look at just what you disagree with him on, take a look at his entire platform.

His beliefs on all issues is what's important, because come election time you're not going to be able to pick just the one or two viewpoints you agree with, you have to take along the entire bag of ideas each candidate carries. If you're a financial conservative, but disagree with the war, are you willing to forfeit that disagreement to get the financial policies that you'd like? That is the kind of question that everyone should be struggling with. But the people hardly ever are torn in this manner. How can that be? How can so many people agree on the exact same ideas on every issue? It's not probable. I wouldn't want a country whose population thinks the exact same things anyway, because then there's no debate, there's no questions asked, and there's no criticism. People need feedback, without it, people continue to make the same stupid mistakes or the same sorts of actions that could be corrected or improved.

Right now, the Democrats correct the Republicans, and the Republicans correct the Democrats. But what if they're both wrong? Who's correcting the both of them? I urge you to take a look at the different platforms that exist in the United States. Do a Wikipedia search on all of the major political parties and then on some of the other independent candidates. Get to know where you truly stand on the issues and which party satisfies a particular issue the best. Then decide where your alignment truly is. No stupid online quiz is going to be able to tell you what party you belong to, it's nonsense. It would take a very long time for a quiz to know absolutely how you feel on every possible issue. It's hard for a quiz to know how you feel about even a single issue! Feelings are hard to use as empirical data. Only you can know where you are on the political spectrum.

Knowledge is power here, and the power to change the social and political climate in the United States should be a powerful motivator for anyone. Why should anyone pick the better of two evils? Why can't someone pick the best candidate for their own views? Why should two parties influenced heavily by lobbyist's control be what the American people want? Why do people have such a poor view of government? Could it possibly be because they were forced to choose a candidate they did not much want, because they wanted the other candidate even less?

THE 3 C'S

If you want to become more than what you are, first you have to develop the 3 C's. My Three C's are Character, Communication and Commitment toward excellence. As I travel around the country and give my lectures and motivational talks, I always leave my audience with my Three C's. It's amazing to me after people listen to my P.R.I.D.E. CD series they always remember the Three C's. I truly believe that if we teach our children the Three C's and we live by them, we will have a great life, not only in business, but in our personal life as well.

The first C is Character. This is the fundamental foundation of all of them. The granddaddy, the big Kahuna - if you miss this one you need to crawl in a hole, go away and resurface after you have fixed this big C. If you don't have this one, your kids, your family, and your business life will suffer from mediocrity. You will be labeled mediocre and unreliable; a big mark on your forehead. Character is who and what you are when no one else is looking. It's going back to the cashier when she gives you too much money in change. Character is the stuff that makes a strong leader. It's not only doing the "Right Thing" it's doing what is Right ALL THE TIME. You can have very little talent and lack all the skills to have a good life, but if you are a person who possesses a strong Character you will develop the abilities and hone the life skills to become a success in your life. What a great legacy to leave to your children, to be passed on generation to generation.

The second C is Communication. This is a skill that is required to do well in business and life. You must master not only good, but great communication skills. This skill can be taught and mastered to perfection. I have always believed that the world is not run by the academics, but by the great communicators. Study history and you will find the giant leaders of this great nation all had the ability to move mountains with their communication abilities. It is truly the art of persuasion at its best. As expressed by the many speeches presented in this book, this is a very powerful skill to possess. Over time, it has and always will be, used for the good and unfortunately for evil as well. This is why the first C of Character must be in place before moving on to the second C. It is a truism. You will get 90% of what you ask for when you ask well.

The third C and equally important as the other two is COMMITMENT TOWARD EXCELLENCE. When I ask my audience how well should your children do? Easy answer, ALL THAT THEY CAN! Why would we as adults do anything less, fall short of the mark? Could of would of should of? You have got to be kidding me, leave it better then you found it. I write my books, produce my CD's and lecture around the country, because I believe that anything is possible in America. The foundation of this country was founded on flat out going for it ALL, ALL OF IT; never backing down, going for it and getting everything that is yours. Not what you deserve, but what you have skillfully and competently created for your life. Whatever it is you do, do it well and do it all. Many times, in hotels, I have seen the bellman who becomes the General Manager. I have seen a homeless man on a five year educational plan (no, not college but 5 years to get through high school) two dollars in his bank account, become a millionaire by forty, running his own companies, authoring books, CD's series and lecturing at major universities on leadership topics. If this person can do

it so can YOU. But you must master my Three C's. You can do well in any economy if you bring extraordinary value to the market place, do it better than your competition, do it better than any person before you; do it better than the person sitting next to you. This is America, anything is possible when you work hard at what you do, and more importantly work harder on yourself.

THE 3 T'S

I have developed the 3 T's of social and political change: Truth, Trust, and Tactics.

Truth is the FOUNDATION of your personal philosophy. It is based on the one thing you value above all else, such as: God, justice, fairness, wealth, family, popularity, honor, etc. You must have a strong FOUNDATION in Truth if you want to influence others. Do your homework. Dig deep to find the facts, but more importantly, find out what is really going on. Find out what motivates people. Understand the big picture. How does everything fit together? You may not know all the answers, but as you move forward, you will learn what questions to ask. Wisdom is less about knowing the right answer and more about asking the right question and knowing where to go to find the answer. Truth is more than just a passionate conviction. It is a statement that when others hear or read it, they will know exactly what you stand for and why. Truth provides clarity and understanding. It lets others know what you believe in and why you believe in it.

In chapter 1, I discuss the possibility of a Universal Morality. Related to this concept is Universal Truth. You cannot have one without the other. There are certain actions that most people would consider to be wrong, such as theft, kidnapping and murder. If you go on TV or radio and state that kidnapping is good, you will find that people will not listen to anything else you say because your version of morality is the exact opposite of most others. If, however, you create a non-profit organization that has a mission to reduce bullying, you will find many people agreeing with you and even perhaps willing to give you money to help you. The closer your message is in tune with this concept of Universal Truth, the easier it will be to find followers and assistants to help you accomplish your goals.

If you want others to follow you, they must Trust you. They must perceive that you have the ability to lead and accomplish the necessary goals. To build trust, you must have a strong track record. Trust is the result of the Three C's of Character, Communication and Commitment toward excellence. If you have good Character, are able to properly Communicate your thoughts and ideas, and are Committed to accomplishing your mission and your goals, people will perceive that you have leadership qualities and will rally behind both you and your cause.

You will always have your detractors. There are people who want to see you fail. Those who can disarm their opponents, while at the same time rally their supporters, are the ones who will eventually find success. For example, a professional such as a doctor has built a rapport with his/her patients over a period of time. Let's say a disgruntled patient files a lawsuit against the doctor and also decides to post negative comments online. A modern doctor now has to fight a battle on two fronts: the court room and the online community of public opinion. I cannot give legal advice, but I do know some techniques that can help shape public opinion (which I discuss in chapter 11). A doctor who has a great relationship with existing patients will have an easier time combating against negative press and public opinion than one who has a poor relationship with his/her patients. Trust is a valuable commodity in the business world. There are times you will need to leverage it to keep your doors open. If you have ever seen *It's a Wonderful Life* (1946) with Jimmy Stewart and Donna Reed, there is a scene where there is a run on his small family owned bank. Because of the strong positive relationships he built with his clients throughout the years, he was able to properly negotiate with his existing clients to keep his doors open after a scandal that almost destroyed his reputation and his business.

Tactics are procedures and strategies that when properly executed are designed to create the desired end result. Modern businesses will always run the risk of negative press and publicity. There are specific Tactics, or strategies, you can implement to accomplish specific goals, such as making it difficult to find negative comments about your business. Remember that a goal is an objective result. For example: I want to be employed within the next 30 days. It is an objective question that you can answer with a "yes" or "no". Did you get a job within 30 days, Yes or No? However, subjective wishes are not goals for they cannot be reached. For example: I want world peace. It would be very difficult to develop a way to test if this was accomplished. Chapters 11 and 12 describe a number of Tactics to help you improve your personal and professional life.

SPOTLIGHT ON RALPH NADER

Ralph Nader is one of the most well-known social and political activists for consumer protection, humanitarianism, and environmentalism. He truly believes in his mission. He has campaigned in every election for President of the United States between 1992 and 2008, written several books, and has started many non-profit organizations. He was born on February 27, 1934, to immigrant parents from Lebanon. In 1951 he graduated from Gilbert School (a quasi-public school founded by owner of the Gilbert Clock Company in 1895 – William Gilbert). He graduated *magna cum laude* from Princeton University in 1955 in government and economics, and he received his law degree with distinction from Harvard Law School in 1958.

Nader served six months on active duty in the United States Army in 1959, then became a lawyer in Hartford, Connecticut. He was a professor of history and government at the University of Hartford from 1961 to 1963, and served on the faculty at the American University Washington College of Law. In 1964, he moved to Washington, DC, where he worked for Assistant Secretary of Labor Daniel Patrick Moynihan (remember Moynihan defeated William F. Buckley's brother as Senator from New York) and also advised a US Senate subcommittee on car safety.

In 1965, Nader published a book called *Unsafe at any Speed*. In it he argued the reluctance of automobile manufacturers to spend money to improve car safety features, such as seat belts. This book made Ralph Nader a household name. As a result of this book, hundreds of young activists flocked to Washington, DC, to help Nader with other projects, in which they investigated government corruption and wrote over a dozen books.

Nader has stated, *"The consumer must be protected at times from his own indiscretion and vanity."* In 1971, Nader co-founded Public Citizen which is an organization currently with over 225,000 members that investigates congressional, health, environmental, economic, and other issues.

In the 1970s and 80s he was a key leader in the movement against the use of nuclear power. The Critical Mass Energy Project was formed by Nader in 1974 and was one of the largest national anti-nuclear energy groups in the United States with over 200,000 supporters. According to the mandatory financial disclosures he filed related his Presidential campaigns, in 2000, he owned more than $3 million worth of stocks and mutual funds with a third invested in Cisco Systems. The report stated that he lives on $25,000 a year and the rest of his money goes to the over four dozen non-profit organizations he has founded. His speech in 2000 at a International Monetary Fund meeting describes some of his political views.

My Thoughts on Ralph Nader

Below I provide direct quotes from Ralph Nader during the International Forum on Globalization in Washington, D.C., on April 14, 2000. Ralph Nader is the head of the Green Party, which is focused on environmentalism, social justice, respect for diversity, and nonviolence. In his speech he talks about allying progressives with some conservatives on some issues, such as subversion of our local, state and federal sovereignty, corporate welfare, cleaner air and drinking water, and the high cost of health care.

I would best describe myself a constitutional libertarian conservative. I am in favor of low taxes, minimal government regulations, limited government spending, free market capitalism, American exceptionalism, strong national defense and a strict interpretation of the US Constitution. I strongly agree with the liberal use of all Constitutional rights, including freedom of speech, the ability to own a gun, and freedom of religion. As a conservative, I would agree with Ralph Nader that certain progressives and certain conservatives could work together to resolve certain issues. But there is one major problem standing in the way – WHY?

Many conservatives want to end corporate welfare in order to reduce government spending and to reduce government involvement in the free market system. Progressives want to end corporate welfare because corporations take advantage of employees and exist solely for profit. If, at the end, corporate welfare is terminated as a direct result of progressives and conservatives working together, is that a good enough reason to work together? The answer would also be dependent upon how the objectives are met. If progressives want to end corporate welfare simply by terminating government subsidies to all businesses and organizations, including corporations, unions, non-profit organizations, and religious institutions, that is something that many Americans could support, including myself. However, if they want to end corporate welfare by banning the formation and use of corporations without any discussion of unions and other organizations that donate large sums of money to political interests, there would be very strong opposition. So how can we change and improve the country? The US Constitution through Article 5 was designed to only allow the enactment of laws that have broad public support.

The Constitution, its amendments, our representatives, and the laws we enact, are just a reflection of our society as a whole. If we as a nation could band together to find common ground and support laws & actions that benefit our country as a whole, regardless of who proposed it or why they proposed it, we might be able to improve the welfare of the entire nation. The primary question is can we find that common ground? As a libertarian fiscal conservative, I do agree with some of Nader's ideas, even though he has a progressive anti-corporate philosophy.

Ralph Nader
IFG IMF/World Bank Teach-In
Washington D.C.
April 14, 2000

"Thank you very much, Jerry, and all the people who work with the International Forum on Globalization. It really does take a huge amount of work to arrange these kind of gatherings. We hope that these proceedings for the past 12 hours will be put on the Internet so people all over the world can see and hear them. Not that we expect any of the major networks or cable companies to be here. They're into other priorities.

I'd also like to thank the panel for their very precise expressions and they've all worked so hard. All of this doesn't get done by a few people but by a lot of people. The few people may get much of the credit, but to those of you who are under 30 or under 25, let me tell that **the key here is stamina. It's commitment. It's diligence. It's realizing that throughout the world's history, the reason why the few dominate the many is because the few are organized and the many are not organized. It is because the few disorganize the many.**

All of this increasing critique of corporate globalization - we should always use the adjective - comes from a long overdue pattern of research to discern the systems of control. Make no mistake about it. Although the shibboleths of free trade are tossed in front of an often misinformed media, **the issue with the IMF and World Trade Organization and World Bank is governance. It's the governance systems for global corporations that we're really dealing with.**

The fundamental issue we face is the autocratic systems of governance that undermine democracy, that subordinate human rights and the rights of people for decent standards of living and for decent standards of justice. This is what is at stake here: Challenging international systems of autocratic governance that serve, overwhelmingly, the interests of giant global corporations who dominate and seek to dominate everything in their path.

They want to dominate governments. They want to dominate the workplace. They want to dominate the marketplace. They want to dominate the universities by corporatizing them. They want to dominate the very concept of childhood with their brazen commercial exploitation of small children. They want to dominate the shaping of the environment. They want to control the genes of the natural world. They want to control the human genes. They want to control the seeds. They want to control the future.

We have to make sure that this relentless drive for control by the commercial instinct - which every major religion in the world has warned us about for two thousand years - should never be given excessive power. Because in its singular focus and drive and lack of respect for other values, it destroys these other values in a paroxysm of greed that implodes on itself.

This is the church where President Clinton comes to pray almost every Sunday that he is in town. He listens to sermons on spirituality, on religion, on various elaborations of the golden rule: Do unto others what you wish others to do unto you. Then, he gets into his limousine and goes down 16th Street of the White House where decisions are made by another golden rule: They who have the gold, rule.

In watching President Clinton coming to this church over the years, I kept asking myself, "What is it that intercepts what he absorbs here by the time he goes down there?" Here, he meets spirituality and communes with it. There, he meets corporations who have turned the White House into a corporate prison. In between, he doesn't meet the people. That's what we're all about. Because that in-between, is the major democracy-gap that must be filled by all generations and peoples from all over the world.

In Seattle, I sat on a panel with Undersecretary of Commerce David Aaron. Some of you may remember. He was short-changing the dialogue in my judgment. In my frustration, I challenged him to a structured, 5-hour debate and he agreed. On the way out from that auditorium, he reiterated his agreement. So I wrote him a letter when I came back and said let's sit down so we can work out the rules, and who is going to debate, over what topics, etc.

Just last week-and-a-half ago, on his last day in office, he wrote me a little note saying that he is leaving the Department of Commerce and is joining a firm - it turns out to be a law firm specializing in global trade. And while he would have loved to engage in the debate, he has to pass it on someone else. There it is. The shuttle at work. The merry-go-round at work between the corporate government and the political government, back to the corporate government to the political government.

Now, let me put before you briefly some of the major problems affecting the world and ask yourself: to what extent does the IMF, The World Bank, The WTO, and global corporations, who, as David Korten has said, `seek to rule the world' - to what extent they either contribute to these problems, worsen them, or even cause them or are indifferent to them?

Poverty is a massive problem in the world. As you know, a couple billion people trying to eke it out on less than the equivalent of a dollar a day. **Authoritarian regimes. Environmental destruction. Multiple epidemics of diseases. Horribly inadequate housing. Inadequate food, ranging from malnutrition to starvation - in terms of inadequate distribution of the available food. The massive military arms trafficking in the world.**

Check out these big corporations. These giant food-grain exporters. These giant food-processing companies. Their main attention to world poverty is to see how much fat and sugar they can pump in to third world people. The tobacco industry. What's their contribution to health? It is to increase the level of cancer and other tobacco-related diseases. How about the housing industry? They could care less. There's not much money in that. The pharmaceutical industry. They're great at producing life-style drugs. They love to develop drugs like Viagra and restoring bald-headed men and harmful anti-obesity drugs. But for decades now, even though they are subsidized by taxpayers, they do not do any research in drugs and vaccines for the major global infectious diseases such as tuberculosis and malaria.

In fact, unfortunately, most of the malaria research for anti-malarial drugs is concentrated in this country and it is over in the Pentagon at The Walter Reed Institute of Health with the Army and Navy scientists. They are the ones who are doing this work.

Isn't it interesting regarding this giant profitable pharmaceutical industry? They are not interested in drugs and vaccines for alleviating the tremendous world mortality and morbidity rates. Malaria itself takes two million lives a year including one million African children.

We see this with the arms traffic. Who is fueling the arms traffic? The giant military arms producers - with your tax dollars. In this country $6 billion of tax subsidies a year for private exports of jets and tanks and ammunition, etc., to countries that aren't exactly governments of, by, and for their people. We see this situation in every area.

Now, when are these companies ever going to lose their credibility? Every major social movement in United States history was opposed by the dominant business firms. Whether it was the abolition of slavery, the trade union movement, the farmer progressive populist movement, even the women's suffrage movement, the environmental consumer movements (the more recent vintage) - all were opposed by the dominant business community. When are these people in the business community going to lose their credibility?

Corporations are chartered by us. We give them the charter. They don't exist without the charter by state and federal governments. We can condition the charter, suspend the charter, pull the charter for corporate recidivism and other misbehaving corporations and throw them into trusteeships and reorganize them so that they behave. We must remember that.

We know how the IMF and World Bank work. It's no mystery. They're funded by taxpayers with very little informed consent. Billions of dollars of U.S. tax dollars for example go into the IMF. This big money-pumping machine as it was called - the IMF and the World Bank - extends loans. They have a model of economic development that is grotesque. Not only in it's damage as you heard earlier repeatedly: damage to human beings, to environment, to the sustainable wisdom of the ages as it replaces it, etc. But it doesn't have any standards for failure.

What do you do about institutions that do not have explicit standards of failure by which they must be judged? Ask the IMF. Let's take the last three years. Here's the last three years very briefly: It's contributed to and worsened financial crises in Asia and elsewhere, and served primarily to bailout the western banks who helped cause the crisis in the first place. The second is, it has wasted billions of our taxpayer dollars and other country's taxpayer dollars, pumping this money into Russia; a tormented land with a tormented people, once governed by criminal communism and now governed by criminal capitalism. Billions of these IMF dollars right down the drain. They disappeared before they were almost deposited into the oligarchies and into the networks.

Where is the accounting system of the IMF? They're supposed to have auditors and accountants. They have admitted they were taken to the cleaners. But when do they admit more structural failure in their operation? Who made that decision to send all that money over there? They knew what the corruption was like. They knew what the practice was like. They knew it wasn't going to get to the people in Russia. But they went ahead and did it.

Did any of their paychecks down the street here bounce? Of course not. Maybe that's the problem. The IMF has bailed out the big banks while impoverishing the poor. It has continued to push its environmentally destructive export-led development trade.

There are a lot of things we all can do about this, obviously. I want to suggest, especially to the young people here - and whoever watches this very wonderful long day event - that, first of all, it is not enough just to be concerned and informed. It is not enough just to be concerned, informed and serious. **It is not enough to be concerned, informed, serious with a sense of urgency. You have got to reach out to other people. You have got to organize your acquaintances, relatives, friends, co-workers all over the country.**

And stop feeling sorry for your selves. Oh! Those overwhelming odds - the IMF, the World Bank, the WTO, the corporations, what can we do, oh-me oh-my, que sera sera. When you see what your forebears were up against for two hundred years and the advanced social justice which you benefit from; when you see what our brother from Bolivia has just gone through with his co-workers and friends - how can you feel sorry for yourself? If you do you're a jerk!

Now we need to emphasize the entry of the labor unions into this fight. This is a dramatic new development. The labor unions have been led for too many years by leaders who see their position as a sinecure and who were much more indentured to corporate power than they should be. Now labor is beginning to rediscover the demonstration, the picket, the rally, locking arms with all the rest of you.

Workers bring great credibility to movements that involve human rights groups and environmental groups and consumer groups and church groups and student groups. They give great credibility because they have all the symbols. The Wall Streeters cannot damage those symbols. They've got all the symbols: they fought in the wars for corporate interests; they built the factories; they sustain the economy. They sweat day-to-day while their CEOs are making 415 times more than the entry-level wage in these companies. Keep that in mind.

The second is, what is wrong with allying ourselves with more conservative interests? Conservative interests who are not corporatists - they don't like this any better than we do. They don't like where their taxes are going. They don't like the subversion of our local, state and federal sovereignty - the largest relinquishment in our history - to the World Trade Organization. They don't like all this corporate welfare aid to dependent corporations - without even a 5-year cutoff if I might add.

They want their children to breathe cleaner air and drink cleaner water. They don't like to get ripped off by higher pharmaceutical prices or have to go up to Canada to get lower prices. Right Maude?. "Not for long," she says. And in Congress now, there is a strong core of conservatives that are very critical of the IMF.

The other thing that young people need to do more of is read. Read! Yes, read. Reading informs. Reading motivates. The Multinational Monitor is our our contribution to your reading. Rob Weissman is the editor here who puts it out with his cohorts 10 times a year. It's all over the place now.

Also, don't underestimate the vote. There is nothing worse than to see young people who are very, very active - as Carol Miller told me a few minutes ago - and then they don't bother to vote, like `Ahh!' - it's beneath them. You have got to register. Go right across the college campuses and register the vote. **Develop a block of informed voters and if you vote and nothing happens, at least it gets you angry. You can be more motivated and more mobilized.**

Now let's look at the IMF and World Bank briefly through the eyes of the people who go to work there everyday. They are paid very well - tax free. They know what it's like to go around in a limousines. They actually have good cafeterias, if you ever sneak in there. It's good food, all kinds of indigenous foreign cuisine.

They read about what the World Bank is supposed to be in college. The World Bank is supposed to fight poverty. It is supposed to build infrastructure that private investment eschews as not being profitable. Roads and dams and water systems, electrification systems, etc. They say, 'Well that's what it is isn't it? That's what it says in the charter, and in the speeches.' And so they go to work for the IMF as well. These institutions live by these myths. **They live by these myths because on paper they have abstracted these cumbersome models of economic development quite inaccurately.** They have abstracted them saying, 'Electrification projects, dams, water, irrigation - who can be against this?' Part of it is that there is a deep set ignorance about how economies develop, especially poor economies.

Giant projects funded on the western model do not work in third world countries. Poverty can be alleviated only by cottage-level projects. For example, look what happened in our country at its best - and why don't we project that for models of economic development with proper indigenous inputs, of course. We had land reform - it's called the Homestead Act of 1863. It broke up the potential for giant plantations as occurred in the South. What people in the third world need is land reform - fundamental land reform. **They need systems that encourages land used to grow food for needy and hungry people. Not to grow cash crops to be exported to the West to earn hard currency to pay debts to foreign banks.**

The second is microcredit. The democratization of credit which occurred in our country with credit unions, agricultural credit banks, producer credit banks in the farm area.

They don't need these giant loans to oligarchs and governments that misuse them and only entrenches the oligarchs and the dictatorial regimes. They need the democratization of credit. It goes right to people - $200, $300, $100 like the Grameen Bank has shown - which by the way, was not an IMF idea, was it?

People need technical assistance and not just western science and not corporate science. When are we going to realize the value of indigenous science and technology? It doesn't come in fancy names and publications and fancy journals. It simply is the result of thousands of years of knowledge. Look at the Neem tree in India, for example. Look at the great Egyptian architect, Hassan Fathy who developed systems for building homes made from the soil underneath the feet of the Egyptian peasants. And whose teachings are spreading around the world. That was not an IMF or World Bank or a consulting firm idea.

How about Nestle? And all the infinite formula that the World Health Organization has said has destroyed the lives of millions of children in the third world. Promoted as Nestle did, knowing that it would be so expensive that it had to be mixed with contaminated water leading to horrendous tragedies for little children and infants. What was that kind of contribution? And what did it replace? It replaced mother's milk. That's real western science isn't it?

How about water safety? Where is the IMF and World Bank in the last 30 to 40 years knowing from their own studies, the huge mortality levels from contaminated water - especially for small children. Where are they? Why is that such a big deal? It's a big deal because **they only think in terms of big projects. They don't think in terms of letting these societies breathe themselves democratically so they can solve their own problems. They don't think of getting off the back of third world people instead**

of constantly shoring up the authoritarian regimes and the oligarchs who benefit from the corporatization, that is often called privatization of public institutions like water companies.

What about cooperatives? We had cooperatives in our country. They were tremendous, especially in the farm and rural areas. Why aren't we saying that the third world needs help in terms of cooperatives? Only a dabble here and a dabble there for that kind of institution.

How about public health and infections? Can you imagine? It was James Grant - any of you heard of James Grant of UNICEF? He passed away a few years ago. He was a Harvard-trained lawyer who in the last few years of his life, went all over the world trying to get regimes to let in public health workers, both indigenous and exogenous, for immunization. It is so easy to save the lives of these children and infants. Pennies per life! Pennies per life! Where are they with their billion dollar loans, that they don't pay attention to this?

What about public education? What about public school systems in our country? One of the great institutions - the G.I. Bill of Rights. Why aren't we saying that other countries deserve those kind of assists, as well, to fulfill human possibilities from early age on?

What about giving people in the third world the right to form independent trade unions? In this country, it built the middle class.

How about the rule of law and due process? And the access to free and independent courts which helped us? Why aren't we fostering and why aren't we supporting efforts in those countries, as well?

What about the whole idea of self-reliance and self-sufficiency? We talk about energy independence in our country but we haven't done much on that although it was talked about in the '70s. What is this emphasis on the inevitability of global trade? Most countries can be self-sufficient in most of the necessities. They may not have manganese mines. But for heaven's sake look at our country. Why do we have to import British biscuits, French drinking water and Swedish ice cream? We have to challenge the very fundamental premise of trade. There is bad trade: there is trade in tobacco; there is trade in munitions; there is trade in prostitution across boundaries. What is this blanket idea that all trade is good? I favor self-sufficient communities. **I favor self-reliant communities to the maximum feasible extent.** We should work for that.

The most prosperous economies are those who build domestic markets, from the grassroots up. Not those who go into debt chattel, debt servitude to foreign banks, and IMFs, and World Banks and develop an export-oriented trade dependency on a boom-and-bust basis where the strings are pulled thousands of miles away by absentee corporate executives and their government allies on the 30th floor of some skyscraper in London, New York or Tokyo.

We have to develop, in other words, a democratic model of self-sufficient, sustainable economic progress. That is what we have to talk about and hurl against the IMF, and the World Bank and the WTO. They either don't have a clue of how democratically-structured economies develop from the community, the neighborhood, the soil, the rural, the cities. Or they don't want to have a clue.

What we have to do is not simply deconstruct their systems of control - and the often brutal consequences that come from their systems of control - for which

they are not accountable. But we have to demonstrate again and again from our own history and from the history of the best practices in our country of the ways we developed economically, to build a higher standard of living and a higher standard of justice.

Mark Hertsgaard is going around the country with his paperback book, Earth Odyssey, after traveling around the world for five-six years. He saw the enormous damage to the poorest people, the most defenseless people, from environmental ravages. He saw it and documented it and now is trying to get the IMF and World Bank to accept a green deal. While I sympathize with his ability to try to reform these institutions, it is quite clear that internally, they are not capable of regeneration. They are capable of new slogans, of new speeches that display 'Care For The Poor Of The World', but they are not capable of internal regeneration. They have to be withdrawn in terms of the funding from the various contributing countries and shrunken into institutions that finally transform themselves, and give up their original impact, and transform themselves into these kinds of promoters of sustainable economic development. Or just close up completely and start new from scratch.

You can critique the IMF, and the World Bank, and WTO, and that is becoming more and more penetrating and more destabilizing for them. But we've got to work with people in other countries around the world as this coalition has demonstrated, and as you have demonstrated, to show that the alternative is superior in every way. It is superior for people today. It is superior for future generations. It is superior for the free play of non-commercial values that build a great culture and a great democracy.

Remember, every country will do it differently. They have different cultural traditions and different priori-

ties. **But there are certain common survival programs in terms of food and housing and health care and education that we must try to foster between nations and between societies.** Let us not adopt the dictionary of the oligarchs and of the international organizations. The dictionary is not privatization, it is corporatization. **The distinction between economic growth and economic justice should be made very clear. Economic growth is not necessarily economic progress or justice for the mass majority of the people.**

I hope that you have a very "compelling weekend," shall we say. **I hope you show your self-restraint as well as your eagerness to communicate throughout the country over the media what you are all here for. I hope you will send your signals to the White House as well as to the Congress. But I hope you'll go back so metabolized that you will multiply your efforts in church basements and union local halls and university auditoriums and through your e-mail, so that this time it is not just a surge. It's not just a movement. Not just a demonstration. It is a permanent transformation of the way we use our time and our knowledge and our estimate of our own significance. Estimate of our own significance.**

You are in the top percent or two of people around the world in terms of health, education, and the ability to make a difference. That gives you a moral imperative to do so. You have even a higher responsibility to do so. We are blessed in this country. We have to make sure we stop the reverse slide that is occurring even here. We have to go back home and develop our own systems of influence, our own compelling networks, whether through the Internet or through person-to-person contact.

Remember, over two thousand years ago, it was the Roman lawyer, **Marcus Cicero, who defined freedom for the**

ages. He defined it this way: "Freedom is participation in power." Everything else is just the symbolism of the oppressors over the oppressed when they talk about liberty and freedom, etc. Freedom is participation in power.

Thank You."

Chapter 10

CATALYTIC CONVERTERS

"Be the change you want to see in the world."
— **Mahatma Gandhi**

The main purpose of this book is to encourage you to get involved within the United States political system so that you can create positive change in the world. Creating positive change is so much more than just having a great idea in your mind. If you want to create change, you have to be equipped with the right tools. The remaining chapters in this book are designed to help you develop some of those tools.

CHANGING YOURSELF

You may have heard part of the quote that states, *"Accept the things you cannot change and the courage to change the things you can."* Have you ever read or heard the quote in its entirety? On its face, this quote can be used for multiple purposes. There is a basic type of wisdom that rings true, regardless of your convictions.

"God, give us grace to accept with serenity
the things that cannot be changed,
Courage to change the things
which should be changed,
and the Wisdom to distinguish
the one from the other.

"Living one day at a time,
Enjoying one moment at a time,
Accepting hardship as a pathway to peace,
Taking, as Jesus did,
This sinful world as it is,
Not as I would have it,
Trusting that You will make all things right,
If I surrender to Your will,
So that I may be reasonably happy in this life,
And supremely happy with You forever in the next."

The Serenity Prayer (1934) – Reinhold Niebuhr

The purpose of this was not to preach to you, it was designed to illustrate a point that you need to dig below the surface to find facts and truths. Find out what is really going on. You cannot become an instigator of change by following everyone else.

There are two perspectives when it comes to changing the world: changing yourself and gathering your groupies. In **Left-Center-Right: What is BEST for America?**, I talk about the importance of changing yourself if you want to see a change in the world. I still stand by that.

If we can accept and embrace the things we cannot change, and instead work on changing ourselves, we could capitalize on our situation and change our lives for the better. You can control your destiny and gain all those benefits life has to offer. It doesn't mean you are a failure if you aren't where you want to be in your life right now. If you want a better life (you would not be reading this book if you didn't), you'll have to spend the energy to change yourself, to educate yourself, and to be around people who can help you get to where you want to be. Then the world will change for you, because you have changed.

Many years ago I said to a friend of mine, *"You can't have an ego in the journey to success."* My friend did not comprehend this concept. He was one of those people who felt they knew everything. He didn't study when he was supposed to. He blamed others when he didn't succeed. He couldn't understand why he failed. It never occurred to him that his ego was not allowing him to succeed. Humility is the key: To know what we do not know. The "ego philosophy" is very simple. Put your ego in your back pocket when it comes to the journey of success. Later you can take a little ego out and put it in front of you, because you need a little ego to carry you forward, but not all your ego. Do not think you know it all. Always be open to new ideas and learning new things. You need to learn more so you can become more.

Top leaders are never finished. Do you think because you have $200,000 in the bank that you would want to stop there, and not earn anymore? Do you think that because your "guy" became President of the United States that all your personal and political problems will be solved? Success is a journey and not a destination. Success will put you in touch with who you are. It will put you in places that you can't see right now, and when you get there you will realize that the process of getting there is more important than arriving. That's why successful people keep striving: it keeps them growing. It is a part of their personality. It's that simple.

In the Introduction, I talked about some of the accomplishments of Steve Jobs. When Apple went public on December 12, 1980, Steve Jobs owned 7.5 million shares which had a stock IPO price of $22 per share. As a result, Jobs was worth more than $165 million. In May 1985, Steve Jobs was stripped of his duties as CEO of Apple. He could have stopped working and walked away from everything, and he would have had a very comfortable life. If he did, there would be no iPads or iTunes or Pixar today.

Innovation thrives in a culture in which people are allowed to maintain control over their own time, money and property. Steve Jobs lost control of Apple for 11 years. He was eventually able to regain control of Apple through a series of business decisions. It was not his thirst for money that kept him going.

It was his singular desire to change the world that lead him on the path towards completely redefining humanity's relationship with technology.

CHANGING YOUR FOUNDATION

I needed to give this couple some advice; I saw very clearly where they were going wrong. I said, *"Listen, you're a wonderful couple, let me give you something that you can take back with you to change your life, because I can tell you both want to succeed in life: You have to develop a stronger FOUNDATION than what you have. You're coming to me because you think that I can make you a lot of money. But what do you have to offer me?"* He said, *"An opportunity we're involved with."* When I asked him if they succeeded yet, he said, *"Well no, we're just getting started."* And I said, *"Well, I don't want to bust your bubble, you're excited, and that's okay, but chances are a year from now you won't be in the same business."*

A year later, guess what? They're not in the business, because it just didn't work out for them. Why didn't it work out, because they're not who they said they were. If you have a really solid FOUNDATION, you're going to make it, and it does not matter what business it is. If you change your job before you change your FOUNDATION, it's not going to work, it's that simple. This couple had not changed their work ethic and they were inconsistent, so they were destined to fail regardless of the opportunity.

There are many aspects to a solid FOUNDATION: spiritual, family, physical and career. When I used to interview sales people for positions throughout the country, I asked them, *"How much money do you want to make for the year?"* Their comment was usually between seventy to hundred thousand a year".

I was not familiar with their FOUNDATION, or their ability at that time, so I would ask them, *"Why do you feel that you want to make that, and why do you feel you're worth that type of income.*" If the year before, they had made thirty thousand, the question would stump them.

If you want to DO more, or if you want to HAVE more, you have to BE more, it's that simple. If you want to increase your income, you have to develop a value to the market place, it's not simply a matter of wanting it, showing up, or setting goals for it. You have to educate yourself to become more in order to earn more and give back. The action you take to achieve your goals is what will get you where you want to be in life.

If you work hard and show up everyday to the job, you are not necessarily guaranteed a raise or even a career for the rest of your life. From the business owner's point of view, an employee is considered a liability, not an asset. An employee takes away from the bottom line and is there primarily to perform specific tasks. If you want job security... if you want a raise... if you want better working conditions, you have to add value to the marketplace. If you are a sales person, and are able to bring in more business, you are an asset. If you have a list of people that you know, and are great at motivating them to donate to a cause, you are an asset.

To truly make a difference, check your FOUNDATION. Are you who you say you are? Are you an asset, or are you a liability? Ask yourself, *"What is my value?"* What is my net worth from an employer's standpoint, or a customer's standpoint. If you weighed 190 pounds, would you be 190 pounds of in-shape muscle, able to pull your load, and able to carry your weight and be productive, or 190 pounds of fat taking up space. Do the action it takes to become that valuable person.

Again look at all areas in your life: spiritual, family, career, and health. All are very important. Where are you right now? Are you able to maximize what you want out of life? If the answer is "no," you might need to move on, and that's okay. But remember, the opportunity does not lie within others, it lies within you. Look at that couple I mentioned earlier where the woman got into the multi-level program. Someone promised her the "pie in the sky," and because she was looking for the easy way out, she fell into the trap of changing the job, rather than changing her FOUNDATION and her work ethic.

SPOTLIGHT ON THE TEA PARTY AND OCCUPY WALL STREET MOVEMENTS

Tea Party Movement

On January 24, 2009, Trevor Leach, chairman of Young Americans for Liberty in New York State organized a "Tea Party" to protest obesity taxes proposed by New York Governor David Paterson and called for fiscal responsibility on the part of the government. Several of the protesters wore Native American headdresses similar to the band of 18th Century colonists who dumped tea in Boston Harbor to express outrage about British taxes.

Leaders within the Tea Party movement credit Seattle blogger and conservative activist Keli Carender with organizing the first Tea Party in February 2009. Carender first organized what she called a *"Porkulus Protest"* in Seattle on Presidents Day, February 16, the day before President Barack Obama signed the stimulus bill into law. Carender said she did it without support from outside groups or city officials. *"I just got fed up and planned it."* Carender said 120 people participated. *"Which is amazing for the bluest of blue cities I live in, and on only four days notice! This was due to me spending the entire four days calling and emailing every person, think tank, policy center, university professors, etc. in town, and not stopping until the day came."*

Carender contacted Steve Beren who promoted the event on his blog four days before the protest and agreed to be a speaker at the rally. Carender also contacted conservative author and Fox News contributor Michelle Malkin, and asked her to publicize the rally on her blog, which Malkin did the day before the event. The following day, the Colorado branch of Americans for Prosperity held a protest at the Colorado

Capitol, also promoted by Malkin. Carender held a second protest on February 27, 2009, reporting *"We more than doubled our attendance at this one."* Those involved in the movement are angry about two issues: federal taxes and spending are too high, and no one in Washington is listening to them.

The Tea Party movement has no central leadership and is composed of a loose affiliation of national and local groups that determine their own platforms and agendas. The Tea Party movement is an example of grassroots political activity. The movement is organized around a vision and core set of principles, and these are listed on the movement's primary website: www.teapartypatriots.org.

Our Vision: We envision a nation where personal freedom is cherished and where all Americans are treated equally, assuring our ability to pursue the American Dream.

Core Principles:

Tea Party Patriots stands for every American, and is home to millions who have come together to pursue the American Dream and to keep that Dream alive for their children and grandchildren. What unites the tea party movement is the same set of core principles that brought America together at its founding, that kindled the American Dream in the hearts of those who struggled to build our nation, and made the United States of America the greatest, most successful country in world history. At its root the American Dream is about freedom. Freedom to work hard and the freedom to keep the fruits of your labor to use as you see fit without harming others and without hindering their freedom. Very simply, three guiding principles give rise to the freedom necessary to pursue and live the American Dream:

Constitutionally Limited Government or your Personal Freedom and Your Rights

Free Market Economics or Economic Freedom to Grow Jobs and Your Opportunities

Fiscal Responsibility or very simply, a Debt Free Future For You and Generations To Come

Personal Freedom: We support personal freedom so all Americans can live life the way they want as long as it does not harm others, or infringe on another's rights.

Economic Freedom: We stand for economic freedom which means a growing economy with reduced tax rates and reduced government spending so we all have a chance to earn more money and businesses can hire more people.

Debt Free Future: We support a debt free future because it is only fair and right to pay the debt we have incurred so our children and grandchildren are not stuck with our bills.

The Tea Party movement has received significant funding since 2010. Sarah Palin was involved in four bus tours to raise money for candidates. One of the tours visited 30 towns and covered 3,000 miles. Following the formation of the Tea Party Caucus, Michele Bachmann raised $10 million for a political action committee, MichelePAC, and sent funds to the campaigns of Sharron Angle, Christine O'Donnell, Rand Paul and Marco Rubio. In September 2010, the Tea Party Patriots announced it had received a $1,000,000 USD donation from an anonymous donor.

On August 30, 2010, Jane Mayer in a NewYorker.com article claims that multibillionaire David Koch has provided a significant amount of funding to the Tea Party movement. Rich Fink, executive vice president of Koch Industries, released a statement reading, *"We have not provided funding to the tea party organizations which are being organized throughout the country and, until recently, we had never been approached by a tea party group for funding. We have publicly supported Americans for Prosperity Foundation since 1984 and Americans for Prosperity since 2004. We have never considered these institutions to be tea party organizations. Whether or not they are considered to be tea party organizations will not affect our support of them. We believe the tea party movement is a response to the growing frustration of many Americans to government overspending. We share these concerns and encourage citizens to express their opinions in a respectful and civil manner."*

I could have sworn that I still live in the United States of America and live under the US Constitution and its Amendments which allow for certain freedoms. If a billionaire wants to fund a political action committee that wants to elect certain conservatives, I say let him. If a group of Hollywood stars and other wealthy Angelinos (those from Los Angeles) want to host 5 parties in one year for both Democratic Presidents Bill Clinton and Barack Obama, I say let them. This is all part of the political process and freedom of expression. Both sides should have the freedom to assemble, donate money, and sponsor bills.

It is the American people, not political insiders, who should determine the fate of candidates and legislation. That is how it has been for over 200 years, and that is how it should be in the future. In a democratic society, money does not win elections, ideas do. Texas billionaire Ross Perot ran for President of the United States twice in 1992 and 1996. If money alone were enough to elect someone, he would have become President, but he didn't. Also, in the 2010 Governor of California election, Meg Whitman spent over $119 million of her own money to defeat Jerry Brown. Yet, Jerry Brown won the election.

The Tea Party movement has become a legitimate movement because they have successfully elected candidates into higher office that believe in their principles of Fiscal Responsibility, Constitutionally Limited Government and Free Markets. Some 2010 winners include: Michele Bachmann (MN), Rand Paul (KY), Trent Franks (AZ), Tom McClintock (CA), Ron Paul (TX), Mike Pence (IN), Jim DeMint (SC), Marco Rubio (FL), Jan Brewer (AZ), and Bobby Jindal (LA).

Occupy Wall Street Movement

In mid-2011, the Canadian-based Adbusters Foundation, best known for its advertisement-free anti-consumerist magazine, proposed a peaceful occupation of Wall Street to protest corporate influence on democracy, address a growing disparity in wealth, and the absence of legal repercussions behind the recent global financial crisis. On their website they wrote: *"Beginning from one simple demand - a Presidential commission to separate money from politics - we start setting the agenda for a new America."* They promoted the protest with a poster featuring a dancer atop Wall Street's iconic Charging Bull.

On September 17, 2011, activists from the internet group Anonymous encouraged its followers to take part in the protests, calling protesters to flood lower Manhattan, set up tents, kitchens, peaceful barricades and occupy Wall Street. Other groups began to join in the organization of the protest. The protest was held at Zuccotti Park since it was private property and they could not be legally forced to leave. At a press conference held on September 17, New York City mayor Michael Bloomberg said, *"People have a right to protest, and if they want to protest, we'll be happy to make sure they have locations to do it."* The term, *"We are the 99%"* was a political slogan used by demonstrators involved in the Occupy protests to state that since the 1970s, wealth and income have become concentrated within the top 1% of the United States population. By October 9, 2011, similar demonstrations had been held in 70 major cities and over 600 communities in the US. Other "Occupy" protests modeled after Occupy Wall Street have occurred in over 900 cities worldwide.

The Bill of Rights allows for peaceful demonstrations and freedom of speech. It does not, however, allow for the purposeful creation of health hazards. Although initially willing to work with the protestors, many cities began to crack down on the protests and disband the occupiers a few weeks later due to the risk of the spread of diseases due to unsanitary conditions where they have set up tents. New York Police arrested 200 as they restored order to Wall Street on November 15, 2011. The Los Angeles Police Department arrested 300 on November 30, 2011, as they restored order near city hall.

As posted on their website (OccupyWallSt.org) on October 4, 2011, they do have a list of demands that, according to them, would create a new economy that will benefit the entire population and not just a small few. The following was posted along with this list of demands: *"Admin note: This is not an official list of demands. This is a forum post submitted by a single user and hyped by irresponsible news/commentary agencies like Fox News and Mises.org. This content was not published by the OccupyWallSt.org collective, nor was it ever proposed or agreed to on a consensus basis with the NYC General Assembly. There is NO official list of demands."*

1. Restoration of the living wage. This demand can only be met by ending "Freetrade" by re-imposing trade tariffs on all imported goods entering the American market to level the playing field for domestic family farming and domestic manufacturing as most nations that are dumping cheap products onto the American market have radical wage and environmental regulation advantages. Another policy that must be instituted is raise the minimum wage to twenty dollars an hour.

2. Institute a universal single payer healthcare system. To do this all private insurers must be banned from the healthcare market as their only effect on the health of patients is to take money away from doctors, nurses and hospitals preventing them from doing their jobs and hand that money to Wall St. investors.

3. Guaranteed living wage income regardless of employment.

4. Free college education.

5.   Begin a fast track process to bring the fossil fuel economy to an end while at the same bringing the alternative energy economy up to energy demand.

6.   One trillion dollars in infrastructure (Water, Sewer, Rail, Roads and Bridges and Electrical Grid) spending now.

7.   One trillion dollars in ecological restoration planting forests, reestablishing wetlands and the natural flow of river systems and decommissioning of all of America's nuclear power plants.

8.   Racial and gender equal rights amendment.

9.   Open borders migration. Anyone can travel anywhere to work and live.

10. Bring American elections up to international standards of a paper ballot precinct counted and recounted in front of an independent and party observers system.

11. Immediate across the board debt forgiveness for all. Debt forgiveness of sovereign debt, commercial loans, home mortgages, home equity loans, credit card debt, student loans and personal loans now! All debt must be stricken from the "Books." World Bank Loans to all Nations, Bank to Bank Debt and all Bonds and Margin Call Debt in the stock market including all Derivatives or Credit Default Swaps, all 65 trillion dollars of them must also be stricken from the "Books." And I don't mean debt that is in default, I mean all debt on the entire planet period.

12. Outlaw all credit reporting agencies.

13. Allow all workers to sign a ballot at any time during a union organizing campaign or at any time that represents their yeah or nay to having a union represent them in collective bargaining or to form a union.

These demands will create so many jobs it will be completely impossible to fill them without an open borders policy.

Conclusion

The Tea Party Movement has a fiscal conservative philosophy of free trade, limited government, and fiscal responsibility. It has had some success in electing candidates into higher public offices that agree with their philosophy, such as Rand Paul and Bobby Jindal.

The Occupy Wall Street Movement has a progressive philosophy. Individuals within the movement have developed their own list of demands, but no such official list was ever made. Although many believe in some of their demands, many others see the Occupy Wall Street Movement as nothing more than a group of uneducated, unmotivated, and disrespectful individuals who would rather invoke Squatter's Rights (ownership of property simply by living there) and live in tents than to be responsible, educate themselves and work hard.

The Tea Party Movement has been successful in moving their agenda forward, because they have a message that appeals to many people, and the messengers are again perceived by many as informed and concerned American patriots. The Occupy Wall Street Movement has had little to no success because of two reasons: 1) If they get everything they ask, many believe it would completely destroy our Nation; 2) The messengers are perceived as lazy, disrespectful and unsanitary.

Our Solution

Late one Friday night in early November 2011 after a hard week of work, we (Randy and Michael) bounced ideas off each other related to the Occupy Wall Street Movement. The end result was something part humorous and part serious.

We developed the Occupy the Library Movement...

In honor of the 99% that are being represented by the men and women that are selflessly working on creating a brand new form of government on the now dead grass and trash-filled streets of Los Angeles, New York, Oakland, et al, the producers of StoriesofUSA.com are officially kicking off our Occupy the Library Movement.

It is our hope that through free education, hard work, clear minds and clean bodies, people will absorb the knowledge they need to truly create an exciting future for themselves, their friends, their family and their community.

Please join our cause to educate the world about what Government Of the People, By the People, For the People truly means by spreading our message of education and hard work to all of your friends and family.

My Public Library "Rules of Conduct"

Be considerate and respectful of all users and staff, and behave in a manner that does not disturb other persons. Unacceptable conduct includes, but is not limited to:

1. Loud, disruptive and inappropriate behavior that would be annoying to a reasonable person using this library
2. Damaging or stealing property
3. Sleeping
4. Use of tobacco products
5. Possession of firearms, weapons or illegal substance

Other rules include:

6. Treat library property with respect
7. Dress appropriately. Person whose bodily hygiene is offensive so as to constitute a nuisance to other persons shall be required to leave building
8. Supervise your children and assist them in observing appropriate conduct
9. Silence your cell phone
10. Leave bicycles and gasoline-powered vehicles outside

11. Personal items are not to be left unattended. Carry or keep items with you at all times. The library is not responsible for items left unattended

12. Comply with staff requests with regard to library policies

13. Assistance dogs are the only animals permitted in the library

Noncompliance with the Rules of Conduct may result in expulsion from the Library and/or suspension of library privileges.

THANK YOU FOR YOUR COOPERATION

Chapter 11

TIME TO MAKE A CHANGE

*The one unchangeable certainty is that nothing
is certain or unchangeable.*

— **John F. Kennedy**

If you have a computer (or smart phone), Internet connection and electricity, you can wield a very powerful tool from the comfort of your own home just by using your fingers. The only questions become: What message do I want to broadcast? How do I broadcast my message? And how do I convince others to do what I want them to do? The following information will get you on that journey towards discovering the answers to these and other related questions.

WHAT MESSAGE DO I WANT TO BROADCAST?

To properly answer this question, you must be willing to take a journey of self-realization and spend a significant amount of time learning and researching. You must also be willing to take some risks by going outside your comfort zone and do things you may have never done before. The ultimate purpose in this process is for you to set a goal (especially one that you want to accomplish but don't think you can) and achieve it. This, for the purpose of this book, is success. There is a book and video produced by Simon Sinek that talks about the Golden Circle. The following is an edited version of that video.

Simon Sinek: Golden Circle

"How do we explain when others are able to achieve things that seem to defy all of the assumptions? Why is Apple so innovative? They are just a computer company. They have the same access to the same talent, the same agencies, the same consultants, the same media. Then why is it that they seem to have something different.

Why is it that Martin Luther King led the Civil Rights Movement? He wasn't the only man who suffered in a pre-civil rights America. And he certainly wasn't the only great orator of the day. Why is it that the Wright Brothers were able to figure out controlled powered man flight when there were other teams that were better qualified, better funded, and they didn't achieve. And the Wright Brothers beat them to it.

As it turns out, there is a pattern. All the great and inspiring leaders and organizations think, act, and communicate the exact same way. And it's the complete opposite to everyone else. And its probably the world's simplest idea. I call it the Golden Circle.

Draw a diagram like a bulls-eye with three concentric circles. Write "Why" in the inner circle, "How" in the middle circle, and "What" in the outer circle. This little idea explains why some organizations and leaders are able to inspire where others aren't.

Every single organization on the planet knows what they do. Some know how they do it. Very few people or organizations know why they do what they do. And I don't mean to make a profit. that's a result. By "Why" I mean what's your purpose, what's your cause, what's your belief. Why does your organization exist? Why do you get out of bed in the morning, and why should anyone care?

The inspired leaders and organizations all think, act, and communicate from the inside out. Let me give you an example. If Apple were like everyone else, a marketing message from them might sound like this...

We make great computers. They're beautifully designed, simple to use, and user friendly. Want to buy one?

It's uninspiring.

Here's how Apple actually communicates...

Everything we do, we believe in challenging the status quo. We believe in thinking differently. The way we challenge the status quo is by making our products beautifully designed, simple to use and user friendly. We just happen to make great computers. Want to buy one?

Totally different, right? You're ready to buy a computer from me. All I did was reverse the order of the information. People don't buy what you do, they buy why you do it."

Apple Inc provides a variety of computer gadgets from Ipods to Iphones to Imacs. They are known more for superior quality and functionality rather than affordability. To compare Apple products to a car, Apple is more like a Ferrari Testarossa than a Geo Metro. Their products are sleek in design and come with a lot of added features. Their basic laptop computer is about three times more expensive than a basic PC laptop. However, if you have ever been to a mall and walked by an Apple store, you will notice that they are always extremely busy. As of June 25, 2011, according to CNN.com Apple's holdings in cash and marketable securities stood at $76.2 billion; and according to the NYTimes.com, Apple became the most valuable business in the world, surpassing Exxon-Mobile for a period of time on August 9, 2011. Apple did not generate this kind of popularity by creating the cheapest products. They did it through innovation, great customer service and products that people are willing to spend good money for. (Read about the history of Apple at: http://storiesofusa.com/ greatest-american-entrepreneurs-and-business-professionals-in-the-usa/#steve-jobs).

How did Steve Jobs get people to do what he wanted them to do? He started with a message that answered "Why" people should purchase his products. That is the most important thing to remember when you develop your message. You need to ask yourself, what value do I add to a person's life? And why should they listen to my message? If you manage a political campaign or a non-profit organization, you need to have a message that will not only get people to notice, but will get them to want to help you spread that message.

Let's face it, people are busy worrying about their own lives. Many do not vote and many more do not donate any money or time, and they think they do not have any surplus time or money. If you want to accomplish specific tasks in order to move your social or political cause forward, you will need both. You want to tailor your message so that it not only tugs on people's emotions, but also creates real solutions to real problems. Make A Wish foundation makes it possible for a person with a terminal disease to have the ability to make one of his/her dreams come true before he/she passes away. Just like any other non-profit organization, they need money and volunteers to accomplish their mission. They were able to gain a significant amount of support because they created a message of hope that reverberated throughout a large portion of society.

So what is your message?

HOW DO I BROADCAST MY MESSAGE?

In this modern environment, people are bombarded daily with numerous advertisements through email, telephone, television, radio, standard mail, magazines, movies, and so on. We live in a time of advertisement overload. People will delete unread emails, toss unopened envelopes, fast forward through commercials on the TV and change radio stations during commercial breaks. With all these seemingly impenetrable walls in between your message and a possible client, donor or vote, how do you get others to pay attention?

The answer can be summed up in four words: RELEVANCY, COMMUNITY, AUTHORITY and TRUST.

Relevancy – People will seek you out if you provide a product or service that is related to what they are interested in. You want to create a product or service that improves the lives of and creates solutions for individuals or groups.

Community – It is a group of similar-minded individuals who communicate with each other related to a specific subject matter or idea. You want to build a community of like-minded individuals that know what products/services you offer.

Authority – It has several meanings and they are all relevant to this discussion:

- the power or right to give orders, make decisions or control someone or something.
- the confident quality of someone who knows a lot about something or who is respected or obeyed by other people.
- a quality that makes something seem true or real.

Trust – It is the belief that someone or something is reliable, good, honest, effective, valuable, etc.

If you master these four concepts, you will have the ability to achieve many of your goals and objectives. To provide some clarity let's briefly compare the influence of Steve Jobs versus a homeless person. My goal here is to clearly describe the importance of these four factors.

Relevancy:

A homeless person may offer services, such as selling newspapers, fruit or flowers. He / She may wash your window, beg or recycle materials for small amounts of cash. Steve Jobs / Apple owns numerous patents and produces many high-value products, such as the iPhone.

Community:

A homeless person is fairly isolated and does not have many strong friendships with people of influence. Steve Jobs is surrounded by influential people, such as government officials, investment bankers, lawyers, inventors, etc.

Authority:

A homeless person would enter a room and either be ignored or ushered out. Steve Jobs would enter a room and be surrounded by numerous people who truly care about what he has to say.

Trust:

Whether financial, emotional, spiritual, etc., a homeless person is perceived as not having much value, whereas Steve Jobs is perceived as having an extremely high amount of value.

Building trust, which is based on individual perception, is the objective. To get results, you have to engender trust.

The following information takes these four concepts and turns them into specific task-oriented activities that will, over time, generate results, and save you a lot of time, money and headaches. Though this process, ask yourself why you purchase something or get involved in something.

1) Purpose, Goals, Passion

It is critical that you believe in your product or service, be willing to put in the effort, and have the passion and commitment to see it through. Technique is important, but without the desire to succeed, nothing else truly matters. It is important to develop those intangibles, such as integrity, persistence, confidence, positive mental attitude, etc.

Action Item(s):
- Read List of Characteristics of Successful People (Taken from: http://storiesofusa.com/top-characteristics-of-successful-people/):
- Develop Intangible Characteristics: Passion, Purpose, Creative, Integrity, Initiative, Character, Dream Big, Hard Work, Innovative, Persistence, Clear Vision, Independent, Self-Confident, Inquisitiveness, Strong Leadership, Tolerance for Failure, Calculated Risk Taker, Goal Oriented Behavior, Positive Mental Attitude and Commitment to Excellence.

2) Get Organized

Being organized is the first and most critical strategy for managing any campaign or event. The more difficult the endeavor, the more crucial it is that people know exactly what is going on. During the Summer Olympics, there is much to do and keep track of. There are dozens of competitions with thousands of athletes, trainers, and employees, not to mention the millions of fans who will be attending events in multiple venues.

So how does one get organized? The most fundamental of tools is the business plan. Before you spend a large amount of money and time, both you and your investors want to know what you plan on doing with the money, equipment and labor that is, or will be, available to you. The business plan is generally organized into the following sections: Executive Summary, Company Description, Products and Services, Marketing Plan, Operational Plan, and Financial Plan. There is another section I would strongly recommend adding: Technology Plan.

Action Item(s):

- Create a Business Plan

3) Technology Infrastructure Recommendations

You will want to determine the hardware and software you will want and need to efficiently and effectively operate and manage your organization. How many computers will you need? Will you need a server? What software do you need? What other equipment will you need? Do you have a person that will manage your technological infrastructure?

The #1 mistake I see organizations make when it comes to technology is to hire or contract someone who does not have integrity. Integrity is much more important than ability. Your "Tech Guy" will often have access to credit card information, personal emails, login passwords, customer contacts, etc. They could easily, and often legally, control your access to the technology that you paid for. You as the leader of the organization must be able to trust that person to not only get the job done, but to not take advantage of you in the process. The #2 mistake I see organizations make is that the business owner does not have access to the technology being developed. The business owner should use a business or personal credit card to purchase items. Time and time again I have had to work with business owners and organization leaders who do not know the login to the website or where everything is located. I do not expect the leader to know how to build a website or setup a server network, but a good leader should have the login and important contact information related to these technologies.

Here is some more advice that could save you thousands of dollars. Software can become very expensive. Microsoft, Adobe, and Norton are companies that provide common mainstream software solutions. The price tag for each of these products can run into the hundreds of dollars. There are free alternatives to these products, but keep in mind that free software does usually not have all the features paid software has. However, if you are on a tight budget, they are good enough to at least get you going.

Brand Software	Free Alternative
Microsoft Office	Open Office (openoffice.org)
Adobe Photoshop	Gimp (gimp.org)
Miva Merchant	Zen-Cart (zen-cart.com)
Norton Antivirus	AVG (free.avg.com)
Adobe Acrobat	Open Office (openoffice.org)

Some other free software includes: Audacity (sound editing), Filezilla (ftp file management), Malwarebytes (Anti Malware), and Windows Movie Maker. I also recommend installing all three major web browsers: Google Chrome, Windows Internet Explorer and Mozilla Firefox. If one gets corrupt, you have another browser to use to download fixes from the Internet. If you are using a Windows operating system, I would recommend downloading and keeping the following software up to date: Adobe Flash Player, Adobe Reader, antivirus, Java, web browsers, and Windows Operating System (7, 8 etc). Also, avoid installing unnecessary software, which will slow your system down and potentially open you up to spyware and viruses.

Action Item(s):
- Setup Your Technology Based Systems (Internet, Document Development, Websites, Financial Tracking, Customer Relations, etc.)

4) A Memorable Name

Create a business name that people will remember and that reflects the product or service you provide. When selecting a name for your website, there are 2 trains of thought:

A) Choose a domain with your business name (ex: facebook.com)

B) Choose a domain that contains keywords associated with the product or service you provide (ex: socialnetworking.com)

Branded domains may have a harder time ranking in search engines versus keyword rich domains. However, branded domains over time offer more flexibility and authority within the marketplace. I would actually recommend buying and developing both types of domains, but use them for different purposes.

Now that you have chosen a domain name, go to Godaddy. com and register it. I recommend Godaddy over the other website domain and hosting companies because of their pricing, reliability and customer service. There are many other options such as BlueHost, 1 & 1, and Host Gator. I can also recommend other hosting companies depending on your requirements. Avoid Network Solutions. Something else to consider is hosting. A company like Godaddy offers inexpensive shared hosting, but this type of service may reduce the speed in which your website loads. You may also be limited in resources, such as bandwidth. A dedicated server offers many more options, such as increased load time, larger bandwidth, increased storage, etc. Its major drawback is the cost. I strongly recommend talking to a technology consultant to determine what type of hosting is best for you, but be aware if that consultant gets financial benefits from converting you into a customer of a specific service. This may not always be a bad thing, but it may cause the consultant to get you to make decisions based on his/her best interest and not yours.

Action Item(s):
- Register Domain and Hosting with GoDaddy.com

5) Websites

Over the last decade, I have built hundreds of websites in which many rank very high in Google searches, automate the ability to purchase products online, manipulate data, and send direct messages to and from clients. A website is part of the marketing arm of an organization. It, if designed and operated properly, will do much of the heavy lifting necessary to create social and political change. If you plan on operating a business, non-profit organization or political campaign, it is critical that you have a website that accomplishes 3 goals:

a) Branding

People need to quickly look at your logo and website and instantly recognize who you are and what products or services you provide. Many American political campaign websites are in various shades of red, white and blue with a visible American flag. When you look at the top of Storiesofusa.com, you will see American patriotic symbols and images, such as the American flag, Abraham Lincoln and the Liberty Bell. Also, users need to quickly determine if they can trust you. Trust signals depend on your industry and marketing objectives, and may include things like: logos of trusted organizations that you do business with, industry awards, easy to find contact information, useful reviews, structure of the site, etc.

b) Usability

The site must be easy to use. You want to make it easy to receive feedback from people that are using your website. Put yourself in the shoes of a visitor. Can you find the information you are looking for? Are all the links working? Does it load quickly? Is all the content spelled correctly and easy to understand? You will want to make sure you add photos, graphs, and videos to improve the comprehension of the ideas you are trying to explain. StoriesofUSA.com contains hundreds of photos and videos. The website is composed of thousands of pages of content. If I had thousands of links on every page, a visitor would quickly feel intimidated and would quickly leave the site. There is a visual menu on top with seven choices. If you click on the image of Abraham Lincoln, it takes you to a page with a list of major historical events in US history that are in chronological order. A person looking for information on the Civil War can quickly find it. You must also make sure that people can access and use your site with a variety of different devices, such as laptops, tablets and mobile phones.

c) Searchability

A website must be tailored for a human being. It must also be developed to be compatible with search engines, such as Google and Bing. Content must be visible and organized properly. Content on a website is not all treated equally. I could write an entire book on the subject of the relationship between a website and a search engine. I will instead try to highlight the most important items. If I were to tell you that StoriesofUSA.com gets thousands of visitors daily and that we do not pay for any of that traffic, would you believe me? So how did I accomplish this?

Action Item(s):
- Create a Properly Designed Website

6) On Page Content

HTML (Hyper Text Markup Language) was initially developed to put newspaper articles online. HTML provides the ability to control style and position of content on a web page. Great content is the most important part of great search engine rankings. If people like your content, they will read it. If they love your content they will link to it and tell others about it.

Writing for the Internet is much different than writing for printed media, such as postcards. At the heart of Internet search is keywords. Keywords are words or phrases that people input in search engines such as Google.com to find information online. Make sure you choose keywords and phrases that are searched often (ex: car repair, auto repair). You will also want to use keywords that are searched often that have less competition than other terms (ex: bmw auto parts, auto repair los angeles).

Google is undergoing a significant change in philosophy. Google's current fundamental philosophy of search engine rankings is AUTHORITY and TRUST. Content posted by the Wall Street Journal or the White House will generally rank higher than similar content re-posted by a journalist. This is due to a number of indicators that the search engine tracks. Some of these indicators are discussed below.

The following is a checklist that will help you identify which strategies to work on. This list is organized into three sections: Extremely Important, Very Important and Somewhat Important. Remember, this is an overview – not a detailed discussion. If any of this confuses you, consult someone who specializes in Search Engine Optimization (SEO).

Extremely Important:
- Use keywords and brand name throughout website pages (There is a balance between too little and too much).
- Write fresh unique content (Do not just copy and paste other content).
- Let your domain age (Mature sites rank better than new sites).
- Reduce the number of coding errors and broken links on a page (Tools I use: Xenu Link Sleuth, Validator.w3.org).

- Make your site friendly for both standard and mobile devices.
- Make sure your website has an RSS feed and link to it.
- Decrease page load time.
- Provide things that increase user time on page, such as: videos, graphs and surveys.
- Write content that is thorough (Avoid writing content that is short or full of spelling / grammar errors).
- Targeted keyword phrase (such as "Auto Car Repair Los Angeles") needs to be in Title (first words), Description, Primary Header, within the first 100 words of main content and page url.
- Post images correctly: image name, alt / title tags.
- Use text-based links as much as possible.
- Minimize or eliminate the amount of Flash (programming language) used on the site.
- Generate separate sitemaps for both the user and the search engine.
- Increase the number of internal links to important pages and decrease the number of links to unimportant pages.
- User variations of your keyword on page (ex: auto repair, car repair, auto mechanic, auto shop).

Very Important:

- Improve quality of or eliminate other websites hosted in the same account.
- Do not use hyphens (-) in the domain name.
- Avoid long domain names.
- Page contains structured data: header tags (h1, h2, h3), rich snippets (schema.org), meta tags, etc.
- Find the right balance between ads and content.
- Be aware of the reading level of your audience.
- Use of Facebook Open Graph Data and/or Twitter Cards
- Use of targeted keyword in on-page link text.
- Less than 100 links per page.

- Create tools that encourage on-page user engagement and backlinks.

Somewhat Important:
- Increase the length of time in which domain expires.
- Use of targeted keyword in bold/italics.
- Use a "New Content" section on your web page.

Action Item(s):
- Use the checklist.

7) Offsite Content

Once you have your website up and running, it is now time to get your message out there. The basic concept is to cast a wide net, and do it over and over again. There are a number of strategies that can be used to increase both website traffic and authority.

A) Register your website domain name with search engines and directories, such as Google, Yahoo, Bing, DMOZ and Ask. There are search engine submitters that will submit to many search engines at the same time. You only need to submit your domain name to search engines once. Use http://www.submitexpress.com/free-submission.html.

B) List the website on all marketing material, including emails and business cards.

C) Link Building – A link placed on another website that points back to your website is called a backlink. Talk to your friends and associates. If they have a website, have them place a link that points back to you. This is an ongoing process. Keep in mind that a backlink from a company like Google.com is better than a backlink from a brand new website. You can use tools like Google Webmaster Tools and ahrefs.com to identify your backlinks.

Backlink Checklist:

- Backlinks from high-quality sites are much better than from low-quality sites.
- Maintain a steady pace in order to increase Link Velocity or the rate in which you get backlinks.
- Get backlinks from quality sites like Wikipedia, DMOZ, .edu/.gov sites, etc.
- Vary the link text and what pages are linked.
- Get backlinks from your industry leaders.
- Get backlinks from other local businesses.
- Do not link to penalized or "spammy" sites.

D) Article Submission and Content Syndication – Although this has been a good way to get backlinks, it is a strategy that you have to implement properly or it can harm you. Article Submission is when you post content onto another website. Content Syndication is when you post the same or similar content across a number of different websites. Content includes: articles, newsletters, and press releases related to services you provide, the industry that you are in, and events that you will be hosting. There are two primary issues of concern: 1) It is not good to post duplicate content across a large number of websites; 2) Backlinks from low quality "spammy" sites could harm your rankings. Once the articles are written, you can distribute them to many locations. http://www.styopkin. com/article_submission_sites.html contains a large list of sites to submit to. You will want to setup accounts for sites like BlogCatalog and Codango. Then you can automatically submit your content to these sites. There is a site I use (moonsy.com/domain_authority) that tells you the authority of any given website. BlogCatalog.com has a domain authority of 86 out of 100. Article submission to and backlinks from this site are very good. ArticleShelf. com, on the other hand, only has a domain authority of

27 out of 100. I would not recommend submitting articles to this site.

E) Blog Commenting – This is another strategy you need to be careful with. As previously discussed, not all backlinks are good. The most important part of this strategy is that you are having conversations with others on high traffic sites. In some cases you can submit a backlink. In other cases you can submit text-based content. You want to portray yourself as someone who is professional and knowledgeable in a subject. Engage in positive conversation with others through blog comments and you will eventually gain on online reputation. Don't just leave a comment that says, "Look at me. Buy my product."

F) Search Maps – Both Bing and Google generate maps in search. For example, they will identify and plot grocery stores near you when you search for them in your local area. BingPlaces.com and Google.com/business provide instructions for how to accomplish this.

G) Videos, Images, Podcasts and mp3s – Create or leverage existing video and audio files. Create accounts on Youtube, iTunes, Vimeo, Metacafe and other sites where you can upload media files. You can often link back to your website from these accounts. You can advertise your website within these media files. These forms of media make your content more interactive and increase the opportunities for others to easily find you and tell others about you. This is the essence of Viral Marketing. People like to share interesting content and links with their friends. So go and create interesting content, post it to your website, and share it with your friends.

Action Item(s):
• URL submission for new website - http://www.submit-express.com/free-submission.html

- Create profiles and content with backlinks on MercantCircle.com, W3sites.org, Bloglines.com, Angelfire.com, Yellowpages.com, Manta.com, Craigslist. org, Yola.com, Squidoo.com, Hubpages.com, Blogger. com / Blogspot.com, Wordpress.com, Tumblr.com, etc.
- Research competition and place links where they have links
- Place backlink to your website on other websites, such as industry related sites, friends, clients
- Create accounts and submit articles as found on http:// www.styopkin.com/article_submission_sites.html
- Comment on other blogs and online news articles with a link back to your site
- Create a profile on Google Places, Bing Places, etc.
- Viral Marketing through video, podcasts and mp3s - Submit to Youtube.com, Vimeo.com, Metacafe.com, iTunes.com, Buzznet.com, Blip.tv, Dailymotion.com, Veoh.com, Flickr.com, PhotoBucket.com, etc.

8) Standard Networking

Join business networking organizations and online groups, such as a chamber of commerce and Meet Up to create business connections and opportunities with local and similar minded individuals.

Action Item(s):

- Join Groups: Chamber of Commerce, MeetUp.com, Business Networking Organizations, Non-Profit Organizations, Political Organizations

9) Public Relations, Social Media and Bookmarking

There are numerous ways to improve relationships with the general public and your client base, including newsletters, email campaigns, blogging, bookmarking and online social media.

A) Newsletters and Email Campaigns – Capturing email through your website and then sending follow up information to them through email is an important element of Internet marketing - sites that make this easier are: MobileStorm.com, ContantContact.com, Aweber.com and iContact.com. Some content management systems (such as Wordpress) have the ability to integrate these features. There are many sites that do this, so do your homework and find one that works for you.

Also, keep your emails simple. Most people will not take the time to read every word that you write in the email. Your main goal in the email is to get them back to your website and to follow further instructions. Setup a web page that has a clear Call to Action (What do you want them to do once they are there?). Then in your email that you submit, create short, but interesting, content that links to this Call to Action page on your website.

You will want to create a campaign in Google Analytics to track email campaigns and use a url tracker. (http://www.google.com/support/analytics/bin/answer.py?hl=en&answer=55578)

One last thing. Everyone's email is setup differently. Some can receive fully formatted emails with embedded images, links and videos. Others receive text only email, that have no formatting. You will have to develop emails that are flexible enough in design that will still be able to get your message to them, no matter what type of email system the recipient has.

B) Blogging - Blogging is a science and an artform. Essentially, you want to create relevant content that is related to your industry, that people want to read about, that will create positive name recognition, and that will drive traffic to your website. If you are in the insurance industry, you will want to write about new insurance laws, new insurance companies, and new types of insurance programs that are available. There are numerous easy-to-use blog platforms to choose from, including: Blogger.com and Wordpress.com.

C) Social Media Optimization - Facebook, Twitter, YouTube, Google+, Pinterest, Linkedin, Foursquare and others help create social connections and a following of like minded individuals. It is not enough to just create a profile. It is an ongoing process of generating contacts, describing yourself and fostering stronger relationships. These are great places to foster niche and relationship marketing. Find like-minded individuals with similar hobbies and interests. Encourage them to be your "friend." As a friend, you can send out info to them. Like-minded people are more willing to purchase from you, vote for you, or give you money. I strongly recommend starting with a Facebook Fan Page. - http://www.facebook.com/help/?page=904 and joining a Facebook "Group". Once you get a lot of "friends", you can send them messages to encourage them to do what it is you would like them to do. Also, Twitter can be a way to encourage backlinking. Create a bit.ly account (url shortener). When you want to post a website, post it as a bit.ly. It will shorten your url and it will allow you to track where you are receiving Twitter traffic from. Use the search features (http://search.twitter.com, etc.) to find discussions related to your topic. I strongly recommend limiting yourself to one or two social media accounts when you first start out. Become proficient at these, and then increase your sphere of influence where necessary. Remember that people will buy more from people they like or want to be around. Do not be pushy or overly aggressive. Social media is a complex area, not because of its difficulty to use, but by its myriad of options and the complex social interactions involved. Use a service like IFTTT.com to coordinate your postings with various social media accounts.

D) Google+ and Authorship – This is an important enough element in search engine rankings that it requires its own section. There are two types of Google+ profiles: author and publisher. The author is a person and the publisher is a business / brand. You will want to create and manage both of these profiles. Refer to https://plus.google.com/authorship and http://www.google.com/webmasters/tools/richsnippets. These sites will help you understand, setup and test Authorship. Essentially, you cross link your web pages with your Google+ profiles. You will want to get +1 referrals to your page of content. You will also want to build relationships, especially through Google+ and Linkedin, with those who are influential and have authority.

E) Social Bookmarking – It is a very simple concept. People use their accounts to mark which sites they like. The more your content is "bookmarked," the better your changes of higher rankings in the search engines. Social bookmarking sites include: Delicious, Digg and Stumbleupon.

F) TV, Radio, Newspaper - There are cost effective and creative ways to get media attention without having to spend a large amount of advertising dollars. If you get media attention, exploit it by posting the image, video or podcast on your website. Encourage them to link back to your website.

G) Be an Expert – Display your knowledge of a certain field. There are various ways to do this, but the bottom line is that you want to be perceived by a lot of people that you know what you are talking about related to concepts that they want to know about. Here are some suggestions: Be an expert on a radio or TV program, setup a profile on Yahoo Answers and answer some questions, etc. If you are a plumber or electrician you might want to be a keynote speaker at a Home Owners Association meeting.

H) S.U.C.C.E.S.S. - Secrets of Viral Marketing – Submit content that is Simple to follow, Unexpected, Concrete and tangible concepts, Credible thoughts and results, Emotional connection, tells a Story and is Shareable.

* Special Note: You will notice little to no mention of "Reviews." There are a number of factors involved in the ranking and social value of reviews. Many reviews are fake. Business owners may insert positive reviews, whereas competitors may write negative reviews. Also, reviews on a website with high authority (such as Google) may be ranked higher than reviews on a low authority website. Never take reviews as truth. Reviews are opinions. As the owner / manager of a business or organization, you want to manage the impact of these reviews. If you follow the guidelines laid out in this chapter, you can begin to reduce the negative impact of bad or hostile reviews.

Action Item(s):
- Create newsletters and email campaigns
- Blog for more content – Blogger.com, Wordpress.com
- Leverage social media for relationship marketing: Facebook.com, Twitter.com, Youtube.com, Google+, LinkedIn.com, Pinterest.com, etc.
- Use Delicious, Digg, Stumbleupon and other book-marking sites.
- Use IFTTT.com to coordinate posts on various accounts
- Leverage Google+ Authorship tools
- Find creative ways to be mentioned in TV, radio or newspaper
- Be an expert and answer questions
- Viral Marketing SUCCESS (Simple – Unexpected – Concrete – Credible – Emotional – Story - Shareable)

10) Track and Analyze

It is critical to be able to objectively analyze where you are obtaining your clients from – http://www.google.com/analytics/. This tool, once integrated onto a website, provides a wealth of information about traffic on a website. Also, if you are spending money on banner ads, directories, etc., you need to make sure you are tracking the response.

Action Item(s):
• Attach Google Analytics tracking code to your website

GATHERING YOUR GROUPIES

If you truly want to create social and political change, you have to do a whole lot more than stand on a street corner with a sign. You have to be able to engage and persuade. You cannot move a mountain by yourself. It takes a team effort. You have to put in effort to train and develop a team that will help you move that mountain. The good news is that you do not need hundreds or thousands of people to get things moving. You just need a handful of dedicated individuals to start getting results, and once you have a core group, that group will begin to do more of the heavy lifting for you.

Justin Bieber is currently a very popular teenage vocalist. He is a social media success story. When he was twelve years old, he began to post videos of himself singing on YouTube.com. He also created a Facebook account to interact with people and to encourage them to view his posted videos. By creating videos that displayed his talents and taking time to nurture a quality base of supporters, Bieber was able to obtain tens of thousands of video views. These videos and the support he had from his fan base caught the eyes of two prominent performers: Usher and Justin Timberlake. After a high-profile bidding war, Bieber signed with Usher.

There are many techniques and strategies that can be used to find and gather followers, groupies, or like-minded individuals. In order for you to find them, you have to learn and develop certain skills. You also have to have the right message. Would Justin Bieber be as popular as he is if he didn't have some ability to sing and perform?

You will gain more support from a position of strength. If people perceive that you are beautiful, intelligent, confident, experienced, courageous, capable or popular, they will be more willing to interact with you, be around you, and be more willing to tell their friends about you, your business, or your cause. Any political or social change must have a large enough base of support in order for it to develop its own wings. For without friends encouraging friends to take action, there is no change.

Here is a list of some strategies and techniques that will help persuade others:

Assertiveness:	Be bold and direct
Body language:	Stand tall
Closing techniques:	Close the deal
Confidence:	Appear calm, cool and collected
Conversation:	Chat with people
Conversion:	Get them to say yes
Happiness:	Smile
Hypnotism:	Subconscious suggestions
Interrogation:	Ask questions
Negotiation tactics:	Know what you want
Language:	Speak clearly
Listening:	What are people saying
Objection-handling:	Overcome "Not Interested"
Propaganda:	Effective Marketing
Public speaking:	Talk to a lot of people
Self-Development:	Develop skills
Stress Management:	Relax

Tipping: Show me the money
Using humor: Laugh it up fuzzball
Willpower: Self-control

SPOTLIGHT ON AJ BOMBERS

Posted by Augie Ray on March 28, 2010 (Forrester.com)

"I moved to the Bay Area from Milwaukee about five months ago. Among the things I miss from my hometown are my two favorite burger restaurants - AJ Bombers and Sobelman's. Both have used Word of Mouth (WOM) to become successful small businesses, but while one built its buzz over 10 years, the other used social media to become a success in just one year. The stories of these two businesses can provide insight and inspiration to much larger brands seeking to create benefits with social media.

Sobelman's is a little hard to find - it's located in an industrial part of the city rather than in a fashionable neighborhood - but that didn't prevent it from building a broad-based following since opening in 1999. Sobelman's created its success the old-fashioned way - with a great story (Dave and Melanie Sobelman worked the grill and took orders), a delicious product and a smart mix of traditional marketing, such as sponsoring Marquette University events.

The road to success for AJ Bombers was considerably shorter, although there were plenty of reasons to think the business would fail quickly: It was launched in the middle of the worst recession in generations and was located at an address that had seen at least five businesses fail in recent years. AJ Bombers' one-year path from grand opening to the pages of the Wall Street Journal speaks volumes about the way social media is changing business.

Of course, just like Sobelman's, AJ Bombers' success starts with a great experience and a great product. (All the tweets in the world won't overcome a poor consumer experience.) But while the two restaurants share that much in common, it is AJ Bombers' use of social media that demonstrates the power of the medium. The restaurant's constant attention toward building awareness and energizing fans has included:

Active engagement on Twitter and Facebook. On Twitter, AJ Bombers has tweeted more than 10,000 times to its 3,000 followers. On Facebook, the restaurant updates its status several times a month and engages with 1,000 fans. Offering new FourSquare mayors a free burger and fries, encouraging repeat visits and checking among its fan base.

A special event drew a mass of FourSquare users who earned the midwest's first "Swarm Badge." Over 150 people turned out for the event - more than one-quarter of all FourSquare users in Milwaukee - and AJ Bombers saw revenue more than double from the same day the previous week. (AJ Bomber's innovative use of FourSquare will continue: The restaurant was recently among 30 small businesses to test new FourSquare analytics technology to track user data and create more engagement.)

A promotion launched with a YouTube video, creating a contest that permitted one lucky winner to earn free burgers for a year. Regular tweetups to draw fans to different events, such as a holiday party and Bloody (Mary) Brunch. Turning a stolen sandwich board into a local news item thanks to a reward offer and smart use of Twitter. A new campaign (in partnership with Sobelman's) to attempt to bring the Travel Channel's "Food Wars" to Milwaukee for a showdown between the two competing burger bars.

While it's interesting to point out everything AJ Bombers has done, it's what they haven't done that is worth noting.

For example, the restaurant has not spent a great deal of cash on their social media success (although time is money, and clearly there's been significant time invested into these efforts.)

Even with little monetary outlay, success can breed problems. I spoke with Joe Sorge, owner of AJ Bombers, and he noted that "in some ways we backed ourselves into a corner - guests expect immediate responses in social media" but he added, "I don't mind the corner!" Sorge still enjoys personally monitoring Facebook and Twitter every day as often as possible, but he is beginning to delegate some of the responsibility. Sorge is training others to monitor and respond to fans on Twitter (with individuals' initials at the end of tweets to make it clear the human behind the tweets).

Another thing AJ Bombers hasn't done is turned their Twitter and Facebook stream into a string of direct marketing offers. Unlike some brands that use their Twitter and Facebook profiles as a replacement for FSIs (Free Standing Inserts) and direct email marketing, Sorge instead points to inspiration from Seth Godin to pursue "the opposite of interruption-style marketing."

Sorge isn't interested in one-way communication but instead praises the value he receives from input and feedback. "Customers are becoming the business," he says. "We had no idea that the 'Burger of the Month' would be so popular and that we'd have to change it to the 'Burger of the Moment.'" In fact, one of their most popular burgers was created by a customer, @KateBarrie; the Barrie Burger features peanut butter, bacon and cheese.

Another thing Sorge does not (and cannot) do is measure ROI. He says he measures what he can - for example, he notes that FourSquare promotions have allowed AJ Bombers to increase sales 30% on select items - but that isn't what Sorge sees as the true value of social media to his business. "This is a restaurant built by social media. This is the only way we know it. We can't say what it would be like without it."

The final thing AJ Bombers isn't doing is waiting for someone else to prove ROI before experimenting with different social media programs. Sorge is unafraid to try new things in inexpensive and small ways. The owner of AJ Bombers knows his customers, understands his brand and recognizes that social media is a way to connect the two. Really, how hard is that?"

Chapter 12

FUND YOUR CAUSE FOR POSITIVE CHANGE

*"Money is only a tool. It will take you wherever you wish,
but it will not replace you as the driver."*

— Ayn Rand

GETTING MONEY IS EASY, JUST ASK!
AND BRING LOTS OF ROI

The most difficult job of chambers of commerce, associations, non-profit organizations, and political campaigns is to ask for money! The other difficulty is: *"How do we do a better job of asking for and raising more money?"* After twenty–three years the song remains the same. I first entered the world of raising money with a large non-profit organization at twenty-five years of age. It was the best training anyone could have. It was always *"How much money are you going to bring us?"* Tom Donahue, the president of the US Chamber of Commerce, would always start our conversations with, *"How's the money?"* Today that training has served me well. Peter Drucker once said, *"Business should study successful Nonprofits."* As president and CEO of several performance enhancement companies, I teach how to do a better job of raising money. If you master this area all your programs and projects get completed; and that leads to more money. In membership organizations if you have the members you can get the money, and if you have the money you can develop programs that will bring in the members. When I lecture and consult around the country I am amazed how the money challenge always comes up. The money will always be there for the ones that can get it.

You Must First Believe in What You Do and Know What You Do

You first have to believe in what it is that you are asking for. To start with, the biggest question that I ask is, *"what is the Organizational Value (OV) to the person that you asking the investment or money from."* The value must be on the same level as, if not more than, the dollar amount you are asking for. Always remember a rule that I have taught for years and truly believe myself. *"Chase the mission and the dollars will come."* In other words, constantly talk about what the organization can do for them!

Constant high value proposition statements.

P.A.R.M.

- Prepare; Make a contribution yourself so you know what it feels like, so you understand the psychology of giving, and so that you have more credibility when asking. Practice your presentation to make yourself more comfortable. If it's not someone you already know well, do a little research (or ask staff) to get a sense of the potential donor's giving ability and tendencies. Make sure your staff knows who you intend to ask, so we don't overwhelm any one donor with multiple requests, or ask someone who just gave. Set goals for you and your organization, and set aside time to do this.
- Ask; in person, if possible. Bring materials, such as brochures, flyers, newspaper clippings about your organization etc.

- Relax; establish rapport with your "prospect" - a person you think might give your organization money. Talk about common interests and ask what the prospect knows about why you are doing this project.
- Make; sure they know the basics. Mention your organization's name many times. If you use an acronym, say it and the full name.

Understanding why people and businesses give is a key to understanding *"show me the money."*

In an article by Charles Bartling CAE, *The Psychology of Asking and Giving*, describes 13 points of understanding:

1. People give because they feel they have an obligation to pay back their profession, their community, their school, or society in general.

2. Much of philanthropy is in the genes of the giver.

3. Corporate giving is different than individual giving.

4. The quality of the organization's management is a significant factor in making the gift decision.

5. The solution is a more powerful motivator than the need.

6. Fund-raising is really friend-raising.

7. The attitude of the ask will result in the quantity of the gift.

8. Maintain optimism in your approach, but reinforce the good that will come from the gift.

9. You can never embarrass a potential donor by asking for too much. You can only embarrass him or her by asking for too little.

10. When asking for money, it's as important to listen as it is to talk.

11. Find a champion to set the bar.

12. Say "thank you" again and again.

13. The most important motivator of them all is - The final and perhaps the most important lesson - There is perhaps nothing as satisfying to an individual as knowing that he or she made a difference in someone else's life.

Placing a Monetary Value on What You Do

I am asked many times how do we place a value (Price) on what it is that we are asking for.

"When the Price isn't Right"

— Andrew Lang

1. While the association's goal is to fulfill its mission and serve its members, to do this well in the long run requires that we avoid under pricing and that we make profits where we can.

2. It is always best to set prices after some input is given by those outside of the department responsible for creating the product.

3. It is essential to know the full cost of a product before you begin to set a price for it.

4. Never price a product without knowing what the market is paying for similar products.

5. The more important the potential revenue stream, the more thorough the testing of potential pricing should be.

6. Be sensitive to buyers' perceptions of the price you are considering. To what extent can you raise it without changing that perception?

7. Work to identify all your premium products and be sure to price them accordingly.

8. Non-member prices should always encourage non-members to become members.

9. Think in terms of the actual dollar value to the purchaser when setting or revising discounts.

10. It is important to review your pricing annually. If a product has strong demand, raise the price. If a product is selling poorly, consider discounts.

11. Remember not to "jar" your marketplace when raising prices or reducing discounts. Move in steps when necessary.

The Points to Importance

Before anything else will work we first have to establish a few points of importance. I was at a major Association conference as one of the guest speakers. My first test question that I love to place in my audiences' hands is:

If we had 4 hours to give our entire story as to why they should join; or give; or sponsor; to 100 non-members, decision makers, or someone that has never heard of what we are doing, how many of those 100 would say *"YES; Here is my money."*

You would be amazed at the answers. One CEO said; *"Probably less than 20%."* This is where the problems are. Give me those same 100 and I promise you that I would capture over 70% of the money!

Here is how the above test works - it's a simple rule - strong Organizational Value will equal strong dues and non-dues revenue.

So you have to look down deep and ask the big question, on a scale of 1 to 10, how much value do we bring the end user (our community)? If we are asking for money on a certain project, does this project tie into the persons YES side of their brain?

Have Clarity as to What Your Value Is to Your Business Community

I have run into many organizational leaders that have a hard time understanding what their value is to the community. When I run into this, I have a Discovering the Value in My Organization Workshop. Line by line we outline the items their organization has to offer its customers or members. After the so called "audit," we then place a value (direct or indirect), on each item. At all times, the Return on Investment (ROI) ratio should be as high as 10 to 1. In other words for every dollar the business or person gives, their return benefit should be ten-fold. In one of my educational CD's, *Join, Stay & Pay,* I go into detail about this.

In the present time and for a very long time to come, businesses are demanding more ROI for their money! Being able to clearly articulate and demonstrate the value of the organization's membership and sponsorship programs will be its survival. I truly believe that if your organization conducted a 4 hour non-member orientation on what the value of their membership would bring to their organization and the overall community, 70% to 80% would join.

That is the good news! Here is the bad news: You don't have 4 hours to conduct the orientation. You rely on referrals, volunteers, a sales force, and your reputation (your branding). Having clarity on what it is you do, and the Call to Action is very important when it comes to bringing in members, and retaining the ones that you have.

Make Sure Your Message and Messenger Are Clear and Concise with Passion and Conviction

Your story had better be crisp and concise. Your marketing pieces that you are showing your member/potential member had better clearly shout: WOW I need to join and stay with this organization! You must have a good story!

Who is telling the story and what is being heard and interpreted within that message? Is it congruent with the organization's message? Does it clearly show that the value of membership overrides the money that you are asking them to invest? Yes, they are investing because they know you will do the right thing with their money. Always remember, it is about the upfront experience that the business or person has with your organization.

After twenty-three years of selling memberships and advertising programs to members and non-members, the questions still remains the same: What have you done for me lately? And what are you going to do for me now? The member and potential member has to hear and see what is taking place within your organization.

Running your organization like a business demands: overcoming objections, bringing strong product value to your potential client base, constantly being on the cutting edge of market and product development, getting your message out to the market place, and letting your community know and understand what it is you sell and why they should buy.

YES, you do sell a product! And part of it is your Passion and a belief structure! Make sure the two are STRONGLY COMMUNICATED!

Don't Be Afraid to Flex Your Organization's Muscles

You cannot be afraid to Flex Your Muscles to the community and show your VALUE to your members and potential members! People are looking for a trusted solution to their personal and professional challenges and you are it!

When the US Chamber of Commerce went from $75 million to raising $200 million, they accomplished this with a new leader. Tom Donahue was not afraid to tell his potential market place and current customers: *"We are worth the money and here is why,"* every chance he got. He Flexed His Muscles, and the business community stepped up to the plate and gave him what he was after, Members and Money!

How did Tom Donahue do this? VP's were required to go out and get the money and ask for big money. The US Chamber's capital campaign was and is a huge success. With an over $250 million budget today, Tom was able to push the value, create more value, and communicate the value to the World. Once again the Organizational Value will bring in the money.

Know the Compelling Reasons to Make It Easy to Say Yes

Clarity in what you do with compelling reasons to say YES is do or die. Know the Message! Understanding why, what, and how much is key. During my last 2 years with the US Chamber I was National Senior Project Leader of the Major Metro Project. I would go out from time to time with a team of three and ask for large membership dues. We knew exactly what we needed and why we needed it - Very clear and to the point. The prospect on the other end of the boardroom table understood the need!

Understanding Communication and Conversation

3 parts of communication according to Aristotle
1. Ethos – character/credibility of the person
2. Pathos – connecting with the emotions – we tune into them and their needs
3. Logos – factual content

3 elements of conversation
1. Words = 7%
2. Tone of voice = 37%
3. Body language = 56%

The Messenger - the Most Important Key

Now, for some words about the Messenger. You could have great Organizational Value and unbelievable C (communication) and M (message), but if the Messenger does not communicate well, you will have problems. Tom Donahue's success is all wrapped up in a great system: Great Organizational Value + Great Communication to the business community + Fantastic Message + Great Messenger!

I have always said, *"communication rules the world and raises money."* Take a look at these areas and use the test and rank yourself in all areas of your Organization.

Communicating For Profit

The 7 Fundamentals of a Perfect Presentation

1. Body Language/Energy Level/Transference of Feeling
2. Rapport
3. Third Party
4. Gain Control
5. Create Need
6. Build Value
7. Assume the Sale

The 5 tools that must be included in your script in order to give perfect presentations are:

1. Initial Benefit Statement (IBS)
2. Show and Tell (if in person)
3. Reason Why
4. Gain Control
5. Create Urgency

In my research in the field and on the phone, here are some of the biggest mistakes that I see when asking for the MONEY!

1. They don't ask.
2. They under ask for the MONEY.
3. They don't understand the 3 communication and 3 conversation rules as I discussed earlier.
4. They don't ask thought provoking questions.
5. They forget it's about them, not you.
6. They do not have a flexible Money option (game plan).
7. You have to TRAIN the messengers.
8. They don't do the homework on the potential money giver.
9. Rejection – Rejection – Rejection! Remember, money is not a rejection, it is a condition.

Golden Rule: As Long As There Is an Agreement in Concept, You Have Permission to Move Forward with Alternatives

1. Talk about what you have accomplished this year and what you plan on doing.
2. Listen. Find out why they do or should care about what you do.
3. Tell them why you are involved in the project, and why you are investing your time in the project. Share your passion - it's infectious. Name all the reasons, but focus on the ones you think your prospect values. If you aren't sure - ask!
4. Tell the truth. Don't promise more than you can deliver.
5. Focus on the cause, and what you can accomplish.
6. Tell a success story.

Objections, Learn to Love Them

If they have questions or objections, use it as an opportunity to clear up any misconceptions. If you don't know or don't have an answer, don't make things up, but promise to get back to them later. Numbers oriented people may be interested in your financial picture. Be prepared to talk about your budget, where your money has come from in the past (individual donations, etc), and who has sponsored or joined to date. People like to get involved with a program that is new, or has momentum, and is likely to succeed.

Get the Commitment Now

Ask for their pledge of financial commitment. Once you've presented your case and dealt with any objections, it is then time to get a commitment. Don't be apologetic; if you don't ask for contributions, most people will not give them. Explain why a new donation (or an increase) is needed. State and Federal cutbacks, economy is challenging - turns such losses into issues to be solved instead of failures of your organization. DON'T PLEAD FOR A "BAIL OUT."

Ask for a specific amount that is high, but not outrageous. It's easier to bargain down than up. Also, according to United Way, *"studies have shown that solicitors, who ask for more, get more."* After you ask for the money, say nothing more. Smile, Relax. It's better to let the silence make them a little uncomfortable than jump in with an excuse that gets them off the hook, or distracts them from their answer. They have the right to say no. You have the right to ask.

When you have secured their financial investment/commitment or better yet, their check, thank the person for the important role he or she is playing in meeting the needs of your organization and their community.

If they pledge support, but are not specific, ask for a dollar amount. If it is a large amount, ask if they would prefer you to send them an invoice or pick the check up personally? Thank them again. I recommend that people who give donations should be thanked seven times for each gift/donation. Send an official thank-you for their tax records. Send them updates periodically. If you have a newsletter, be sure they receive it, and that you acknowledge their financial involvement in the newsletter.

When you are ready to ask again, you will want to say thanks again for their last financial involvement, and would they consider giving a larger amount.

If they say no, thank them for letting you present them your case. Ask why, if it's not too awkward. Maybe they'd like to be involved in some other way - donate time, or materials - or perhaps the timing is wrong this year, but they'd be interested in the future if you approach them at a different time of year etc. Don't forget – Say THANK YOU!!

SUMMARY

How to Ask for Money – building the foundation for the YES!

1.   Repeat the name of your organization often.

2.   Say your name, the name of your group and your position: *"Hello, my name is Joe Jones, Executive Director of the Organization."*

3.   Describe your group's activities and its effectiveness (maximum of five sentences): *"The Organization provides training and technical consulting services to non-profit groups in the areas of leadership development, empowerment, board development, and financial self-sufficiency. The Organization works with neighborhood groups, rural organizations, churches, minority constituencies, seniors, and organizations for the disabled."*

4.   Describe your budget: *"It costs $900,000 to operate the Organization for one year."*

5.   Describe your Financial funding Strategy: *"The Organization receives 70% of its funding budget from workshop and training fees, consultant contracts from our constituencies, and earned income projects. We receive 10% of our funds from state and federal sources."*

Asking for Money - the presentation

1. Always ask for a specific amount of money.

2. If the donation is tax-deductible, say so.

3. Always ask for money for a specific part of your program.

4. Ask for the dollar amount again.

5. Try to break down your request into cause and effect terms: *"Your $100 contribution will enable us to mail our 300 newsletters."*

6. Smile - stop talking. Wait for a response.

7. Answer questions briefly.

8. Explain why you need the money NOW.

9. Repeat steps 1-5 until they say YES.

Role Play

Pick a friend or colleague to play a potential funder. Role-play steps 1-7 and actually ask for money for a real project in your group. Switch off. You may even exchange money during this role-play. Allow five minutes for each person.

Why are people afraid to ask for money?

Answer: They are not trained properly.

The 3 C's: Building Blocks of a GREAT Organization

Congruency
- In order for us to GROW, we must know: Is everyone on the same page?

Communication

Messaging
- Message to our customers
- Message of ROI
- Message to the community
- Message to potential customers

Commitment toward Excellence
- Mission
- Vision
- Values
- Leadership, at ALL levels

Over the past many years, I have raised tens of millions of dollars and trained thousands of people on how to raise money selling memberships, sponsorships, and advertising. When I conduct training seminars and lecture on how to "Get the Money," there are several rules that have served me well. I always make sure that I pass them on to my Students and audience:

Attitude - yes I can!

Urgency - yes it will!

Conviction - I believe it will!

Assumption - I am expecting it will!

Now, go out and get the MONEY!!

SPOTLIGHT ON ZACHARY COVE AND EMILI CABRERA

Zachary Cove is the great grandson of former Beaumont, California, Mayor Albert "Happy" Haskell (who served on city council or as mayor from 1963-1976). He is also one of the co-founders of Kids Cures Foundation. When he was five years old, he was diagnosed with terminal brain cancer. At the same time, twenty-three year old Shannon Smith was diagnosed with a rare and deadly form of cervical cancer in which there is only a 3% survival rate. It was touch and go for awhile, but both eventually overcame their cancers and began to regain their strength. It was during this time that Zachary and Shannon met each other and developed a strong and lasting friendship. Out of that bond they decided to start a non-profit organization focused on advocacy for children's wellness – Kids Cures Foundation. This was in 2004.

Today, Kids Cures Foundation has become a positive force in the lives of many children and their families. Kids Cures Foundation has worked tirelessly to develop positive relationships with strategic partners and donors. They are aligned with Loma Linda and San Gorgonio Hospitals, Arthritis Foundation, Ronald McDonald House, American Lung Association, Angel Flight, Mercy Medical Airlift, and Angel Bus to name a few. Sara Price, one of the top motocross racers, is their current ambassador, and R & B artist LyNe' developed a song specifically for them. Kids Cures Foundation does what it can to improve the health and wellness of children in their community.

On Valentine's Day the doctors and nurses at Riverside County Regional Medical Center were all working diligently to heal the 20-some ill children in the pediatric, intensive care pediatric, and neonatal intensive care units. Walking onto the floor, there were smiles and looks from the nurses and doctors. One of the lead doctors came to inspect the situation. Noticing the colorful homemade Valentine cards with candy attached in the big box, he flashed a smile. He looked around the nurse's station and realized that there were no cheerful decorations. A helpful social worker came over to escort us from room to room. There were surprised faces in the first room and the little ones began smiling. Every family got cards and were completely taken back and surprised by the gesture of community volunteers creating handmade Valentine wishes. Some even created little googly-eyed, pipe-cleaner-eared buddies with big feet to sit on the table to remind them about fun.

Every little youngster was handed several Valentine cards consisting of fairies, motor cross, dinosaur, puppies, and cartoon characters. After they were passed out to the kids, there were some left over. So the best course of action was to now remind the hospital staff that today was a holiday. Little red-cupped, paper-legged, googly-eyed characters were placed around the nursing stations and then the entire pediatric staff was given cards and candy. It was great. Everyone took a breath and remembered that today was a holiday, smiled and started exhibiting cheer. Because Kids Cures Foundation was able to gather both the money and the volunteers required to make this special event happen, there are a number of kids and adults who were offered a day of positive emotions and thoughts, which has been proven to improve overall health.

Kids Cures Foundation has expanded outside of California and it has done so through the efforts of Emili Cabrera and her mother Jennifer. Emili is my 'ahijada' or goddaughter. Although not blood related, I have always treated her like my own daughter. She is now in high school and is developing into a wonderful young lady. She has been developing her entrepreneurial skills for several years now providing both baby-sitting and culinary services. This is merely the beginning. Because of her academic success, she was given an opportunity to travel to Europe for four weeks. The only catch is that she has to come up with her share of the costs prior to the trip. What she did next absolutely amazed me. She made it her singular mission to raise money from local sponsors to fund her trip. She arose early in the morning, wrote letters to approximately 100 local businesses and individuals, and hand delivered them. She even made follow up calls, but she didn't want to stop there. She wanted to expand the program to include others that have qualified to go, but are otherwise unable to afford it. The main issue she ran into is that many wanted to help, but preferred to donate to established non-profit organizations. That is when she called me to ask for advice. What she needed was the ability to work through an existing non-profit organization so that she could offer tax incentives and credits. It would also demonstrate more legitimacy than her trying to do it on her own. I had the perfect solution – Kids Cures Foundation. Over the last few years I have been able to make a significant positive impact on the value of Kids Cures Foundation. When I talked to them about my idea of allowing Emili's project to fall under their scope, they embraced it with open arms. Emili has the ability to leverage a non-profit organization, and Kids Cures Foundation has the ability to expand their mission into Texas.

Currently, Emili, her younger brother Joseph, and their mother Jennifer are involved in an anti-bullying campaign in El Paso. They told me that this is only one of two in the entire state of Texas. They have gained much support from local residents, including police officers, teachers, school administrators and judges. In one of their first meetings designed to organize and develop the program, hundreds of people showed up and dozens volunteered to be involved in leadership positions. They also have my backing and that of Kids Cures Foundation. What this means is that most of their infrastructure is taken care of. They can focus on developing programs, volunteers and donations. Again remember that Emili and Joseph are in high school. They have a long life ahead of them to Make a Difference!

Chapter 13

WHAT IS BEST FOR AMERICA—7 POINT PLAN

*"When ancient opinions and rules of life are taken away,
the loss cannot possibly be estimated. From that moment,
we have no compass to govern us, nor can we know
distinctly to what port to steer."*

— Edmund Burke

When we (Randy and Michael) met outside a print shop (University Printing) in the spring of 2010, we talked about promoting Randy's children's ebook – AmericanPrideeBook. com. It is now four years later, and together we have produced three books, positively impacted numerous lives, and developed a website that has gained the attention of the world.

The part we both laugh about now is that Randy truly thought that I was blowing smoke up his you know what. He didn't think I had it within me to deliver. It was not an easy journey I assure you. I was up until the wee hours of the morning (many times over) developing the site, creating content, and doing the marketing to bring in traffic. Through this hard work and dedication to building something greater than ourselves, everyone has benefited.

After a joint meeting with the Young Republicans and the Republican Women of Prescott, he and I had a serious talk about our vision and purpose. Out of that conversation, Randy basically said that I understand him well and that he would like to see what I come up with for a social/political platform that engenders the philosophy of Randy E. King, StoriesofUSA.com, and Dream2Achieve.

I knew what his convictions were. I knew his strengths, and I tailored his platform accordingly. I did not expect perfection out of the gate. I just wanted to create something that we would only need to make minor adjustments to.

Through this we were able to develop a platform that clearly defined who Randy is and what he stands for. It is not our goal to convince you that our political beliefs are better than yours. We are using this as a guide for you to develop your own message. What do you believe in? Why do you believe that your message and vision are important?

The following is what several of us have developed as his 7 Point Plan. This has become our message and our mission.

VISION:

I believe America is unique and rare, not because of its government, but because of our shared values of Liberty, Justice, Hard Work, Compassion, Respect for Life, and Personal Responsibility. We must all play our part in protecting what makes America great.

MISSION:

To promote the concepts that personal growth, self-education, hard work, and winning strategies lead ultimately to success in these United States of America.

GUIDING PRINCIPLES:

1.   Strong Personal Integrity and Accountability: Stay true to your convictions, remain consistent, and de-

velop external systems of checks and balances to keep everyone accountable.

2. Limited Government: The role of government is to create a strong platform for both individual and collective growth and development. It is also to create limits and boundaries that protect and promote the general welfare of all our residents and citizens. The role of the individual is to exercise his / her rights and to keep all levels of government accountable.

3. Free Market System: The entrepreneurial spirit is one of the most powerful engines America has to generate prosperity for all. The individual has the capacity to move faster, be more creative, and be more flexible in the economic market than government. The role of government is to promote the rights of the individual to be an entrepreneur and to only restrict activities that cause significant harm to the rest of society.

4. Personal Faith: The Declaration of Independence says that people are created and endowed by their Creator with certain unalienable rights. The Bill of Rights states that Congress shall make no law respecting an establishment of religion, or prohibiting the free exercise thereof. It is not the role of Government to promote one faith or religion over another, but to secure the ability for individuals to practice their faith as they see fit, as long as it brings no harm to other individuals.

SPECIFIC ISSUES:

National Security and National Defense:

One of the primary duties of the federal government, as listed in the Preamble of the US Constitution, is to provide for the common defense of the Nation. We must support our military forces with the best training, equipment, technology and infrastructure necessary to allow them to protect its citizens. When we are engaged in military action abroad, we must have a clearly defined mission and objectives. We must allow our ambassadors and diplomats to negotiate from a position of strength, not weakness, and we must have systems in place that reach a balance between national security & secrecy and the rights of the individual to know what the government is doing. The rights of the individual trump the needs of national security, and we must never forget about our men and women in uniform that protect us.

Energy:

Domestic energy production and consumption have become national security issues. It is imperative that enough energy, in the forms of gasoline, electricity, etc., is available to meet our growing demands. Currently, our top foreign sources for oil are (in order): Canada, Mexico, Saudi Arabia, Nigeria, and Venezuela. Although Canada is one of our staunchest allies, Venezuela is not. In order to decrease potential political and security issues abroad, we must encourage increased energy production at home. Environmentally friendly renewable energy production, such as solar and geothermal, is part of the solution. However, it by itself is not enough to fulfill the country's needs. Each type of energy production has its strengths and weaknesses, but it is not the role of government to choose winners and losers. Allow private individuals to bring various forms of energy to the market, and let the market decide. The primary role of the federal government in this case is to ensure the safety of individuals. Certain forms of energy production, such as nuclear fission, can be extremely dangerous. Laws and regulations should be in place to significantly reduce the risks. However, the federal government should not be directly funding specific businesses or organizations. It should be focused on encouraging innovation.

Energy distribution is another significant issue. In 2003, much of the Northeast (about 55 million people) was without power for about two days. It was caused by a power surge that made a power plant in Ohio shut down. In 2011, a severed power line in Arizona forced the San Onofre nuclear power plant near San Diego to go offline. This terminated electrical power to about 5 million people in Arizona, California and northern Mexico for almost a day. It is imperative that a plan is implemented which improves the efficiency and redundancy of these electrical distribution channels.

Economy:

I have been involved with the business community since I was 19 years old. I worked my up through the US Chamber of Commerce to become one of its most successful leaders, developed my own successful corporations, and became a speaker and author on business strategies and business leadership. I have been working directly with lobbyists, Congressional leaders, business owners, and non-profit organizations for many years. The solution to our current economic problems is simple: Allow private-sector innovators to do what they do best and get government out of the way. The federal government needs to do the following:

1. Eliminate many government programs that are obsolete or counterproductive to private-sector market growth.

2. Develop fiscally sound financial budgets for all aspects of the federal budget that must be adhered to.

3. Make it easier to bring a product or service to the marketplace by reducing or eliminating requirements created by the federal government.

Immigration:

Legal immigration has been a part of our American heritage since the birth of our Nation. We pride ourselves in both diversity and the rule of law. We cannot financially support a policy that allows everyone who wants to be here to freely enter the country without restrictions. We must have adequate and efficient systems in place that regulate our borders to reduce and prevent foreign nationals from entering the country without prior permission. We are also a compassionate country. The 14th Amendment states, *"All persons born or naturalized in the United States, and subject to the jurisdiction thereof, are citizens of the United States."* If we want to adhere to the laws that we ourselves as a country have voted into place, we must find a way to integrate the millions of children that are born here from both legal and illegal immigrants into our society. The best way to do this is to encourage them to become well-adjusted, educated, and active tax-paying participants of our local communities and our Nation as a whole.

Education:

I am co-producer of a website that directly tackles issues within our current educational system. The website (StoriesofUSA.com) is in fourteen languages and gets thousands of visitors daily from all over the world. It has received a commendation from the US Department of Education. I have also written or co-authored ten books on the subjects of business leadership, youth leadership, American patriotism, politics and education. It is our collective duty to ensure that the next generation is able to compete in the global marketplace. The federal government must set the example and establish and maintain national standardized tests in which all students across the country must pass in order to graduate with a high school diploma. These educational goals can be accomplished, however, without any significant expenditures from the federal government. If we establish base level curriculum standards at the collegiate level, these standards will then be passed down to K-12 schools through the accreditation process. And the federal government should issue tax credits to legitimate businesses and organizations that assist in the development of any non-payroll infrastructure development within any accredited public or private school. This will foster involvement between our schools and their local communities.

Environment:

We must strike a balance between the needs of our current generation to expand and the desires to protect our lands and our environment for future generations. I encourage funding and protecting our current National Park System. I would like to make other underdeveloped federal lands (especially those that fall under the jurisdiction of the Bureau of Land Management) open to joint business opportunities, such as timber production and mining. The land would be leased to businesses that qualify. They would manage daily operations of that business, and in return, would pay royalty fees back to the federal government. I am also adamantly against any form of carbon cap and trade policy. There is not enough scientific evidence to show that controlling carbon emissions would significantly alter global climates, especially when many other highly populated countries like China and India do not have such regulations in place. And this cap and trade policy could increase production costs for a business. I do understand the need to protect endangered species, and I respect the actions of groups like the Sierra Club and the Audubon Society. They try to create legislation through legitimate grassroots support. I respect the current environmental laws that are in place, as long as they have broad national support.

Health Care:

The federal government should not be directly involved in the operational management of hospitals and doctors. Health care is a highly specialized field that requires years of scholarship and practical experience. The high cost of insurance is due in part to the significant risk of lawsuits and the way that health insurance companies and government health plans pay out on claims. The federal government should work with organizations like the American Medical Association to consider eliminating regulations that either directly or indirectly increase the cost of health care and do not add any significant protection to the individual. The government should also work with these same organizations to develop laws and regulations that find a balance between consumer protection and reduced risk of consumer litigation that in the end will significantly reduce the costs involved in providing medical care.

Chapter 14

HOPE AND MAYBE YOU'LL CHANGE

"He conceives of, mentally builds up, an ideal condition of life; the vision of a wider liberty and a larger scope take possession of him; unrest urges him to action, and he utilizes all his spare time and means, small though they are, to the development of his latent powers and resources."

— James Allen

When Democratic Candidate Barack Obama campaigned for President of the United States in 2008, his mantra was Hope and Change. When I hear this, I immediately think hope for what and change into what? I do not vote for someone simply because of skin color, gender, religious affiliation or political party. We live in the melting pot that is the United States of America, not a country where religious and ethnic affiliations are of premiere importance. I want to know exactly what that person stands for, and I want to vote for the best person for the job. Chapter 4 contains Obama's speech, "Audacity of Hope." So I analyzed the content of his speech to see if I can find some answers. In his speech he states:

"This year, in this election, we are called to reaffirm our values and our commitments, to hold them against a hard reality and see how we are measuring up, to the legacy of our forebearers and the promise of future generations. And fellow Americans, Democrats, Republicans, independents, I say to you, tonight, we have more work to do - more work to do, for the workers I met in Galesburg, Illinois, who are losing their union jobs at the Maytag plant that's moving to Mexico, and now they're having to compete with their own children for jobs that pay 7 bucks an hour; more to do for the father I met who was losing his job and chocking back the tears wondering how he would pay $4,500 a months for the drugs his son needs without the health benefits that he counted on; more to do for the young woman in East St. Louis, and thousands more like her who have the grades, have the drive, have the will, but doesn't have the money to go to college."

This portion of his speech tells me much about his political philosophy. He believes that it is the federal government's responsibility to involve itself in the job market, increase the security of union jobs, increase the minimum wage, pay for health care benefits, and pay for college. Knowing what I know about political philosophies, I now determine that he is closely associated with the progressive philosophy. If I believed, like progressives do, that government action and intervention is important and necessary to improve opportunity and personal security, I might consider voting for Barack Obama and those similar to him.

I was asked what I think the most important parts of the US Constitution are. Since I have spent a lot of time studying this exact question, I was able to quickly answer the question: First Amendment, Second Amendment and Tenth Amendment. The First Amendment is an expression of our freedom and liberty: speech, religion, press, assembly, and petition the Government for grievances. The Tenth Amendment limits the powers of the federal government and empowers states and individuals. It describes a Balance of Power and through it encourages the Rule of Law. Should all else fail in limiting the power of the federal government, the Second Amendment is in place to enforce that ideal. It is not there to protect ourselves from an individual who wants to hurt us, it is there to protect us from a federal government that is attempting to usurp more power than the majority of Americans are willing to provide it with. I truly believe that the federal government was empowered by Americans to provide specific services, and not the reverse.

LETTER TO THE PRESIDENT #1

On that note, we, the authors of this book, did petition the federal government on June 20, 2011, as protected by the First Amendment. It was primarily addressed to the US Secretary of Education, and submitted to all of the following:
Barack Obama, President of the United States
Arne Duncan, US Secretary of Education
Diane Ravitch, Assistant Secretary of Education (former)
Duncan Hunter, US Congressman
Lee White, National History Coalition Executive Director
Linda Salvucci, National Council for History Education Vice Chair
Ted McConnell, Campaign for the Civic Mission of Schools Executive Director
Jim Grossman, American Historical Association Executive Director
The letter states:

StoriesofUSA.com is Tackling the US History Education Issue Head On

"Children are the world's most valuable resource and its best hope for the future."

— President JFK

To: **Arne Duncan**, US Secretary of Education
The Problem:
In February 2011, the Thomas B. Fordham Institute released a report stating that almost 60% of states received a D

or F in US History instruction. And recently, the National Assessment of Educational Progress released a report stating that 20% of 4th-graders, 17% of 8th-graders and 12% of 12th-graders performed at or above the Proficient level on the 2010 US History assessment. 27% of 4th-graders, 22% of 8th-graders and 24% of 12th-graders performed at or above the Proficient level on the 2010 US Government Civics assessment. There is enough blame to go around for the lack of knowledge and understanding of US History.

The Solution:

History is more than memorizing names and dates. Its purpose is to create understanding as to who we are and where we come from. In this modern era of hand-held computers, mobile internet access and self-produced videos, it is easier than ever to create a dynamic, interactive and engaging system that not only teaches US history and government, but through a multimedia approach, students are able to envision themselves at the steps of the Lincoln Memorial listening to Martin Luther King, Jr., say, "Free at last! Free at last! Thank God Almighty, we are free at last!." The goal is to not only gain an appreciation for past events, but through it, gain an understanding of our American Heritage.

Who We Are:

StoriesofUSA.com is a multimedia website that provides an interactive approach towards learning about US History from ~13,000 B.C.E. to current events. It is a viable solution to the dilemma of how to effectively teach US History, in that it is a tool designed to engage and lead the student through an interactive process focused on the major transformative people, places and events in US History. The site has just celebrated its one year anniversary, and in that year, over 90% of the world's nations and territories have visited our site. The website is in 14 languages. Over the past year, we have received hundreds of thousands of website visitors, emails and comments, most of them essentially telling us "Thank you" and "Keep up the good work." The producers of this website are collectively an author, business professional, public speaker, high school teacher and technical consultant. StoriesofUSA.com is more than a US History website, it is our collective Story of America. StoriesofUSA.com is committed to educating our youth about our American Heritage.

WE CAN HELP!

Please email us at storiesofusa@gmail.com to discuss how we can help you.

With my regards,

Randy E King

Co-producer and founder of StoriesofUSA.com

On July 25, 2011, Randy E. King received a letter from the US Department of Education.

The letter states:

United States Department of Education

Office of Innovation and Improvement

To: Randy E. King

Co-Producer and founder of StoriesofUSA.com

Dear Mr. King:

Thank you for your letter to Secretary Arne Duncan describing your multimedia website, StoriesofUSA.com. Secretary Duncan forwarded your letter to my office and I am happy to respond. We appreciate you sharing information about your program with us. As you may already know, we provide resources for history teachers in a number of ways. Through the Teaching American (TAH) program, the Department has awarded a number of grants to school districts for them to develop and provide professional development activities for teachers to strengthen their content knowledge of American history. For more information about the TAH program including abstracts of funded projects please visit our website, http://www2.ed.gov/programs/teachinghistory/index.html. Additionally, we support the National History Education Clearinghouse (NHEC) site, which is funded through a contract with George Mason University's Center for History and New Media. The site, www.teachinghistory.org, is a single destination for K-12 American history content, teaching methods, and current research.

I will share the information about your program with the members of our TAH team. While we are unable to endorse individual programs or materials, we are interested in learning about education resources that may inform or be informed by our work here. We commend you for your efforts to develop and improve access to high-quality history education resources that will enhance the teaching and learning of history in schools across the nation. If I can be of any further assistance, please do not hesitate to contact me.

Sincerely,
Margaret A. Zelinko
Director – Teacher Quality Program Office
400 Maryland Ave SW, Washington, DC 20202

Because of my background as a teacher, website developer and content manager, I could discuss in detail how effective these government programs are, but I think in this case a simple single question would be much more effective... With all the energy you have put into history education, why are the results so poor? What is more important, HOPE that things will CHANGE because of good intentions, or real CHANGE because of an effective performance that creates true HOPE for a bright tomorrow?

LETTER TO THE PRESIDENT #2

The following is another letter to another President. As you read it can you determine who is writing it, who it is addressed to, and why he wrote it?

"Will you, after the great political defeat we have suffered, listen a moment to the words of a true friend who means to serve you faithfully, and in whose judgment you once, perhaps, reposed some confidence? The defeat of the Administration is owing neither to your proclamations, nor to the financial policy of the Government, nor to a desire of the people to have peace at any price. I can speak openly, for you must know that I am your friend. The defeat of the Administration is the Administration's own fault.

It admitted its professed opponents to its counsels. It placed the Army, now a great power in this Republic, into the hands of its enemies. In all personal questions to be hostile to the party of the Government seemed to be a title to consideration. It forgot the great rule, that, **if you are true to your friends, your friends will be true to you, and that you make your enemies stronger by placing them upon an equality with your friends.** Is it surprising that the opponents of the Administration should have got into their hands the government of the principal States after they have had for so long a time the principal management of the war, the great business of the National Government?

Great sacrifices and enormous efforts had been made and they had been rewarded only by small results. The people felt the necessity of a change. Many of your friends had no longer any heart for the Administration as soon as they felt justified in believing that the Administration had no heart for them. I do not speak of personal favors but of the general conduct of the war. A change was sought in the wrong direction. This was the true cause of the defeat of your Government.

You have now made a change. This evening the news reaches us that the command of the Army... has passed into new hands. But the change of persons means little if it does not imply a change of system. Let us be commanded by generals whose heart is in the war, and only by such. Let every general who does not show himself strong enough to command success, be deposed at once. Let every trust of power be accompanied by a corresponding responsibility, and all may be well yet.

There is but one way in which you can sustain your Administration, and that is by success; and there is but one thing which will command success, and that is energy. In whatever hands the State governments may be, – as soon as you are victorious, they will be obliged to support you; and if they were all in the hands of your friends, – if you do not give them victories, they will after a while be obliged to oppose you. Therefore let us have energy without regard to anything that may stand in your way. Let not the Government be endangered by tender considerations. If West Point cannot do the business, let West Point go down. Who cares? It is better that a thousand generals should fall than that the Republic should be jeopardized a single moment.

Today we are still strong enough to meet the difficulties that stand against us. We do not know what we shall be tomorrow."

These are strong and direct words to a leader of a country. In other countries this person might be imprisoned for such a letter, but the First Amendment protects this kind of communication. Except for the slightly archaic way of stating his ideas, you might think that this is a modern person speaking about the modern problem of executing a war properly. This was actually a letter sent to President Abraham Lincoln about seven and a half weeks after the bloodiest single day of battle in American history – the Battle of Sharpsburg / Antietam (September 17, 1862). There were 3654 killed, 17,292 wounded and 1771 captured or missing. The letter was dated November 8, 1862, and written by Major General Carl Schurz (aka two-star general). If you haven't heard of Carl Schurz, he is a man who has almost completely faded into the background of history. During my research for this book, I came across his name and decided to dig a little deeper. After reading his accomplishments I became enthralled with this "friend" of President Abraham Lincoln.

Carl Schurz was born in Liblar (now part of Erftstadt), Germany on March 2, 1829. During the German revolution of 1848, Schurz and Gottfried Kinkel (University of Bonn professor) founded the Bonner Zeitung, a paper advocating democratic reforms. When the Frankfurt parliament called for people to take up arms in defense of the new German constitution, Schurz, Kinkel, and others from the University of Bonn community did so. During this struggle, Schurz became acquainted with Franz Sigel, Alexander Schimmelfennig, Fritz Anneke, Friedrich Beust, Ludwig Blenker and others, many of whom he would meet again in the Union Army during the US Civil War. The revolution in Germany failed when the fortress at Rastatt surrendered with Schurz inside. Schurz escaped to Zurich, Switzerland. He married fellow revolutionary Johannes Ronge's sister-in-law, Margarethe Meyer, in July 1852, and then moved to the United States. In 1861, President Abraham Lincoln sent him as ambassador to Spain. He succeeded in quietly dissuading Spain from supporting the Confederacy. Persuading Lincoln to grant him a commission in the Union army, Schurz was commissioned Brigadier General of Union volunteers. He took part in the Second Battle of Bull Run, Battle of Chancellorsville, Battle of Gettysburg and Battle of Chattanooga. When Rutherford B. Hayes was named the 19th President of the United States, Schurz was named the 13th

United States Secretary of the Interior. Margarethe Schurz, his wife, was instrumental in establishing the kindergarten system in the United States.

In 1848 Carl Schurz was a man who had HOPE for CHANGE in Germany to support increased political freedom, democracy, and freedom from censorship from an autocratic government. The end result is that he barely escaped out of Germany with his life. When he came to the United States, armed with the knowledge of what a strong centralized government is like, he was able to flex his freedoms to support a strong existing Republic. He created CHANGE in order to generate HOPE. The end result is that he eventually became a US Senator from Missouri and part of a Presidential administration. He advocated for: fiscal responsibility, anti-imperialism, integrity in government, the removal of political patronage, and forest preservation. Even though he was but one voice, he was able to exercise his constitutional rights to Reclaim America.

ALL THE DIFFERENCE IN THE WORLD – THE ROAD LESS TRAVELED

When you read the following story, replace the turtle for anything that you truly care about, such as a whale, a dog, or a child.

> Every Saturday morning I take a brisk walk around a park near my home. There's a lake located in one corner of the park. Each time I walk by this lake, I see the same elderly woman sitting at the water's edge with a small metal cage sitting beside her. This past Saturday my curiosity got the best of me, so I walked over to her. As I got closer, I realized that the metal cage was in fact a small trap. There were three turtles, unharmed, slowly walking around the base of the trap. She had a fourth turtle in her lap that she was carefully scrubbing with a spongy brush.

"Hello," I said. "I see you here every Saturday morning. If you don't mind, I'd love to know what you're doing with these turtles."

She smiled. "I'm cleaning off their shells," she replied. "Anything on a turtle's shell, like algae or scum, reduces the turtle's ability to absorb heat and impedes its ability to swim. It can also corrode and weaken the shell over time."

"Wow! That's really nice of you!" I exclaimed.

She went on: "I spend a couple of hours each Saturday morning, relaxing by this lake and helping these little guys out. It's my own strange way of making a difference."

"But don't most freshwater turtles live their whole lives with algae and scum hanging from their shells?" I asked.

"Yep, sadly, they do," she replied.

I scratched my head. "Well then, don't you think your time could be better spent? I mean, I think your efforts are kind and all, but there are fresh water turtles living in lakes all around the world. And 99% of these turtles don't have kind people like you to help them clean off their shells. So, no offense… but how exactly are your localized efforts here truly making a difference?"

The woman giggled aloud. She then looked down at the turtle in her lap, scrubbed off the last piece of algae from its shell, and said, "Sweetie, if this little guy could talk, he'd tell you I just made all the difference in the world."

This story provides the proper perspective. Your personal actions are not about saving all the _____ (fill in the blank). It is about having a positive impact on one and then another and then another. As you improve your FOUNDATION as described in Chapter 10, you will be able to make a larger impact. A person is not born President of the United States,

CEO of a corporation, or President of an organization. It is a position to work towards. You have to have vision, a message, experience, and enough influence. It is a position that may take decades to work yourself into.

The lady in this story had a clear vision and mission to assist those turtles. She applied herself on a regular basis to fulfill her personal mission. Even though many others did not understand her, and may have even made fun of her, she found contentment in what she was doing. I want to encourage you to develop your own vision and mission statement. Chapter 13 provides an example of these. They do not have to be political in nature. These statements provide clarity of purpose. It allows you to answer: Why am I doing certain tasks? Am I headed in the right direction? Are there ways to improve upon what I am doing to make a larger positive impact? If you make personal vision and mission statements, they will help guide you through the difficulties of life.

The Road Less Traveled is taken from a famous poem by Robert Frost. The following is this poem in its entirety, and I find it strong encouragement to find your own path:

The Road Not Taken

TWO roads diverged in a yellow wood,
And sorry I could not travel both
And be one traveler, long I stood
And looked down one as far as I could
To where it bent in the undergrowth;

Then took the other, as just as fair,
And having perhaps the better claim,
Because it was grassy and wanted wear;
Though as for that the passing there
Had worn them really about the same,

And both that morning equally lay
In leaves no step had trodden black.

Oh, I kept the first for another day!
Yet knowing how way leads on to way,
I doubted if I should ever come back.

I shall be telling this with a sigh
Somewhere ages and ages hence:
Two roads diverged in a wood, and I—
I took the one less traveled by,
And that has made all the difference.

Chapter 15

OUR FOUNDING DOCUMENTS YOU SHOULD KNOW

"Many a revolution started with the actions of a few. Only 56 men signed the Declaration of Independence. A few hanging together can lead a nation to change."

— Wynton Marsalis

DECLARATION OF INDEPENDENCE

IN CONGRESS, July 4, 1776.

The unanimous Declaration of the thirteen united States of America,

When in the Course of human events, it becomes necessary for one people to dissolve the political bands which have connected them with another, and to assume among the powers of the earth, the separate and equal station to which the Laws of Nature and of Nature's God entitle them, a decent respect to the opinions of mankind requires that they should declare the causes which impel them to the separation.

We hold these truths to be self-evident, that all men are created equal, that they are endowed by their Creator with certain unalienable Rights, that among these are Life, Liberty and the pursuit of Happiness.--That to secure these rights, Governments are instituted among Men, deriving their just powers from the consent of the governed, --That whenever any

Form of Government becomes destructive of these ends, it is the Right of the People to alter or to abolish it, and to institute new Government, laying its foundation on such principles and organizing its powers in such form, as to them shall seem most likely to effect their Safety and Happiness. Prudence, indeed, will dictate that Governments long established should not be changed for light and transient causes; and accordingly all experience hath shewn, that mankind are more disposed to suffer, while evils are sufferable, than to right themselves by abolishing the forms to which they are accustomed. But when a long train of abuses and usurpations, pursuing invariably the same Object evinces a design to reduce them under absolute Despotism, it is their right, it is their duty, to throw off such Government, and to provide new Guards for their future security.--Such has been the patient sufferance of these Colonies; and such is now the necessity which constrains them to alter their former Systems of Government. The history of the present King of Great Britain is a history of repeated injuries and usurpations, all having in direct object the establishment of an absolute Tyranny over these States. To prove this, let Facts be submitted to a candid world.

He has refused his Assent to Laws, the most wholesome and necessary for the public good.

He has forbidden his Governors to pass Laws of immediate and pressing importance, unless suspended in their operation till his Assent should be obtained; and when so suspended, he has utterly neglected to attend to them.

He has refused to pass other Laws for the accommodation of large districts of people, unless those people would relinquish the right of Representation in the Legislature, a right inestimable to them and formidable to tyrants only.

He has called together legislative bodies at places unusual, uncomfortable, and distant from the depository of their public Records, for the sole purpose of fatiguing them into compliance with his measures.

He has dissolved Representative Houses repeatedly, for opposing with manly firmness his invasions on the rights of the people.

He has refused for a long time, after such dissolutions, to cause others to be elected; whereby the Legislative powers, incapable of Annihilation, have returned to the People at large for their exercise; the State remaining in the mean time exposed to all the dangers of invasion from without, and convulsions within.

He has endeavoured to prevent the population of these States; for that purpose obstructing the Laws for Naturalization of Foreigners; refusing to pass others to encourage their migrations hither, and raising the conditions of new Appropriations of Lands.

He has obstructed the Administration of Justice, by refusing his Assent to Laws for establishing Judiciary powers.

He has made Judges dependent on his Will alone, for the tenure of their offices, and the amount and payment of their salaries.

He has erected a multitude of New Offices, and sent hither swarms of Officers to harrass our people, and eat out their substance.

He has kept among us, in times of peace, Standing Armies without the Consent of our legislatures.

He has affected to render the Military independent of and superior to the Civil power.

He has combined with others to subject us to a jurisdiction foreign to our constitution, and unacknowledged by our laws; giving his Assent to their Acts of pretended Legislation:

For Quartering large bodies of armed troops among us:

For protecting them, by a mock Trial, from punishment for any Murders which they should commit on the Inhabitants of these States:

For cutting off our Trade with all parts of the world:

For imposing Taxes on us without our Consent:

For depriving us in many cases, of the benefits of Trial by Jury:

For transporting us beyond Seas to be tried for pretended offences

For abolishing the free System of English Laws in a neighbouring Province, establishing therein an Arbitrary government, and enlarging its Boundaries so as to render it at once an example and fit instrument for introducing the same absolute rule into these Colonies:

For taking away our Charters, abolishing our most valuable Laws, and altering fundamentally the Forms of our Governments:

For suspending our own Legislatures, and declaring themselves invested with power to legislate for us in all cases whatsoever.

He has abdicated Government here, by declaring us out of his Protection and waging War against us.

He has plundered our seas, ravaged our Coasts, burnt our towns, and destroyed the lives of our people.

He is at this time transporting large Armies of foreign Mercenaries to compleat the works of death, desolation and tyranny, already begun with circumstances of Cruelty & perfidy scarcely paralleled in the most barbarous ages, and totally unworthy the Head of a civilized nation.

He has constrained our fellow Citizens taken Captive on the high Seas to bear Arms against their Country, to become the executioners of their friends and Brethren, or to fall themselves by their Hands.

He has excited domestic insurrections amongst us, and has endeavoured to bring on the inhabitants of our frontiers, the merciless Indian Savages, whose known rule of warfare, is an undistinguished destruction of all ages, sexes and conditions.

In every stage of these Oppressions We have Petitioned for Redress in the most humble terms: Our repeated Petitions have been answered only by repeated injury. A Prince whose character is thus marked by every act which may define a Tyrant, is unfit to be the ruler of a free people.

Nor have We been wanting in attentions to our Brittish brethren. We have warned them from time to time of attempts by their legislature to extend an unwarrantable jurisdiction over us. We have reminded them of the circumstances of our emigration and settlement here. We have appealed to their native justice and magnanimity, and we have conjured them by the ties of our common kindred to disavow these usurpations, which, would inevitably interrupt our connections and correspondence. They too have been deaf to the voice of justice and of consanguinity. We must, therefore, acquiesce in the necessity, which denounces our Separation, and hold them, as we hold the rest of mankind, Enemies in War, in Peace Friends.

We, therefore, the Representatives of the united States of America, in General Congress, Assembled, appealing to the Supreme Judge of the world for the rectitude of our intentions, do, in the Name, and by Authority of the good People of these Colonies, solemnly publish and declare, That these

United Colonies are, and of Right ought to be Free and Independent States; that they are Absolved from all Allegiance to the British Crown, and that all political connection between them and the State of Great Britain, is and ought to be totally dissolved; and that as Free and Independent States, they have full Power to levy War, conclude Peace, contract Alliances, establish Commerce, and to do all other Acts and Things which Independent States may of right do. And for the support of this Declaration, with a firm reliance on the protection of divine Providence, we mutually pledge to each other our Lives, our Fortunes and our sacred Honor.

Georgia:
    Button Gwinnett
    Lyman Hall
    George Walton

North Carolina:
    William Hooper
    Joseph Hewes
    John Penn

South Carolina:
    Edward Rutledge
    Thomas Heyward, Jr.
    Thomas Lynch, Jr.
    Arthur Middleton

Maryland:
    Samuel Chase
    William Paca
    Thomas Stone
    Charles Carroll of Carrollton

Massachusetts:
    John Hancock

New Hampshire:
    Matthew Thornton

New York:
    William Floyd
    Philip Livingston
    Francis Lewis
    Lewis Morris

Massachusetts:
    Samuel Adams
    John Adams
    Robert Treat Paine
    Elbridge Gerry

New Hampshire:
  Josiah Bartlett
  William Whipple

Rhode Island:
  Stephen Hopkins
  William Ellery

Connecticut:
  Roger Sherman
  Samuel Huntington
  William Williams
  Oliver Wolcott

New Jersey:
  Richard Stockton
  John Witherspoon
  Francis Hopkinson
  John Hart
  Abraham Clark

Deleware:
  Caesar Rodney
  George Read
  Thomas McKean

Pennsylvania:
  Robert Morris
  Benjamin Rush
  Benjamin Franklin

Virginia:
  George Wythe
  Richard Henry Lee
  Thomas Jefferson
  Benjamin Harrison
  Thomas Nelson, Jr.
  Francis Lightfoot Lee
  Carter Braxton

  John Morton
  George Clymer
  James Smith
  George Taylor
  James Wilson
  George Ross

UNITED STATES CONSTITUTION

We the People of the United States, in Order to form a more perfect Union, establish Justice, insure domestic Tranquility, provide for the common defence, promote the general Welfare, and secure the Blessings of Liberty to ourselves and our Posterity, do ordain and establish this Constitution for the United States of America.

ARTICLE. I.
Section. 1.

All legislative Powers herein granted shall be vested in a Congress of the United States, which shall consist of a Senate and House of Representatives.

Section. 2.

The House of Representatives shall be composed of Members chosen every second Year by the People of the several States, and the Electors in each State shall have the Qualifications requisite for Electors of the most numerous Branch of the State Legislature.

No Person shall be a Representative who shall not have attained to the Age of twenty five Years, and been seven Years a Citizen of the United States, and who shall not, when elected, be an Inhabitant of that State in which he shall be chosen.

Representatives and direct Taxes shall be apportioned among the several States which may be included within this Union, according to their respective Numbers, which shall be determined by adding to the whole Number of free Persons, including those bound to Service for a Term of Years, and excluding Indians not taxed, three fifths of all other Persons. The actual Enumeration shall be made within three Years after the first Meeting of the Congress of the United States, and within every subsequent Term of ten Years, in such Manner as they shall by Law direct. The Number of Representatives shall not exceed one for every thirty Thousand, but each State shall have at Least one Representative; and until such enumeration shall be made, the State of New Hampshire shall be entitled to chuse three, Massachusetts eight, Rhode-Island and Providence Plantations one, Connecticut five, New-York six,

New Jersey four, Pennsylvania eight, Delaware one, Maryland six, Virginia ten, North Carolina five, South Carolina five, and Georgia three.

When vacancies happen in the Representation from any State, the Executive Authority thereof shall issue Writs of Election to fill such Vacancies.

The House of Representatives shall chuse their Speaker and other Officers; and shall have the sole Power of Impeachment.

Section. 3.

The Senate of the United States shall be composed of two Senators from each State, chosen by the Legislature thereof for six Years; and each Senator shall have one Vote.

Immediately after they shall be assembled in Consequence of the first Election, they shall be divided as equally as may be into three Classes. The Seats of the Senators of the first Class shall be vacated at the Expiration of the second Year, of the second Class at the Expiration of the fourth Year, and of the third Class at the Expiration of the sixth Year, so that one third may be chosen every second Year; and if Vacancies happen by Resignation, or otherwise, during the Recess of the Legislature of any State, the Executive thereof may make temporary Appointments until the next Meeting of the Legislature, which shall then fill such Vacancies.

No Person shall be a Senator who shall not have attained to the Age of thirty Years, and been nine Years a Citizen of the United States, and who shall not, when elected, be an Inhabitant of that State for which he shall be chosen.

The Vice President of the United States shall be President of the Senate, but shall have no Vote, unless they be equally divided.

The Senate shall chuse their other Officers, and also a President pro tempore, in the Absence of the Vice President, or when he shall exercise the Office of President of the United States.

The Senate shall have the sole Power to try all Impeachments. When sitting for that Purpose, they shall be on Oath or

Affirmation. When the President of the United States is tried, the Chief Justice shall preside: And no Person shall be convicted without the Concurrence of two thirds of the Members present.

Judgment in Cases of Impeachment shall not extend further than to removal from Office, and disqualification to hold and enjoy any Office of honor, Trust or Profit under the United States: but the Party convicted shall nevertheless be liable and subject to Indictment, Trial, Judgment and Punishment, according to Law.

Section. 4.

The Times, Places and Manner of holding Elections for Senators and Representatives, shall be prescribed in each State by the Legislature thereof; but the Congress may at any time by Law make or alter such Regulations, except as to the Places of chusing Senators.

The Congress shall assemble at least once in every Year, and such Meeting shall be on the first Monday in December, unless they shall by Law appoint a different Day.

Section. 5.

Each House shall be the Judge of the Elections, Returns and Qualifications of its own Members, and a Majority of each shall constitute a Quorum to do Business; but a smaller Number may adjourn from day to day, and may be authorized to compel the Attendance of absent Members, in such Manner, and under such Penalties as each House may provide.

Each House may determine the Rules of its Proceedings, punish its Members for disorderly Behaviour, and, with the Concurrence of two thirds, expel a Member.

Each House shall keep a Journal of its Proceedings, and from time to time publish the same, excepting such Parts as may in their Judgment require Secrecy; and the Yeas and Nays of the Members of either House on any question shall, at the Desire of one fifth of those Present, be entered on the Journal.

Neither House, during the Session of Congress, shall, without the Consent of the other, adjourn for more than three days, nor to any other Place than that in which the two Houses shall be sitting.

Section. 6.

The Senators and Representatives shall receive a Compensation for their Services, to be ascertained by Law, and paid out of the Treasury of the United States. They shall in all Cases, except Treason, Felony and Breach of the Peace, be privileged from Arrest during their Attendance at the Session of their respective Houses, and in going to and returning from the same; and for any Speech or Debate in either House, they shall not be questioned in any other Place.

No Senator or Representative shall, during the Time for which he was elected, be appointed to any civil Office under the Authority of the United States, which shall have been created, or the Emoluments whereof shall have been encreased during such time; and no Person holding any Office under the United States, shall be a Member of either House during his Continuance in Office.

Section. 7.

All Bills for raising Revenue shall originate in the House of Representatives; but the Senate may propose or concur with Amendments as on other Bills.

Every Bill which shall have passed the House of Representatives and the Senate, shall, before it become a Law, be presented to the President of the United States: If he approve he shall sign it, but if not he shall return it, with his Objections to that House in which it shall have originated, who shall enter the Objections at large on their Journal, and proceed to reconsider it. If after such Reconsideration two thirds of that House shall agree to pass the Bill, it shall be sent, together with the Objections, to the other House, by which it shall likewise be reconsidered, and if approved by two thirds of that House, it shall become a Law. But in all such Cases the Votes of both Houses shall be determined by yeas and Nays, and the Names of the Persons voting for and against the Bill shall be entered on the Journal of each House respectively. If any Bill shall not be returned by the President within ten Days (Sundays excepted) after it shall have been presented to him, the Same shall be a Law, in like Manner as if he had signed it, unless the Congress by their Adjournment prevent its Return, in which Case it shall not be a Law.

Every Order, Resolution, or Vote to which the Concurrence of the Senate and House of Representatives may be necessary (except on a question of Adjournment) shall be presented to the President of the United States; and before the Same shall take Effect, shall be approved by him, or being disapproved by him, shall be repassed by two thirds of the Senate and House of Representatives, according to the Rules and Limitations prescribed in the Case of a Bill.

Section. 8.

The Congress shall have Power To lay and collect Taxes, Duties, Imposts and Excises, to pay the Debts and provide for the common Defence and general Welfare of the United States; but all Duties, Imposts and Excises shall be uniform throughout the United States;

To borrow Money on the credit of the United States;

To regulate Commerce with foreign Nations, and among the several States, and with the Indian Tribes;

To establish an uniform Rule of Naturalization, and uniform Laws on the subject of Bankruptcies throughout the United States;

To coin Money, regulate the Value thereof, and of foreign Coin, and fix the Standard of Weights and Measures;

To provide for the Punishment of counterfeiting the Securities and current Coin of the United States;

To establish Post Offices and post Roads;

To promote the Progress of Science and useful Arts, by securing for limited Times to Authors and Inventors the exclusive Right to their respective Writings and Discoveries;

To constitute Tribunals inferior to the supreme Court;

To define and punish Piracies and Felonies committed on the high Seas, and Offences against the Law of Nations;

To declare War, grant Letters of Marque and Reprisal, and make Rules concerning Captures on Land and Water;

To raise and support Armies, but no Appropriation of Money to that Use shall be for a longer Term than two Years;

To provide and maintain a Navy;

To make Rules for the Government and Regulation of the land and naval Forces;

To provide for calling forth the Militia to execute the Laws of the Union, suppress Insurrections and repel Invasions;

To provide for organizing, arming, and disciplining, the Militia, and for governing such Part of them as may be employed in the Service of the United States, reserving to the States respectively, the Appointment of the Officers, and the Authority of training the Militia according to the discipline prescribed by Congress;

To exercise exclusive Legislation in all Cases whatsoever, over such District (not exceeding ten Miles square) as may, by Cession of particular States, and the Acceptance of Congress, become the Seat of the Government of the United States, and to exercise like Authority over all Places purchased by the Consent of the Legislature of the State in which the Same shall be, for the Erection of Forts, Magazines, Arsenals, dock-Yards, and other needful Buildings;--And

To make all Laws which shall be necessary and proper for carrying into Execution the foregoing Powers, and all other Powers vested by this Constitution in the Government of the United States, or in any Department or Officer thereof.

Section. 9.

The Migration or Importation of such Persons as any of the States now existing shall think proper to admit, shall not be prohibited by the Congress prior to the Year one thousand eight hundred and eight, but a Tax or duty may be imposed on such Importation, not exceeding ten dollars for each Person.

The Privilege of the Writ of Habeas Corpus shall not be suspended, unless when in Cases of Rebellion or Invasion the public Safety may require it.

No Bill of Attainder or ex post facto Law shall be passed.

No Capitation, or other direct, Tax shall be laid, unless in Proportion to the Census or enumeration herein before directed to be taken.

No Tax or Duty shall be laid on Articles exported from any State.

No Preference shall be given by any Regulation of Commerce or Revenue to the Ports of one State over those of another; nor shall Vessels bound to, or from, one State, be obliged to enter, clear, or pay Duties in another.

No Money shall be drawn from the Treasury, but in Consequence of Appropriations made by Law; and a regular Statement and Account of the Receipts and Expenditures of all public Money shall be published from time to time.

No Title of Nobility shall be granted by the United States: And no Person holding any Office of Profit or Trust under them, shall, without the Consent of the Congress, accept of any present, Emolument, Office, or Title, of any kind whatever, from any King, Prince, or foreign State.

Section. 10.

No State shall enter into any Treaty, Alliance, or Confederation; grant Letters of Marque and Reprisal; coin Money; emit Bills of Credit; make any Thing but gold and silver Coin a Tender in Payment of Debts; pass any Bill of Attainder, ex post facto Law, or Law impairing the Obligation of Contracts, or grant any Title of Nobility.

No State shall, without the Consent of the Congress, lay any Imposts or Duties on Imports or Exports, except what may be absolutely necessary for executing it's inspection Laws: and the net Produce of all Duties and Imposts, laid by any State on Imports or Exports, shall be for the Use of the Treasury of the United States; and all such Laws shall be subject to the Revision and Controul of the Congress.

No State shall, without the Consent of Congress, lay any Duty of Tonnage, keep Troops, or Ships of War in time of Peace, enter into any Agreement or Compact with another State, or with a foreign Power, or engage in War, unless actually invaded, or in such imminent Danger as will not admit of delay.

ARTICLE. II.
Section. 1.

The executive Power shall be vested in a President of the United States of America. He shall hold his Office during the Term of four Years, and, together with the Vice President, chosen for the same Term, be elected, as follows:

Each State shall appoint, in such Manner as the Legislature thereof may direct, a Number of Electors, equal to the whole Number of Senators and Representatives to which the State may be entitled in the Congress: but no Senator or Representative, or Person holding an Office of Trust or Profit under the United States, shall be appointed an Elector.

The Electors shall meet in their respective States, and vote by Ballot for two Persons, of whom one at least shall not be an Inhabitant of the same State with themselves. And they shall make a List of all the Persons voted for, and of the Number of Votes for each; which List they shall sign and certify, and transmit sealed to the Seat of the Government of the United States, directed to the President of the Senate. The President of the Senate shall, in the Presence of the Senate and House of Representatives, open all the Certificates, and the Votes shall then be counted. The Person having the greatest Number of Votes shall be the President, if such Number be a Majority of the whole Number of Electors appointed; and if there be more than one who have such Majority, and have an equal Number of Votes, then the House of Representatives shall immediately chuse by Ballot one of them for President; and if no Person have a Majority, then from the five highest on the List the said House shall in like Manner chuse the President. But in chusing the President, the Votes shall be taken by States, the Representation from each State having one Vote; A quorum for this purpose shall consist of a Member or Members from two thirds of the States, and a Majority of all the States shall be necessary to a Choice. In every Case, after the Choice of the President, the Person having the greatest Number of Votes of the Electors shall be the Vice President. But if there should remain two or more who have equal Votes, the Senate shall chuse from them by Ballot the Vice President.

The Congress may determine the Time of chusing the Electors, and the Day on which they shall give their Votes; which Day shall be the same throughout the United States.

No Person except a natural born Citizen, or a Citizen of the United States, at the time of the Adoption of this Constitution, shall be eligible to the Office of President; neither shall any Person be eligible to that Office who shall not have attained to the Age of thirty five Years, and been fourteen Years a Resident within the United States.

In Case of the Removal of the President from Office, or of his Death, Resignation, or Inability to discharge the Powers and Duties of the said Office, the Same shall devolve on the Vice President, and the Congress may by Law provide for the Case of Removal, Death, Resignation or Inability, both of the President and Vice President, declaring what Officer shall then act as President, and such Officer shall act accordingly, until the Disability be removed, or a President shall be elected.

The President shall, at stated Times, receive for his Services, a Compensation, which shall neither be increased nor diminished during the Period for which he shall have been elected, and he shall not receive within that Period any other Emolument from the United States, or any of them.

Before he enter on the Execution of his Office, he shall take the following Oath or Affirmation:--"I do solemnly swear (or affirm) that I will faithfully execute the Office of President of the United States, and will to the best of my Ability, preserve, protect and defend the Constitution of the United States."

Section. 2.

The President shall be Commander in Chief of the Army and Navy of the United States, and of the Militia of the several States, when called into the actual Service of the United States; he may require the Opinion, in writing, of the principal Officer in each of the executive Departments, upon any Subject relating to the Duties of their respective Offices, and he shall have Power to grant Reprieves and Pardons for Offences against the United States, except in Cases of Impeachment.

He shall have Power, by and with the Advice and Consent of the Senate, to make Treaties, provided two thirds of the Senators present concur; and he shall nominate, and by and with the Advice and Consent of the Senate, shall appoint Ambassadors, other public Ministers and Consuls, Judges of the supreme Court, and all other Officers of the United States, whose Appointments are not herein otherwise provided for, and which shall be established by Law: but the Congress may by Law vest the Appointment of such inferior Officers, as they think proper, in the President alone, in the Courts of Law, or in the Heads of Departments.

The President shall have Power to fill up all Vacancies that may happen during the Recess of the Senate, by granting Commissions which shall expire at the End of their next Session.

Section. 3.

He shall from time to time give to the Congress Information of the State of the Union, and recommend to their Consideration such Measures as he shall judge necessary and expedient; he may, on extraordinary Occasions, convene both Houses, or either of them, and in Case of Disagreement between them, with Respect to the Time of Adjournment, he may adjourn them to such Time as he shall think proper; he shall receive Ambassadors and other public Ministers; he shall take Care that the Laws be faithfully executed, and shall Commission all the Officers of the United States.

Section. 4.

The President, Vice President and all civil Officers of the United States, shall be removed from Office on Impeachment for, and Conviction of, Treason, Bribery, or other high Crimes and Misdemeanors.

ARTICLE III.
Section. 1.

The judicial Power of the United States shall be vested in one supreme Court, and in such inferior Courts as the Congress may from time to time ordain and establish. The Judges, both of the supreme and inferior Courts, shall hold their Offices during good Behaviour, and shall, at stated Times, receive for their Services a Compensation, which shall not be diminished during their Continuance in Office.

Section. 2.

The judicial Power shall extend to all Cases, in Law and Equity, arising under this Constitution, the Laws of the United States, and Treaties made, or which shall be made, under their Authority;--to all Cases affecting Ambassadors, other public Ministers and Consuls;--to all Cases of admiralty and maritime Jurisdiction;--to Controversies to which the United States shall be a Party;--to Controversies between two or more States;-- between a State and Citizens of another State,--between Citizens of different States,--between Citizens of the same State claiming Lands under Grants of different States, and between a State, or the Citizens thereof, and foreign States, Citizens or Subjects.

In all Cases affecting Ambassadors, other public Ministers and Consuls, and those in which a State shall be Party, the supreme Court shall have original Jurisdiction. In all the other Cases before mentioned, the supreme Court shall have appellate

Jurisdiction, both as to Law and Fact, with such Exceptions, and under such Regulations as the Congress shall make.

The Trial of all Crimes, except in Cases of Impeachment, shall be by Jury; and such Trial shall be held in the State where the said Crimes shall have been committed; but when not committed within any State, the Trial shall be at such Place or Places as the Congress may by Law have directed.

Section. 3.

Treason against the United States, shall consist only in levying War against them, or in adhering to their Enemies, giving them Aid and Comfort. No Person shall be convicted of Treason unless on the Testimony of two Witnesses to the same overt Act, or on Confession in open Court.

The Congress shall have Power to declare the Punishment of Treason, but no Attainder of Treason shall work Corruption of Blood, or Forfeiture except during the Life of the Person attainted.

ARTICLE. IV.
Section. 1.

Full Faith and Credit shall be given in each State to the public Acts, Records, and judicial Proceedings of every other State. And the Congress may by general Laws prescribe the Manner in which such Acts, Records and Proceedings shall be proved, and the Effect thereof.

Section. 2.

The Citizens of each State shall be entitled to all Privileges and Immunities of Citizens in the several States.

A Person charged in any State with Treason, Felony, or other Crime, who shall flee from Justice, and be found in another State, shall on Demand of the executive Authority of the

State from which he fled, be delivered up, to be removed to the State having Jurisdiction of the Crime.

No Person held to Service or Labour in one State, under the Laws thereof, escaping into another, shall, in Consequence of any Law or Regulation therein, be discharged from such Service or Labour, but shall be delivered up on Claim of the Party to whom such Service or Labour may be due.

Section. 3.

New States may be admitted by the Congress into this Union; but no new State shall be formed or erected within the Jurisdiction of any other State; nor any State be formed by the Junction of two or more States, or Parts of States, without the Consent of the Legislatures of the States concerned as well as of the Congress.

The Congress shall have Power to dispose of and make all needful Rules and Regulations respecting the Territory or other Property belonging to the United States; and nothing in this Constitution shall be so construed as to Prejudice any Claims of the United States, or of any particular State.

Section. 4.

The United States shall guarantee to every State in this Union a Republican Form of Government, and shall protect each of them against Invasion; and on Application of the Legislature, or of the Executive (when the Legislature cannot be convened), against domestic Violence.

ARTICLE. V.

The Congress, whenever two thirds of both Houses shall deem it necessary, shall propose Amendments to this Constitution, or, on the Application of the Legislatures of two thirds of the several States, shall call a Convention for proposing Amendments, which, in either Case, shall be valid to all

Intents and Purposes, as Part of this Constitution, when ratified by the Legislatures of three fourths of the several States,
or by Conventions in three fourths thereof, as the one or the
other Mode of Ratification may be proposed by the Congress;
Provided that no Amendment which may be made prior to
the Year One thousand eight hundred and eight shall in any
Manner affect the first and fourth Clauses in the Ninth Section
of the first Article; and that no State, without its Consent,
shall be deprived of its equal Suffrage in the Senate.

ARTICLE. VI.

All Debts contracted and Engagements entered into, before
the Adoption of this Constitution, shall be as valid against
the United States under this Constitution, as under the
Confederation.

This Constitution, and the Laws of the United States which
shall be made in Pursuance thereof; and all Treaties made, or
which shall be made, under the Authority of the United States,
shall be the supreme Law of the Land; and the Judges in every
State shall be bound thereby, any Thing in the Constitution or
Laws of any State to the Contrary notwithstanding.

The Senators and Representatives before mentioned, and
the Members of the several State Legislatures, and all executive and judicial Officers, both of the United States and of
the several States, shall be bound by Oath or Affirmation, to
support this Constitution; but no religious Test shall ever be
required as a Qualification to any Office or public Trust under
the United States.

ARTICLE. VII.

The Ratification of the Conventions of nine States, shall be
sufficient for the Establishment of this Constitution between
the States so ratifying the Same.

The Word, "the," being interlined between the seventh and eighth Lines of the first Page, the Word "Thirty" being partly written on an Erazure in the fifteenth Line of the first Page, The Words "is tried" being interlined between the thirty second and thirty third Lines of the first Page and the Word "the" being interlined between the forty third and forty fourth Lines of the second Page.

Attest William Jackson Secretary

done in Convention by the Unanimous Consent of the States present the Seventeenth Day of September in the Year of our Lord one thousand seven hundred and Eighty seven and of the Independance of the United States of America the Twelfth In witness whereof We have hereunto subscribed our Names,

G°. Washington
Presidt and deputy from Virginia

Maryland:
James McHenry
Dan of St Thos. Jenifer
Danl. Carroll

Virginia:
John Blair
James Madison Jr.

South Carolina:
J. Rutledge
Charles Cotesworth Pinckney
Charles Pinckney
Pierce Butler

North Carolina:
Wm. Blount
Richd. Dobbs Spaight
Hu Williamson

Georgia:
William Few
Abr Baldwin

New Jersey:
Wil: Livingston
David Brearley
Wm. Paterson
Jona: Dayton

New Hampshire:
  John Langdon
  Nicholas Gilman

Massachusetts:
  Nathaniel Gorham
  Rufus King

Delaware:
  Geo: Read
  Gunning Bedford jun
  John Dickinson
  Richard Bassett
  Jaco: Broom
  James Wilson

Pennsylvania
  B Franklin
  Thomas Mifflin
  Robt. Morris
  Geo. Clymer
  Thos. FitzSimons
  Jared Ingersoll

Connecticut:
  Wm. Saml. Johnson
  Roger Sherman
  Gouv Morris

New York:
  Alexander Hamilton

Amendment 1: Congress shall make no law respecting an establishment of religion, or prohibiting the free exercise thereof; or abridging the freedom of speech, or of the press; or the right of the people peaceably to assemble, and to petition the Government for a redress of grievances.

Amendment 2: A well regulated Militia, being necessary to the security of a free State, the right of the people to keep and bear Arms, shall not be infringed.

Amendment 3: No Soldier shall, in time of peace be quartered in any house, without the consent of the Owner, nor in time of war, but in a manner to be prescribed by law.

Amendment 4: The right of the people to be secure in their persons, houses, papers, and effects, against unreasonable searches and seizures, shall not be violated, and no Warrants shall issue, but upon probable cause, supported by Oath or affirmation, and particularly describing the place to be searched, and the persons or things to be seized.

Amendment 5: No person shall be held to answer for a capital, or otherwise infamous crime, unless on a presentment or indictment of a Grand Jury, except in cases arising in the land or naval forces, or in the Militia, when in actual service in time of War or public danger; nor shall any person be subject for the same offense to be twice put in jeopardy of life or limb; nor shall be compelled in any criminal case to be a witness against himself, nor be deprived of life, liberty, or property, without due process of law; nor shall private property be taken for public use, without just compensation.

Amendment 6: In all criminal prosecutions, the accused shall enjoy the right to a speedy and public trial, by an impartial jury of the State and district wherein the crime shall have been committed, which district shall have been previously ascertained by law, and to be informed of the nature and cause of the accusation; to be confronted with the witnesses against him; to have compulsory process for obtaining witnesses in his favor, and to have the Assistance of Counsel for his defence.

Amendment 7: In Suits at common law, where the value in controversy shall exceed twenty dollars, the right of trial by jury shall be preserved, and no fact tried by a jury, shall be otherwise re-examined in any Court of the United States, than according to the rules of the common law.

Amendment 8: Excessive bail shall not be required, nor excessive fines imposed, nor cruel and unusual punishments inflicted.

Amendment 9: The enumeration in the Constitution, of certain rights, shall not be construed to deny or disparage others retained by the people.

Amendment 10: The powers not delegated to the United States by the Constitution, nor prohibited by it to the States, are reserved to the States respectively, or to the people.

Amendment 11: The Judicial power of the United States shall not be construed to extend to any suit in law or equity, commenced or prosecuted against one of the United States by Citizens of another State, or by Citizens or Subjects of any Foreign State.

Amendment 12: The Electors shall meet in their respective states, and vote by ballot for President and Vice-President, one of whom, at least, shall not be an inhabitant of the same state with themselves; they shall name in their ballots the person voted for as President, and in distinct ballots the person voted for as Vice-President, and they shall make distinct lists of all persons voted for as President, and all persons voted for as Vice-President and of the number of votes for each, which lists they shall sign and certify, and transmit sealed to the seat of the government of the United States, directed to the President of the Senate.

The President of the Senate shall, in the presence of the Senate and House of Representatives, open all the certificates and the votes shall then be counted.

The person having the greatest Number of votes for President, shall be the President, if such number be a majority of the whole number of Electors appointed; and if no person have such majority, then from the persons having the highest numbers not exceeding three on the list of those voted for as President, the House of Representatives shall choose immediately, by ballot, the President. But in choosing the President, the votes shall be taken by states, the representation from each state having one vote; a quorum for this purpose shall consist of a member or members from two-thirds of the states, and a majority of all the states shall be necessary to a choice. And if the House of Representatives shall not choose a President whenever the right of choice shall devolve upon them, before the fourth day of March next following, then the Vice-President shall act as President, as in the case of the death or other constitutional disability of the President.

The person having the greatest number of votes as Vice-President, shall be the Vice-President, if such number be a majority of the whole number of Electors appointed, and if no person have a majority, then from the two highest numbers on the list, the Senate shall choose the Vice-President; a quorum for the purpose shall consist of two-thirds of the whole number of Senators, and a majority of the whole number shall be necessary to a choice. But no person constitutionally ineligible to the office of President shall be eligible to that of Vice-President of the United States.

Amendment 13:

Section. 1. Neither slavery nor involuntary servitude, except as a punishment for crime whereof the party shall have been duly convicted, shall exist within the United States, or any place subject to their jurisdiction.

Section. 2. Congress shall have power to enforce this article by appropriate legislation.

Amendment 14:

Section. 1. All persons born or naturalized in the United States, and subject to the jurisdiction thereof, are citizens of the United States and of the State wherein they reside. No State shall make or enforce any law which shall abridge the privileges or immunities of citizens of the United States; nor shall any State deprive any person of life, liberty, or property, without due process of law; nor deny to any person within its jurisdiction the equal protection of the laws.

Section. 2. Representatives shall be apportioned among the several States according to their respective numbers, counting the whole number of persons in each State, excluding Indians not taxed. But when the right to vote at any election for the choice of electors for President and Vice President of the United States, Representatives in Congress, the Executive and Judicial officers of a State, or the members of the Legislature thereof, is denied to any of the male inhabitants of such State, being twenty-one years of age, and citizens of the United States, or in any way abridged, except for participation in rebellion, or other crime, the basis of representation therein shall be reduced in the proportion which the number of such male citizens shall bear to the whole number of male citizens twenty-one years of age in such State.

Section. 3. No person shall be a Senator or Representative in Congress, or elector of President and Vice President, or hold any office, civil or military, under the United States, or under any State, who, having previously taken an oath, as a member of Congress, or as an officer of the United States, or as a member of any State legislature, or as an executive or judicial officer of any State, to support the Constitution of the United States, shall have engaged in insurrection or rebellion against the same, or given aid or comfort to the enemies thereof. But Congress may, by a vote of two-thirds of each House, remove such disability.

Section. 4. The validity of the public debt of the United States, authorized by law, including debts incurred for payment of pensions and bounties for services in suppressing insurrection or rebellion, shall not be questioned. But neither the United States nor any State shall assume or pay any debt or obligation incurred in aid of insurrection or rebellion against the United States, or any claim for the loss or emancipation of any slave; but all such debts, obligations and claims shall be held illegal and void.

Section. 5. The Congress shall have power to enforce, by appropriate legislation, the provisions of this article.

Amendment 15:

Section. 1. The right of citizens of the United States to vote shall not be denied or abridged by the United States or by any State on account of race, color, or previous condition of servitude.

Section. 2. The Congress shall have power to enforce this article by appropriate legislation.

Amendment 16: The Congress shall have power to lay and collect taxes on incomes, from whatever source derived, without apportionment among the several States, and without regard to any census or enumeration.

Amendment 17: The Senate of the United States shall be composed of two Senators from each State, elected by the people thereof, for six years; and each Senator shall have one vote. The electors in each State shall have the qualifications requisite for electors of the most numerous branch of the State legislatures.

When vacancies happen in the representation of any State in the Senate, the executive authority of such State shall issue writs of election to fill such vacancies: Provided, That the legislature of any State may empower the executive thereof to make temporary appointments until the people fill the vacancies by election as the legislature may direct.

This amendment shall not be so construed as to affect the election or term of any Senator chosen before it becomes valid as part of the Constitution.

Amendment 18:

Section. 1. After one year from the ratification of this article the manufacture, sale, or transportation of intoxicating liquors within, the importation thereof into, or the exportation thereof from the United States and all the territory subject to the jurisdiction thereof for beverage purposes is hereby prohibited.

Section. 2. The Congress and the several States shall have concurrent power to enforce this article by appropriate legislation.

Section. 3. This article shall be inoperative unless it shall have been ratified as an amendment to the Constitution by the legislatures of the several States, as provided in the Constitution, within seven years from the date of the submission hereof to the States by the Congress.

Amendment 19: The right of citizens of the United States to vote shall not be denied or abridged by the United States or by any State on account of sex. Congress shall have power to enforce this article by appropriate legislation.

Amendment 20:

Section. 1. The terms of the President and Vice President shall end at noon on the 20th day of January, and the terms of Senators and Representatives at noon on the 3d day of January, of the years in which such terms would have ended if this article had not been ratified; and the terms of their successors shall then begin.

Section. 2. The Congress shall assemble at least once in every year, and such meeting shall begin at noon on the 3d day of January, unless they shall by law appoint a different day.

Section. 3. If, at the time fixed for the beginning of the term of the President, the President elect shall have died, the Vice President elect shall become President. If a President shall not have been chosen before the time fixed for the beginning of his term, or if the President elect shall have failed to qualify, then the Vice President elect shall act as President until a President shall have qualified; and the Congress may by law provide for the case wherein neither a President elect nor a Vice President elect shall have qualified, declaring who shall then act as President, or the manner in which one who is to act shall be selected, and such person shall act accordingly until a President or Vice President shall have qualified.

Section. 4. The Congress may by law provide for the case of the death of any of the persons from whom the House of Representatives may choose a President whenever the right of choice shall have devolved upon them, and for the case of the death of any of the persons from whom the Senate may choose a Vice President whenever the right of choice shall have devolved upon them.

Section. 5. Sections 1 and 2 shall take effect on the 15th day of October following the ratification of this article.

Section. 6. This article shall be inoperative unless it shall have been ratified as an amendment to the Constitution by the legislatures of three-fourths of the several States within seven years from the date of its submission.

Amendment 21:

Section. 1. The eighteenth article of amendment to the Constitution of the United States is hereby repealed.

Section. 2. The transportation or importation into any State, Territory, or possession of the United States for delivery or use therein of intoxicating liquors, in violation of the laws thereof, is hereby prohibited.

Section. 3. This article shall be inoperative unless it shall have been ratified as an amendment to the Constitution by conventions in the several States, as provided in the Constitution, within seven years from the date of the submission hereof to the States by the Congress.

Amendment 22:

Section. 1. No person shall be elected to the office of the President more than twice, and no person who has held the office of President, or acted as President, for more than two years of a term to which some other person was elected President shall be elected to the office of the President more than once. But this article shall not apply to any person holding the office of President when this article was proposed by the Congress, and shall not prevent any person who may be holding the office of President, or acting as President, during the term within which this article becomes operative from holding the office of President or acting as President during the remainder of such term.

Section. 2. This article shall be inoperative unless it shall have been ratified as an amendment to the Constitution by the legislatures of three-fourths of the several states within seven years from the date of its submission to the states by the Congress.

Amendment 23:

Section. 1. The District constituting the seat of Government of the United States shall appoint in such manner as the Congress may direct:

A number of electors of President and Vice President equal to the whole number of Senators and Representatives in Congress to which the District would be entitled if it were a State, but in no event more than the least populous State; they shall be in addition to those appointed by the States, but they shall be considered, for the purposes of the election of President and Vice President, to be electors appointed by a State; and they shall meet in the District and perform such duties as provided by the twelfth article of amendment.

Section. 2. The Congress shall have power to enforce this article by appropriate legislation.

Amendment 24:

Section. 1. The right of citizens of the United States to vote in any primary or other election for President or Vice President, for electors for President or Vice President, or for Senator or Representative in Congress, shall not be denied or abridged by the United States or any State by reason of failure to pay any poll tax or other tax.

Section. 2. The Congress shall have power to enforce this article by appropriate legislation

Amendment 25:

Section. 1. In case of the removal of the President from office or of his death or resignation, the Vice President shall become President.

Section. 2. Whenever there is a vacancy in the office of the Vice President, the President shall nominate a Vice President who shall take office upon confirmation by a majority vote of both Houses of Congress.

Section. 3. Whenever the President transmits to the President pro tempore of the Senate and the Speaker of the House of Representatives his written declaration that he is unable to discharge the powers and duties of his office, and until he transmits to them a written declaration to the contrary, such powers and duties shall be discharged by the Vice President as Acting President.

Section. 4. Whenever the Vice President and a majority of either the principal officers of the executive departments or of such other body as Congress may by law provide, transmit to the President pro tempore of the Senate and the Speaker of the House of Representatives their written declaration that the President is unable to discharge the powers and duties of his office, the Vice President shall immediately assume the powers and duties of the office as Acting President.

Thereafter, when the President transmits to the President pro tempore of the Senate and the Speaker of the House of Representatives his written declaration that no inability exists, he shall resume the powers and duties of his office unless the Vice President and a majority of either the principal officers of the executive department or of such other body as Congress may by law provide, transmit within four days to the President pro tempore of the Senate and the Speaker of the House of Representatives their written declaration that the President is unable to discharge the powers and duties of his office. Thereupon Congress shall decide the issue, assembling within forty-eight hours for that purpose if not in session. If the Congress, within twenty-one days after receipt of the latter written declaration, or, if Congress is not in session, within twenty-one days after Congress is required to assemble, determines by two-thirds vote of both Houses that the President is unable to discharge the powers and duties of his office, the Vice President shall continue to discharge the same as Acting President; otherwise, the President shall resume the powers and duties of his office.

Amendment 26:

Section. 1. The right of citizens of the United States, who are eighteen years of age or older, to vote shall not be denied or abridged by the United States or by any State on account of age.

Section. 2. The Congress shall have the power to enforce this article by appropriate legislation.

Amendment 27: No law, varying the compensation for the services of the Senators and Representatives, shall take effect, until an election of Representatives shall have intervened

THOMAS JEFFERSON'S RULES OF CONDUCT

1. Never put off to tomorrow what you can do today.
2. Never trouble another with what you can do yourself.
3. Never spend your money before you have it.
4. Never buy a thing you do not want, because it is cheap, it will be dear to you.
5. Take care of your cents: Dollars will take care of themselves.
6. Pride costs us more than hunger, thirst and cold.
7. We never repent of having eat too little.
8. Nothing is troublesome that one does willingly.
9. How much pain have cost us the evils which have never happened.
10. Take things always by their smooth handle.
11. Think as you please, and so let others, and you will have no disputes.
12. When angry, count 10. before you speak; if very angry, 100.

CREATING LEGISLATION: AN OVERVIEW

Local Law:

1. A member of the community or a council member has an idea for a law.
2. A council member proposes or introduces the idea.
3. City council members (or village trustees) often form a committee to evaluate the proposed law, or assign the proposal to an appropriate committee. This step is not required.

4. A public hearing is required for some ordinances, such as zoning ordinances. Citizens must have at least 10 days notice of the hearing.

5. The members of the committee vote on whether or not to adopt the ordinance.

6. The committee recommendation goes to the Council. A majority of the Council must approve the ordinance for it to pass. Usually the mayor or village president does not vote except in the case of a tie.

7. The mayor or village president can veto an ordinance, but only if it
    - Creates liability against the city
    - Provides for spending of money
    - Involves selling any city property

8. The members can override the executive's veto with a 2/3 vote.

Federal Law:

The detailed process for how a bill becomes a law can be complicated and tedious. The system of checks and balances is designed to make sure that there is significant agreement before a new law is enacted. If you have ever watched *Mr Smith Goes to Washington* (1939), there is an entertaining scene describing how a bill becomes federal law.

1. Where does a bill start? An individual or group gets an idea for a new law or a change to an old law.

2. What is a bill? An idea that is written as a proposed law.

3. After a bill is drafted, Representatives (either Congresspersons or Senators) propose a bill in the House or Senate.

4. The bill is read to the representatives on the floor of the House or Senate (a proposed bill must be read

into the Congressional record three times before it moves forward).

5. The bill is sent to the appropriate House or Senate committee (For example, an issue dealing with education would be sent to the Education Committee; an issue dealing with the interstate highway system would be sent to the Transportation Committee).

6. The committee holds public hearings on the bill where individuals or interested groups can give public comment or testimony on their opinions of the bill.

7. The committee debates and votes on whether to approve the bill and send the bill back to the floor (with or without amendments), or to "kill" the bill by keeping it in committee for further debate.

8. If the committee approves the bill, it goes to the floor of the originating house where it is read a second time. At this point, any amendments made to the bill are debated by the members of this house of Congress.

9. After the debate is finished, the bill is read a third time. The members debate again, and vote on the bill.

10. If the first house passes the bill, it goes to the second house (for example, if the bill started in the House of Representatives, it would then go on to the Senate).

11. The whole process starts over again in this second house.

12. If the House and Senate pass different versions of the same bill, the bill is sent to a conference committee made up of members from both houses to try to reach a compromise on the bill. Both houses must then agree to the compromise by majority vote.

13. If both houses agree on a final version of the bill, it goes to the President for his or her signature.

14. The President can sign the bill into law or veto the bill.

15. If the President vetoes the bill, it is sent back to Congress. Congress can then re-vote on the bill. If each house of Congress votes to override the veto by a 2/3 majority vote, the bill becomes a law.

Voting is a Right, not a Privilege

A right is something you are born with. A privilege is something you are given. Election Day in the United States of America is the day set by law for the election of public officials, initiatives and referendums. For federal offices (United States Congress, President and Vice President), it occurs on the Tuesday after the first Monday of November in even-numbered years; the earliest possible date is November 2 and the latest is November 8. Presidential elections are held every four years, elections to the United States House of Representatives are held every two years, and a US Senator runs for election every six years. General elections in which Presidential candidates are not on the ballot are referred to as midterm elections. Many state and local government offices are also voted upon on Election Day as a matter of convenience and cost savings. Election Day is a civic holiday in some states, including Florida, Hawaii, Illinois, Indiana, Louisiana, Maryland, Michigan, Montana, New Hampshire, New Jersey, New York, and Wisconsin. I encourage everyone who is qualified to exercise your right to vote.

EPILOGUE

The journey towards writing this book started in May 2010 when I met Randy E. King outside University Printing in La Habra, California. Over the next four years, we have developed something that is greater than ourselves as individuals. We have a website, three books, an ebook, and an audio CD that actively promotes the concepts that personal growth, self-education, hard work, and winning strategies lead ultimately to success in these United States of America. At first, I started developing this book into a list of ways in which government has overreached its authority. It quickly morphed into something greater. The primary purpose of this book is to show you that one person can make a difference and to give you some tools to go out there and make it happen. More importantly, it shows you WHY you should be involved in this Nation's social and political environment and HOW to Reclaim America.

If you do nothing, you will lose everything. A Republic based upon justice, liberty and the Rule of Law must be actively protected. Freedoms are like a muscle. In order to keep it healthy and strong it must be flexed and exercised. There are many entities in the world, both internal and external, that do not want us to have a healthy representative Republic and constitutional government. If you are one of them, than I apologize for wasting your time. If you want to protect our culture, our heritage, and what it means to be American, you must educate yourself, create your own personal message and get involved. Remember that there are a lot of great ideas out there that can improve who we are as a nation.

Both authors of this book have our individual philosophies on life. It is not our goal to make you think like us, but rather, to get you to think and do for yourself in such a way that positively infects others and, in return, makes you successful and creates a better Nation for all of us.

Just like any other tool, information can be used for good or for evil. This book is not just about information. It is about Truth and the American Way. We still live under a Constitution. We still have the right to vote. We still have the ability to educate ourselves, and with the many new technologies at our disposal, we have the ability to communicate with anyone and everyone. Through this, we have the ability to create positive political and social change.

Neither of us know what the future has in store, but we do know what the past and present represent. We also know that education, hard work, integrity, personal liberty, personal freedom, and the pursuit of justice have made America successful in the past and will continue to make it successful into the future as long as we, its citizens, continue to embrace and cherish our National identity as just and free.

I will leave you with this. American Patriotism is not a blind adoration towards something we are told to appreciate. American Patriotism is an outward expression of our inward love and admiration for the culture, laws, and ideals of what the United States of America represents.

Now Go Reclaim America!

BIBLIOGRAPHY

Introduction

Wikipedia. (04.20.2014). *September 11 attacks*. Retrieved from http://en.wikipedia.org/wiki/September_11_attacks

Wikipedia. (04.20.2014). *Attack on Pearl Harbor*. Retrieved from http://en.wikipedia.org/wiki/Attack_on_Pearl_Harbor

Wikipedia. (04.20.2014). *Moon landing*. Retrieved from http://en.wikipedia.org/wiki/Moon_landing

Gallup. (01.11.2009). *Presidential Approval Ratings -- George W. Bush*. Retrieved from http://www.gallup.com/poll/116500/presidential-approval-ratings-george-bush.aspx

Gallup. (04.13.2014). *Presidential Approval Ratings -- Barack Obama*. Retrieved from http://www.gallup.com/poll/116479/barack-obama-presidential-job-approval.aspx

Wikipedia. (04.20.2014). *Patient Protection and Affordable Care Act*. Retrieved from http://en.wikipedia.org/wiki Patient_Protection_and_Affordable_Care_Act

Worldometers. (04.20.2014). *World Population Clock: 7 Billion People (2014)*. Retrieved from http://www.worldometers.info/world-population/

Orwell, George. (1948). *1984 (page 191)*. Retrieved from http://books.google.com/books?id=w-rb62wiFAwC&pg=PA191&lpg=PA191

Free Online Dictionary. (2009). *Duplicitous - Definition*. Retrieved from http://www.thefreedictionary.com/duplicitous

Camus, Albert. (born 1913, died 1960). *Albert Camus Quotes*. Retrieved from http://www.brainyquote.com/quotes/quotes/a/albert-camu104177.html

Wikipedia. (04.20.2014). *Steve Jobs*. Retrieved from http://en.wikipedia.org/wiki/Steve_Jobs

Morgan, George. (10.05.2011). *Steve Jobs, RIP*. Retrieved from http://patentaz.com/872/steve-jobs-rip/

Stanford University. (05.14.2008). *Steve Jobs' 2005 Stanford Commencement Address (with intro by President John Hennessy)*. Retrieved from https://www.youtube.com/watch?v=Hd_ptbiPoXM

Chapter 1

Rector, Robert. (08.27.2007). *How Poor Are America's Poor? Examining the "Plague" of Poverty in America*. Retrieved from http://www.heritage.org/research/reports/2007/08how-poor-are-americas-poor-examining-the-plague-of-poverty-in-america

ABC Real Estate Directory. (04.21.2014). *Texas Real Estate Prices*. Retrieved from http://www.abcrealestatedirectory.com/prices/states/Texas.htm

Los Angeles Almanac. (11.2008). *Historical Median Home Sales Prices in Southern California By County, 1982-2008*. Retrieved from http://www.laalmanac.com/economy/ec37.htm

Diamond, Diane. (09.15.2011). *The Real Grifter of Beverly Hills*. Retrieved from http://www.thedailybeast.com/articles/2011/09/15/russell-taylor-armstrong-s-business-associates-friends-on-financial-legal-troubles.html

Wikipedia. (04.20.2014). *September 11 attacks*. Retrieved from http://en.wikipedia.org/wiki/September_11_attacks

ABC News. (11.01.2004). *Full Transcript of Bin Laden Video*. Retrieved from http://abcnews.go.com/International/story?id=215913

Drac, Michel. (09.01.2011). *le 11 septembre n'a pas eu lieu*. Retrieved from http://www.amazon.fr/11-septembre-pas-lieu/dp/2355120412

The History Place. (1996). *The Rise of Adolf Hitler*. Retrieved from http://www.historyplace.com/worldwar2/riseofhitler/

Robbins, Stephen P. (2001). *Organizational Behavior, Ninth Edition*. Prentice Hall International, Inc. Retrieved from http://wwwuser. gwdg.de/~uwuf/pdfdatei/orga/Chapt1.pdf

Schweizer, Peter; Hall, Wynton C. (03.06.2007). *Landmark Speeches of the American Conservative Movement*. Texas A&M University Press. Retrieved from http://books.google.com/ books?id=SZbijMUHMQMC&pg=PA55

Wikipedia. (04.23.2014). *Theodore Roosevelt*. Retrieved from http:// en.wikipedia.org/wiki/Theodore_Roosevelt

Roosevelt, Theodore. (04.23.1910). *Citizenship in a Republic*. Retrieved from http://design.caltech.edu/erik/Misc/Citizenship_ in_a_Republic.pdf

Chapter 2

Madison, James. (11.22.1787). *The Federalist No. 10*. Retrieved from http://www.constitution.org/fed/federa10.htm

Wikipedia. (04.23.2014). *Theodore Roosevelt*. Retrieved from http://en.wikipedia.org/wiki/Theodore_Roosevelt

Wikipedia. (04.23.2014). *Republican Party presidential primaries, 2008*. Retrieved from http://en.wikipedia.org/wikiRepublican_ Party_presidential_primaries,_2008

Wikipedia. (04.23.2014). *Democratic Party presidential primaries, 2000*. Retrieved from http://en.wikipedia.org/wiki/ Democratic_Party_presidential_primaries,_2000

Wikipedia. (04.23.2014). *Democratic Party presidential primaries, 2004.* Retrieved from http://en.wikipedia.org/wiki/Democratic_Party_presidential_primaries,_2004

Wikipedia. (04.23.2014). *Bernie Sanders.* Retrieved from http://en.wikipedia.org/wiki/Bernie_Sanders

Forbes. (04.23.2014). #1 *Bill Gates.* Retrieved from http://www.forbes.com/profile/bill-gates/

Wikipedia. (04.23.2014). *Bill Gates.* Retrieved from http://en.wikipedia.org/wiki/Bill_Gates

Bill & Melinda Gates Foundation. (04.23.2014). *Foundation Fact Sheet.* Retrieved from http://www.gatesfoundation.org/who-we-are/general-information/foundation-factsheet

Gates, Bill. (06.07.2007). *Bill Gates Speech - Harvard Commencement 2007.* Retrieved from http://www.youtube.com/watch?v=qBoa8ujU_fs; http://www.youtube.com/watch?NR=1&v=AS8PyuafC0E; http://www.youtube.com/watch?v=cAmyWaMylWk

Chapter 3

Wikipedia. (04.23.2014). *Progressivism.* Retrieved from http://en.wikipedia.org/wiki/Progressivism

Archives.gov. (04.23.2014). *The Constitution: Amendments 11-27.* Retrieved from http://www.archives.gov/exhibits/charters/constitution_amendments_11-27.html

Wikipedia. (04.23.2014). *W. E. B. Du Bois.* Retrieved from http://en.wikipedia.org/wiki/WEB_Du_Bois

Boyden, Wallace C.; Boyden, Merill N.; Boyden, Amos J. (1901). *Thomas Boyden and His Descendants.* Retrieved from http://storiesofusa.com/images/thomas-boyden-genealogy-1634.pdf

Wikipedia. (04.23.2014). *Horace Mann.* Retrieved from http://en.wikipedia.org/wiki/Horace_Mann

Wikipedia. (04.23.2014). *Frank Johnson Goodnow*. Retrieved from http://en.wikipedia.org/wiki/Frank_Johnson_Goodnow

Wikipedia. (04.23.2014). *Woodrow Wilson*. Retrieved from http://en.wikipedia.org/wiki/Woodrow_Wilson

Goodnow, Frank_J. (1914). *Politics and Administration: A Study in Government*. The MacMillan Company. Retrieved from http://books.google.com/books?id=NVoPAAAAYAAJ

University of Vermont. (01.30.2002). *A Brief Overview of Progressive Education*. Retrieved from http://www.uvm.edu/~dewey/articles/proged.html

Wikipedia. (04.23.2014). *Labor unions in the United States*. Retrieved from http://en.wikipedia.org/wiki/Labor_unions_in_the_United_States

Wikipedia. (04.23.2014). *Franklin D. Roosevelt*. Retrieved from http://en.wikipedia.org/wiki/Franklin_D._Roosevelt

Wikipedia. (04.23.2014). *Lyndon B. Johnson*. Retrieved from http://en.wikipedia.org/wiki/Lyndon_B._Johnson

Social Security Administration. (2011). *Frequently Asked Questions - Ratio of Covered Workers to Beneficiaries*. Retrieved from http://www.ssa.gov/history/ratios.html

Adams, Abigail. (03.31.1776). *LETTERS BETWEEN ABIGAIL ADAMS AND HER HUSBAND JOHN ADAMS*. Retrieved from http://www.thelizlibrary.org/suffrage/abigail.htm

Wikipedia. (04.23.2014). *Abigail Adams*. Retrieved from http://en.wikipedia.org/wiki/Abigail_Adams

Wikipedia. (04.23.2014). *Susan B. Anthony*. Retrieved from http://en.wikipedia.org/wiki/Susan_B._Anthony

Kerr, Andrea M. (1995). *Lucy Stone: Speaking Out for Equality*. Retrieved from http://books.google.com/books?id=bvPpRyMcQzoC&pg=PA60

Anthony, Susan B. (1873). *On Women's Right to Vote*. Retrieved from http://www.historyplace.com/speeches/anthony.htm

Chapter 4

Wikipedia. (04.23.2014). *First inauguration of Franklin D. Roosevelt*. Retrieved from http://en.wikipedia.org/wiki/First_inauguration_of_Franklin_D._Roosevelt

Roosevelt, Franklin D.; Rosenman, Samuel. (1938). *The Public Papers of Franklin D. Roosevelt, Volume Two: The Year of Crisis, 1933*. New York: Random House. Retrieved from http://historymatters.gmu.edu/d/5057/

Wikipedia. (04.23.2014). *Anna Howard Shaw*. Retrieved from http://en.wikipedia.org/wiki/Anna_Howard_Shaw

Shaw, Anna H. (06.21.1915). *The Fundamental Principle of a Republic*. Retrieved from http://gos.sbc.edu/s/shaw.html

Wikipedia. (04.23.2014). *United States presidential election, 1932*. Retrieved from http://en.wikipedia.org/wiki/United_States_presidential_election,_1932

Wikipedia. (04.23.2014). *Great_Depression*. Retrieved from http://en.wikipedia.org/wiki/Great_Depression

United States History. (04.23.2014). *Unemployment Statistics during the Great Depression*. Retrieved from http://www.u-s-history.com/pages/h1528.html

Walsh, Kenneth T. (02.12.2009). *The First 100 Days: Franklin Roosevelt Pioneered the 100-Day Concept*. US News & World Report. Retrieved from http://www.usnews.com/news/history/articles/2009/02/12/the-first-100-days-franklin-roosevelt-pioneered-the-100-day-concept

Roosevelt, Franklin D. (03.04.1933). *First Inaugural Address*. Retrieved from http://www.americanrhetoric.com/speeches/fdrfirstinaugural.html

Wikipedia. (04.23.2014). *Lyndon B. Johnson*. Retrieved from http://en.wikipedia.org/wiki/Lyndon_B._Johnson

Johnson, Lyndon B. (03.15.1965). *We Shall Overcome*. Retrieved from http://www.americanrhetoric.com/speeches/lbjweshallovercome.htm

Wikipedia. (04.23.2014). *Barack Obama*. Retrieved from http://en.wikipedia.org/wiki/Barack_Obama

Obama, Barack H. (07.27.2004). *Audacity of Hope*. Retrieved from http://www.washingtonpost.com/wp-dyn/articles/A19751-2004Jul27.html

Chapter 5

Wikipedia. (04.25.2014). *Ronald Reagan*. Retrieved from http://en.wikipedia.org/wiki/Ronald_Reagan

Reagan, Ronald W. (10.27.1964). *A Time for Choosing*. Retrieved from http://www.americanrhetoric.com/speeches/ronaldreaganatimeforchoosing.htm

Wikipedia. (04.25.2014). *American exceptionalism*. Retrieved from http://en.wikipedia.org/wiki/American_exceptionalism

Jefferson, Thomas. (07.04.1776). *Declaration of Independence Transcript*. Retrieved from http://www.archives.gov/exhibits/charters/declaration_transcript.html

Madison, James, et al. (09.17.1787). *Constitution of the United States Transcript*. Retrieved from http://www.archives.gov/exhibits/charters/constitution_transcript.html

Key, Francis S. (1814). *The U.S. National Anthem*. Retrieved from http://www.music.army.mil/music/nationalanthem/

Bellamy, Francis, et al. (08.1892). *The Pledge of Allegience*. Retrieved from http://www.ushistory.org/documents/pledge.htm

Bellis, Mary. (04.25.2014). *19th Century technology, science, and inventions*. Retrieved from http://inventors.about.com/od/timelines/a/Nineteenth.htm

Bellis, Mary. (04.25.2014). *19th Century technology, science, and inventions*. Retrieved from http://inventors.about.com/od/timelines/a/Nineteenth.htm

Bellis, Mary. (04.25.2014). *20th Century technology, science, and inventions*. Retrieved from http://inventors.about.com/od/timelines/a/twentieth.htm

Wikipedia. (04.25.2014). *List of Nobel laureates in Physiology or Medicine*. Retrieved from http://en.wikipedia.org/wiki/List_of_Nobel_laureates_in_Physiology_or_Medicine

Photius. (01.2005). *GDP 2005*. Retrieved from http://www.photius.com/rankings/economy/gdp_2005_0.html

Wikipedia. (04.25.2014). *All-time Olympic Games medal table*. Retrieved from http://en.wikipedia.org/wiki/All-time_Olympic_Games_medal_table

US Census Bureau. (2012). *U.S. Census Bureau, Statistical Abstract of the United States: 2012*. Retrieved from https://www.census.gov/compendia/statab/2012/tables/12s1229.pdf

Federal Office for Migration. (2014). *FAQ – Frequently asked questions: Swiss citizenship / Naturalization*. Retrieved from https://www.bfm.admin.ch/content/bfm/en/home/themen/buergerrecht/faq.0002.html

Wikipedia. (04.25.2014). *Languages of the United States*. Retrieved from http://en.wikipedia.org/wiki/Languages_of_the_United_States

Wikipedia. (04.25.2014). *Timeline of United States inventions*. Retrieved from http://en.wikipedia.org/wiki/Timeline_of_United_States_inventions

Forbes. (03.10.2010). *The World's Billionaires.* Retrieved from http://www.forbes.com/lists/2010/10/billionaires-2010_The-Worlds-Billionaires_Rank.html

Lilly Family School of Philanthropy. (06.09.2010). *U.S. charitable giving falls 3.6 percent in 2009 to $303.75 billion.* Retrieved from http://www.philanthropy.iupui.edu/news/article/us-charitable-giving-falls-36-percent-in-2009-to-30375-billion

Wikipedia. (04.25.2014). *List of countries by past and future GDP (nominal).* Retrieved from http://en.wikipedia.org/wiki/List_of_countries_by_past_and_future_GDP_(nominal)#IMF_estimates_between_2000_and_2009

Conservapedia. (11.02.2013). *Conservative.* Retrieved from http://conservapedia.com/Conservatism

Hoover Institution, Stanford University. (09.23.2013). *Shelby Steele.* Retrieved from http://www.hoover.org/fellows/10347

Steele, Shelby. (09.01.2011). *Obama and the Burden of Exceptionalism.* Wall Street Journal. Retrieved from http://online.wsj.com/news/articles/SB10001424053111904787404576532623176115558

Wikipedia. (04.25.2014). *Alexander Hamilton.* Retrieved from http://en.wikipedia.org/wiki/Alexander_Hamilton

Wikipedia. (04.25.2014). *Henry Clay.* Retrieved from http://en.wikipedia.org/wiki/Henry_Clay

Wikipedia. (04.25.2014). *Abraham Lincoln.* Retrieved from http://en.wikipedia.org/wiki/Abraham_Lincoln

Wikipedia. (04.25.2014). *George Mason.* Retrieved from http://en.wikipedia.org/wiki/George_Mason

Wikipedia. (04.25.2014). *Thomas Jefferson.* Retrieved from http://en.wikipedia.org/wiki/Thomas_Jefferson

Wikipedia. (04.25.2014). *Republicanism.* Retrieved from http://en.wikipedia.org/wiki/Republicanism

Wikipedia. (04.25.2014). *Thomas Jefferson*. Retrieved from http://en.wikipedia.org/wiki/Thomas_Jefferson

Wikipedia. (04.25.2014). *Federalism*. Retrieved from http://en.wikipedia.org/wiki/Federalism

Wikipedia. (04.25.2014). *Separation of powers*. Retrieved from http://en.wikipedia.org/wiki/Separation_of_powers

National Archives and Records Administration. (03.04.1779). *Bill of Rights Transcript*. Retrieved from http://www.archives.gov/exhibits/charters/bill_of_rights_transcript.html

Wikipedia. (04.25.2014). *Andrew Jackson*. Retrieved from http://en.wikipedia.org/wiki/Andrew_Jackson

Wikipedia. (04.25.2014). *Whig Party (United States)*. Retrieved from http://en.wikipedia.org/wiki/Whig_Party_(United_States)

Wikipedia. (04.25.2014). *United States presidential election, 1840*. Retrieved from http://en.wikipedia.org/wiki/United_States_presidential_election,_1840

Wikipedia. (04.25.2014). *United States presidential election, 1844*. Retrieved from http://en.wikipedia.org/wiki/United_States_presidential_election,_1844

Wikipedia. (04.25.2014). *United States presidential election, 1848*. Retrieved from http://en.wikipedia.org/wiki/United_States_presidential_election,_1848

Wikipedia. (04.25.2014). *Compromise of 1850*. Retrieved from http://en.wikipedia.org/wiki/Compromise_of_1850

Wikipedia. (04.25.2014). *United States presidential election, 1852*. Retrieved from http://en.wikipedia.org/wiki/United_States_presidential_election,_1852

Wikipedia. (04.25.2014). *List of Presidents of the United States*. Retrieved from http://en.wikipedia.org/wiki/List_of_Presidents_of_the_United_States

Wikipedia. (04.25.2014). *United States presidential election, 1860.* Retrieved from http://en.wikipedia.org/wiki/United_States_presidential_election,_1860

Wikipedia. (04.25.2014). *American Liberty League.* Retrieved from http://en.wikipedia.org/wiki/American_Liberty_League

Wikipedia. (04.25.2014). *William F. Buckley, Jr..* Retrieved from http://en.wikipedia.org/wiki/William_F._Buckley,_Jr.

Wikipedia. (04.25.2014). *Young Americans for Freedom.* Retrieved from http://en.wikipedia.org/wiki/Young_Americans_for_Freedom

Buckley Jr, William F. (06.11.1950). *Today We Are Educated Men.* Retrieved from http://storiesofusa.com/william-buckley-today-we-are-educated-men-june-11-1950/

Chapter 6

Wikipedia. (04.25.2014). *Ronald Reagan.* Retrieved from http://en.wikipedia.org/wiki/Ronald_Reagan

Reagan, Ronald W. (06.12.1987). *Remarks at the Brandenburg Gate.* Retrieved from http://www.americanrhetoric.com/speeches/ronaldreaganbrandenburggate.htm

Kommersant. (09.19.2008). *Mikhail Gorbachev award.* Retrieved from http://www.kommersant.com/p-13256/r_500/Mikhail_Gorbachev_award/

C-SPAN. (06.01.1990). *Wellesley College Commencement.* Retrieved from http://www.c-span.org/video/?12521-1/wellesley-college-commencement

Reagan, Ronald W. (10.27.1964). *A Time for Choosing.* Retrieved from http://www.americanrhetoric.com/speeches/ronaldreaganatimeforchoosing.htm

Wikipedia. (04.25.2014). *Marco Rubio.* Retrieved from http://en.wikipedia.org/wiki/Marco_Rubio

Rubio,   Marco.   (08.24.2011).   *Prosperity   and Compassion*. Retrieved from http://storiesofusa.com/marco-rubio-prosperity-and-compassion-august-24-2011/

Wikipedia. (04.25.2014). *Mitt Romney*. Retrieved from http://en.wikipedia.org/wiki/Mitt_Romney

Romney, Willard M. (01.10.2012). *Tonight We Made History*. Retrieved from http://storiesofusa.com/mitt-romney-new-hampshire-victory-speech-tonight-we-made-history-january-10-2012/

Wikipedia. (04.25.2014). *Newt Gingrich*. Retrieved from http://en.wikipedia.org/wiki/Newt_Gingrich

Gingrich, Newt. (01.04.1995). *Contract With America*. Retrieved from http://storiesofusa.com/newt-gingrich-contract-with-america-january-4-1995/

Chapter 7

Wikipedia. (04.25.2014). *United States presidential election, 2000*. Retrieved from http://en.wikipedia.org/wiki/United_States_presidential_election,_2000

Wikipedia. (04.25.2014). *Battle of the Little Bighorn*. Retrieved from http://en.wikipedia.org/wiki/Battle_of_the_Little_Bighorn

Wikipedia. (04.25.2014). *Ulysses S. Grant*. Retrieved from http://en.wikipedia.org/wiki/Ulysses_S._Grant

Wikipedia. (04.25.2014). *United States presidential election, 1868*. Retrieved from http://en.wikipedia.org/wiki/United_States_presidential_election,_1868

Wikipedia. (04.25.2014). *United States presidential election, 1876*. Retrieved from http://en.wikipedia.org/wiki/United_States_presidential_election,_1876

Wikipedia. (04.25.2014). *39th United States Congress*. Retrieved from http://en.wikipedia.org/wiki/39th_United_States_Congress

Wikipedia. (04.25.2014). *40th United States Congress*. Retrieved from http://en.wikipedia.org/wiki/40th_United_States_Congress

Wikipedia. (04.25.2014). *41st United States Congress*. Retrieved from http://en.wikipedia.org/wiki/41st_United_States_Congress

Wikipedia. (04.25.2014). *42nd United States Congress*. Retrieved from http://en.wikipedia.org/wiki/42nd_United_States_Congress

Wikipedia. (04.25.2014). *43rd United States Congress*. Retrieved from http://en.wikipedia.org/wiki/43rd_United_States_Congress

Wikipedia. (04.25.2014). *Ulysses S. Grant presidential administration scandals*. Retrieved from http://en.wikipedia.org/wiki/Ulysses_S._Grant_presidential_administration_scandals

New York Times. (03.31.1875). *The Canal Frauds*. Retrieved from http://query.nytimes.com/mem/archive-free/pdf?res=9E0DEED61338EE3BBC4950DFB566838E669FDE

Wikipedia. (04.25.2014). *Samuel Tilden*. Retrieved from http://en.wikipedia.org/wiki/Samuel_Tilden

Wikipedia. (04.25.2014). *Gangs of New York*. Retrieved from http://en.wikipedia.org/wiki/Gangs_of_New_York

Wikipedia. (04.25.2014). *Oligarchy*. Retrieved from http://en.wikipedia.org/wiki/Oligarchy

Wikipedia. (04.25.2014). *List of Presidents of the United States*. Retrieved from http://en.wikipedia.org/wiki/List_of_Presidents_of_the_United_States

Wikipedia. (04.25.2014). *Communism*. Retrieved from http://en.wikipedia.org/wiki/Communism

Wikipedia. (04.25.2014). *Fascism*. Retrieved from http://en.wikipedia.org/wiki/Fascism

Madison, James. (12.02.1829). *Speech in the Virginia Constitutional Convention*. Retrieved from http://www.constitution.org/jm/18291202_vaconcon.txt

Brainy Quote. (04.25.2014). *Lord Acton Quotes*. Retrieved from http://www.brainyquote.com/quotes/authors/l/lord_acton.html

Wikipedia. (04.25.2014). *Abraham Maslow*. Retrieved from http://en.wikipedia.org/wiki/Abraham_Maslow

Orwell, George. (1948). *1984 (page 263)*. Retrieved from

http://books.google.com/books?id=yxv1LK5gyV4C&pg=PA263&lpg=PA263

US Government Spending. (04.25.2014). *Federal debt chart*. Retrieved from http://www.usgovernmentspending.com/federal_debt_chart.html

US Government Spending. (04.25.2014). *Federal deficit chart*. Retrieved from http://www.usgovernmentspending.com/federal_deficit_chart.html

US Government Spending. (04.25.2014). *Government Spending in United States: Federal State Local for 1910*. Retrieved from http://www.usgovernmentspending.com/total_spending_1910USrn

US Government Spending. (04.25.2014). *Government Spending in United States: Federal State Local for 2010*. Retrieved from http://www.usgovernmentspending.com/total_spending_2010USrn

Welch, Robert. (12.1958). *Robert Welch predicted Insider plans to destroy America in 1958*. Retrieved from https://www.youtube.com/watch?v=79Vow-huxfQ

Cohen, Ariella. (01.13.2007). *Slow Roasted Fine*. Brooklyn Paper. Retrieved from http://www.brooklynpaper.com/stories/30/2/30_02coffee.html

Lifsher, Marc; Chang, Andrea. (07.01.2011). *Amazon fights California sales tax requirement*. Los Angeles Times. Retrieved from http://articles.latimes.com/2011/jul/01/business/la-fi-amazon-sales-tax-20110701

Lifsher, Marc. (09.15.2012). *Free ride is over -- Amazon.com collecting California sales tax*. Los Angeles Times. Retrieved from http

://articles.latimes.com/2012/sep/15/business/la-fi-mo-amazon-collecting-ca-sales-tax-20120915

Wikipedia. (04.25.2014). *Americans with Disabilities Act of 1990.* Retrieved from http://en.wikipedia.org/wiki/Americans_with_Disabilities_Act_of_1990

Stateman, Allison. (12.29.2008). *Lawsuits by the Disabled: Abuse of the System?.* Time. Retrieved from http://content.time.com/time/nation/article/0,8599,1866666,00.html

Grimes, Katy. (07.08.2011). *Democrats Kill Abusive Lawsuit Bill.* Retrieved from http://calwatchdog.com/2011/07/08/democrats-kill-abusive-lawsuit-bill/

Highland Community News. (03.2014). *Dutton/Steinberg Legislation to Curb ADA Lawsuit Abuse Signed by Governor.* Retrieved from http://www.highlandnews.net/news/article_8413f9a4-cd30-5501-a248-5c9687e88599.html

Norby, Chris. (09.2007). *Redevelopment: The Unknown Government.* Retrieved from http://www.cotce.ca.gov/meetings/testimony/documents/CHRIS%20NORBY%20-%20ATTACH.PDF

National Archives. (04.25.2014). *The Constitution: Amendments 11-27.* Retrieved from http://www.archives.gov/exhibits/charters/constitution_amendments_11-27.html

Wikipedia. (04.25.2014). *Andrew Napolitano.* Retrieved from http://en.wikipedia.org/wiki/Andrew_Napolitano

Napolitano, Andrew. (02.13.2012). *5-Minute Speech that Got Judge Andrew Napolitano Fired from Fox News.* Retrieved from http://www.washingtonsblog.com/2012/02/the-5-minute-speech-which-got-judge-napolitano-fired-from-fox-news.html

Chapter 8

Brainy Quotes. (04.25.2014). *Benjamin Franklin Quotes.* Retrieved from http://www.brainyquote.com/quotes/authors/b/benjamin_franklin.html

Wikipedia. (04.25.2014). *Statism.* Retrieved from http://en.wikipedia.org/wiki/Statism

Teachers Union Exposed. (04.25.2014). *Dues and Don'ts | Teachers Union Facts.* Retrieved from http://teachersunionexposed.com/dues.cfm

Wikipedia. (04.25.2014). *K Street Project.* Retrieved from http://en.wikipedia.org/wiki/K_Street_Project

Forbes. (04.25.2014). *The World's Most Powerful People.* Retrieved from http://www.forbes.com/powerful-people/list/

US Census Bureau. (04.25.2014). *Consumer Income.* Retrieved from http://www2.census.gov/prod2/popscan/p60-093.pdf

US Census Bureau. (04.25.2014). *Median and Average Sales Prices of New Homes Sold in United States.* Retrieved from http://www.census.gov/const/uspricemon.pdf

US Census Bureau. (04.25.2014). *Income, Earnings, and Poverty Data From the 2006 American Community Survey.* Retrieved from http://www.census.gov/prod/2007pubs/acs-08.pdf

Jefferson, Thomas. (05.28.1816). *Private Banks (Quotation).* Retrieved from http://www.monticello.org/site/jefferson/private-banks-quotation

Wikipedia. (04.25.2014). *Federal Reserve System.* Retrieved from http://en.wikipedia.org/wiki/Federal_Reserve_System

Bagwell, Tyler. (2008). *The Jekyll Island duck hunt that created the Federal Reserve.* Retrieved from http://www.jekyllislandhistory.com/federalreserve.shtml

Wikipedia. (04.25.2014). *Republican Party presidential primaries, 1912.* Retrieved from http://en.wikipedia.org/wiki/Republican_Party_presidential_primaries,_1912

Wikipedia. (04.25.2014). *Charles August Lindbergh.* Retrieved from http://en.wikipedia.org/wiki/Charles_August_Lindbergh

Federal Reserve Board of Governors. (01.09.2009). *FRB: Press Release--Reserve Bank income and expense data and transfers to the Treasury for 2008.* Retrieved from http://www.federalreserve.gov/newsevents/press/other/20090109a.htm

Federal Reserve Board of Governors. (01.10.2011). *FRB: Press Release--Reserve Bank income and expense data and transfers to the Treasury for 2010.* Retrieved from http://www.federalreserve.gov/newsevents/press/other/20110110a.htm

Appelbaum, Binyamin. (01.10.2012). *Fed Turns Over $77 Billion in Profits to the Treasury.* The New York Times. Retrieved from http://www.nytimes.com/2012/01/11/business/economy/fed-returns-77-billion-in-profits-to-treasury.html

Federal Reserve Board of Governors. (01.10.2013). *FRB: Press Release--Reserve Bank income and expense data and transfers to the Treasury for 2012.* Retrieved from http://www.federalreserve.gov/newsevents/press/other/20130110a.htm

Federal Reserve Board of Atlanta. (04.26.2014). *FRB: Press Release--What institutions are members of the Federal Reserve System, and what does membership entail?.* Retrieved from http://www.frbatlanta.org/fedfaq/search/Dsp_itempopupUFAQ.cfm?ID=635F7444-AB06-4884-A31D-CD2C29038E15

Doctor Housing Bubble. (01.2009). *Total Assets of Each Federal Reserve Bank as of January 2009.* Retrieved from http://www.doctorhousingbubble.com/wp-content/uploads/2009/02/total_assets_of_each_federal_reserve_bank.jpg

Youtube. (03.09.2010). *Nancy Pelosi Pass the Bill to find out what's in it.* Retrieved from https://www.youtube.com/watch?v=QV7dDSgbaQ0

Wikipedia. (04.25.2014). *John F. Kennedy.* Retrieved from http://en.wikipedia.org/wiki/John_F._Kennedy

Kennedy, John F. (04.27.1961). *The President and the Press.* Retrieved from http://www.jfklibrary.org/Asset-Viewer/Archives/JFKPOF-034-021.aspx

Moyer, Liz; Shumsky, Tatyana. (01.29.2008). *Where The World's Wealth Is Stored*. Forbes. Retrieved from http://www.forbes.com/2008/01/29/gold-silver-diamonds-biz-cx_lm_0129vaults.html

US Treasury. (03.31.2014). *Status Report of U.S. Treasury-Owned Gold*. Retrieved from http://www.fms.treas.gov/gold/current.html

Wikipedia. (04.27.2014). *Gold reserve*. Retrieved from http://en.wikipedia.org/wiki/Gold_reserve

Tax Foundation. (10.17.2013). *U.S. Federal Individual Income Tax Rates History, 1862-2013 (Nominal and Inflation-Adjusted Brackets)*. Retrieved from http://taxfoundation.org/article/us-federal-individual-income-tax-rates-history-1913-2013-nominal-and-inflation-adjusted-brackets

Lubin, Gus. (04.14.2010). *25 Scandalous Examples Of Government Pork That Will Drive You Crazy*. Retrieved from http://www.businessinsider.com/the-worst-pork-of-2010-2010-4?op=1

Wikipedia. (04.27.2014). *Dwight D. Eisenhower*. Retrieved from http://en.wikipedia.org/wiki/Dwight_D._Eisenhower

Eisenhower, Dwight D. (01.27.1961). *Eisenhower's Farewell Address to the Nation*. Marquette University. Retrieved from http://mcadams.posc.mu.edu/ike.htm

Wikipedia. (04.27.2014). *Zimbabwe*. Retrieved from http://en.wikipedia.org/wiki/Zimbabwe

Wikipedia. (04.27.2014). *Hyperinflation in Zimbabwe*. Retrieved from http://en.wikipedia.org/wiki/Hyperinflation_in_Zimbabwe

Rove, Karl. (04.27.2014). *Biography*. Retrieved from http://www.rove.com/bio

Wikipedia. (04.27.2014). *Karl Rove*. Retrieved from http://en.wikipedia.org/wiki/Karl_Rove

Rove, Karl. (01.16.2014). *Independents Will Decide The 2014 Elections*. Wall Street Journal. Retrieved from http://www.rove.com/articles/511

Chapter 9

King, Randy E. (01.2011). *Left-Center-Right: What is BEST for America?*. Road Scholar Publishing Group LLC

Wikipedia. (04.27.2014). *Political parties in the United States.* Retrieved from http://en.wikipedia.org/wiki/Political_parties _in_the_United_States

Hahn, Martin. (04.21.2007). *Top 5 historical facts of the U.S democratic party.* Retrieved from http://en.articlesgratuits.com/top-5-historical-facts-of-the-us-democratic-party-id1508.php

Cohen, William A. (1998). *The Critical Importance of Integrity.* Retrieved from http://www.stuffofheroes.com/critical_importance_ of_integrity.htm

Wikipedia. (04.27.2014). *Ralph Nader.* Retrieved from http:// en.wikipedia.org/wiki/Ralph_Nader

Nader, Ralph. (04.14.2000). *Challenging Autocratic Governance That Serves The Interests Of Global Corporations.* Retrieved from http://www.ratical.org/co-globalize/RalphNader/ifg041400RN.txt

Chapter 10

Wikipedia. (04.27.2014). *Serenity Prayer.* Retrieved from http:// en.wikipedia.org/wiki/Serenity_Prayer

King, Randy E. (01.2011). *Left-Center-Right: What is BEST for America?*. Road Scholar Publishing Group LLC

Wikipedia. (04.27.2014). *Tea Party movement.* Retrieved from http://en.wikipedia.org/wiki/Tea_Party_movement

Tea Party Patriots. (04.27.2014). *Our Vision.* Retrieved from http:// www.teapartypatriots.org/ourvision/

Mayer, Jane. (08.30.2010). *Covert Operations.* Retrieved from http:// www.newyorker.com/reporting/2010/08/30/100830fa_fact_mayer

Lafferty, Elaine. (09.10.2010). *'Tea Party Billionaire' Fires Back.* Retrieved from http://www.thedailybeast.com/articles/2010/09/10/billionaire-david-koch-fires-back-at-the-new-yorker.html

Bio. (04.27.2014). *Ross Perot Biography.* Retrieved from http://www.biography.com/people/ross-perot-9438032#awesm=~oCGaKPvrln0kA5

Bio. (04.27.2014). *Meg Whitman Biography.* Retrieved from http://www.biography.com/people/meg-whitman-20692533#political-ambitions&awesm=~oCGaWscOryrLCG

Wikipedia. (04.27.2014). *Occupy Wall Street.* Retrieved from http://en.wikipedia.org/wiki/Occupy_Wall_Street

Occupy Wall Street. (09.25.2011). *Proposed List Of Demands For Occupy Wall St Movement!.* Retrieved from http://occupywallst.org/forum/proposed-list-of-demands-for-occupy-wall-st-moveme/

Chapter 11

mentorwithmahdi. (08.14.2012). *Simon Sinek - The Golden Circle - TedTalks 2009.* Retrieved from https://www.youtube.com/watch?v=fMOlfsR7SMQ

Elmer-DeWitt, Philip. (08.08.2011). *Why isn't Apple AAAA?.* Retrieved from http://tech.fortune.cnn.com/2011/08/08/why-isnt-apple-aaaa/

Bilton, Nick. (08.09.2011). *Apple Is the Most Valuable Company.* Retrieved from http://bits.blogs.nytimes.com/2011/08/09/apple-most-valuable-company/

Ray, Augie. (03.28.2010). *Word of Mouth and Social Media: A Tale of Two Burger Joints.* Retrieved from http://blogs.forrester.com/augie_ray/10-03-28-word_mouth_and_social_media_tale_two_burger_joints

Chapter 14

Schurz, Carl. (11.08.1862). *Letter from Carl Schurz to Abraham Lincoln.* Retrieved from http://en.wikisource.org/wiki/Letter_from_Carl_Schurz_to_Abraham_Lincoln,_November_8,_1862

Wikipedia. (04.27.2014). *Carl_Schurz* . Retrieved from http://en.wikipedia.org/wiki/Carl_Schurz

Wikipedia. (04.27.2014). *Battle of Antietam.* Retrieved from http://en.wikipedia.org/wiki/Battle_of_Antietam

Frost, Robert. (1920). *The Road Less Traveled.* Retrieved from http://www.bartleby.com/119/1.html

APPENDIX

Gettysburg Address
13th, 14th, 15th Amendments
Indian Wars
Plessy v. Ferguson
Spanish American War
World War 1
Great Depression
World War 2
Industrial Revolution
Civil Rights Movement
Amendment 18, 19, 21, 26
Cold War
Global War on Terror
Information Age Inventions

US Historical Icons
(http://storiesofusa.com/us-historical-icons/)
   Pilgrim Memorial State Park
   Mount Vernon Memorial Park
   Liberty Bell, Independence Hall
   Valley Forge National Historical Park
   Monticello National Historical Landmark
   Lewis and Clark Journey
   Alamo
   Gettysburg National Military Park
   Little Big Horn
   Statue of Liberty
   Kittyhawk, NC
   Mt Rushmore National Memorial Park
   USS Arizona Memorial
   World Trade Center Ground Zero Museum & Memorial
   Arlington National Cemetery
   Washington DC Monuments
   Kennedy Space Center
   Great Seal of the United States of America

American Patriotism
(http://storiesofusa.com/patriotic-america/)
   Famous Patriotic Quotes About America
   American Patriotic Songs
   Patriotic Books for Adults
   Patriotic Books for Children
   Top American Patriotic & Historical Movies
   American Patriotic Videos
   4th of July
   September 11
   Veterans Day

Dream 2 Achieve (http://storiesofusa.com/dream-2-achieve/)
   Dream 2 Achieve Program
   Is Anybody Listening?
   In Bullhead City AZ
   Resources

Success in America
(http://storiesofusa.com/success-in-america/)
   Business 101
   Greatest American Entrepreneurs
   Top 10 Most Patriotic Speeches in American History
   Top Characteristics of Successful People
   Raising Successful Children
   Translations
   Arabic
   Chinese
   English
   Farsi
   French
   German
   Greek
   Hindi
   Korean
   Japanese

Portuguese
Russian
Spanish
Tagalog

Other
(http://storiesofusa.com/behind-the-red-white-and-blue/)
Media:
    Media Coverage & Events
    Is Anybody Listening?
    Left-Center-Right: What is BEST for America?
    CD & mp3 Digital Media
Practice Quizzes:
    US History
    US Constitution
    US Presidents
Other Articles and Subjects:
    Our Vision
    Educational Links
    Become a Sponsor
    Donate Now
    Sponsor Links
    American Patriotism Blog
    News
Articles of Interest:
    Patriotic Public Speaker
    Diamond Crest Consulting
    PO2 EOD2 Mike Monsoor
    Army Spc Michael Dahl
    Lesson Plans for Kids
    Pocahontas Geneology
    Boyden Genealogy
    US History National Public School Curriculum Standards
    50 States Game
    Major Important Events in US History

What 4th of July Means to Me
F5 Tornado in Joplin, MO
First Women in the Military
Letter from the Department of Education
10th Anniversary of September 11
Burden of American Exceptionalism
Tribute to Veterans Day
Free US Constitution Course
California Amazon Tax
Americans with Disabilities Act Frivolous Lawsuits
Donald Shoenholt Fined as Air Polluter for Brewing Coffee
Andrew Carnegie Wealth Speech
I Broke Away from the Communist Party Speech
How to Take Action and Get Your Political Opinions Heard

SPOTLIGHT ON
STAFF SERGEANT JOHN BRADEN

"Freedom requires no effort to enjoy but requires heroic efforts to preserve."

— **Richard G. Scott**

RestoreOurPride.us

John Braden, the illustrator of this logo, won an Art Scholarship and served as Infantry in the Army & Military Police in the Air Force. He is an Iraq War veteran and left active service with the rank of Staff Sergeant.

The authors of this book respect all who protect and serve the US Constitution, freedom, liberty & justice both here and abroad.